CROSSING CENTURIES

CROSSING CENTURIES:

THE NEW GENERATION IN RUSSIAN POETRY

Edited by John High

Vitaly Chernetsky · Thomas Epstein · Lyn Hejinian
Patrick Henry · Gerald Janecek · Laura Weeks

with Edward Foster · Vadim Mesyats
and Leonard Schwartz

Talisman House, Publishers • Jersey City, New Jersey

Published in the United States of America by
Talisman House, Publishers
P.O. Box 3157
Jersey City, New Jersey 07303-3157

Manufactured in the United Sates of America
Printed on acid-free paper

The publisher would like to acknowledge the support and encouragement given this project by the Russian Academy of Sciences and the William and Mary Greve Foundation. The publisher would also like to thank Vadim Mesyats, Leonard Schwartz, Elena Pahomova, Dmitry Kuzmin, Arkadii Dragomoschenko, and Katya Kapovitch for their work in helping to resolve some of the complex problems that arose in preparing the final version of this book

Library of Congress Cataloging-in-Publication Data

Crossing centuries : the new generation in Russian poetry / edited by John High . . . et al.].
  p. cm.
  ISBN 1-883689-90-2 (cloth : alk. paper) — ISBN 1-883689-89-9 (pbk. : alk. paper)
  1. Russian poetry--20th century--Translations into English. I. High, John Alexander.

PG3237.E5 C76 2000
891.71'4408--dc21

00-028695

Acknowledgements

Most of the translations and all of the introductory essays were prepared especially for this volume. Particular attention has been given to identifying those who control copyright material reproduced here. Should any have been inadvertently missed, the error will be corrected in future printings. Unless otherwise indicated, works appear by permission of the authors, their translators, and/or their representatives. • Vladimir Aristov, "Baltic Reflections" (translated by Donald Wesling) is reprinted from Kent Johnson and Stephen M. Ashby, eds., *Third Wave: The New Russian Poetry* (Ann Arbor: The University of Michigan Press, 1992. Copyright © 1992 by the University of Michigan Press). Reprinted by permission of the publisher. • Yuri Arabov's "Windy" and "Initiation into the Circle of Poets" (both translated by Forrest Gander and Sara Dickinson) and A Monument (translated by Cole Swensen and Aleksei Andreev) are reprinted from Kent Johnson and Stephen M. Ashby, eds., *Third Wave: The New Russian Poetry* (Ann Arbor: The University of Michigan Press, 1992. Copyright © 1992 by the University of Michigan

Continued on the following page,
which constitutes an extension of the copyright page

Nina Iskrenko (1951-1995)

To talk with you is like burning in the marsh
like climbing head and all into a roll-your-own-smoke
like looking at the sky through a black cat
and peeing in the meat grinder.

—translated John High and Patrick Henry

Andrei Turkin (1962-1998)

I bought Lenin's *Works* (Selected)
and the more I read, the more I
stopped being a thorny delinquent
and became an uncluttered young man.

No longer a misfit, a paranoid freak,
I was calm as your pet mouse.
When I save up enough for his *Works* (Complete)
what kind of man will that make me?

—translated by Paul Schmidt

Genrikh Sapgir (1928-1999)

I am Adonis!
Nothing in common with these streets and shops
Nothing in common with people drunk or sober
Railways televisions telephones
Cigarettes newspapers fogs and dawns.

—translated by J. Kates

CONTENTS

I. PRELUDES OPENING THE DOOR TO THE UNDERGROUND
(1960s- 1970s)

II. Cracks in the Communist Wall:
Reinventing the Avant-Garde

Conceptualism

III. New Territories (1970s-1980s)

Polystylistics

A Leap into Emptiness

Disappearing Space

In Places Far From Perfection

IV. From The Underground Into the Open (1880s-1890s)

After the House Arrest
(Glasnost & the Resurfacing Gay Poetic)

Speaking Through the Veil:
The Dilemma of Women s Voices

Beyond the Ring Road

Thomas Epstein, "Miracles of Russian Poetry" • 419

AFTERTHOUGHTS

Contributors

JOHN HIGH

CROSSING CENTURIES: THE NEW RUSSIAN POETRY

> .... Blood floods the main arteries.
> Along their rows, a whispered orchestration:
> —I was born in '94,
> —I was born in '92 . . .
> Herded with the crowds, I utter through
> a bloodless mouth, fists clutching
> the worn out year of my birth:
> Born the 2nd or 3rd night
> of the unreliable year — January 1891,
> these centuries now surround me with fire.
> —Osip Mandelstam, *Lines of the Unknown*
> *Soldier* (Voronezh, 1937)

The Talisman Project

THE FIRST NIGHT WE GATHERED in Moscow to announce the Talisman anthology project, we ironically found ourselves in the Central House of Writers — once a private club for members of the infamous Soviet Writers' Union — before a crowded hall of poets, journalists, editors and drunkards. "In Russia you could always bum a smoke," as Nina Iskrenko once wrote, but to catch the attention of its poets and lovers of poetry — sober or drunk — something real or honest has to occur. There has been too much tragedy and vodka for the frivolous. Notorious for their brusque manners, these crowds will simply talk over or even heckle the reader if they're not caught by the poetry. Strange to me as well that night, as it was to many of the Russian poets assembled there, that this opening gala should be held in this former place of privilege, pride of the writers' union that collaborated in the deaths of so many of its members. Nowhere in known history has a nation of writers been so systematically brutalized, tortured and murdered than in twentieth-century Russia. Murdered, but not silenced or stopped at the boundaries of language, where another world converges. So abandoning my prepared text as I stood before the noisy crowd, I cited the lines above by the revered poet Osip Mandelstam. Mandelstam died in the camps a year after writing the poem.

"In many respects what we're doing here is absurd," I then said. "A tragic, if not absurd, century is coming to a close, and we are here to do an anthology. Anthologies, like translations, are still another exercise in failure." As the room grew still, I added with less cynicism in my voice, "But the project also offers *possibilities*. If you will help us, this anthology will offer possibilities of exposing the cracks, ruptures and lies of what has been presented as your poetry not only in the West, but here in Russia as well."

ৡ ৡ ৡ

There is no way to separate my personal and "professional" life in Russia. The day the Berlin Wall came down, just eight years before, I found myself in this same hall for a wedding reception. The wedding was my own, and several of the poets found in these pages — poets already famous though for the most part unpublished in the Soviet Union — were there with me. Dmitry Prigov sang in his dramatic baritone. Only a few years earlier he had been sent to a mental institution for writing his conceptualist verse. My then wife and I borrowed rings for the ceremony from Nina Iskrenko and her husband Sergei Kuznetsov for it was still illegal for foreigners to marry under the Stalinist constitution, and hence, to buy rings. While checking our coats after taking taxis from the Trinity Church on Lenin Hills, where I had been baptized the night before the wedding in the same church as Pushkin, the poet Yury Arabov came up to me and said: "I can't help but feel uncomfortable here. This is where they killed our poets. You can't imagine."

> According to custom, everything's kept dark here,
> Our deadened life and square-ruled notebooks.
> And slavery's the best defense;
> Don't remove your head, just your cap.
> —Yury Arabov

I could imagine what Yury was saying as we later passed the champagne, but only as an outsider. Not long after Stalin created the Soviet Writers' Union, one of his apparatchiks gave the dictator a poem Mandelstam had written in secret and only shared with a few supposed friends. "One gets it in the balls," Mandelstam wrote of Stalin's victims, "the other in the forehead, one split between the eyes." None of the poets who are included in this anthology can forget that past. Even as I write this the country spirals deeper and deeper into ruin, hypocrisy and deception. Yet as the poetry within *Crossing Centuries* reveals, Russia's writers have never been negligent about their art.

> Darkness
> of a fast-flying cloud, a trace of glass, the whiteness.
> The clock-faced rim.
> Death's grandeur and insignificance: the stewing
> of garbage in the scorching fog of dragon-flies,
> and some word or other, like a copy of an agreement, the world
> is revealed in the mirror image along the axis of matter.
> > --Arkadii Dragomoshchenko

These poets could not publish, so they met in their apartments — the fabled late-Soviet "kitchen culture." They copied out their poems for one another (samizdat), even put out underground journals in minuscule numbers to avoid Soviet publishing restrictions. In an article Chris Reiner asked me to write in 1991, when I was in Moscow, I observed the following about the changes afoot in Russia right after the failed putsch:*

> Fate hasn't turned out as most expected. A revived mysticism is afoot in Russia, both in daily life as well as in the arts. The new poetry I'm reading and hearing indicates that this is at least partially true. . . . The euphoria over the failed coup attempt has passed, and the talk of new coups continues on the streets and in the press on a daily basis. Nonetheless, there is an energy and excitement among many about the possibilities that may be born of this 'corpse' of a culture. And at the moment, I'm looking out my window at a 16th century Orthodox Church (known as Tolstoy's church, as he lived nearby) with its five golden cupolas & massive dome, its stark & almost mysterious beauty in this surrounding of white & expanding fields of Constructivist buildings, thinking about what Mark Shatunovsky told me drinking vodka by Gogol's statue.
>
> "First you decide one thing & then God decides another for you. We exist between the worlds of the East and West. Fate is not what we thought it would be. There is no freedom but within."

---

*I have here and elsewhere throughout this essay excerpted from my writings in *WITZ, A Journal of Contemporary Poetics,* Volume I, Number two, FALL 1992; Polycontexts: Working Notes From Moscow, *the Five Fingers Review* while under my editorship, and *The Right to Err,* translations of Nina Iskrenko's writing. All poems cited without attribution were done by myself and Patrick Henry.

Shatunovsky later poignantly wrote in one of his recent poems:

. . . we came together so that, once parted,
we'd not see the washed-out features in the other,
still how were we to know that from now on two parentheses
of emptiness would be our punctuation mark.

it appears that we, like water, were spilled
in the past tense, in relic-like forests,
yet memory is still capable at half-speed
within me sustaining an oblong fear.

—Mark Shatunovsky

A Century Circling on Itself

MYSTICISM AND FEAR are inherent features of Russian literature. Critical to note as well, however, that in spite of this twentieth-century Russian poetry has been imbued with a fierce and spiritual utterance. Russia has produced some of the world's most outstanding verse with poets as diverse as Akhmatova, Mayakovsky, Khlebnikov, Tsvetaeva and Pasternak, whose influence is once more at work in the new poetry found in *Crossing Centuries*. For close to half a century, however, simply possessing copies of many of these great writers' poetry could lead to serious problems with the authorities, even in some cases to imprisonment.

When Stalin read Mandelstam's poem, incidentally, he even phoned the very respected and still prominent poet Boris Pasternak, a poet who was later vilified for writing *Doctor Zhivago* and publishing it abroad.

Stalin began by telling Pasternak that Mandelstam's case had been reviewed, and that everything would be all right. This was followed by a strange reproach: why hadn't Pasternak approached the writers' organizations, or him (Stalin), and why hand't he tried to do something for Mandelstam. "If I were a poet and a poet friend of mine were in trouble, I would do anything to help him."

Pasternak's reply to this was: "The writers' organizations haven't bothered with cases like this since 1927, and if I hadn't tried to do something, you probably would never have heard about it." Pasternak went on to say something about the word "friend," trying to define more precisely the nature of his relations with M., which were not, of course, covered by the term "friendship." This digression was very much in Pasternak's style and had no relevance to the matter in hand. Stalin interrupted him: "But he's a genius, he's a genius, isn't he?" To this Pasternak replied: "But that's not the point." "What is it, then?" Stalin asked. Pasternak then said that he would like to meet him and have a talk. "About what?" "About life and death," Pasternak replied. Stalin hung up.

  —Nadezhda Mandelstam, in her memoir *Hope Against Hope*.

It is widely believed that because of this incident, Mandelstam was spared execution and sent into internal exile instead, during which time he wrote many of his best poems. In countless incidents such as this, the poetry of the first half of the century survived to profoundly influence and help shape the poets found in the present book.

As Russia crosses the boundaries of another bloody war and a series of revolutions into the dawn of another millennium, the old and the new have merged. Ivan Zhdanov echoed the sentiments of a new generation when he wrote nearly a quarter century ago:

> I'm not the branch, only the prebranchness.
> Nor a bird, simply the bird's name.
> Not even a raven, though somewhere in the prewind
> the horde of ravens is discussing my fate.

What is that fate? In effect, this is a question we asked ourselves going into this project, one I continue to ask myself. And, of course, it is a question that remains, as we have found no "answers," though the reader will find many possibilities in the generation of poets found within. As Nina Iskrenko so aptly wrote in her essay "We Are The Children of Russia's Dull Years":

> The artists of today, just as the naturalists, are spurred on by one task: the quest for the unity of the world, that is, for concrete signs which confirm the general nature of things. . . . There follows from this a shift in interest, from that which separates the hero (or event) from the crowd, the mass, and from chaos, and which makes him unique, to that which, by contrast, unites him with his surroundings. Such a perception of reality is not connected with concrete particularities of identity or fate, but rather reflects some more general regularities in the spiritual life of man.

Splits from the Center

THE STRIPPING AWAY OF THE LYRICAL HERO Iskrenko alludes to in the new Russian poetry provides a key to reading, to uncovering the intersections of its language, poetics, and stance in a violated world. Soviet critics were furious and frustrated when they first began to see the manifestations of the new poetry, for on one hand the poetry was 'apolitical'. It becomes difficult to point fingers and judge poets as subversive when the narrator or speaker of the poem simply exists in a relative frame of relations with all of the objects around her. What were Brezhnev's censors to do? Unlike Brodksy and other poets from the 1960s, the majority of these new poets made no outward jabs at the state. To the contrary, the writing enters into the roots of poetic composition to extremes, as Rea Nikonova's writing radically demonstrates in "Poem explaining the process of literary work":

$$\frac{\begin{array}{cccc} a & c & f & e \\ b & d & g & m \end{array}}{}$$

```
  a   c   f   e
-
  b   d   g   m
  ─────────────
  ab  cd  fg  em
+
   b  cd      m
  ─────────────
  a      fg  e
```

—translated by Gerald Janecek

Can a censor read a subversive message in such a text? It's a stretch. On the other hand, the goal of Socialist Realism as implemented under Stalin was not eliminate the individual will, but rather to coerce it into becoming a more subservient lyrical self — a self singing the glory of the working stiff, the average communist citizen striving toward the goal of the communist state — which became a metaphor for the new ruling class.

In the new poetry, the censors were seeing poets who moved away from the lyrical, authoritarian "I" altogether. The self seemed to vanish. These were not protest poems; they contained a spiritual force indifferent to the political mechanisms of communism or capitalism. So the censors began to simply label the poets of the 1970s and 1980s as "perverse," "decadent," these new "citizens of the night" (the average reader certainly recognized the reference to whores) were not worth reading.

Even during the Thaw period, when Evtushenko and Voznesensky, Sosnora, Akhmadulina, Okudzhava and others were reading their poetry to stadiums of fans in the late 1950s and 1960s, their vaguely anti-Soviet poetry was something the critic and censor could understand, identify and control. Khrushchev could parade before the Party and pound his shoe on the podium, saying, "Enough!" In the last days of the communist period, the censors were left with branding this young avant-garde with banal epitaphs, which naturally spurred a great interest from the public.

As the philosopher and critic Mikhail Epshtein pointed out over a decade ago in "Like a Corpse I Lay In the Desert":

> The new Moscow poetry provokes in the reader a feeling of aesthetic unrest — a certain loss of orientation. Complaints can be heard about its code and its over-complexity. However, the complexity doesn't come from the language itself, but rather from the principal loss of a solid center, which was previously embodied by the lyrical hero.

If the poets of the last quarter century stand in reaction to the previous generation of writers from the 1960s who sang with the voices of proud resisters, the new poets flair for the verbal arts — for discovering in language a reality in & of itself — hearkens back to the major avant-garde movements of the first quarter of the twentieth century: the Symbolists, Futurists, Acmeists, and, later, the Oberiu. Most of the poets of these schools were eventually wiped out by Stalin, or as in the case of Mayakovsky and Tsvetaeva, killed themselves.

The thing "wants to have its say," as Marina Tsvetaeva expressed it before hanging herself.

Again referring to Iskrenko's essay:

> Mandelstam understood his age in terms of the unremarkable details of a half-starved city life, that is, of things. . . . He pointed in silence to his clock face, where "life began in a wash-tub with a wet, burring whisper, and continued in the kerosene's soft soot. . . ." A handsome, twenty-two year-old Mayakovsky literally incarnated the world and the real object, appealing to it as if to a living being, and seeing in it not only a living soul, but also living flesh. With the arrival of the Oberiu group (Zabolotsky, Harms, et al), the border dividing artistic space into heroes and non-heroes finally came up against its own most extreme contingency: a man has collided head to head with a quickly strengthening, full-blooded thing grown to obscene dimensions.

In those "obscene dimensions"of the new poetry the 'self' begins to disappear into language itself. Hence, the absence of a hero. Neither can the symbolist striving toward another world, a near Platonic embellishment of a 'religious' life, be ignored in this new writing. Contemporary poets such as Zhdanov, Parshchikov and Eremenko make metaphors inside metaphors, and in effect, layer the language of poetry, making of it, a scheme of words that requires the reader to leave the ordinary realm of syntax. The reader has to accept, or endure, a mysterious framing for both spiritual language and experience:

I look at you from such deep graves,
that before my glance can reach you, it splits in two.
We'll hoax them now as always by playing a comedy:
that you were not there at all. And so, neither was I.
We didn't exist in the inaudible chromosomal bustle,
in this large sun or the large white protoplasm . . .
Here are the conditions of the first move:
if you illuminate the nearest stretch of road,
I'll call you a noun of the feminine gender.
                                        —Aleksandr Eremenko

In his introduction to the section of metarealist poems in this anthology, Thomas Epstein reveals the spiritual underpinnings of this work:

Socially invisible, this band of metaphysicians and metaphorists, Leningraders and Muscovites, sought to awaken the slumbering Russian language with charges of electrical-poetic energy. This energy surged in all directions; backward into tradition and myth; forward, into the linguistic and social realities of the Soviet and world present; upward, into the heavens; downward, into murky earth. For these poets, both defined by and cut off from Soviet realities, art's primary goal was neither cognitive nor ideological; rather, in the works of Elena Shvarts and Olga Sedakova, Viktor Krivulin and Arkadii Dragomoshchenko, Vladimir Aristov and Nadezhda Kondakova, Aleksandr Eremenko and Aleksei Parshchikov, in Ilya Kutik and Ivan Zhdanov, the poetic word was both an end in itself, revealing riches, both comic and tragic, suppressed by the one-dimensionality of the official culture; and a vehicle for travels to other worlds, invisible and perhaps incomprehensible, but nevertheless real or potentially so.

Cracks in the Wall

A POETRY THAT ABANDONED THE SOVIET MASTER NARRATIVE, that even subsumed the identity of the poet in this linguistical barrage of tropes, confused the censors, but it excited young readers and precipitated an explosion in the arts by the late 1980s. The official language of the state held no meaning. Slogans were manipulated and privately mocked. The material trappings of that language had no signification, no place to go. The young poets, on the other hand, looked back into the pantheon of great poetry from the century's beginning and expanded the boundaries of expression, as well as experimentation. They not only deconstructed the official language, they began to create a new one. (One cannot underestimate the effect this had on the ultimate fall of the regime itself. Quite simply put, the new generation no longer believed in propaganda.) Eremenko observed in his essay "Twelve Years In Literature":

> They (the critics and editors as one) were cynical enough to pretentiously discuss for 10-15 years whether young poetry existed or not. My friends' poetry lay around in editorial offices for years — so there was no poetry. . . . One poet on the editorial board said that the suggested selection of authors couldn't be published: it'd be noticed in the West. He's afraid of the West? He's not afraid of the devil, or the West, East, North or South. . . . He's afraid that an enlightened public will stop listening to his inventions about how he drank vodka with the classics of Soviet poetry. . . . But are they not afraid of each other, when they publicly announce that rock music is a manifestation of "satanism"?

In the new poetry the reader finds a mockery and renunciation of Soviet oppression itself.

Nero's battling with the cat.
Attila's battling with the cat.
Ivan the Fourth's battling with the cat.
Lavrenti's battling with the cat.
Korea's battling with the cat.
Kotov's battling with the cat.
The cat's battling with the cat.

And the cat's karate is nothing
compared with the statues of dictators.
—Aleksei Parshchikov, "Cats"

Already the dictators are viewed as simply "statues." Already the poetry is linguistically verging off into its own created universe while dismissing the political dictates of official culture. By the time of Brezhnev's death and Gorbachev's introduction of glasnost, it was too late to stop the recreation of poetic language.

> Colonel Bokov, the Bureau of Disinformation Chief
> gets up early —
> he's got a lot of catching up to do.
> The Bureau of Disinformation Chief despises the information
> coming from our t.v. screens.
> But then, for the Chief of the Bureau of Disinformation
> the absence of information — means death.
> —Aleksandr Eremenko

An Abandoned Ideology

THE CONTEMPORARY CONCEPTUALIST, not wholly unlike the Futurist poets, took the raw propaganda of this official Soviet language and turned it against itself, making absurd jokes of the regime that on the surface appeared to be simple and humorous verse. The Futurists' verbal dramatization of 'defamiliarization' (ostranenie) and zaum' (transsense), as found in the poetry of Khlebnikov and Kruchenykh at the start of the century, is echoed in contemporary conceptualism as well as in the poetry of the polystylists. The Conceptualists strip the Soviet vocabulary down to a series of clichés, revealing its natural meaning — *nothing*. The Soviet propagandists attempted to make a false reality endure by constructing a language to support it. If a storefront sign read "Cheese" then it meant cheese was sold inside. As Lev Rubinstein once said, no one questioned it, even though there was no cheese. Everyone knew there was no cheese.

"We only have ideas of nomination and pathos. . . . The Party has said, for instance, the main task of the Party is to build communism. From the Western point of view you have to ask where is this communism it has proclaimed? But in Russia if the Party has said the aim is to build communism, communism appears at once. Once you nominate the subject, it appears," poet and artist Dmitry Prigov once told me in an interview. In short, communism never existed except as a language:

26 -"Within this space language neither lives nor dies — it, so to speak, vegetables."

27 -"Vegetates" . . . I get it . . .

28 -"Various styles and indices of genre embodied in the form of extracts, fragments, quotes and pseudo-quotes are lifted from this space irrespective of the local hierarchy . . ."

29 -Not so fast . . .

30 -"Their recoding occurs without any surgical intervention — simply through their transfer from one context to another."

31 -Take it easy

32 -"In their new context all the hidden drama of language is turned inside out, as if revealed."

—Lev Rubinstein, translated by Michael Molner

During the 1970s-1980s, to witness a conceptualist reading was to join in a performance. (In this I can't help but think of Daniel Harms of the Oberiu group a half a century earlier, reading his poetry from a window sill, precariously balancing both body and language.) The Conceptualists, fifty years later, unveiled the hypocrisy of the Soviet slogans by using them directly in their writing, showing the underlying nature of daily Soviet life. Prigov pokes fun at every level of Soviet society. As one of the masters of conceptualism's irony, he pushes the borders of accepted speech into a series of puns, mockery and comedy itself:

The people after all doesn't only drink
Although not many people know that
It labors and it lives
Not like the little insects with lots of legs

And into the bottom-of-the-page articles in newspapers
Where they write that it works
You should read that it doesn't only drink
But that in fact it does work
                    —Dmitry Prigov, translated by Gerald Smith

While Russian conceptualism is distinct from its Western counterpart, both share a resistance to dead language. As Gerald Janecek substantiates in his introduction to the conceptualist poets found in *Crossing Centuries*, each avant-garde movement shared an underlying basis:

Both the Russian and Western variants were reacting against the incursion of propaganda into the arts. In the West this was primarily commercial propaganda (advertising, art marketing, etc.), while in Russia the propaganda was overwhelmingly political and cultural, with ideological clichés saturating virtually every aspect of public life. By the 1960s the emptiness of these formulas was becoming more and more obvious and at the same time their availability for artistic manipulation as cultural artifacts ("ready-mades") became clearer to artists and poets.

The regime had little life left in it by the end of the Brezhnev period. The leadership was simply going through the gestures, portraying the earlier acts of Lenin and Stalin in pomp and stereotyped ceremony. Conceptualist poets enacted games and performances — in bathhouses, on the streets, in the forests — that parodied the dying regime as well as language in such a way that it could appear as a variant of Socialist Realism to the unsuspecting critic.

The poet Andrei Turkin wrote, perhaps anticipating his own death:

I bought Lenin's Works *(Selected)*
and the more I read, the more I
stopped being a thorny delinquent
and became an uncluttered young man.

No longer a misfit, a paranoid freak,
I was calm as your pet mouse.
When I save up enough for his Works *(Complete)*
what kind of man will that make me?
                    —translated by Paul Schmidt

Roman Jakobson wrote shortly after Mayakovsky' death, "Every man when he finds himself becomes a myth, and then his death is predictable." The same message rang true in contemporary Soviet life. Propaganda, or meaningless mockery? Inquiry, or the empty shells of language speaking of themselves? Language is not only the subject and end, it is the means of unlocking a vast and meaningless reality that supported itself on the blood of its own people as well as the emptiness of its own vocabulary.

There is in conceptualism something similar to Buddhism or Zen Buddhism: a certain reality discloses its own illusoriness and ghostliness, making way for the perception of emptiness itself. Conceptualism is the reign of petty, boring trifles, behind which opens one great summoning emptiness.
    —Mikhael Epstein, *The Avant Garde Art and Religious Consciousness.*

The void. thorna of
Tarkovsky?

As far as I know, Andrei Turkin's death still remains a mystery. On New Year's night in 1997 he plunged to his death from a Moscow apartment balcony.

Converging Paths

BY THE LATE 1970S, with the Soviet regime severely feeling the signs of its own exhaustion — there were deep cracks in the wall. The time was ripe. The poets from *Crossing Centuries* picked up and developed the traces and prints left from the Symbolist, Futurist, Acmeist as well as Oberiu experiments. In the 1980s, writers from a diversity of styles and schools came together to read their poetry and find solace outside of any official dogma in a group that came to be known as the Poetry Club. The "club" provided a space for contemporary writers who were conceptualist or metarealist, and for those who felt uncomfortable with either of these orientations. The same was true of the Stray Dog Salon, where poets as diverse as Osip Mandelstam, Velimir Khlebnikov, Vladimir Mayakovsky, Anna Akhmatova, and others read and drank and argued about writing before World War I in St. Petersburg. (At one of those recitals, during one of Mayakovsky's notorious declarations as a young Futurist, the shy and withdrawn Acmeist poet Osip Mandelstam stood up and shouted, "Mayakovsky! Stop reading your poems like you're some Hungarian Orchestra!") I have witnessed many such episodes at the Poetry Club readings, where poets of opposing aesthetics took turns reading and badgering one another.

In tracing the work of the poets from *Crossing Centuries* the ghosted language from the century's beginning echoes, but with a haunting verve and renewed vitality. The early Acmeist aim to rename and in doing so, re-discover and invent the physical world, can be seen in much of the writing.

> . . . hey, come on, what's the big deal,
> won't you let 'em root-a-toot-toot?
> hey, come on, what's the big deal,
> won't you let 'em out to shoot?
>
> can we catch our goals in flight
> across the board's black and white
> in the crosshairs of a sight?
> we've yet to scatter like type
> we've yet to flee, yet to fly

it's the finish, too close to call
black raven falcon bright
every songbird stoned or mauled
plagued to death, you can't make it right

here a chick there a chick. . . .
—Vladimir Druk, translated by Thoreau Lovell and Patrick Henry

It is, of course, too reductive to simply compare the movements of the
century's close with those of its beginning, but parallels can be found through-
out the literature of both periods. The truth is that while overlaps between the
different groups exist, they should be seen not as a restrictive closure, but
rather as an opening set of boundaries in which the abyss of the Stalinist era
was bridged. Propaganda made language itself suspect. Since the ego-based
"I" behind the words of Stalin's Socialist Realism played such a significant role
in destroying culture and literature, poets brought their distrust wholeheart-
edly into the poetry itself. The Acmeist aim (particularly Mandelstam's) to
rename and in so doing to re-discover and invent the physical world, can be
seen in many of the poets from *Crossing Centuries*.

In effect, the century was circling back on itself and expanding into a new
language of being, one that offered an exit from official dogma as well as any
set identities:

Where to begin?
Everything cracks and shakes.
The air quivers with similes.
No one word is better than any other.
The earth is humming with metaphor . . . .
Osip Mandelstam, translated by Michael Molner

As Michael Molner recognized in his introduction to Dragomoshchenko's
"Description," translated by Lyn Hejinian and Elena Balashova:

The "beginning" occurs in the middle of the (Mandelstam's) poem and at the
end of an era and the question it raises is ontological. The world is saturated
with imagery and signification: there is no room left for the old poetic self
which "only connects." It has been crowded out and the poem finishes with
the words ". . . and there is not enough of me left for myself." The moment of
consciousness marked by this poem recognizes thematic exhaustion and the
end of language as self-expression. It might have founded a new poetics, but
the time was wrong.

xxxviii

Yet as the empire crumbled, so did the material trappings of communist speech. Now the time was right. Iskrenko's own "Hymn to Polystylistics" made way for a cross-fertilization of poetic 'talk' which became its own sign of meaning. Concept and mystery converge, the inanimate takes on its own life, and the narrator only appears as a figure of language itself.

Polystylistics   is when all the girls are as cute
                     as letters
                     from the Armenian alphabet composed by Mesrop Mashtoz
                     & the cracked apple's
                     no greater than any one of the planets
                     & the children's sheet music is turned upside down
                     as if in the air it would be easier to breathe like this
                     & something always humming
                                                  & buzzing
                     just over the ear

A poetic trope is grounded in the sheer vibrancy of the object, sign and signification. Unity has become more a horizon of interactions now, a communication between the "things," the words themselves with ideas — this obvious paradox between characters and their worlds. The ghosts of each word await the reader. Still, these "things" are alive, and when they're allowed to live in the text and its talking, their particular (or should I say, peculiar) story, symmetry, balance, plausibility find themselves.

The poets who gathered under the banner of the Poetry Club experienced a profound loss with the death of Nina Iskrenko in 1995. For several years the group often met at my apartment in Moscow, bringing together established and younger poets, much of whose writing is found in *Crossing Centuries*. Iskrenko, as Andrei Voznesensky wrote years earlier, was the "soul" of the club, organizing bizarre readings in the subways, in train stations, in line at MacDonald's. . . . Patrick Henry's introduction to the club's work reveals the loss her contemporaries experienced when she died of breast cancer in 1995:

On that evening, a sense of weary grief prevailed. Without Iskrenko, whom he called "perhaps the most significant poet of my generation," satirist Igor Irtenev said with evident regret that "the Poetry Club existed — now we can probably say this in the past tense, because any efforts to reanimate it without Nina I think would be touching, naive, simple and still-born. She is gone, and our youth has gone with her. The club has assumed the existence of a legend." The Poetry Club appeared just once more as a group, when, in February 1996 on the first anniversary of Iskrenko's death, its members came one last time to the Mayakovsky Museum.

I have been at the gravesite where family members and poets sometimes meet to pray, reminisce, and tend to the grave, and I can attest that her death was a difficult passage for both Russian and American poets.

During her several visits to the United States over the past decade, Iskrenko had garnered a readership and many deep friendships here as well. Her vitality and explorative verse brought a unique presence to her readings and performances. In the end, her death became a metaphor for the passing of the regime and communist culture, in all of its decadence and discovery.

As the poet Bunimovich said:

> Today, by a stroke of fate, everything has overlapped. As my generation bids farewell to youth, no single path has emerged; rather, each writer has found his own. We have also parted with context. Alas, my generation is not the first free generation, as it seemed to us, but rather the last generation of Soviet poetry, closing the tragic and farcical circle.

Thanks to the financial contributions of both Americans and Russians, poets and lovers of poetry from diverse backgrounds from both countries, a tombstone sculpted in the shape of an egg stands at the site of Iskrenko's grave in Moscow. Along with Andrei Turkin, this anthology is dedicated to her — two extraordinary poets who met premature deaths but profoundly affected the course of poetics around them.

Breaking Codes

AS THE LANDSCAPE OF POETICS DIVERSIFIES AND BRANCHES OUT, it is impossible not to acknowledge the rise of ontological as well as phenomenological manifestations in the new poetry as well: that of emerging gender and gay writing long suppressed in the century of tyranny that has ruled in the language as well as politics of the Russian people. In May of '97 I traveled to Moscow two months before the conference Talisman Press and the Russian Academy of Sciences sponsored there. I wanted to arrive early in order to meet with the poets, to garner some advance support for the anthology, and to attempt to bring the different groups into a dialogue, one that would help the American editors and translators find the work needed for *Crossing Centuries.*

Many of the poets in this anthology will not talk to one another. The rivalries and diverse poetics have sadly separated them, though most if not all did read and meet in the panels and discussions, providing a lively and contentious diversity of views and poetry.

Of all the controversial topics we discussed, the question of a gay or feminist poetic, or of new voices among women, brought the most tension, and even hostility into these early dialogues. This did not surprise me. Over a decade before I had found it nearly impossible even to get names of women writers who were not already included in the official canon. As far as gay writers were concerned, they seemed not to exist. I only learned of writers like Elena Shvarts and Nina Iskrenko after bringing Ivan Zhdanov, Aleksandr Eremenko and Aleksei Parshchikov to my room in the Ukraine Hotel — along with several bottles of whiskey. Even then, it wasn't until the booze was consumed that I pried lose some information. It is critical to understand that whereas it is changing, Russia is still a backward, almost medieval world, rooted in the mysticism that often informs the work and in the religious bigotry that often accompanies it. That bias, even among some of my closest friends, continues to disturb me. Now as a new generation expands the limits of poetic composition, a Dmitrii Volchek can write verse that crashes against these boundaries:

the further it is the faster   what will be   what used to happen
an anxious kiss faster under the blanket
to writhe there to submit
to shameless piercing waves

was trying on a wig or looking at medussa
all the tight billiard pockets all the cracks and moans
who could have thought they'd come
from such a chest so slanted so manly

love I have lost and also the grass and the blanket
what had drowned was much more difficult to raise
under the canopy a young eye opened up
filled itself with water
    —translated by Vitaly Chernetsky and Aaron Shurin

I know where you are now, Ganymede
It's a different night, and I follow your path
by the movement of tea
leaves on the surface of the

water. Soon we'll meet again. One after another,
I burn the matches & finish your
drawing: the face, the rose,
the cry of horror & indignation,
the wind, the eagle & the boy.
                    —Sergei Kruglov, translated by Lewis Walsh and Vitaly Chernetsky

Not so long ago, such open declarations of love between men could not only bring prison, they brought torture or death. Even among the former underground poets of the nation, it is generally shunned. The sodomy laws which were repealed with the Communist revolution, were put back into law by Stalin in 1933, and only repealed again in 1993. Nonetheless, both the gay and feminist writing have long traditions in Russian poetry. Having run directly up against this other form of censorship, editor Vitaly Chernetsky writes in *After the House Arrest: Russian Gay Poetry*:

> In Pushkin's own work, gay themes are represented by poems of a different genre, namely, by the imitations of classical Greek and medieval Arabic poetry. . . . It is only after the relaxation of tsarist censorship after the revolution of 1905 that we see a sudden emergence of self-conscious, assertive, outspoken gay and lesbian literature.

Chernetsky cites the work of the Vyacheslav Ivanov and Lidiya Zinoveva-Annibal and goes on to trace the writing to that of the "two most important figures of gay writing: Mikhail Kuzmin and Sophia Parnok." Kuzmin's association with Acmeism as well as Symbolism is essential as well. Yet the force of invisible censorship has denied gay writers both publication and the acknowledgment of a tradition that Simon Karlinsky for one, has tried to restore. Chernetsky observes: "In the case of other prominent Russian poets of that era who at various points explored gay desires and homoerotic imagery in writing, we also see a pattern of forced erasure of that aspect of their legacy (as it happened with Tsvetaeva, Sergei Esenin, Nikolai Gumilev, Nikolai Kluev and many others.)"

To be identified as a so-called 'gay writer' continues to create barriers in Russian poetry — rejection of the poet — just as it does for women who associate their writing with feminist or gender-related issues. Laura Weeks writes in "Speaking Through the Veil":

> The position of the woman behind the veil, forced to speak through a device that both deflects and attracts attention, accurately describes the position of

Russian women poets writing today. Most Russian women poets are reluctant to be immediately identified as women. True, there is an active and articulate feminist movement in Russia with a long tradition behind it. True, there is a growing body of gendered lyric. But the majority of women poets avoid stepping into this charmed circle for fear of several things: that their female-ness will be dismissed as "femininity," that their poetry will somehow become circumscribed as "female experience."

What is this female experience, what in the syntax as well as gender creates a wall, and hence, hidden border, to be crossed. Is there such thing as a "woman's poetry" in Russia? Why does the mere idea bring up such strong resistance? Lyn Hejinian proposes a similar question, and quest, in her "Preludes" essay:

> In American postmodern poetry, borders have been at stake, under scrutiny and up for reshaping, transgressing, or destroying — borders delimiting genre, borders delimiting style, borders delimiting personhood (voicings of ethnicity, class, gender, and life style). American postmodern poetry has undertaken a great deal of border crossing. Is this true, I wondered, of Russian postmodern poetry?

It is true, but to find it in Russian poetry one often has to look below the threshold of what is "accepted" poetry, even in today's writing where the censor includes the poets themselves. The best censors in Russia were always the poets. Yet women and homosexuals also face the institutionalized prejudice of journals and publishing houses that keeps their work from reaching a wider public. This response of the new literary establishment deals more with the writer's "personality" than the actual work, and the chauvinistic, anti-Semitic and overall nationalistic nature of much public discourse is particularly disturbing.

In this respect, the revised "unofficial" officials resemble the old adherents of Socialist Realism, choosing to move against the body, the race, the sex, the personality, or even the "politics" of the writer, rather than to confront the writing directly. Perhaps because the aesthetic is open, aware of formerly censored traditions as well as the text's sexuality, its potential material trappings are broad enough in approach to include the world itself. Dialogues, ruptures and interruptions — ones serving as signals of communion — attempt to move the poetry past these ideological borders. And the poetry flourishes; its manifestation is undeniable. Part of the endeavor of those

xliii

working on the *Crossing Centuries* anthology was to find, uncover, and translate it.

It was also part of our goal to find writers existing and working in the provinces outside Moscow or St. Petersburg. Those two cities might, for instance, represent New York and San Francisco on the American landscape. But in America writing centers or pockets of poets, and journals for their work, exist throughout the country. The same is less true in Russia, though it is changing. The bias against poets living outside these two cities is so severe that more often than not they are considered failed writers by the literary powers-that-be.

> A book, a gesture tossed off by the right hand (Whose?
> Take a guess!) Trampled by the coupling, copulating, naked throng.
> A voice tattooed onto the pages —
> a stupid trope, but a right hand has neither timbre nor throat.
> —Vitaly Kalpidi, translated by Laura Weeks

> Life looks too haughtily towards the traces of particles flying past,
> leaving behind the legacy of the fleeting empires'
> lead water pipes, whose essence would have been like a gasp of breath,
> if someone had only responded to the echo of the repeated gasp.
> —Vadim Mesyats, translated by Margarita Zilberman

A failed poetry? Again referring to Thomas Epstein,

Outside the capitals lies a vast, impoverished nation land known as the Russian provinces. For the poets of these regions, the choice has often been stark: either make their mark on the capital or suffer the fate of obscurity. Nevertheless, cities like Samara (Ulanov, Yermoshina, Kekova), Chelyabinsk (Kalpidi) and Sverdlovsk (Mesyats, Kurytsyn, Tkhorzhevskaya), to name but a few, have produced vital poetic communities and poets of real worth. Indeed some of these "provincial poets" have demonstrated more poetic freedom than their capital-bound counterparts, some of whom can be said to suffer from the provincialism of the capital (that is, the illusion of being at the center of "everything that matters"). Poets like Ulanov, Zhdanov, Abulldaev, Kal'pidi, and Mesyats have used their experience in the capital as a pole, not of imitation, but tension. Of equal significance, one can see in them the sheer diversity of Russian poetry and therefore the limitations of the very rubric "provincial."

Beyond the Rings

THERE ARE TWO STATUES OF GOGOL in Moscow. Stalin thought the first one, erected in the nineteenth century, was too "sad." So he had a more heroic structure mounted on the boulevard and removed the original to the small courtyard of the house where Gogol actually died. The paradox evident in such acts continues today. But the dead and the living, the animate and the inanimate, the past and the present, occupy equal ground in the poetry. Neither the self's singular absence or singular control can populate the corollaries which create an "arched" dialogue between the mythic and the real in the new Russian poetry. The question Osip Mandelstam proposed to himself a half a century ago is still relevant in this world: "Which tense do you want to live in? I want to live in the imperative of the future passive participle — in that 'what ought to be. . . .' I feel like breathing that way. There exists such a thing as mounted, bandit-like equestrian honor. That's why I like the fine Latin gerundive — that verb on horseback . . ."

The critical question involving the new poetry issues from a "sliding" between the culture's fragmentation and identity, the momentary ruptures and movement of a world which is itself fractured. As Paul Celan wrote:

Speak you too
Speak as the last
Say out your say.

Culture itself necessitates some kind of reinvention of itself and a subsequent understanding of the changes brought about in the stripping away of its external fabric: the sham of an entire history, one which perhaps, evolved out of "the same lack of judgment, the same superstition if you like, that consists in believing in a political solution to the personal problem," as Marguerite Duras so aptly wrote before her death.

In Russia, one immediately senses among writers and artists the need to grapple with the "ghosts" of history and memory — not in the grandiose heroic monuments of Pushkin or Mayakovsky, but in the once forbidden words and quotes and collages, for instance, painted on the walls of the apartment building where Mikhail Bulgakov lived and wrote the once censored *The Master and Margarita.* ("Then writing would mean opening, with every stroke, a new day which the worlds take into their keeping. . . . We will never be done with hope," Edmund Jabes wrote. Or from Bulgakov's novel, this line comes to mind: "Manuscripts don't burn.")

What connects the subjective and the objective, the self and its othering in the flux of these changing contexts? The question itself becomes a paradox that evades definition when one goes out on the streets and with each week witnesses the seemingly perpetual shifting of the Russian landscape, it's unpredictability.

The Soviet Corpse? Vanishing histories. Paradox?

JH: In all of this, in your writing process, where is Prigov?

Dmitry Prigov: Prigov is above all the images. He's like the director who directs all the images and gives them the stage where they can meet.

Lev Rubinstein: In their new contexts all the hidden drama of language is turned inside out, as if revealed.
—Why "as if"?
—Ideally, this is a linguistic mystery.

—translated by Michael Molner

JH: What determines the "order" in your own personal poetic process?

Aleksei Parshchikov: For me, it's important that one who sees order in things understands that the sequence of these things composes a certain drama . . .

Yury Arabov: One crow/or maybe a flock/But a flock cannot be/a crow/And having pecked the barren field/nearly to ash/we fly off somewhere else.

Nina Iskrenko: Art provides us with a unique opportunity, first of all to believe in everything, and second, third, and forty-ninth of all to tell everyone about it. What's to be done; the world has to be maintained in some sort of equilibrium, however unstable that may be. . . . Why have the innumerable attempts to narrow the gap between art and life come to nothing? Might not the reason be that we're constantly dealing with a Moving Frame, as well as the gradual, but steady, disappearance of a reality we can only approach at sufficient distance in order to disappear along with it?

FINALLY, I WOULD PERSONALLY like to thank each of the editors as well as coordinators for the project, and especially Ed Foster, whose tireless work as a poet and editor is changing the landscape of available reading in the United States. While Leonard Schwartz helped bring together dozens of American poets to translate the work, Vadim Mesyats vigorously collected and corresponded with the Russian poets before and after our conference in Moscow in 1997. No one was paid for any of the work. Laura Weeks, Lyn Hejinian, Patrick Henry, Jerry Janecek, Thomas Epstein, and Vitaly Chernetsky worked for almost three years to provide literal translations of the writing, in many cases to translate the writing, and to edit the diversity of sections that appear in *Crossing Centuries*. In many cases, their sections do not reflect all of their editorial prowess, as I have organized the sections, and created sections from all of the writing gathered. In many cases, I have also added poets to their sections, for during the past three years many of the poems that have come into the anthology have arrived thanks to the helpful suggestions of both Russian and American writers not directly involved with the project. It was also our goal to bring as many American poets into the translation process in order to create vital poems and as well, to further the cultural interchange between American and Russian writers. I have been amazed at the number of fine American poets willing to lend their time and effort to the arduous task of translation.

As I have noted before, and said that first night in Moscow at the Central House of Writers, translation can at best echo the original of a poem, and there is inevitable violence that is done to the text in the process. If successful, however, a relationship between the original and the translation is developed, a kind of marriage that by necessity creates more echoes of the interaction between languages. Cultural and linguistic equivalents simply do not always exist, so we have tried to stay as close to the *intention* of the work as possible. Rhyme and meter have generally been sacrificed in the English, sometimes whole fragments of a given poem have appeared untranslatable. Each translator has followed his or her separate approaches, attempting to breathe vitality and life into the English variant. By including so many American poets in this process, we hope to have produced not only translations, but *poems* that stand on their own in English.

A translation is never completely faithful to its original. As in any relationship it is something to be worked on, nurtured, and gradually, perhaps, understood and rendered. Often a rupturing of the senses is involved, an overlapping of genres and folds of meaning, abandoning of a literal or any "master narrative" that a culture imposes through syntax or propaganda. As Octavio Paz had reckoned, each language has its own world, and maybe Schopenhauer was right when he wrote that we think differently in different languages. A guiding light throughout the work has been to stay clear of any imposed ideology. We have not attempted to erase the foreignness of the text, the boundaries between languages, or to avoid the inevitable transformation that evolves in the process of rendering a poem. Of course, we've had our disappointments. Sacrifices are almost always involved. But the parts reflect the whole as they will in any given body, and that is our hope with this anthology. We have done our best to let the translations breathe their own transmuted life into the poems. With the help of too many Russians and Americans to mention, the result is *Crossing Centuries: The New Generation in Russian Poetry.*

PRELUDES:
OPENING THE DOOR
TO THE UNDERGROUND
(1960s-1970s)

LYN HEJINIAN

PRELUDES

A**N ANTHOLOGY IS INEVITABLY LOCAL** to two times and places, that of its publication and that of the work collected in it. This situation is further complicated when an anthology of work from one language culture is edited and published in that of another, as is the case here. This is an end-of-the-century postmodern (or post-postmodern?) American anthology of Soviet and post-Soviet Russian poetry written over the span of the last half century and translated into English. These multiple placements and displacements are, in many ways, what the anthology turns out to be about, although I, at least, didn't foresee this when first agreeing to act as one of its many sub-editors.

In American postmodern poetry, borders have been at stake, under scrutiny and up for reshaping, transgressing, or destroying — borders delimiting genre, borders delimiting style, borders delimiting personhood (voicings of ethnicity, class, gender, and life style). American postmodern poetry has undertaken a great deal of border crossing. Is this true, I wondered, of Russian postmodern poetry?

The adventurousness (and it truly is that) of border crossing is, within American terms, at the same time quite traditional: American culture has always been charged with the task of going over horizons, moving outward and onward. Literal mobility is seen as the heart of American cultural experience.

This has not been the condition of Russian experience, where the possibilities for travel, and even for change of apartment, have, for political and/or economic reasons, been extremely difficult. The result has not been immobility, however. Mobility of persons may be circumscribed, but their ability to carry out conceptual shifts, to move ideas, has flourished. In Russian postmodern poetry, too, then, borders have been at stake, but they are interior borders. Russian poetry has undertaken to cross the concentric rings of perception, going inward across waves of effects to the instant the stone first drops into the pond.

Russian poetry has also adventured through layers of language and across overlapping borders of social, ideological, and linguistic contextuality that are situated in it.

This has produced a poetry of lexical and syntactic depth; it has also resulted in semantic density.

It may seem that these would be difficult to carry over in translation — and, in some sense, this is certainly the case — but that displacements are constantly occurring in and through Russian poetry is clearly perceptible even in English. And in the course of perceiving the moving of borders within Russian poetry, it becomes evident that what is at stake is reality — how realities are cast, where they fall, how they radiate inward, how they are perceived.

The task of the editors and translators of this anthology was to move the realities of realities. It seems a truly postmodern and truly intercultural task. I hope we have succeeded.

Were is chuvash?

⊠⬦⊠ GENNADY AIGI ⊠⬦⊠

Winter Marked By God

loaded title.

a second white luminous one
the land was at rest

it was cause of darkness at table
and for its own sake making peace
gave not knowing where or to whom

not food
less desylvan

awe.

and god came close to his own being
already allowing us to touch
his enigmas

God! *man?* *seeing God in the world*

and sometimes in jest
gave back life to us
just slightly cold

cut up.

understood afresh

becoming spring

why hazel Aidu? *no Aidu*

TRANSLATED BY PETER FRANCE

awe.

Viola

to F. Druzhinin

a black bird has lost itself here
oh bright monk of the galleries
and fragment of snow like star of reward !

forest people activity

detaching themselves from the fingerboard
here planks of villages fall
in the yard long since deserted

and the tree is pleased by the tree's dislocation
the velvet by pieces of silk

but the strings would lie more clearly on books
lit by snow on the roof
through the window

Kolomenskoe Church
to Igor Vulokh

oats
copying you in its grains
were reflected in a red stain
on us both together
when we were first seen in the likeness of thought
by the Saviour

a net
in autumn heat upon berries is possible
over skin with your clangour
but the message
going up to the heights
is a single essence

the wind
the bluetit and my friend
I asked them if we are forever
and sadly she answered from outside
"three"

Crossing Centuries:

Degree: Of Stability

foward smses of light

to V. Shalamov

You yourselves are visited already by something like skyglow

and the image perhaps
has been made real for all:

independent of all:

is this not the unseen flame of poverty
in the noiseless wind:

of the shortlived features ? —

or possibility of the perilous it is :

in faces illumined —

as if waiting to be opened:

like those who guard something ? —

or — with un-clear incandescence (as if staring with a kind of vision of
unhurried illness):

everywhere — unseen — illuminating all:

the ultimate *it*
of the Fire-Word:

which long ago seized
the very places of out thoughts ? —

everywhere as if in a noiseless wind:

without word without spirit:

has it come into being ?

Translated by Peter France

Again: Places in the Forest

again *they are sung* ! yes ! again it is they
everywhere — sounding — at once ! —

again at the same hour
at awakening:

bright
— as a clearing — suffering! —
unmoving
and clear — unending ! —
and as if steadfast was the morning
in me: as in the world — entire:

and there they have placed that place
between others related
to them:

that at one time I knew ! —

it seemed the hour
of happiness shone:

with a high
clear centre:

hawthorn — silent in singing
like a silent god — behind the sounding Word:

Crossing Centuries:

silent — in intangible self:

just touch — and it will be: *there is no God*

TRANSLATED BY PETER FRANCE

Second Madrigal
to A.B.*

as with blue stone the "special treatment"
was quietly staining your face
and with a green lamp on the watchtower
they loved the fact of your being

but the ash
did it touch you on the neck in sleep
like children — weakly then more strongly !
and a handful of it fitting as a tree
in festive light it is it is
perhaps near the poplar oh over the yard by the path
or somewhere birds will start singing again

but at evening the metal of trolleys is pitiful
— who more than they can forgive
why do such stabs bring joy
and they all wanted themselves to adorn you
but many not knowing how

oh I shall preserve this wound as a centre
I shall say let it shine
let it shine with existence
you slide away and already a star

---

*the poet Anna Barkova, a victim of Stalinist repression

and so that it alone should be
it is time to quench the end where I am

TRANSLATED BY PETER FRANCE

Crossing Centuries:

They say to me
what poverty of words, of words!
Yes, poverty, poverty
The meanness, rottenness of barracks,
grayness,
deathly wheyness;
and eternal fear: and how.
yes, poverty, now.

TRANSLATED BY J. KATES

Visiting came comrade Strakhtenberg.
How old he is,
just grin and sin.
Comrade Strakhtenberg,
comrade Mandragé,
sit down please — doesn't sit; — already I . . .

TRANSLATED BY J. KATES

The farther along to age and death
(alaverdy, alaverdy)
the nearer to tears in Gennesaret
and the blubbering of Bluebeard
      — alive we weren't —
      — we weren't alive —

      — we learned to wive —
      — why didn't ye —

TRANSLATED BY J. KATES

Eh, Mandelstam did not see
any pigeon on the Moscow pavement,
did not hear
any rustling
and knocking
coming from below,
did not take into his hand
the blue-gray bird,
did not begin to blow into her pennywhistle beak,
coo coo, little pigeon, coo coo,
he died Osip Emilevich, he died.

TRANSLATED BY J. KATES

I have nothing against realism in art.
Life
is more important than appearance.
Having tricked
my gullible vision
I will dip
my eyes
into a Marquet landscape,
I will swim
on the watercolor float
in three dimensions easy to take in.

TRANSLATED BY J. KATES

Poetry

I say to you: miracles don't happen.
Me,
they call me chicken pox.
I'm no chicken pox,
but the Black Plague.
You will understand, too late.

TRANSLATED BY J. KATES

Crossing Centuries:

Ask them, go ahead and ask the cripples,
those for whom war has ended forever,
how long is the peaceful day, how lengthy the night,
and how does it look when the clouds open up,
when they break apart — the descending moon.

Translated by J. Kates

Yes, my dreams testify that I lived among people.

Translated by J. Kates

Marble

The left breast is half broken off
Pallas Athena
Kissed there
By long-haired maidens —
A chip from inside has turned pink
From the x-raying of Aphrodite by mature women —
Hugging the armless woman from behind
It looked as though the goddess were caressing herself
These full hands sliding
Along her marble belly!
Those round knees four of them!
This doubled flank!
But the one who is always running with a beautiful noseless face
Diana enticed the virgins
In the moonlight her hair
The silent hounds slipped away
And the nubile girls — the lunatics went
With their unwilling shoulders lowered
Their unwilling hands extended

O goddesses! I know your lovers
They love to please men
But I know how to distinguish them
They calmly take hold of a dress
They lie down — please take me —
Suddenly the centuries open
They grow cold they turn to stone
Stupid boy you lied
This girl is not virginal
This woman not frigid

They were loved by
Goddesses

TRANSLATED BY J. KATES

Adonis Dying

I am Adonis
I limp along blood leaking from my thigh
I contort myself — the worm in my hands
Nature be kind don't turn aside
I am your son Adonis

Destroyed by a stupid girl from the bar
They were all around in gloom and gray
I fail — I'll die before the daylight
Bad for me

Here's the roar of an approaching car
Shining its white light in my face
— Hey buddy what's your name?
— Adonis
"Adonis? That's Estonian or Lett"

I am Adonis
I come from a completely different world
Where Flora scatters oranges
Where Venus waits for me
And soon she will learn misery
Wild boars on the loose
In her beloved Cyprus . . .

— Oh, one in a million!
"I got it! he's Sicilian"

I am Adonis!
Nothing in common with these streets and shops
Nothing in common with people drunk or sober
Railways televisions telephones
Cigarettes newspapers fogs and dawns

"No
I bet you

He's
A Jew"

I am Adonis
I ran trembling through the brake after the boar
Twigs grabbed at and twisted my heels
Beat me! Loved me! Wanted me! Steamed me!
I am the beloved of the goddess of love
I am not here! I am not yours! I don't believe!

— Clearly out of his mind
— But where's he from?
— Who knows

I am Adonis

TRANSLATED BY J. KATES

Childhood

Here in a certain faraway kingdom in forty-five
A bomb fell — glass flew around all the houses
And the surgeon's eyes turned soft and warm
How completely confused this Venice was — look over here

That one slept — face wrapped in gauze — a head-wound
The round-ups got 'em in good time — Where do they go?
      The other world?
A greyhound gazed and panted loudly. They gave me
A silly cap and shoved me along: Shut up and go home

They bartered a woman's shawl for vodka and black bread
From the Sovinformburo: after prolonged resistance
We stood in the snow in front of a blackening chapel.

Crossing Centuries:

We walked and groped teen-agers with our eyes — Oscar and I
On the corner of Sady-Samotechnaya and Kotelnicheskaya
A horse turned around up-ended and splash in the water

Translated by J. Kates

Psalm 117

1. O praise the Lord all ye nations:
heighdy hodey ready body

2. Praise him all ye people
in O
and in U
and in I
and in A

3. for His mercy
even his paucity
even for nothing —
Hallelujah!

4. Desiring nought
Hallelujah
tumble-drunk on the floor I
Hallelujah
And in me — out of me
all eons peoples
howling:
O God! — ha!
Take this! And that!
Hallelujah!

Translated by J. Kates

Psalm 148

1. Praise ye the Lord from the heavens
all angeldemons
all devilarchangels
all sunmolecules
all atomstars

2. He commanded — and they were created
evilgood and goodevil
gathered into a knot
Long live Thy cruelkindness!

3. To praise is dispraise
To dispraise is praise
Praise ye the Lord from the earth
not fearing to dispraise
plainfall
and rainclear
and tigerbull
and sheepfilth
and beggarprince
and holivile
and anglonegro
and germaruss
and veteravirgin
and cleverfool
and every pharynx
and every bellybutton
praise ye the Atheistogod!

4 And earhand
and eyeleg
and tailhorn
Hallelujah!

TRANSLATED BY J. KATES

Crossing Centuries:

Pronouncers and The Pronounced

The director writes a play on the basis of the props available.
What the pronouncers say must be present on stage.

Translated by Gerald Janecek

A Rustle of Steps

Any ballet as a dramatic play
　(slow down everything)

Translated by Gerald Janecek

O, Madness!

Madness, Madem, Midumum, Numima

　　The Action
occurs on a thumbnail
at two minutes after 12 o'clock

The action consists in looks and speeches; gestures and movements
are addressed simply to the audience. The characters are
straight as nails, or bent as nails. There are no speeches and the spectators
are 1000 times bigger in size.
　　Madness begins and ends the play, always remaining on the thumbnail.
　　Madem sings in silence. Midumum is entirely absent, and not present.
Well, Numima is weeping in the moonlet and has hidden under a flake of
nail polish. Her weeping simply smells, and that's all.
　　The whole play is sucked out of a finger (index).

Translated by Gerald Janecek

Paper Angel

make yourself paper wings with fringe
put them on
demonstrate them before God
and if he likes you
work as an angel

TRANSLATED BY GERALD JANECEK

Poem explaining the process of literary work

```
    a   c   f   e
 -
    b   d   g   m
   _____
   ab  cd  fg  em
 +
    b   cd      m
   _____
    a       fg  e
```

TRANSLATED BY GERALD JANECEK

A Free Alphabet

```
A_ _ _ _ _ _ _ _ _ _ _ _
  _ _ _ _ _ _ _ _ _ _ _ _
  _ _ _ _ _ _ _ _ _ _ _ Z
```

TRANSLATED BY GERALD JANECEK

The Seething of a Pause Around Nothing

$((((\qquad\qquad))$

TRANSLATED BY GERALD JANECEK

312 steps by the author
up to a microphone

TRANSLATED BY GERALD JANECEK

550 words
          explaining
vacuum poetry

TRANSLATED BY GERALD JANECEK

Complete Absence

Spectators arrive at the theater.
but the actors do not.

TRANSLATED BY GERALD JANECEK

Traveling Duds

Dormitory monastery or army barracks
good to be a sports instructor at a labor colony!
to buy it for money in train stations
Now he comes to Moscow has no
place to crash the night an acne-covered
face over his fist socks with a hole at
the heel a worn undershirt faded under-
wear hanging at the dorm — breeding
ground. Took off everything — here ain't I
good here touch feel how I am spread
underneath put it on and went
on. That's the best for them Sport!

TRANSLATED BY SAM TRUITT AND VITALY CHERNETSKY

The Poem

A fragile poem from a tender family
can't even drop a word without an introduction
and sees I am there at the side. Did I leave a mark
on his mind? No? Then I'll run before sleep.
This one though right away when he comes in
the children grow quiet exchange a few halting
utterances and I remain invisible. Here no one can lay
hands on each other's heart the unseasoned
shoulder with him over on a lawn out front so light playful
so dreamy you try to do it just like him

TRANSLATED BY SAM TRUITT AND VITALY CHERNETSKY

Vilboa

S calls need to put up a young woman for two nights.
We get there she drops off to sleep he exits
and what's left is enduring — loudspeaker blaring
across the district congratulations songs trucks
squeezing through the crowd that still doesn't feel right
an ante-bellum era siphoned through a horn the poet
has no place in to hide torn into the collective
to laugh at living people the same living people
as you that do not feel they are laughing stock.
She trots onto the platform not young not beautiful in a taut decolletéd dress
& you feel her cold against the crush of overcoats
a love song starts and young men endlessly invite
her to walk into it with her limbs uncrossed
smiling as the song demands her teeth projecting forward
then another tune to remember those who fell
shouts at you but doesn't look into your eye
twisted in a binary of trumpets the old leader commands
and the young pioneer his protegé and
an accompanist with an accordion behind them
where a fourth one holds the notes for that stolid performance artist
his chest covered with fragments of metal
as the sporty professional emcee announces —
"Sailors! Vilboa!" the surnames shouted out but VILBOA!

No one knows him. The old leader and the nit-wit pioneer
begin — the first starting what the other does not pick up.
The citizens notice exploding into wise-arsing and guffaws.
The compassionate old women however accept this.
They have brought their grandkids out for a stroll. They will die soon.
Despite everything the leader remains calm
but the pioneer's choked. Still it remains a means of distraction
separating youths from gangs & booze to play brass
partake of the artistical — Vilboa! And here we go
something closer to the real work at hand —
a boy & a girl 13 or so dancing. Everybody's gaze
riveted the same as the boy dances the girl on his side

the majority of our eyes on him a fragile moving
embryo of masculine lines — I have to dance they say
so I'm dancing like it should be! He's no jelly-belly
but remarkably well proportioned. It is no wonder
a father wants a son. As Efrosinya Nikiforovna said
they had a girl — four years then — without much thought —
a son was born! Brother so-and-so. Hooray!
the sailors' dance! Everyone is in thrall not
me alone. The brothers run out three of them
their age forever mine two of them twins
one of the twins dancing who of the two you
won't guess the third he does not look like them
though all of them good especially the third one
older than the others at that turning point brothers
all of the same blood all good but the third —
thighs squeezed by belts the heart of the program.
War deals precisely with you. It does not let you overripe
but fixes on the eve of blooming so that everyone's
heart would break. The boy in sailor's shirt perishes
the cheeks lose their flush not having blossomed in the trenches
nobody opened his lips. The main show is over
and the emcee invites all to watch the concert again
at the Construction Technology Club.
The children pile into the bus. The eldest he is in the back.
You recognize him by his smile from far off
where a girl chirps to him oh Vilboa! Vilboa!
Here am I in my Dutch scarf more enigmatic than Vilboa.
The participants next to me are walking touching
the exhibit an experimental model of the city
at the House of Construction Technology —
no spectators however just two or three old women
a few kids from an elementary school.
I turn to the woman in charge as she instructs the twins.
The older one has gone downstairs.

(He was not their brother. The emcee is a liar.)
Villebois! I implore you! I have came for the concert.
If it won't take place because there are no people.

Please do at least the sailors' dance! I came just for that!
Please she replies come at such-and-such a date
for now it looks like it's canceled. Indeed the director
all covered with medals for victory emerges and cancels.
Oh Vilboa only to go home where a strange young woman drolls on the pillow!
Woman — give me a son and go leave yourself take a hike!
What moves us to pick up a pen? Correspondences.
In the courtyard I saw a young pioneer made out of plywood
half a pioneer not even painted just seated there
on the grass neck like a bull's. He was sawed out
by clumsy hands. Pioneers do not have necks like that.
Vilboa what a nape that young sailor had. Picked him up just the same!
By the way about the young sailor from Lena Gulyga.
Famine on a ship. They chose to eat the youngest sailor.
I can imagine — to skin a teenager separate his muscles
divide the muscular tissue among the collective
they pulled back the skin on the back of the neck
felt punctured draining blood into a bucket.
The team is at the side. Waiting. And he went to do it himself
stern recognizing the task. Hypothalamus unripe
marrow picked out of a sweet bone boiled chest membrane one for all!

Translated by Sam Truitt and Vitaly Chernetsky

The Grasshopper and the Cricket

"The poetry of Earth is never dead" —John Keats

The poetry of Earth is never dead.
Here up north, when it snows hard
the grasshopper falls silent. But when a blizzard blows,
the cricket starts to strumming like a blind man.
His mind sharp as a sword,
he always keeps his lyre dry and in tune,
the thin wet hair stretched tight.
He is Demodokos among the guests at an invisible feast
and sounds like a whole meadow taken shelter in the house.

The poetry of Earth is not that rich:
a young child and a thin old man,
grasshopper and cricket, follow the same steps
from one place to another —
the distance is vast as a patch
sewn across the gamut of hearing.
Hollow heart-shaped jingle bells
clink like wavy scissors on the golden manes
of young unearthly horses.
Their effigies butt the emptiness in vain.

But the howling chimneys are enough.
Some raise their pale eyes from the snowstorm,
some wander the fields at dawn,
scattering the silver —
the last of it holds everything there is.

The poetry of Earth is never dead,
but when it has an augury of death,
it finds a dependable boat,
throws away the oars and drifts off —
It matters little what befalls it later;
it's beyond all hope already

and never will forget the way
to ride the waves of sound.
Tell me what under heaven
gives a lovelier view of the heavens
than to drift with open eyes
along the bottom of the sea
like a wounded Tristan?

The poetry of earth is terribly monotonous.
Striking tiny anvils of obscure sound
the grasshopper and cricket have shackled the ocean.

TRANSLATED BY GREGORY KAPELYAN AND STEPHEN SARTARELLI

Nor for the Sacred Legends of Obscure Antiquity
to V. Aksyuchits

The loveless and sometimes the doomed
have a strange attachment to the Earth.
Yet I have no great fondness even for
the mother tongue, whose milky darkness
troubles the font. Nor for the timeworn images
of the long forgotten poverty
of a wisdom never revealed.

Nor for the fields all sown with sorrow,
where the unreaped wheat tells tales
of guilt before heaven and earth
more countless than the grains of sand.

— Abandon all hope of salvation,
we are wretched and weak of heart.
Only a saint can love God's judgment
and praise the execution to which he is led
and the wind along the empty road.

TRANSLATED BY GREGORY KAPELYAN AND STEPHEN SARTARELLI

On the Death of Vladimir Ivanovich Khvostin

Your labor is over, poor soul, your labor
of happiness and hope, irreproachable
labor of love. Is that our fate? To be erased
like chalk from slate? A gift
of the heart, the future's charm. A milky way,
the way along which we are led . . .
Or do we never reach the end? My *eternal* friend —
or does eternity exist only here?

Courage is a better thing than life.
Such astonishment as we were born for
does exist. As in the rush
of his first movement
he lies, bearing life
in the arms of benediction.

And like a babe in arms
he shall carry healing and song
and life deep-rooted in the ages
over the burning dust.
He sleeps as if happy in the knowledge
that his dreams reveal
the final affirmation.

TRANSLATED BY GREGORY KAPELYAN AND STEPHEN SARTARELLI

CRACKS IN THE COMMUNIST WALL: REINVENTING THE AVANT-GARDE

CONCEPTUALISM

GERALD JANECEK

CONCEPTUALISM

ONCEPTUALISM WAS ONE of the most prominent and characteristic trends in Russian poetry of the late Soviet period. The term gained recognition in the Russian context as a result of an article by Boris Groys, "Moscow Romantic Conceptualism," published in the first issue of the Paris Russian art journal *A-Ya* in 1979, but its roots were in the 1960s, as was the case of the Western movement of the same name. Both the Western movement and Russian Conceptualism developed at the intersection of the visual and verbal arts. While in its Western variant it was mainly a movement in the visual arts which incorporated textual elements in visual works, sometimes to the total exclusion of other elements, the Russian variant, although it had a number of prominent and influential practitioners among its visual artists (Ilya Kabakov, Erik Bulatov, Victor Pivovarov, Komar & Melamid, Abalakova & Zhigalov among them), was especially rich in its poetic manifestations. As Prigov, one of the leading Russian theoreticians of the movement, put it, "Conceptualism in our condition turns into some strange creature which is in between Pop Art and Conceptualism and postmodernism. Soviet Conceptualism at once began to work with nomination and contraction of languages which is built on this nomination."[*] Both the Russian and Western variants were reacting against the incursion of propaganda into the arts. In the West this was primarily commercial propaganda (advertising, art marketing, etc.), while in Russia the propaganda was overwhelmingly political and cultural, with ideological cliches saturating virtually every aspect of public life. By the 1960s the emptiness of these formulas was becoming more and more obvious and at the same time their availability for artistic manipulation as cultural artifacts ("readymades") became clearer to artists and poets. The late Brezhnev era was a particularly fertile time for this approach, since the geriatric leadership itself appeared to be merely going through the motions of communist propaganda, while declining into comfortable atrophy. Conceptualism provided the opportunity for a witty game in which the prevailing cliches, presented in a subtly distanced, ironic

---

[*]"An Interview with Dmitry Prigov," by John High, *Five Finger Review* No.8/9 (1990), p.79. Prigov explains "nomination" as follows: "in Russia if the Party has said that the aim is to build communism, communism appears at once. Once you nominate this subject, it appears." (Ibid.).

way, could be shown to be empty signs devoid of real meaning. It was a form of social critique that could pass for Socialist Realism, if you didn't look too closely. As the ideological and governmental center of Russia, Moscow naturally became the center of the Russian conceptualist movement, though similar trends could be found elsewhere.

Poetry in the West has probably never had the high status it attained in Russia in the twentieth century, particularly in the Soviet period, both as a form of state-sponsored literary expression and as a form of protest against and escape from the same state-imposed ideological norms. Therefore it provided a well-developed and gratifying medium for conceptualist operations. To the conceptualist, any pre-existing material is usable, the humbler and more ordinary the better, since the initially non-art status of the material is thereby clearer. But even pieces of high art can be used, if they have achieved the status of cliche (e.g. the Mona Lisa, the Pieta, certain Shakespeare quotations, etc.). In the Soviet context, poets such as Pushkin, Mayakovsky and a few others were raised to the status of cultural icons and force-fed to the population, thus turning them into conceptualist material. The conceptualist ostensibly does not invent or create works of art, but rather collects or assembles material from cultural stereotypes and manipulates it, plays with its stylistic properties to reveal the underlying psychological and cultural consciousness. After all, there is probably nothing more revealing about a state of mind or a culture than its cliches, since they are likely to be much more typical of the culture than its most original art, which is by definition exceptional. Hence conceptualist poetry focuses heavily on collage-like assemblages, quotations (hidden or overt), intertextuality, stylistic eclecticism and ahistoricism, making it a quintessentially post-modern trend.

In the selections below are three of the four figures most frequently labeled as conceptualists, Vsevolod Nekrasov, Dmitry Prigov and Lev Rubinstein (the fourth, Vladimir Sorokin, writes prose, not poetry). They more or less accept the label of Conceptualism and have added to the theoretical discussion surrounding the movement as well as exemplifying it in their works. Nekrasov would, however, prefer the term Contextualism, since in his quite correct view, the context or frame of the speech act is what defines it as art, rather than any concept *per se*, since all language is automatically conceptual, whether it is intended to be art or not. Words are defined as ideas or categories, and the conceptualizing process is present in their very creation and selection.

Prigov (b. 1940) is by far the most prolific of contemporary Russian po-
ets, having already written 10,000 poems by 1986 and aiming to reach 20,000
by the millennium (a conceptualist performance in itself). He tends to write
in extensive series of poems based on an organizing principle, such as al-
phabet poems or "banal judgements." In theoretical statements, Prigov has
indicated that he sees himself as a playwrite or stage manager who orga-
nizes encounters or collisions between ways of thinking or speaking. The
selected poems include examples of the early short lyrics that made him
famous, as well as a recent work that has him manipulating text as if
according to computer programming principles. The latter opens with a
typical introductory statement that hides more than it reveals. An interest-
ing and perhaps unintendedly ironic aspect of "Metacomputer Extremes" is
that the original, which is composed in his frequent form of a typewritten
brochure, includes overstrikes of crossed-out letters in a few places, an ef-
fect easy to accomplish on a typewriter but difficult to do in word-process-
ing on a computer without special programming.

Rubinstein (b. 1947) has said that "everything has already been written"
and that the poet's role is only to select and assemble. He gathers his lan-
guage ready-mades on index cards and then organizes them in some way
that emerges as appropriate to a given set of materials. In public he reads
them from these cards, which are his works' ideal embodiment, though for
obvious practical reasons they are rarely published in that way. While os-
tensibly each card holds a collected quotation, in fact many are what Rubin-
stein terms "quasiquotations," i.e. phrases designed to seem like quotations
(commonplace expressions, overheard statements, sentence fragments)
when in fact there is often no specific quoted source. "Sonnet 66" has as its
obvious intertext the given Shakespeare sonnet, but one struggles to find
any direct connections between the two except the elegiac tone. "Melan-
choly Album" consists of short sentences or sentence fragments of mostly
morose content that seem randomly assembled. These are interrupted by
stanzas of a poem in the making with its rhymes provided but with many
lines yet to be filled in. What we seem to be observing is the creation of a
poem from raw material. As is typical of a Rubinstein work, however, we
are left to build our own context for combining these disparate elements
into a meaningful whole. The last line suggests that an element of humor
may be present in the self-indulgent piling on of "tragic" material.

Among the "senior" conceptualists we can also include Andrei
Monastyrsky (b. 1949), leader of the performance group Collective Actions
which was active from 1979 to 1989. Examples are two early works in the

series Elementary Poetry, which, while they had a group action realization, can in fact be read as conceptualist poetry independent of their concrete actualization.

Of the "junior" conceptualists (the quotation marks indicate not relative chronological generations but rather poetic generations), Mikhail Nilin (b. 1945) and Ivan Akhmetev (b. 1950) most closely relate to the Nekrasov manner, Nilin enriching it with greater stylistic scope and narrative content, while Akhmetev moves in the direction of even greater simplicity of speech. Mikhail Sukhotin (b. 1957) is a recognized master of the cento form (i.e. a work consisting mainly of quotations from other sources), which is tricky to deal with in translation, since much of the original material easily recognized by Russians would be entirely unfamiliar to readers of the translations and therefore would not be recognized as quotations. Nikolai Baitov (b. 1956), in one of his many manifestations, provides us with an abstractly structured word-shuffling game whose aleatoric processes lead to striking juxtapositions and chance formulations. Finally, Eduard Kulemin (b. 1960) demonstrates the unexhausted potential of conceptualist collage with fresh and interesting new effects. This younger generation is not strikingly different from the previous one, except that as the Soviet Union recedes into the dead past, it provides less and less interest as a target and source of material. The evolving cultural situation provides other and more varied focal points (technology, commerce, entertainment) familiar to and shared by the West.

Rea Nikonova (Anna Tarshis, b. 1942) can lay claim to a conceptualism independent of and perhaps even prior to the Moscow branch. In Sverdlovsk in the mid-1960s and later in her native Eisk, she produced a huge variety of texts that are conceptualist in essence, but that emerged sui generis from her own inspiration without much foreign or domestic influence. Nikonova's role as Russia's premier avant-gardist goes far beyond her conceptualist works and includes painting, bookworks, quasi-musical literary forms, theory and criticism.

To the extent that Russian Conceptualism depended on Soviet cliches for its vitality, that period of its flourishing has ended with the fall of the Soviet Union, but to the extent that its main interest was not on Soviet realia but on "the problems of the perception and functioning of art" and on art "not as a thing (a work), but as an event (situation)," as Mikhail Aizenberg has put it, then it is likely to bear additional fruit in one form or another.

⬚⬚ DMITRY PRIGOV ⬚⬚

122

An eagle flies over the earth
Isn't Stalin its name?
'Course not, its name is eagle
And Stalin doesn't fly up there
There's a swan flying over the earth
Isn't Prigov its name?
No, Prigov, alas, isn't its name
And Prigov isn't flying up there
What about Prigov? he sits on the earth
And steals a look up at the sky
The eagle and the swan he sees
And Stalin? He's lying in the earth

TRANSLATED BY GERALD S. SMITH

125

Here's me, an ordinary poet let's assume
But the thing is that by the whim of Russian fate
I have to be the conscience of the nation
But how to be that thing, if there is no conscience
Poems, maybe, there are, but a conscience — no
What to do

TRANSLATED BY GERALD S. SMITH

126

When I think about poetry, how it should live from now on
I understand that my contemporaries ought to love me more than Pushkin
I write about what happens to them, or has happened, or will happen, they're

familiar with every fact
And I say this to them in our comprehensible common language
And if they still love Pushkin more than me, then it's because
I'm good and honest, I don't put him down don't make allegations about his
    poetry, his fame and honor
But how could I put all this down when I am that same Pushkin

TRANSLATED BY GERALD S. SMITH

130

We've known since ancient times
That man is stronger than death
But in our times, believe me —
He's stronger than life as well

Life tempts and beckons him
But he just gives it the finger
There is nothing that can seduce him —
He lives in poverty and rejoices
Since he's stronger than anyone

TRANSLATED BY GERALD S. SMITH

131

A raven-bird hangs in the sky
And under the earth lies a dead man
They look each other in the face
They see each other through
everything that may be in the middle
o thou, my native earth!
You hold me here as a singer
Between raven and dead man

TRANSLATED BY GERALD S. SMITH

Metacomputer Extremes

Opening Statement

Among the computer conjurations taking over the modern world and seeking to overwhelm it to the point of its complete subjection, at the same time attenuating the projection of its whole fabric of being and reducing it to the level of agar-agar, I have tried to discover the most extreme, i.e. the unique and superior point that is indeed the extreme of pure computerity. In general, all the arguments for the otherness of the computer world — quick action, the quantity and compactness of memory, the elaboration of multiplicities of space, etc.— are still (viewing the matter from the proud heights of traditional culture) based simply on an intensification and prolongation of the vectors of anthropomorphism and its customary manifestations. Indeed, the man running on foot has been replaced by the horse, then the automobile, then the airplane and the telegraph, the channels of telecommunication. Of course, one is impressed by the almost synchronic simultaneity of a signal's transmission and reception, by the free choice of addressee, by the geographical voluntarism — but everything is laid out retrospectively in a smooth line of sequentiality and undisturbed succession. No! Give us a new anthropology! At least — unlimited virtual worlds! Which of course have analogs in cultural practice, so that the genealogy of the virtual can be traced back through states of meditation, mystical revelations and experiences with states of altered consciousness. In Judeo-Christian culture, where genetic engineering and other neo-anthropological research is at issue, we still encounter fundamental taboos (in regard to "in the image and likeness . . .") All these strategies for exiting from the postmodernist atmosphere of all-encompassing manipulativeness are able to retain a heuristic character; but the resolution will come in some fifth or sixth way (like: life has triumphed in a completely unknown way). But of course one has to admit that the warm-breathing mass of the unknown is already peering through the attenuated membrane of a cultural sphere that seems to have reached its limit: the limit of its variant of the anthropocosmos. And indeed nuclear power has not only simply turned the human fist into a weapon of immense destructive force, but also has determined the limit of its self-reflexiveness, its relation to its own utter annihilation (the fist should also be understood as a preeminently phallic symbol). All this is complicated and hardly consoling, or, on the other hand, complicated *and* consoling, or, on the *other* hand, as uncomplicated as it is unconsoling, or something like that. All the more so, since in the contemporary art world to which I belong, so to say, by dint of to my primary professional gender traits and which I have perhaps a more legitimate right to discuss (all the more since I am discussing every type of computerity without owning my own computer, having become familiar with all sorts of computer problems by listening to others discuss them) thus modern art has discredited textuality in favor of gesture, manipulation and behavior (I, of course, have in mind exclusively so-called *contemporary art*[*], which defines all other practices as crafts from which strategies of action can be extracted), has actualized the operational level for announcing authorial ambitions and even artistic existentialities, thereby preparing for an ideology of new cultural behavior. In general, all these numerous words mean only that I want to identify "operative action" as the unit of computer behavior. This is essentially what I have been trying to demonstrate in this book.

Because this was written a while ago, I can no longer remember the meaning of all the descriptions and so-called quasi-operations employed here. I only remember that everything was carefully planned and honestly prepared. In general, as intended, we are returning to the promised secret and the mysterious realm of cultural activities. Perhaps someone will follow in my steps and be able to go through these texts and explain to me what I had in mind.

ໜໜໜ

If one proceeds to read not by words but by syllables
Adding one at a time
Then as a result much will be revealed to you
Unattainable initially by eye and mind
Like:
Re-Call   Me-Agre
Yes-terday

ໜໜໜ

If one prefers not the first but the second

---

[*]English in original. [trans. note]

And takes the middle first and then returns to
The start
And then finds the end by jumping over the second
Then you will understand what it means to
Get to the heart of the matter —
G-o-ne a-g-es a-d-vancing

∾∾∾

It is necessary to take the third positions from the
                                beginning
Of the two middle numbers in the sequence
2 and 3, then return to the beginning
And then after three numbers go to the end

Bo-a-ts pa-s-sed far-t-her ri-g-ht

Then from the obtained result
Each position will expand its meaning
3, 2, 4, giving rise to

That signal gets answered

From this result one has to seek the positions and
        succession for describing the greatest ecstasy
            at the moment of coincidence

    3   3   3
Amid this concretely
    3   3   3
Spoken passage select
    3
Thirds (end)

They serve as the beginning of the following
        quasisemantic construction,
        without limitation for each
        position (with the prearranged

departure from regularity in the case
of the fifth word)

Hence:

Initiated innovation normalizes
operational licensing initially

Then follows the direct abbreviation
of corresponding positions:

~~Initiated innovation normalizes~~
12   3

45   6
~~operati~~onal ~~licensing initially~~

We get:
       TIZONL —
Illustrating the possibility of practically
           endless development

∾∾∾

Let us enter some initial material:

Day quietly annihilated itself

If we hear the reaction: Oh! — the program is developing
       according to second positions:

Already under night's tent!

If we hear: O-oh! — the program is developing
       according to third positions:

Yet initially negated sleep —

Further developments are similar,
     arbitrary and irrelevant

∾∾∾

Let's take:

Respected Comrade Descendants!

We replace each second position
     with the position following it in the alphabet

Rfspected Cpmrade Dfscendants! —

Every fourth with the second position
     in the following expression:

Desires ontologically anthropomorphic!

We get:

Rfseected Cpmnade Dfsncendants! —

We exchange the fifth position with the sixth:

Rfseceted Cpmndae Dfsnecndants! —

We leave out all the even positions and we get:

     RSCTD CMDE DSFNAT

We exchange the first two positions in the first
     two numbers, and we simply throw out the
     third number:

     CMCTD RSDF

And using unnamed operations we get:

Coming hordes

i.e. Respected Comrade Descendants = Coming hordes

Let's take, for example:

Lexington

We turn around the axis of rotation
running from us through i, and then
around the axis of rotation running
parallel to the position of sight
through the center of all the letters and
we get:

Notgnixel

Then we move the odd positions behind the
even positions and we get:

O G I F (L assumes a zero meaning)

Then we move the even positions behind the odd
positions and we get:

O I

Then we develop each complex
behind the end positions
around a vertical axis which
passes through the central symbol
of each complex and we get:

GON FIN

We combine them:

GNOIFN and L

Which is a genuine name

∾∾∾

We give Y the meaning 2, X the meaning 3, F the meaning 4, S the meaning
5 and we get:

Yyxxxeeeesssss

We attempt to decipher and we get:

Yxesyxes, xes, es, s

or:

Yxyxexesesss

or:

Ysysxsxsxseeee

or:

Eyeseyesxxxsss

But then, establishing that the number is a position shifted by one and re-
verted, we get:

SEXY

All ideas are played out in the sum of ideas —
The sum is equal to 29 and it occurs from the position and number 4, 4, 5, 10,
or 1+3 = 1st word +3 letters; 2+2 = 2nd word +2 letters; 3+3 = 3rd word + 3
letters; 4+4 = 4th word + 1 letter; 5+5 = 5th word + 5 letters
or:
        IDEAS

~~~

A long word

During a momentary turning on and turning off one reads only

      ABRA

Abra - movich
Abra - u Durceau
Abra - cadabra
Abra - sivo

They undergo abbreviation:

Møʋíȼh, UƊuɾȼȼáɥ, Cáɗáɓɾɑ, Sɪ́ɾø

There remains:

      MHUUCBS

We get:

      Aɓɾɑ́mchuusƀs
      MHUUSCS

i.e.
      Many houses up under
      Strong clean skies

again we abbreviate and we get:

      MHPE

One could also get:

      MAHAPE
      MYHYPF

MIHYPE

(Follows abra automatically)

∾∾∾

You think I can be easily fooled
Which means: I adore you completely

We submit this to the program
        two forward the one after next back,
        with several omissions and we get:

  Adryeocu molet

We move the evens behind the odds with a reversion
        after three around the central position as an axis
                and we get:

    ERA LTO

We expand it:

Even really awful lives turn on

Translated by Andrew Joron and Gerald Janecek

Elementary Poetry Number Eight

"BLACK CANNON"

Text-instructions for E. P. No.8 (placed in a box to the right of the tube)

INSIDE A BOX THERE IS ONE ELEMENT OR CONTENT ITEM. TO PERCEIVE IT AN APPARATUS "BLACK CANNON" HAS BEEN CONSTRUCTED. VISUAL PERCEPTION OF THE ELEMENT OR CONTENT ITEM REQUIRES THE PARTICIPATION OF THE VIEWER (READER).

IT IS NECESSARY TO USE THE APPARATUS IN THE CORRECT SEQUENCE: FIRST TO PLACE ONE'S EYE AT THE OPEN END OF THE TUBE AND ONLY THEN TURN ON THE APPARATUS (THE SWITCH IS LOCATED ON THE LEFT SIDE OF THE BOX).

Explanation

1. Inside the box there is an electric bell. The sound of the bell should be no weaker than that of a doorbell, preferably as loud as possible.

2. This version of "Black Cannon" is a basic design. It can be used at home, at small exhibitions and in serial production. The original of "Black Cannon" should be mounted on Red Square in Moscow. The dimensions of the box: 10 cubic meters, the diameter: 50 centimeters. The bell should be audible for a radius of ten kilometers.

3. This work can be correctly understood only if it is examined in the context of poetic art and as a system of coordinates marking a starting point for meditation.

4. Note: this explanation is not a part of "Black Cannon," but is a brief authorial commentary for interested observers.

11 December 1975

TRANSLATED BY GERALD JANECEK

Elementary Poetry Number Nine "The Pile"

Text-instruction for E. P. No.9 ("The Pile") No.1 in its general type

A PILE IS CREATED BY VIEWER-PARTICIPANTS OF THIS COMPOSITION. THE COMPOSITION MATERIALIZES IN THE FORM OF A PILE OF OBJECTS CONTRIBUTED BY THE PARTICIPANTS. THESE OBJECTS CAN BE: CLOTHING, BODY PARTS, THE CONTENT OF POCKETS OR THINGS BELONGING TO THE PARTICIPANTS. EXCEPTIONS ARE DECOMPOSABLE MATERIALS — SALIVA, BLOOD, ETC. OBJECTS MUST BE NO LARGER THAN ONE-TWO CUBIC CENTIMETERS IN SIZE.

EACH PARTICIPANT MUST FEED THE PILE ONLY ONCE A DAY.

THE COMPOSITION IS FINISHED WHEN THE TOP OF THE PILE REACHES THE WHITE LINE ON A RULER.

Order of feeding the pile: THE PARTICIPANT CHOOSES AN OBJECT AND PLACES IT ON THE WHITE PODIUM. THEN HE OPENS THE NOTEBOOK AND NOTES IT DOWN. HAVING NOTED IT DOWN, THE PARTICIPANT TAKES A BLANK FORM FROM THE BOX AND FILLS IT OUT AS INDICATED IN THE MODEL AND KEEPS IT (THE FORM CAN ALSO BE FILLED OUT BY THE AUTHOR OF "THE PILE").

When choosing an object, try not to be repetitious!

Created 12 December 1975

TRANSLATED BY GERALD JANECEK

NOTEBOOK FOR RECORDING CONTRIBUTIONS TO FEEDING THE PILE

Model for records in the notebook

No.	Date	surname, name, patronymic	name of the object
1.	21/1-76	Rubinstein, Lev Semyonovich	bead, black

Explanation

1. "The Pile" was begun on 12 December 1975. To the present (19 February 1976) the pile consists of 77 objects.

2. No.4 in the general form is a small box with blank records.

3. No.5 in the general form is a ruler with a white mark, the attalnment of which signals that the composition of the pile is finished.

TRANSLATED BY GERALD JANECEK

Sonnet 66

1   - Burning tears
2   - From the heavens fall
3   - The forest wears
4   -A dewy veil
5   - Wassat? Ok then . . .
6   - Clouds scurry forth
7   - Flocks fed in air
8   - By separate paths
9   - We are heading there
10   - Where's that, eh?
11   - Wrecking the final dream
12   -She is on her way here
13   -Who?
14   -Hide yourself in vain
15   - She will find out where you are
16   -Who?
17   - Hope of salvation
18   -Can never die
19   -True . . .
20   -I know what must be done
21   -He knows . . .
22   -When they arrive
23   -That's interesting . . .
24   -"And apart from that there is a certain space one might designate 'the realm of the *belles lettres'*".
25   -So what?
26   -"Within this space language neither lives nor dies-it, so to speak, vegetables.
27   -"Vegetates" . . . I get it . . .
28   -"Various styles and indices of genre embodied in the form of extracts, fragments, quotes and pseudo-quotes are lifted from this space irrespective of the local hierarchy . . ."

29 -Not so fast . . .

30 -"Their recoding occurs without any surgical intervention — simply through their transfer from one context to another."

31 -Take it easy

32 -"In their new context all the hidden drama of language is turned inside out, as if revealed."

33 -Why "as if"?

34 -"Ideally, this is a linguistic mystery."

35 -Finished?

36 -Now the waves roll ever onwards

37 -"Ever onward . . ."

38 -Now the waves roll on and on

39 -"On and on . . ."

40 -Now the waves roll on towards their doom

41 -"Towards their doom . . ."

42 -Now the waves roll on and you are saying

43 -"You are saying . . ."

44 -Now the waves roll on and break against the ship

45 -Fine . . .

46 -Now yawns a black, unplummeted abyss

47 -Well . . .

48 -Now life begins with non-existence

49 -To non-existence life returns

50 -Now this is our first meeting, this our native shore

51 -And now the rosy sun arises in the east

52 -But were we to follow that path evermore

53 -Now bitter thoughts trouble the darkened brow

54 - Now death's shadow falls across the track

55 -If only, as if out of nothing, somehow

56 -Oh to forget, to fall asleep

57 -But there's no sleep and no forgetting

58 -Oh to go further and for longer

59 -But it turned out nearer and quicker

60 -Oh but how I longed and longed

61 -Yet somehow everything turned out all wrong

62 -Oh to be wide awake and find the place where time after time

63 -The dust engenders

64 -Both Achilles
65 -And the tortoise
66 -And life
67 -And tears
68 -And love
69 -And! . . .
70 -One! Two! Three! Four!
71 -And now henceforth forever
72 -Yeah!
73 -If not today, when will it ever
74 -Yeah!
75 -Everything passes, dreams will be forgotten
76 -Yeah!
77 - Surely this is not the last
78 -Yeah!
79 -Fishes are not afraid of draughts
80 -Yeah!
81 -The shore will no more see the vanished mast
82 -Yeah!
83 - Surely this is not the last
84 -Yeah!
85 -The bones are rotting underground
86 -Yeah!
87 -Surely this is not the last
88 -Yeah!
89   -Mother, lay me out on my bed
90 -Yeah!
91 -Surely this is not the last
92 -Yeah!
93 -When I am gone my friend will be downcast
94 -Yeah!
95 -Surely this is not the last
96 -Yeah!
97 -Surely without a trace of what has passed
98 -Yeah!
99 -Surely this is not the last
100 -Yeah!

101 -And finally:

102 -Ill-starred Phoebus, play your part

103 -Caesura

104 -You yourself know that when it bids farewell

105 -Period . . .

106 -The soul clings to the body

107 -Comma . . .

108 -In the antheap lies the matchstick

109 -Comma . . .

110 -Thrown there a year ago

111 -Caesura . . .

112 -By somebody into the wet grass

113 -Period . . .

Translated by Michael Molnar

Melancholy Album

1. Speaking quite seriously,
2. Then it's already too late.
3. Otherwise, everything is OK: the wind sometimes howls, sometimes is
     quiet,
4. And a wet branch taps at the window.
5. A wet branch taps at the window —
6. Nothing makes sense;
7. A squashed fly is stuck to the glass —
8. To sleep alone;
9. The child made a puddle in the cradle —
10. Left gets mixed up with right;
11. A dead body on the road —
12. A match breaks;
13. The roof has started leaking in the middle —
14. Attend to the guests;
15. The edge of the roof has started leaking —
16. You will envy a neighbor;
17. A black hound —

18. You will find a mushroom right at the gate;
19. Someone arrived unexpectedly —
20. You will think
      "Aroused by the mighty flapping
      Of an incautious wing,
      You attend with fear and trembling
      ....thing.
      While your soul plays hide and seek,
      Recording every twist of fortune,
      ....without a peek
      ....tomb."
21. A rat drinks the water —
22. A guest will hang around till after midnight;
23. Long hair is made into a braid —
24. The samovar will spring a hole;
25. An old man with a cane —
26. The stomach will turn lax;
27. A boat with one oar —
28. You will fall in love with a one-eyed man;
29. A black cockroach —
30. A strange old man will scare you;
31. A reddish cockroach —
32. You'll forget what you wanted;
33. Instead of honey, you ate crap —
34. A dream will come true;
35. Stubbed a toe on a rock —
36. You will say:
      "Today I'm not in the mood for art.
      Sorry, sorry, it's time to go to bed.
      ....smart
      ....instead.
      But no game of subordination —
      ....no bounds,
      ....animation
      ....not found."
37. A naked girl —
38. To pinch a little finger;
39. A blacksmith goes a-courting —

40. To pinch a ring finger;
41. A gypsy lit a match —
42. To pinch a middle finger:
43. The grain has been scattered —
44. You will awake in darkness;
45. You are reading a book —
46. To wave a handkerchief;
47. You pick flowers in the woods —
48. It will begin too late;
49. You pick flowers in a field —
50. As you go in, so will you go out;
51. Didn't recognize oneself in the mirror —
52. You will remember:

> "Until you ask, they will not respond,
> ....won't distribute.
> ....wind.
> ....contribute.
> ....of hated prose
> ....forever after.
> ....laughter
> With tears the world can never know."

53. Wandered into a swamp —
54. There will be no one to even talk to;
55. The chicken will sing like a nightingale —
56. Death is inevitable;
57. You hope for it's not clear what —
58. To struggle with agonizing doubts;
59. You are amazed at your own indecisiveness —
60. To cling to the pitiful remains of your own ideas;
61. You arbitrarily expand the boundaries of the acceptable —
62. You will approach the fateful moment when everything will clearly lose all meaning.
63. Didn't notice that the wind subsided and the last stars went out —
64. You will forget that everything is behind you and that time has irretriev ably run out;
65. You disappear somewhere and then appear unexpectedly, uninvited —
66. Suddenly you will understand that it's time to leave. But where to go?
67. Nothing makes sense —

68. A wet branch is to tap at the window;
69. The wet branch taps at the window,
70. The wind howls, the water gurgles.
71. And all this has long been quite familiar,
72. For some reason it's still interesting.

TRANSLATED BY GERALD JANECEK

IVAN AKHMETEV

from Poems and Only Poems

(1968-1980)

the immobility of
the hour hand

~~~

it is pleasant
to place a hand
on the table

~~~

be fruitful
multiply
trade apartments

~~~

I met two tiny twins
and though they were exactly identical
only one
looked at me

~~~

we have a despondent look
we hang our heads
and stretch our necks out
waiting for the axe to fall

~~~

evening
I watch silent movies
in the windows of the neighbor's house

∾∾∾

(1980-1985)

immersing myself in memories
I realize
how much was extraordinarily
significant
so far exceeding
the humble proportions
of my person

∾∾∾

    the pause
I will make
before answering
will tell you more

∾∾∾

(1985-1992)

writing in the dark
I didn't notice
the pen wasn't writing

∾∾∾

in those times
to think (so)
was unacceptable

now it's unusual

∾∾∾

I stand out
from most other writers
in that I'm personally acquainted
with all my readers

∾∾∾

people wrote
in labor camps
and in prison
and in the nut house
and where didn't they write

the main thing
was to do it unobtrusively

∾∾∾

Stalin isn't typical

∾∾∾

that single glance
had innumerable consequences

innumerable glances
innumerable embraces
innumerable kisses
innumerable vows
of fidelity to the grave

∾∾∾

Crossing Centuries:

1 what you want
2 what you need

one contradicts the other

~~~

(forgot to write it down)

~~~

the weather was
  so nice
the sun shining

I just had to
go out
and stand in line

Translated by Alex Cigale

from Accidental Selection

Chaadaev's publisher
was *Gershenzon*.

What's the forecast?

What might he . . .
Or . . .
And what about the liqueurs?

Whose wife?
Or later he'll write:
"And the child-wife,
like a dark glass . . ." . . .

The color of drunken sour cherries.

Whitefish,
forgive me.
Have a bite.

∾∾∾

  Kiev.

"February. Obtain ink . . ." . . .
"We have household detergent
continually
on sale."
So that's how it is.
He knew the language
and still didn't run away.
Whose side are you on, commissars of culture?

ᘉᘉᘉ

Kolya,
don't fool around with alcohol.
What are you thinking!
It's no laughing matter.

ᘉᘉᘉ

Orgies —
to the Party organizer
let's give the signal —
he'll organize it.

You know —
with one
of the "book collection's"
whores.

Where's
your Party conscience,
gone?

At government
expense.

ᘉᘉᘉ

Yura's
parents are
crooks.

Vera's
girlfriends are
unsuitable.

(*Lyova's* opinion).

These,
it turns out,
are the examples.

∾∾∾

With black caviar?
And some cognac.
What could be better.

∾∾∾

Nice and accurate —
that's what
can be said
about this book.

∾∾∾

Abraham,
are you coming
to the meeting?

Abraham.

∾∾∾

Comrade,
get to your point.

I earnestly ask you
not to deny
my request.

People in line
are waiting,
comrade.

TRANSLATED BY ALEX CIGALE

Crossing Centuries:

No one has yet spoken like this

Mandelstam said:
　　　. . . caravan-sarai . . .
Oh, forgot.
That is, I forgot,
but it wasn't Mandelstam who said that I forgot.[*]

Aleksandr Ivanovich and Daniil Ivanovich[†]
eye-witnessed:
　　　. . . Ivan Ivanich
Oh, forgot.
Which Ivan Ivanich — Daniil Ivanovich's,
which — Aleksandr Ivanovich's
perhaps someone will tell us?

Yan Abramovich[‡] sensed it
　　　. . . do I want . . .
That is, he,
that is, I,
that is, he,
that is no, forgot again.

Of this I'm certain, I chose the right title:
"no one has yet spoken like this".

∾∾∾

Every booklover submitting to the government
40 kg. of scrap paper is entitled
to acquire 5 kg. of books.

---

[*]As in the other two cases, there is a fragmentary reference to words by the given poet.
[†]Vvedensky and Kharms.
[‡]Satunovsky

∞∞∞

And the reading . . .
What about the reading?
It has begun already,
and perhaps
much earlier
than you noticed.

∞∞∞

Leningrad's Order of Lenin Lenin Metropolitan Subway,
what to call it now — to releninize and reeleninate?

∞∞∞

It seems: somewhere at the test site
on the screen
in every house
2 clowns have taken over:
Bing and Bom
bingbombingbombing.
Bombing.

∞∞∞

Fingers are drawn to pen
pen — to paper
paper — to a flat surface
flat surface — to the cold,
to the cold with the perfected
to the perfected
with a shifted center of gravity
with an optical
scope,
a minute —
and the poetry will flow freely

∾∾∾

the art of success is
in the success of the art

∾∾∾

life expectancy of a dinosaur, 370 years
life expectancy of a crocodile, 65 years
life expectancy of a dog, 16 years
life expectancy of a flea, 1.3 years

a length of legs stretched out on the sand toward the sea
and along their whole length
not a single flea
not one dog
no crocodile either
no dinosaur

TRANSLATED BY ALEX CIGALE

◼◼ NIKOLAI BAITOV ◼◼

from Four Corners: Adventures of Information

TRAJECTORY 61

Glazed tile mouth well fine you envy well plowed skull not looking countertop

glazed stalwart prisoner tile through the mouth well fine already you envy skull well number blanket plowed not looking polecat countertop

glazed here you are tile salubrious stalwart prisoner went through the mouth crookedly well fine already you envy well number polecat blanket went skull not looking well plowed stalwart sickly countertop

glazed here you are tile flowering whom went stalwart salubrious prisoner well fine plowed though the mouth crookedly polecat went like well number whom you envy socle skull already sickly well went stalwart not looking plowed salubrious blanket like countertop

<table>
<tr><td>A</td><td>B</td></tr>
</table>

glazed countertop already flowering well like tile not looking polecat went whom blanket well stalwart hose salubrious

glazed resembling countertop already tile whom flowering not looking well like service went final hose polecat salubrious well whom stalwart already blanket

glazed not looking countertop vainly resembling went polecat final whom already tile flowering whom incident well service went salubrious stalwart like hose well whom polecat blanket already not looking

you envy here you are through crookedly number socle well fine final mouth sickly plowed skull time already prisoner like you laugh

you envy socle crookedly here you and scrap number through the mouth well fine time you laugh sickly socle is it plowed well skull already crookedly like prisoner

you envy next well scrap socle crookedly wilted here you are well fine mouth through number once sickly scrap you laugh socle prisoner well is it plowed already like time crookedly through skull glazed not looking countertop hammered vainly resembling went stalwart incident final polecat whom already soil flowering service whom well tile went salubrious stalwart like polecat hose well whom not looking blanket already service

you envy well fine socle already crookedly wilted is it next prisoner well scrap here you are sawdust time you laugh like number through sickly mouth skull plowed socle well is it crookedly you laugh gauze prisoner next time well fine scrap number

A

glazed whom blanket tsaritsa resembling flowering well not looking went stalwart incident whom hose soil like countertop salubrious

glazed stalwart salubrious well resembling whom hose incident soil well tsaritsa like flowering whom went not looking suggest blanket like countertop

glazed stalwart incident well gently resembling whom flowering tsaritsa like blanket well soil whom salubrious countertop hose not looking to suggest went

glazed gently stalwart well blanket incident resembling

ab

final time is it polecat tile hammered crookedly gauze prisoner well time service well mouth already vainly especially wilted

final time service is it yesterday gauze tile hammered well crookedly already vainly mouth wilted is it especially time prisoner polecat

final time is it gauze yesterday hammered polecat all in all crookedly well already tile mouth especially vainly is it service time prisoner wilted

final time especially yesterday is it gauze hammered all

B

you envy socle sickly here you and next scrap through skull plowed sawdust number honorary well fine you laugh like

you envy number next here you are through socle honorary skull beauty well fine sickly you laugh plowed like scrap sawdust

you envy skull next sickly number here you are through scrap like plowed sawdust across a stump block well fine you laugh honorary socle beauty

you envy sickly across a stump block sawdust next scrap number here you are whom bouquet like flowering soil well tsaritsa hose not looking countertop whom to suggest salubrious went

in all crookedly prisoner looked around tile vainly already mouth is it service well polecat

reliably across skull plowed you like socle honorary well fine beauty

Ab

glazed mouth whom crookedly to suggest is it time gently blanket resembling incident whom tsaritsa well not looking countertop yesterday salubrious like stalwart personally already wilted prisoner went is it bouquet gauze well all in all hose flowering soil

glazed bouquet gauze whom mouth is it prisoner to suggest crookedly yesterday personally blanket gently resembling well tsaritsa like incident soil all in all already wilted flowering stalwart relative is it went time salubrious not looking countertop well hose

glazed bouquet salubrious relative whom gauze is it crookedly to suggest well mouth yesterday prisoner personally stalwart gently hose resembling well tsaritsa like whom incident all in all eternal countertop already wilted soil flowering is it went time not looking plowed

Ba

you envy polecat sickly socle reliably across a stump block looked around next skull final number well like hammered honorary scrap already service vainly you laugh tile especially across sawdust well fine like frequenter already plowed here beauty

you envy across sawdust sickly socle understood reliably looked around polecat across a stump block final number well already like skull hammered honorary frequenter vainly you laugh scrap especially tile like beauty well fine already plowed here you are service

you envy across sawdust like understood honorary frequenter well across a stump block reliably looked around sickly polecat thanks final next number already hammered skull socle especially vainly you laugh tile well fine service like beauty here you are understood scrap already plowed

AB

glazed through sawdust bouquet honorary whom you envy relative service whom like salubrious frequenter time understood his crookedly through gauze is it scrap well across a stump block mouth looked around reliably to suggest yesterday personally well thanks polecat well prisoner eternal stalwart its gently all in all final sickly hose already hammered resembling next skull tsaritsa like socle especially incident vainly already number wilted tile you laugh understood whom soil flowering beauty well fine is it went here you are time understood already countertop not looking plowed blanket

glazed here you are honorary relative personally like understood its incident whom service yesterday already final time well polecat looked around across a stump block reliably hammered through gauze gently whom to suggest is it salubrious number well fine plowed his blanket through sawdust crookedly went prisoner well thanks whom you envy stalwart sickly hose you laugh is it especially tsaritsa all in all flowering tile here you are time bouquet beauty well went next frequenter socle vainly you laugh already wilted mouth resembling well fine llke scrap already not looking understood whom soil eternal countertop

TRANSLATED BY GERALD JANECEK

from One-cocked Ulysses

APPROXIMATELY THUS:

ate times tree equus too tens 'n for
I used the past tense because
my data is possibly out of date
(you do understand what I'm saying)

everything, except anyone

I read: NIPPEL' (Engl. nipple) — . . . 3) mushroom-
shaped part with an inner
thread for tightening
I spokes in the rim of a wheel

wow
what cacophony

awkward, like annulled babble

then why this
daily ritual: breakfast, lunch and supper
a disinterest in going anywhere,
aggravated by an immense desire to travel somewhere,
from and to
and an exceptional mental state

one thing
is uncertain,
if they're blind, then how are they drawn to the light

inarticulately

I read

and the young girls sang each night
at night either scream or be silent
scream don't scream ragmen
will defile you in the night

how 'bout a drink

I read
And he took it into his left hand, so as to place it.
And he took it into his right hand, so as to lay it.
And then he said: "Thus my deed is complete."

these
strange things
are whose?

✳✳✳

OTHERWISE:

A garland made of sargasso
to wipe the floors with.
Quantity of goods: 1 piece.
Quantity in box: 10 pieces.
Unit price per 1 piece — 1 ruble 25 kopeks.

OTHERWISE:

. . . eviscerated, granulation, recklessness
self-spun, to inhale . . .

Tell it to anyone else, he wouldn't believe it.

OTHERWISE:

Two cartridges for a ballpoint pen.
One empty,
the other about half-filled.

OTHERWISE:

They climbed up and did so quickly.
They descended and did so slowly.

OTHERWISE:

With inexplicable satisfaction excavating small-
ish balls of this substance, he intently ex-
amined them, sniffing, experiencing some sort
of peculiar feeling of pleasurable disgust.

OTHERWISE:

Into a matchbox I will place a negative fly.

OTHERWISE:

I turned on the iron.
A good iron.
Electric.

OTHERWISE:

It moves — that means it disappears.

OTHERWISE:

Robbed of their natural function they
reminded one of little metal sculptures.
Sort of pseudo-matréshkas. One larger, two
others smaller. Roundbellied . . .

OTHERWISE:

. . . as many as there are, how many there may be, a few
for each; but: no matter how much money he has, he will
spend it all.

OTHERWISE:

September 11, 1989.

OTHERWISE:

No otherwise is possible.

ༀༀༀ

CONTINUATION OF THAT WHICH.

the plumbers came on time
and installed new faucets
but there is no hot water

how can you sleep so much

twilight

the transom is bigger than an airvent
but smaller than a window

. . . drip-drip-drip . . .

everything is normal
there are already several of us

through her
with baby rattles of internal combustion
dirty-faced eternity chatters

gnawing on the pit
(black plum — night's embryo)

turn the fan on!

what does the Arctic have to do with it

it just so happens

the woman's about thirty and she smokes

so there

now you definitely don't understand a thing

TRANSLATED BY ALEX CIGALE

MIKHAIL EPSTEIN

LIKE A CORPSE I LAY IN THE DESERT

T HE NEW MOSCOW POETRY PROVOKES IN THE READER a feeling of aesthetic
unrest — a certain loss of orientation. Complaints can be heard about
its code and its over-complexity. However, the complexity doesn't come
from the language itself, but rather from the principal loss of a solid center,
which was previously embodied by the lyrical hero. All of poetry's com-
plexities were revealed just as the reader's response coincided with the cen-
tralized system's hero: "I am this way. . . . This is how I see the world."
Whether the hero was diabolical, frightening or cynically empty, fanatically
cruel or naively foolish (as in the poetry from the beginning of the twentieth
century, the Oberiu poets, etc . . .) they somehow gave the reader the happy
possibility of transforming and expanding their own "I" by putting it up for
account before that of another's.

There's no one left to identify with anymore. Poetry has ceased to be a
mirror for the self-loving "ego," and all that remains is a murky spot left
from the last lyrical breath. Now, there's the stone's crystal structure — and
its multiple reflections: perception no longer reflects back on the self. A po-
etry of structure has taken the place of the poetry of the "I." In some deci-
sive historical break-down, the "I" discovered its own unreliability and
falsehood, discovered that it had — treacherously evaded its responsibility,
and the structure then had to take this responsibility upon itself. The social,
the symbolic (signifier), the nuclear, the genetic. . . . People don't speak in
the language of these structures, but Some One speaks to them. It's part of
our desire to understand. But the new lyric represents an experiment at de-
veloping these alienated, these trans-personalized or hyper-personalized
structures, behind which lies the felt presence of a completely different Sub-
ject, not at all in line with the habitual measures of subjectivity, i.e., "hu-
manity — the measurer of all things, etc. . . ." The object itself becomes the
measure of everything human, in that through it this Other's presence can
be sensed and unleashed, and a person can subsequently feel the actual ba-
sis of his or her own "I." The new poetry no longer puts forth the self's ex-
pression, which could really be called the Ego's expression, but moves into
worlds where humanity leaves neither a trace nor footprint, where one can
look through the strangely arranged crystal of the poetic eye.

This is what Blok experienced in his own time as the "Crisis of humanism," the spouting of "Utter cruelty" and "Backward tenderness," the animal and organic forms in a human. In our time this poetic eye has reached its peak, discovering a multitude of self-activating forms of being in place of the old individual. These (manifested) forms co-exist in a joint, "musical" flow (human civilization was conquered by the "spirit of music"). Mandelstam acknowledged the same thing with almost the same words: "In him (the poet), the ideas are singing, the scientific Systems, the governmental theories. . . ." This whole lyrical movement which goes beyond the limits of the lyrical "I" reveals the depth of something completely different, more fundamental — and because of that it presents a more finite experience, a shifting structure and hyper-objectiveness best described in religious terms, though not connected with any concrete religious tradition. The essence is not in the theme but precisely in the subject of expression, to which the new lyric pushes beyond the author's personality and simultaneously, in the outcome of all these processes of disembodiment and "depersonalization," has to accept the qualities of the transcendental Personality.

The structure's nature (now incorporated in contemporary poetry) varies according to the capacities of the replaced center itself. Poets such as the Conceptualists, (Prigov, Rubinstein, Kibirov, Sukhotin), explore the mechanisms of mass consciousness and everyday speech, which automatically influence a person, neither willingly nor consciously, but rather as it is said, "through" the spoken language itself. The bare schemes of divergent ideas, the gutted scarecrow of contemporary world views, i.e.,"concepts," are exposed. "Life is given to man for the rest of his life . . . ," "The outstanding hero moves forward without fear," "Stalin's falcon proudly makes its hawking cry . . . ," "Sing me a song about everything you'd like, the swan song, the bright red cotton flag!" Conceptualism presents a poetry of crossed-out words, words which come apart at the moment of expression, as if they have no meaning whatsoever. Their presence, like the riddle of self-revealing emptiness, should appear directly in this absence or erasure of meaning. Each time something like "absolutely right" or "absolutely banal" is uttered, there's an uncomfortable pause, a strained silence, which uncovers the real presence of the Absolute, yet manifests as its only negative — the void. It seems no one really speaks in this manner now — but Mr. Nobody goes on talking in such a way, having made his claim to the commanding role in literature and life. A number of conceptual poems are written in his name, taking from the reader in the end the chance to relate with *anyone.*

But perhaps the importance of the work lies elsewhere. This deliberate banality hides in itself the reverse idea of deepening the zone of the unspoken. If you don't simply laugh at the Conceptualists' poetry, seeing in them the parody of stereotyped mass consciousness, you may sense something more still: behind this chattering Nobody, there's the authentic lyric of the silent Hyper-subject. After all, only in the relationship to His Hyper-filled silence can all of our words sound so poor, flat, & crude as they intentionally sound when used by the Conceptualists. They sentimentally call their literary group, "The Sincere Chat," but in their playfulness about a "sincere chat," the Conceptualists hem in clearly overused and alien words that lack any meaning in & of themselves. In artistic groups, nothing's really "sincere" or reminiscent of a "chat." Nevertheless, a keener ear will probably catch in their so-called poems an echo that calls to mind a Chekhovian intonation. For instance, when Chebutykin was reading aloud from his newspaper and said, "Tsytsykar. The plague is raging here," or thoroughly convincing his partner: "But I tell you, it was chekhartma," from under the disgusting text, a subtext of misunderstanding, senselessness and loneliness unfolds. In comparison, we have Prigov's: "The chopped up one again is the President, though now it's in Bangladesh . . . ," or from Rubinstein: "Don't talk nonsense!" What does "Woe From Wit" have to do with it when this is the "Dead Souls"? Here again we have all the same empty signs of "useful" information or "meaty" communication. It's true, the Conceptualists' subtexts themselves "like another meaning" have been dissolved, yielding a place for the "no meaning whatsoever." Yet, too many words from the twentieth century's "torrent of words" have flown into the wind; the layer behind them hasn't had time to air out the psychological underpinnings, hasn't had time to expose the writings' deeper metaphysical emptiness. Still more emphatically, the Conceptualists sweep these dead words from the language like "bees from an empty beehive." In this way, we're allowed to listen to the silence itself — along the border of the once deceived sense of hearing.

On the other hand, poets such as Zhdanov, Sedakova, Grimberg, Parshchikov, Kutik, and Aristov, take into their vocabulary, as if into the red book of speech, all those words that remain alive. They squeeze out and even overstrain their meaning in order to unveil the actual structure of reality, which again, doesn't evolve toward the lyrical "I." Nonetheless, it is attained according to the process of affirmation rather than negation. Meta-realism, as the movement can be called, opens a pluralism of realities — those that appear through the perspective of an ant and those which pivot within a mathematical formula, or those that are said to be *in* the "sky-high flight of angels." The Metarealistic image doesn't simply reflect one of these realities (mirror realism), doesn't simply compare, become like (meta-phorism), doesn't simply deliver one to the other by means of allusion, allegory (symbolism): it reveals their authenticity and inescapable wonder through the process of a genuine participation and mutual transformation. "I know something about wonders, they're like sentries on the hours" (Sedakova). Each reality appears in another (reality) by the violation of its own laws, like an exit into a new dimension, which is why the image becomes a chain of metamorphoses, having surrounded Reality as a whole through its dreams and wakenings, through its breaks and ties within the link of the chain. In this way, the words don't crumble in on themselves, can't be discarded like "nobody's," but rather they strive toward the limit of omni-responsiveness and multiple meanings, which are rooted in the very depth of language's memory; the more intermingled the diverse times and diverse nationalities of the layers of the cultural soil, the more fresh the sprout and plentiful the growth. In Metarealism, the poetry of emphatic words, each word should mean more than what it once meant. The characteristics of this poetry can be heard in I. Zhdanov's lines: "Either the letters are not being understood, or perhaps their size is unbearable to the eye . . ./ a red wind remains in the field,/ the name of the rose is on its lips." The meanings acquire such intensity that the difference between signifier and signified disappear. Out of the letters comprising the rose's name, the wind remains, painted in the color of the flower itself: to name it means to acquire its qualities. In this hyper-reality explored by the meta-realist, there is no humanly designated contrast between object and word: they (the object and word) exchange their "attributes" and the world is read as a book, written with letters of incomprehensible measure.

The poets who have been through the experience of timelessness attain a grandness of condensed space. They are distinct from the poets of the 60s, who saw the world as divided into epochs and periods, countries and continents; the poets who began writing in the 70s and publishing in the 80s spiritually exist in the multiple measures of continuum, where all time and consciousness are interconnected, ranging from the neolithic to the neo-avant-garde. The historical stream has lost its monolithic direction called progress. Where it has slowed and expanded, an estuary has formed: "times" no longer follow one another but sway freely in boundless space at the entrance point into the sea.

These new poets catch the impulses pertaining to the tremors of meaning, passing as they do through all of the epochs at once. What was hallowed in the Middle Ages resounds as echos in the twentieth century. They're children of their own timelessness, who have experienced not only the negative effect of historical stagnation — which turned them into the latent "stagnating generation" — but also the positive sensation of the hyper-historical abutment, exposed along the receding waters of the last decade. *Timelessness — this is the parodying monument of eternity.* And if only some poets, like the Metarealists, strive toward this eternity, others such as the Conceptualists uncover its state of "parodyness," and yet a third group commemorate it as a monument.

In the poetry of "Moscow Time" and that of those poets close to the group (Gandlevsky, Soprovsky, Bunimovich, Korkiya, and others) a multitude of sharp, contemporaneous signs appear like an amazingly preserved layer in the zone of some future archaeological findings. ". . . We recognize our years in the concentric rings of the capital" (Bunimovich). The poets of this circle rarely venture into metaphysical questions or the area of distant epochs, but stay closer to the relics of the past found in Moscow's constrained and ghostly lifestyles of the 1970s and 1980s. Yes, "relics of the past," because willingly or unwillingly it has entered into a new hyper-historical dimension where it appears as one of the intricate sediments of passing time, even as we continue to reside in it: the last bittersweet remains of time is as such. It's good to bear in mind with these particular poets that while they still partly maintain the lyrical hero in their poetry, these heroes no longer go through the same kind of experience. They just remember it, adding honest and sad testimony to the precious archive of the museum of deceased Humanity, i.e. "the personality of the twentieth century." "Did I happen to be here or not, making Rhymes across the living thread? And here, up to now, Everything was useful for the loser, for the torment of his heart" (S. Gandlevsky).

Distinct from the archivists, who attempt to override the present with the past and seriously write as they did 100 years ago, the poets of "Moscow Time" show the sense and taste of the *archaeologists* who know how fragile and breakable the decomposed material (the lyrical "I") is and thus don't try to interchange time. With the lyrical "I" they continue their tedious restoration work and show how the material is destroyed from straight contact with the here and now. In their poems, the "I" shines through distinctly, but as a silhouette all the same, as if shining through a transparent fossil. In the densely associated fabric of writing, time congeals as in the cold and pure bullion erupted from the ancient deep. How will future descendants of the epoch remember it? Perhaps they'll call it "the Amber Century" of Russian poetry.

This metapoetry, so removed from any "battle-like" participation in modernity, seems death-like to readers raised on the previous generation's poetry. Where's the passion, the inspiration, the impulse? Instead of a lyrical hero who's enthusiastic, desperate, someone who has traveled the world from Canberra to Calcutta, or who, on the other hand, is committed to the plowed pasture of his native land, or the keenly sensitive "I" or the thoughtfully self-assured "we," we have this strange lyrical "It." "It" is not imaginable in the appearance of any concrete human form. Even love is no longer a feeling, an attraction, but rather more of a contour with a tightly bent, exclusive space of its own, the curve of which is either exploding like an earthquake and separating lovers, or breaking the mirror into pieces which unite them. "The earthquake is in the thudding t's" (A. Parshchikov), or, "The distance between you and me is you. . . ." In Zhdanov's poetry, the works are about love, but it's scrutinized more from the viewpoint of topology or geophysics than from that of the laws of a psychology regarding "human behavior." The new poetry isn't like some offspring of a new time with humanity existing as the central point of the universe's structure, but more like a memory of an earlier time and a premonition of a later time — when humanity will cease to be the inevitable point of departure and may possibly become the inevitable point of arrival.

Just when and why did we decide that poetry has to be cut to the measure of the human "I," that its hero should reach the height of his or her own historical contemporary, that it must possess the same distraught heart, the same eyes clouded with dreams and passion, the same language suitable for the population's consumption? The lyrical "It" has its own prototype resembling wheels connecting with one another, their rims full of eyes, moved by the Spirit of holy animal-cherubs. And didn't the path of the poet-prophet begin after all with the Book of Isaiah and Ezekiel, which charted the path of the high poetry preserved by Pushkin. Let's re-read this "Prophet" with today's eyes, and as if for the first time we are shaken up by the necessity of the destruction of what is human. He was given a snake's sting instead of a tongue, burning coal instead of a heart. That's how the whole human content was killed off within him. What was that monster that lay in the desert with a stinger in its mouth and coal in its rib cage? But he was a prophet on the calling of God; he was ready for resurrection.

Like a corpse I lay in the desert . . .

Contemporary poetry at times reminds us of a corpse in which everything that's alive and human-like has disappeared. What sticks out are the sharp stingers, the webbed tissue, the carbon bodies. But picture it: this whole unimaginable aggregate is ready to rise and announce the truth at the first word from above — he was made to quiver. The Seraph has already concluded its difficult dirty-work: the new superhuman organism is ready for life. And people that see in it only inhuman deformities and a set of mechanical parts don't even suspect that precisely from him they may hear new words, which communicate the thought and the will of God. To reach people, the prophet has to kill the human in itself — in order to burn their hearts. The prophet requires coal instead of a heart.

Maybe we are living in the unknown short pause.

. . . And God's voice was calling me . . .

Now what is left is to listen, to heed, and not miss this voice in the desert, which surrounds the lonely prophet, who looks like a corpse.

TRANSLATED BY JOHN HIGH WITH JULIE GESIN

METAREALISM

THOMAS EPSTEIN

METAREALISM

B Y THE MID 1970s, as the Soviet Union slipped into the Communist utopia
of "post-history," now less kindly looked back upon as a period of so-
cial and political "stagnation," a new generation of poets burrowed under-
gound, creating a body of texts whose significance only became apparent in
the early 1990s. Socially invisible, this band of metaphysicians and meta-
phorists, Leningraders and Muscovites, sought to awaken the slumbering
Russian language with charges of electrical-poetic energy. This energy
surged in all directions; backward into tradition and myth; forward, into
the linguistic and social realities of the Soviet and world present; upward,
into the heavens; downward, into murky earth. For these poets, both de-
fined by and cut off from Soviet realities, art's primary goal was neither
cognitive nor ideological; rather, in the works of Elena Shvarts and Olga
Sedakova, Victor Krivulin and Arkady Dragomoschenko, Vladimir Aristov
and Nadezhda Kondakova, Aleksandr Eremenko and Alexei Parshchikov,
in Ilya Kutik and Ivan Zhdanov, the poetic word was both an end in itself,
revealing riches, both comic and tragic, suppressed by the one — dimen-
sionality of the official culture; and a vehicle for travels to other worlds, in-
visible and perhaps incomprehensible, but nevertheless real or potentially
so.

To talk about these poets as a "group" is something of a misnomer:
they wrote no manifestoes, marched under no banner, created no single
linguistic or symbolic code. However, a certain emphasis can be discerned
among them, which allows us to divide them broadly into two sub-groups.
The first, comprised of Eremenko, Parshchikov, Kutik, Kondakova, and
Dragomoschenko, explores the limits and powers of language to name the
real and of metaphor to link disparate levels of experience. In Eremenko the
prevailing device for this exploration is irony, the inability of language, as
bearer of cultural meanings, to express the meanings it intends: inevitably
there is both excess and deficit, a plenitude which, bordering on chaos,
threatens to be engulfed by a ground-zero of language. Parshchikov, his
friend and nemesis, tends toward a semantically saturated grid of cultural
coordinates. Kutik's genial eye captures a plenitude of worlds in a single
penetrating glance. Kondakova's meta-world takes root at the crossroads of
sound and image. Dragomoschenko, whose connections with American

Language poetry are well documented, is the most philosophically reflective of the group, exploring the meaning-creating powers of language in the very process of poetic creativity.

Zhdanov, Krivulin, Sedakova, Aristov, and Shvarts, poets whose works could never be mistaken one for the other, nevertheless share an abiding faith in the lyric voice, in the myth-making powers of language, in the presence of the past in the present, and of the spiritual mystery of life and death. Zhdanov, the "archaizer" of the group (particularly in form: for example, his poem "The distance between you and me is you" is written in anapestic pentameter) is a poet whose brooding lyrics are rooted in Russia's solemn metaphysical tradition dating back to the 18th-century poet Gavriil Derzhavin. Meditative more than discursive, Zhdanov uses chains of metaphors to link/unlink the personal to the historical and transcendent. Krivulin, inspired by his mentors Blok and Mandelstam, tries to create what may be described oxymoronically as a Leningrad Silver Age: a poetic paradise in the underbelly of a declassé Soviet city. Aristov, a paradoxical lyricist, subverts and enriches the experience of the everyday by submitting it to a variety of discourses, linguistic registers, humor and pathos. Sedakova, by contrast, is a cool and controlled, classicizing talent whose religiously inspired verse combines the quiet grace of Akhmatova with a neo-Symbolist awareness of the infinite depths that lie beyond and within. Shvarts, perhaps the single most talented poet of her generation, is simultaneously a formal innovator, a metaphysically charged myth-maker, and a lyric seeker for whom no subject is "below" poetry: everything is recuperable, everything is real.

Having reached their maturity in obscurity or amidst the unwanted attentions of the cultural (and civil) police, these poets are rightly considered living classics to the poets who have followed behind. Thank God, they are all of them still alive, and most of them still writing.

Untitled

To Hieronymus Bosch,
inventor of the projector

1.
I look at you from such deep graves,
that before my glance can reach you, it splits in two.
We'll hoax them now as always by playing a comedy:
that you were not there at all. And so, neither was I.
We didn't exist in the inaudible chromosomal bustle,
in this large sun or the large white protoplasm.
They're still accusing us of such senility,
standing watch with their upraised oars in a primeval soup.
We'll as always now again attempt to bring together
the bodies' trajectories. Here are the conditions of the first move:
if you illuminate the nearest stretch of road,
I'll call you a noun of the feminine gender.
Of course in this rubbish I'll find — plain as day —
the appropriate conflict, one corresponding to the assigned scheme.
So, floating up from the bottom, the triangle will forever stick
to its theorem. You still need to be proven.
We'll still have to drape over you some combination of morphemes
/the morphine that has lost its way in the dazzling form of a wasp/
so that the bodies' possessors would recognize you in the appropriate shape
on every occasion. My glance has now returned to the first stanza.
l look at you from such deep . . .
The game continues — the move will grow out of me, like a gun port.
Take away the convoy. We're acting out a hoax.
I was sitting on a mountain, depicted where the mountain is.

I was sitting on a mountain, depicted where the mountain is.
Below me/if I spit — I'd hit/
the crowd of runners passing through an impenetrable and dark blue hell,
the numbers on their shirts wiggling like fine lice.

Behind my back a painted paradise rustled,
now it's trumpeting along the edge, now ringing so that you could hear it a
   mile away.
It was an angel that floated by, or it was a brand new clean streetcar,
like a cross-eyed little boy, with a metallic pipe in his mouth. . . .
And like an antenna, the empty hand will turn the altar
and the son who combined with himself there within
will wander on — lost in the wet and flabby aspens' structure,
like a paper hockey goalie unfurled by the wind.
Who today can pare down this language — folded over 2-3 times, complete
yet simple — this meaning that's wound itself around the theorem's screw
with its length, width, height — this 3-fold horror
of a system built into the mind?
Here's a heavenly sign — hell's making progress,
concentric cold circles approaching us.
I look at you — and my glance bends,
biting its own tail, stomping on the nape of my neck with its boots.
And the last days are stuck in the bellowing tableau,
the running deer imprinted on frozen firewood.
Surfacing from the bottom — beneath the ice, go ahead, push apart the
   year-old ring
and it'll rejoin, bringing you to your knees,
where the three-dimensional well isn't worth a spit.
Archimedes up to his own knees in mud — the secant flatness of the Tatars.
A direct pistol shot does exist in this cross-eyed world,
but even it is no straighter than a straight intestine.
Just as a wolfhound would never strangle a desert wolf —
in the empty skies the skyscraper is scraping nothing but the sky. And
when /I forget the word/ your spine will end up
in this meat and grinder —
and then your gullet will sing for sure!

2.

A nightingale expands in the bushes.
A star spins over it.
Water's crammed into the marsh,
as an electrical transformer.

The moon flying over our heads.
A projector burning on the vacant lot
delineating this sector,
from where the angle's given.

TRANSLATED BY JOHN HIGH

Fragment

The translucent wires of the forest are crumbling,
The leaves waver slightly, nothing ever in working order for long.
There a silent *lemma* sagging along a straight road
The straight lines of the telegraph give one a headache.

The air's unclear, there's a broken connection
Between the circuitry and the flower
And the river is haphazardly crawling under itself,
And it too rustles, at least all things are in phase.

The electric wind is tied in empty knots
and if the top layers of the red dirt were stripped away
the pine trees would be masts held to the ground with bolts
the tops are half twisted and the thread of the bolt gummed with clay.

As soon as the stamped out rows
of fir trees fly away I will see through the window
a factory village torn and sinking in the thick mud by the river,
and a small brickyard with an even smaller hole in its side.

Does is matter that I haven't been here in eleven years,
the autumn thicket by the side of the road is still as clean and well tended.
And the spot's still there, where Kolka Zhadobin by a campfire
one night molded me a pistol from a piece of lead.

There's my wife knitting on a long boring couch.
There's my bride sitting in a wooden chair
There's my mother at work and lost in rising fog
and my grandson peering through the window into the ruined air.

I died there yesterday. And I could hear
horrible and clear an old horse along the road
a workhorse, and I could hear as it climbed the hill
the "horsepower," whirring and choking like a chainsaw.

TRANSLATED BY JOSEPH DONAHUE AND ALEKSANDR KALUZHSKI

The Length of a Look

The look that inducts men for war
taking their height, the look of a T-Square
the long look that underlies the world and supports it
like an old bracket, the long look out the window.

Glimpse of the beyond, Einstein saw it,
but did Einstein really amount to much?
He flipped the bracket over like an empty glass,
but — it was the same old bracket. As in an old myth

the world kept resting on the backs of whales.
But for us the importance is in the look,
and then all that it observes in the dark.
Length alone has meaning: a long, empty look.

With it one can gaze into a well for water
though it's no good for showing how to get to the recycling center with old
                                                                    paper.
And if one spends the time working on one's looks at a health club
this long, empty look will vanish.

From all this we derive our view
on how to truly measure the length of an empty look
whether the sum of these lengths, when each is a single book
equals one length, the length of an empty look

Crossing Centuries:

. . . underlies the world, so that the cities
can stand level and secure in their places.
An empty movie house, the dredges of the supermarket
and the metronome of the branches, which ticks unnoticed between the walls.

TRANSLATED BY JOSEPH DONAHUE AND ALEKSANDR KALUZHSKI

Untitled

A horizontal country.
Verticals moving by.
Here, the diagonal and its side always
exist as an immeasurable continuum.

At the house, a garden
square of a window.
Snow falls along the diagonals.
As for tomorrow, the snow will only be a heap
piled there . . . against the other side.

Satan is omniscient in fact
within the depth of the draftsman's tools.
Today's genius — is still a genius,
but he doesn't remember a fucking thing.

There's truth in everything
so drink up, friend.
At the house, a garden — making whatever noise it wants.
Who can understand its language
when awakening . . .

TRANSLATED BY JOHN HIGH AND KATYA OLMSTED

Untitled*

And Schubert on the water, and Pushkin living on rations,
and Lermontov's eye grown accustomed to the darkness . . .
I've learned you, blissful swingsets
loafing about the illusive boundary line without a knife.

It's as if I were strung up in a public toilet
on a long vector which splashed in the heat of the moment.
And already I'm up to my elbow in that black swill
plunging deeper on up to the shoulder.

TRANSLATED BY JOHN HIGH AND KATYA OLMSTED

Untitled

Igor Alexandrovich Antunov,
your death isn't far off.
In other words, after a few eons
you'll fly over us like a light-emitting body.

A simple Moscow guy, you'll fly over us
complete, like a transfigured Buddha.
Rama Krishna, Kedrov, and Gagarin
each watching in amazement.

A long time now I haven't trusted my own heart,
yet I clearly remember where you
puked, having opened the small door — so cultured
and flowers growing through the asphalt!

Kali Yuga — there's the centrifuge.
So as not to spin out of orbit
we stand, clutching one another
at this remote reach of the Milky Way.

---

*The poem makes reference to Osip Mandelstam's "Solomnika" ("Straw") and Zabolotsky's "Vchera o smerti razmyshliaia" ("Musing Yesterday on Death").

Crossing Centuries:

And when the infinite astral plan
converges with the earth's crashing,
you'll go like Christ through the beer halls
in your foreign bell-bottom jeans.

You'll go down among the drunks and the barnacles*
Go to those who don't have any legs at all.
And the one who refuses you
won't be able to call himself a yogi.

You'll walk up to a telephone in the middle of the night —
eyes practically crawling out of their orbits:
Igor Alexandrovich Antonov, as if one of the living
talks to the living!

And during the final incarnation,
gathering all of yourself into a fist,
may your impotent glow
strike down ignorance and darkness!

Your genius can't be measured.
From the southern mountains to the northern seas
you've infinitely paralleled yourself
with my immeasurable motherland.

TRANSLATED BY JOHN HIGH

Pieter Breughel

A tavern
and behind it, the drunk tank
and above it, an iron weathervane.
Pieter was wandering down the road,
down the long, great road he came

---

*A paraphrase of Mandelstam's line in his poem "Lamarck": "I'll go down to annelids and barnacles."

just like on the globe, sliding
half-drunken, there goes Europe
and the cavern, groping toward Lyon
and from there, hitching rides

and then by any means possible
and on; shitting in Anvers, pissing in France
while in the head, the promenade of the wind
and on the slopes, the rain razing the grasses.

Oh yes, his son is marching well.
Pieter is painting well.
In the Netherlands, a tangible boredom,
books being burned and everybody's pleased.

In Italy, the heat is unbearable,
and their paintings, inconceivable. It should be impossible
and yet there, and like nowhere else.
But can they paint like Pieter?

Farther south, more pepper,
more alcohol and Bosch.
While Pieter the younger dead drunk and asleep
under a cart in a field.

There he will sleep through the peace of four centuries
and there he will wake, shockingly sober
and from there he will walk
laughing, down the road, the railroad

past a garden exploding with produce
past the sauna — cafés
ah, past a hydrogen bomb
ah, past the whores at the harbor.

TRANSLATED BY COLE SWENSEN

Crossing Centuries:

Philological Verse

"A step sideways is an escape."
Probably restful though —
to be born on Earth
an armed guard and a Descartes.
Such a hussar of theorems!
Strolling around with
a loaded gun
and Spartan computers!

What a poet has perished
in the ship's regulations!
Why even one of
the assorted knives
aimed deep inside you
like a homemade laser,
is manufactured like delirium,
like your pet snake's ultimate hell.

And so language, having lost its essence,
brings the delirium of proverbs out
upon the dictionaries' sandbars,
like a Rome turned loose.
In my own barely living blood
electrolysis roams among
the unbearable trash,
we use in conversation . . .

Some kind of idiot
invented idioms,
one unable to beat the burden,
of the anchors' rasping,
and so that you and I have to talk
on different wavelengths.
The reader waits for a rhyme.

Well take it then, jerk. . . .*

A step sideways is an escape.
Look at things directly:
Breton was a surrealist,
while Pushkin was a mason.
And if it's a Dalai,
it's absolutely got to be a Lama,
and if it's the spaceship "Soyuz"
then it's — "Apollo" as well.

And if it's Bret, well then, it's Harte,
If you say Maria, then it's Remarque,
and if somebody's a buddy, then he's a king's buddy,
and if you say skiing, then it's got to be a lodge,
and if it's a crank, then it's a shaft,
an archipelago . . . step
just slightly to the side, and pardon me,
that's much too clever, by half.

TRANSLATED BY JOHN HIGH

---

*A reference to lines from Pushkin's *Eugene Onegin*: "The reader waits for a rhyme for a rose /
Well here it is, grab it."

Crossing Centuries:

Poetica — More Geometrico

St. Petersburg

perfection

geometry

Parallel lines converged.
In the corner where they crossed the shelter blushed.
The soul set off like train lights, leading
In every direction — but they converged,
And all my souls suddenly collided
Smashed against a sturdy dark
The mind could no longer comprehend.

Lost in the woods, drowned in oceans
O my soul, you called up from a pit
But the poems, like dogs, flew headlong in mad sleighs,
Parallel tropes converged.

They met from where they set out —
In this obtuse angle,
Lancing subcutaneous life.
Now I live at their convergence —
A lump of coal sudders in each letter.

But the mind was given clothes
Against the stitched, living dark —
The wind blows too hard
In this blessèd corner of words.

TRANSLATED BY THOMAS EPSTEIN

Elegy on the Fifth Cardinal Point of the Earth

As if streaming together, all the cardinal points of the earth were reduced
To a single point — whence they were carried off to meet the dawn.
Farewell, turn back from the West and the East.
It's time. Rotate backwards — there's no longer anywhere to go.

The New Generation in Russian Poetry

From the North, from the South, turn the oar back.
You know, that our world is a cross is not news.
Four beasts guard it on all sides.
But suddenly they arose from their well-armed bastions
And set off for the central point — as if someone were calling to them,
And there, on nobody's earth, the chasm mouth opened.

From the laurel-draped south on a thickly-maned black lion
I travelled across a brutally magnetic blade of grass.
It was a midnight full of the fiery pleasures of intoxication
In translucent alembics a crimson flame stretched
Suddenly there was thunder, noise — a waterfall lay ahead.

I was embraced and dragged down but not like everyone else is dragged:
Like those who, with closed eyes, hurl themselves into eternity from a roof top.
But I struggled, jumping up and to my left.
And that was the West, where there's cold, languor, and sin.
As I jumped I lost all memory of nights,
Rubies and stars, the blushing, the bunch of keys.
The windmill of wings turned, and I was already
In the South, in a yurt, where the head governs amidst the snows.
But again I slid across that same watery table
Books went flying with me and the unstoppable table cloth.
Then to the East I strained with final hope
There where there are mountains, rest, and saffron-clothed gods.

But no matter how much you turn on the millwheel of the points of the earth
There are only two ways out, the first: in falling, the downward slope.
The other is to be thrown into the outer darkness.
I reject that one, there's nothing there to feed the Mind.
There are no refuges, no landmarks, no fences there.
None at all! There's only a waterfall.
That terrifying point is the heart of the Cross,
Where the heart is like a piece of coal, all pain and emptiness.
But in that same heart the blood roars, it seethes —
Carrying the hope of love dressed in wrath.

Farewell, my mill, wheel of the cardinal points!
I'm already being hauled and dragged, I remember you like a dream.
Neither keys nor stones, names or bones
Will ever again be returned to me.
With a spark of light in my palms I'll fly amidst a storm of shadows.
O storm, O mill, O waterfall!
Ground to ashes and dust we will settle at the bottom.
Lion, angel, eagle, and calf have all dissolved within me.
But if you are able to glance skyward once more, toward the source —
The cardinal points are spinning like a black flower,
And if I'm able to swallow it with the spark of light in my palms
A miracle will occur — I will fly upward, to the center.

A rising stream is already beginning to carry me back,
Propelling me, and in its center there's a record player
(The music can be heard from both sides).
Now I'm flying into dawn's joy, the watermelon East.
I immediately remember that the world is a Cross,
Four beasts guard it on all sides.
At its center lies a heart, its beat ever more terrifying.
I remembered memory, found the golden keys.

The four beasts fled toward the borders of their countries.
Success demands that one be crucified in the beginning.
An angel above my head, a broad-chested lion at my feet,
Two others by my sides, on guard.
Luke, John, Mark, and Matthew —
In the heart's pink dusk they met, carrying bundles of books.
Heart, heart, start seeing clearly!
The heart cast a sidelong glance at them.

Thought, flying high, has wings.
The deeply-penetrating word bears nails.
O, paw of fury, O, beak of radiant frenzy!
But the Angel and Calf willed us pity, meekness.
I pity them all. Suddenly — but why didn't I notice? —
The head was flying North, the feet rushing South.
That's how I was torn apart. Where the heart's a muttering key —

The bush rushes about, beautiful and thorny.
And we are all crushed, ground, and broken
But time gives us a home so we don't notice
Our soaring up and down through golden, blood-rich smoke
We fly above the abyss and circle in the wheel.

On Epiphany Eve savage wolves gather by an ice hole.
Their tails are frozen but the wolves follow the shimmering play
Of stars, which sail downwards, seeing fathomless worlds.
Such pitiful, sharp-sighted beasts — they are not kings.
The wolves are like us, and they nod: Speak.
Their paws muddy the water in which their eyes
Burn like a cold flame. If it's a star, then it's distorted by a tear.
Salvation lies in it alone, look at it
As your entrails are lacerated by the ever widening cross.

TRANSLATED BY THOMAS EPSTEIN

Untitled

When I fly over dark water
And scud above black forests
I have nothing in my pockets — only
Tobacco mixed with Russian verse.

When an angel carries off my soul,
Embracing it in haze and flame —
There's neither a body nor tears,
Just the sack of my heart filled with poems.

But before flying into the unbounded blaze
I plead: Don't burn me, grant me this favor.
And the angel says: leave her, don't touch,
A pure poison permeates her.

TRANSLATED BY THOMAS EPSTEIN

Crossing Centuries:

Birds above the Ganges

In the Ganges birds of prey
Always find reward,
Beggared bodies (and whose is not
Beggared?) swim into sharp beaks.
The soul smoothly rises from the body,
"Eat, birds," it says, "Enjoy,"
Humbly offering its face
Like a practiced servant.
In India people sense
The time to die,
Quietly they approach the water
Quietly the body is removed.
It slips into the water like a mountain.
A wild heron
Circles above, circles
Until it descends alone on the face:
A blue impetuous eye
Unwillingly swallowing,
It repeats, choking: "I must."

TRANSLATED BY THOMAS EPSTEIN

Mind in Search of Mind

Scene of the action: Height of summer. On the banks of the gulf of Finland. A large sporting event. On the sand is an exhibition of diving suits. Among them is a bronze diving bell. The children are trying to put it on. A diver, wearing something dirty and modest, goes under water. He is not expected to reappear.

Dramatis personae: Mind, Madness, a Crowd of Onlookers, the Bronze Diving Bell.

Round, shimmering, bronze
A helmet, glistening in sunlight, gazed out on the Gulf
As the diver, in rubber suit, slipped
Into the water on a threadbare cable.

Who knows what it means to be sane?
O, that circular house!
Eyes cannot come unglued from that beautiful bell.
Like the yoke's dream of its shell,
So the head dreams of the house.

The crowd, from above,
Resembles a billiard table
Without pockets.
O, don't push like that —
We are but a sea of skulls
Where there should be only one.
Nature, division is your madness.

The mind — a circular, bronze bell
Dull and rivetted
An enormous eye.
Wise diver, please give me back
The clothes of reason and house of mind.

The sea, people, dusty flowers, have driven me mad.
But the madness has been drowned,
The madness has slipped away
Into labyrinths of dream and Crete.
Mind is again in the mind of minds.
The mind is again ready
To produce those horrifying leucocytes
That cross from vein to vein — words.

TRANSLATED BY THOMAS EPSTEIN

The Bear's Dream

I don't want the powers to play me
Like a horn.
I won't whistle along to a cheerless
Wretched fate.

In blissful joy I greet
The new day.
A cup of sweet tea:
Its sloth comforts me.

How lucky you are —
Nobody loves you.
In their graves your relatives'
Lips have dried.

Suddenly we're flying — round and sharp
Buck shot
All the brothers and sisters dissolved.
The men departed.

And everything — from the hat down to the boots —
Inside the coat
Crossing into the span of the specks of dust
Becomes a joyful emptiness.

But what is leaning on its shoulders
Rising up on its paws?
Inside me, in this wild den,
Lives a bear.

All life a winter, and all winter
He cries, shrinking in size —
But the moment comes, and like you
He enters the world, breaking bones.

And then it's spring, Hey there! Spring
As if time were singing
Eyes were rolling — he and I
Roaring together.

TRANSLATED BY THOMAS EPSTEIN

◼▰◻ ALEXEI PARSHCHIKOV ◻▰◼

Money

Walking on Stone Bridge
playing at star wars visions
I suddenly felt the air
tissue into whispered layers.
Albania will triumph in global battles,
departing toward the depths of another world,
the wobblings of fleeting ether
amplified, piercing me through.
Within frenzied swarms of multiplication
devoid of primordial zero
a point opened on Stone Bridge
from which I strode through a three-ruble note.

We have an intuition — the more-than
of our very selves. Family of astral figures,
flaring up, snailing helices behind.
Money lacks a more-than. Tempestuous hens
take the Dutch guilder on a stroll
along with the royal family busts —
as many hens as people need
strut about, pecking at eternity's eyes.
The bills are the trace of touch,
they could take the place of eyes, of ears.
Monies, to the State you're the same
as lateral line to a fish.

And I stepped off the bridge on the count of "three."
O golden freebie!
I fell from the inside of money
to the inside-out of money now.
There I strolled the gallery
and saw Presidents from behind
sitting, straighter than hafts,

peering out the windows of their bills.
I saw how easily they change
the world's scales from point zero.
And with a precision that ignites us
they tense like a bullet in a cage.

I understood that money was a sta-
tue jammed together by finger-people,
a passion-hot vacuum,
for Russians and foreigners alike.
Galloping on the final steed and growing brighter,
it stings people's faces,
yet not we, but our figures
of intuition combat it.
Like wind-up messiahs, they race across seas,
tacking nimbly between watermarks,
which darken bicarbonate ships
in sickening chasms.

These figures are not programmed.
They resemble: a stick striking
a light bulb; their traits:
in bondage they don't
create; they hide behind
the belted eight, ahead of
the speeding shell. Like a hole in the chest
they're not interchangeable.
Recorded in the Diamond Sutra,
they're the mere shadow of soul, barely etched.
While we bathe in the nacreous suds
of passivity, they pave our way.

The bills flew, skirting riches,
their shelf-ridges branched.
They appeared to me like tree-mushrooms
robbing the universe of its safe
transported by the horseman of the void, king of finances,
all the world's money on his back.

The Kremlin chimes struck twelve
and the horseman turned to me.
Rippling like a biker's leathers,
an Eagle Scout caught out behind the barn,
I heard his sibylline voice ascending:
Well, why are you stallin' over a three-ruble note?

Figures of intuition! They live
in the desert, their pupils pierced
by spikes. Their holy
communes sit high toward the source
of time's river. We have vistas and e-mail,
embraces and earth, and lightning in a bottle.
Death can't afford
what they have to sell.
They are three-year-old Mozarts.
It's night, the heights exacting, the yearning brute.
Now the figure of intuition grows more visible.
It walks alone from both ends of the bridge.

Lettuce-green three-spot, beet-red twenty
and jaundiced ten!
And wanted to wander free of charge
in those clouds where nothing
resembles them, and where Cinzano still flows
in the Bar of the Beards,
and where our threesome, beneath lightning at Black Station,
is bound tighter than an atom of water.
But again the mimeo machine of People's Freedom
bated the dreams of teens, and the Pale Horse flew in,
his rash gallop so torn from the earth
that each leap was like a trigger squeeze.

The goal draws us on and traps in us
the cold larva of a second goal.
The future's spirit enthralls the eye:
comparing goals creates prices.
One bill admires itself in another, but not eye to eye,

Crossing Centuries:

and from the viewpoint of progress, it seems
to whisk my penniless fate
into a periscope curl. Nevertheless
the bills smell of leather and gasoline,
and if you sleep with an open mouth, they crawl in.
I walked around their property, like Osiris,
backside forward, to deceive them.

History is a sack, an abyss of money inside it.
But the sack has its history.
Who will draw it into a knot? Who will carry
these powerful centuries on a stick?
Where does the bearer go?
And does he know what a mirror is?
And a wheel? And where is his abode?
And how much did he pay for a jar of milk?
Could he have gotten lost or stopped
while I walked along Stone Bridge
and spent violet ink?
And who was a figure of intuition to whom?

TRANSLATED BY MICHAEL PALMER AND DARLENE REDDAWAY

Cow

O cow, embroidered, embossed, bellbottomed at the foot,
anatomized into twelve parts —
formalin bathes you,
between udder and craw the buttery ball stays put.

Like the apostles, your parts, O cow,
scattered, expanding continuously.
Kiev arose from your right and left lung,
exhaling the Lavra and the welded bridge.

Your last glance mesmerized Rome,
Athens, Paris —

The New Generation in Russian Poetry

each of your vertebrae, O cow —
forms one floor of a limpid pagoda.

Translated by Michael Palmer, Eugene Ostashevsky,
and Darlene Reddaway

Prelude, Spoken to My Work Tools

Run, my verse, my hound, — fetch it! —
                     & come back to my heel
with the stick clasped in your jaws, again serve
                    the arc, —
the missile flies off, much to the eye's joy — & to provide some work
                      for your muscles,
I take the sea & toss it — where does it go? — & the sea
                      it adjusts to the flight,

diminishing like a shadow from a pair of eyeglasses
                      on a sultry day,
when someone slips their glasses near to the face,
                      trying them on for size, say —

& the sea hardens just like that shadow
                      only so as to fit
between the paper & the typeface & flicker like a tongue
                      in the mouth at last
a flash! — & the sea widens to its former self, going beyond
                      the edges of the cut pages.

Letters, you're — my army suddenly blinded & ambling along
                      the edges of times,
we see you up close —the rice of the eyelashes, & above them —
                      the notches in the marching columns, —

technology abandoned, & people — as if hanging on a fishing line,
                      are connected by their body temperatures,
but the troops will come to their senses, provided even one makes it

to the 12-layered walls
of the ideal city, & gets their fill of sleep — clean bedding, & turns —
into a cherub,
then the text, inseparable from our faces — will serve us with a new vision.

Everything I see yields an electrical fork from the crystalline lens
into my heart & brain
& after intersecting at my finger tips, pours into the
clanging of
the typewriter. Here it is, the typewriter: an amphitheater with its back
turned to the chorus,
the page moves, like an avalanche in reverse; sideways —
& a correction — then uphill.

Win for me, my instrument, total it all up on your fingers —
a score! — & around
another corner — the same letters fly, like clods of earth,
a hill is sculpted,

& the canon bedplate quivers, & the levers glitter
in the drops of oil,
& above the levers — scented crests of meaning — not open for viewing —
appear,

I, myself, am rather sluggish, needing to exert more force against
this laziness,
but the typewriter, it's loaded with stacks of flights & movement's
leaping means!

Steer toward the south, taking both the direct & carefree path & the
roundabout devious one,
holding on to the key of — Ѣ — we'll leave the once
royal
snow. The heat seduces me. The north as calm
as the knot of a shoelace, —

& the harder you yank on a frosted mustache,
the more self-preoccupied it becomes.

Run, my verse, my hound, Argus.
August on the Dniepr overflows across the fruit bearing
                                        farms.

TRANSLATED BY JOHN HIGH

Untitled

You're a magic lantern
And when you gaze
At the screen on the wall
Then you alone work
Its luminous magic.
Just this way long ago
With your look
You brushed this cloak, this pain
From a dear face
Shoulders unburdened — historical shoulders.

Now you're entirely
The dusty path
Streaming from your eyes
To the colorful wallpaper.

Can you get
The whisper of the man
Who once sat at this table?

For on the wallpaper
Both you and he
Fade beneath your gaze.

For you're far more dear
Than that fire-breathing pot,
Like a small blast-furnace, where
        the light of the past is kept.
Because you're more dear than yourself,
It's not for us to understand.
Because we walk in the daylight
        after you
With milk pails for light

You should shed for us
On that day (and on a pistol's shadow)

But we can't hold that day
Nor sever you from yourself —
        somewhere . . . inside us, most likely.

TRANSLATED BY JULIA WARD AND PATRICK HENRY

To N. I.

There is no hopelessness
If the abyss is
A cross
Of eternal wind
And flickering dimmed

There's a sign by which we'll be recognized

Continuing —
A true word.

And here's a fragment from the world —
With all the azure you can't hold
All the faraway of your colorless eyes
As if the air were forced from rooms beneath a filthy blue.

You're a conversion, you're the current of a way,
The transmission of flame

From the world as from a room —
Where to?
With Shakespeare's hasty rhetoric
Hallway tapping
Changing channels
Fingers playing
The body's quiet keys

Crossing Centuries:

Is it too late?
Ornate formulas come too late
And the sickness of our voices
Echoes
A dream of dreams.

The spirit is shaded in readiness
And matter frozen in place
For our gathering in the dissolving world.

TRANSLATED BY JULIA WARD AND PATRICK HENRY

Untitled

Emerging from this winter, people appear thinner,
From the foggy white gloom,
Where ice blocks, chopped, like retorts, resemble matte milk . . .
They rise at the bus stop
          days of stubble greasy with gasoline,
In blue-black soot,
Their new shadows faded,
In the long skirts of drab Finnish coats
And keeping just on the hand-brake
          their suppressed voices.
And it's the voice out of a dream,
The eye-socket of a sprouted prophet.
Like seed holes leaning toward people,
          suddenly germinated on an iced window.
Nothing good for us to learn
From a coat's fur grown long for the winter
Nothing to cure us of this dim always timid kindness.

TRANSLATED BY JULIA WARD AND PATRICK HENRY

Neva Verses

I

Granite frames.
And within them — maximum distance.

Noon. From grave stone, slowly enduring,
You fly without visible wings.

An angel placed one stocking toe on the path,
Ascending, on a gilded sphere stealing away.

No more wavering reflection
And moist grout of the heavens.
Dissolved frames, empty,
And beyond them — the sea.

From Titian's Venus
Sways a green sort of silence,
And from the Kunstkamera[*] — the porcelain-perfect uniform.

Japan's flag,
A sign of melted ice,
Beyond the consular palace stern
On the Moika.[†]

Sparks from January granite
Fly like the cinnabar of bullfinches
Into our concealed palms
And the summer nights have gone.

---

[*] Peter the Great founded the Kunstkamera, or Museum of Natural History, in St. Petersburg. It contained the usual contemporary collection of curiosities — minerals, shells, stuffed animals, etc. — as well as a public library and observatory.
[†] A small river in St. Petersburg, emptying into the Neva. For most of its course the Moika is lined with fashionable houses and government buildings.

Crossing Centuries:

II

Damned city, crossed out by bullets,
Only the people are alive here.
Hands palm and warm
These hoary green walls.

But the Winter Palace is not taken . . .
And though it's winter still
In the blood returns
Our black spring.

As if hoar-frosted branches also hold
A venous valve. And not in vain
Lives transport gasoline in tankers.
But half a drop of blood
From that citadel's stalwart
Soberness belongs to us
In the flinty stone of a citadel
Under an engineer's invention,
Under the timeless lock of design,
Standing on blood.

TRANSLATED BY JULIA WARD AND PATRICK HENRY

Baltic Reflections

Like daytime walks,
The islands are far away.
And your footsteps are cautious:
Not to leave a print on the world.

There: expanse of seascape over houses,
Of seagulls the resonant babbling,
And sunset doesn't quiet down the dawn,
Like Altdorfev's battle
That pulled itself tight, bunched toward the horizon.

Here: nature of light is pure.
The light coordinates
Have found a home in your face.
But always over your silence and the sea's
Is the beauty of your face.
And the loose little tail of rainbow
That died, beyond the forest.

Only the water retreats
Passing across the salty spikes of grain,
Next to the monuments
Where the children are playing,
Hitting the ball into their reflection on the pedestal.

Still grinding salt, flour, or money
Are mills above the expanse of sea,
And radars like windmills
Turn on a clearing behind the hut.

Only wind circles
Through delicate wings,
Only the children smack their ball
And hide it in the hollow of the hand.

TRANSLATED BY DONALD WESLING

Crossing Centuries:

Before the Word

You — the stage and the actor in the vacant theatre.
You'll pull down the curtain, playing out a form of life,
and the drunk anguish, sizzling like sodium,
will fly about the hall in utter blackness.
Ragged gardens choked with fruit,
when speech stretches your larynx,
and a tin-can pogrom raises you in the play
to pillage and burn, flood the stage corners with light.
Yet the unsound coffins of unoccupied seats
will not yield, or sigh, or snap in two,
or move toward that place where you've again spread
a marked heap, some moth-beaten trash.
And here, the parquet already grows into a mountain,
the stage seized under its foot,
and maintaining a quarrel with the muteness,
you roll your eternal monologue, like Sisyphus.
You — a nightingale's ricocheting whistle.
As if someone's sleeping and dreams this
place where you live alone, unaware that day
after day you wait for the dreamer to awaken.
And your shade took off naked through the city
to indulge the flower vendor, stir up some fun.
No time for boredom, it's altogether different,
it can't blow with you into a single pipe.
The bird and flight are fused in it,
there, the ice and cold drone on in marriage,
the mother and father await the return of their mute son,
and he glances out the window and looks into nowhere.
Still, somewhere to the side of the icy gaze,
the word is born of itself in the dark,
writhing your pungent prison into a tornado,
it reaches out for you, and you go to it.
You crumble like the steppe gnawed away by heat,

and a crowd of horsemen rains down from the clouds,
and with freshness strikes the extendable space,
and the wings of the bank embrace the ray.
O, just give me the cross! And I'll sigh in anguish,
stretching the bottom and causing the banks to heel.
I'll abandon force — and there, in an open field. . . .
But someone's dreaming, and the dream outlasts me.

TRANSLATED BY JOHN HIGH AND PATRICK HENRY

The Mountain

Like a cow's flank, the mountain above my village.
Memory has nothing against warming itself nearby.
From the mountain top, another childhood visible,
or rather, a pre-childhood, an idea between the lines.

But there was a war then. Snake-meat venomously
shot out of the grass, ravaging the countryside,
multiplying itself like a number. One of my names buried
outside Leningrad, so that it might survive in me and sprout.

It means this mountain too, seized by an honest earth,
departs to the depths of that earth, searching for its lost home.
And on it, like a battle, dew gleams beneath a brother's hand,
the dew of a tender grass, a capricious green thunder.

At times Ursa Major disappears beyond the horizon — it's the Earth's
axis shifting, inquiring of beast and spirit: where did the wheat vanish,
the light's guiding adolescence? Where is the sky's customary face,
growing from which gaping hole?

Where is the sky's customary face? The creators
of Babylon's tower sought it above, no hope of finding it,
so they aimed to knit themselves to it, equate it with common flesh,
and they were fated to lose touch, degrading both.

Crossing Centuries:

Now, flying over the place where the tower stood,
a bird could forget whither and why it flies,
the rain vanishes within itself, and emerging as it did
before the world's creation, the grass remains unquivering.

This burden of conjoining walls — and the shield on Constantinople's gates,
the prototype of the Petrine window, glitters from all sides.
Still a trace of Babylon's tower gapes with hell's amnesia
and stalks, staining the roads of time with fist fights and hatred.

He who constructed "you" and became its pedestal
sees the heavenly face through the thickness of walls and times.
A brother goes along the mountains, looking more like you —
and the closer he comes, the more you grieve.

Translated by John High and Patrick Henry

Untitled

The distance between you and me is you,
as when you stand before me, deciding this or that,
as if constructing me from the fragments of your own muteness,
regarding yourself in them, not seeing a whole.

As a mirror shatters itself from thirst,
(this thirst to appoint oneself a spy of various perspectives) —
so the hapless Tree of Longing completes itself in foliage,
in all its multitudes to predict the wind's slope,

and to sing, echo itself, go quiet and hear everyone out,
float, a contrail in the planes of silence —
but a bitter nut, lost spirit, stalks the forest,
as if immured by insomnia in the proximity of war.

Where is it, that paradise and cabin, burning in the hands
of which thief? I am blind for you, yet blinded by your hand,
still water wound like a turban about the mountain,
and the wombs all barren, empty sails in the calm.

Like one of your particles, jealous — searching
my resurrection through you, and I fear it will cost me,
as I see you raise the sling, like jealousy,
beating the dust of a locomotive from the foliage's shame.

As though repeating my gesture, the one to you,
an unknown bird in immortal flight catches a larger
heart in its wing, submitting to its fate,
and it becomes the sky, without dissolving there.

Distance binds us, this is the law,
allowing jealousy's existence, as it does your own truth and will.
Immortal while subjugated, yet not subjugated,
because I love, because I love, because I love.

TRANSLATED BY JOHN HIGH AND PATRICK HENRY

Untitled

In sister's memory

An inconvertible possession, this terrain:
the feathery water of clouds.
Dissolving into a tribe of yore,
there a sister remains as she was in her youth.

Betrothed to an innocent fate,
true wife to an unworthy man,
her love, measured off by the length of days,
she gave in return to infinity.

As she was a schoolteacher,
since that beginning a piece of chalk in her hand
burns wide open in a three-fingered cross,
writes something on the blank blackboard.

Either the letters are unintelligible,
or their sweep continues, unbearable to the eye:

Crossing Centuries:

a reddish wind abides in the field,
the name of the rose on its lips.

And in the breaking of the sacred tablet
a notched wood will be discovered:
a piece of chalk crumbling, or hoarfrost,
or stars falling into sand.

You are one of the yet unknown women,
and for you I am indistinguishable.
In my hand I hold the other fragment —
when we meet we will join them.

TRANSLATED BY JOHN HIGH AND PATRICK HENRY

Complaints of the Game
(*Antihero*)

You — the bush and the robber in the bushes — the wind
and an airpocket, where the funeral granite
caved in, filled it to the edges of absence,
and became a monument, long forgotten.
     And the backs of second-hand cards
          fell over you, tender —
   as the wind's molecules, rumbling like ice,
          began to shuffle you up.

Spinning in their own constructions,
     arbitrary, like death,
the wind's molecules were wound into the plastic vault,
and its staged firmament swallowed you whole,
like floodwater, flowing backwards.
     Shrouded in a mask of silence,
          hurled into the midst of a circle dance, fated
   to swirl about a world that chose dreams
          as its only possibility and law.

Spots from a repeated sun's black nimbus
splattered your eyes, and the day swayed, like a rick —
incarnating you again in infinite clocks,
an already incarnated time crushed the sum.
  Without permission returning to yourself, at random,
    untimely, not in time.
  You woke and understood that you're a vending machine,
    a princeling to these streams of passengers.

You understood that you're a vending machine, but your triumph
tosses you head-long into a dissected heart.
You're the power in whose domain nothing
can be discovered save its own power.
  You're like the hoop on a barrel, yet resemble the crown
    locking its will.
  Doomed to drown in a deluge of shame,
    barren, a glued-together garden.

Yet ever effective — like a powder warding off murder,
the injection against these floods and ointment hexing the judgement,
a bandage to prevent being late for the trains,
a scorching stinger to our fear and knife against this humiliation.
  Your mercy now transformed into an indulgent pampering,
    it grew into a magnetic band,
  and your profession troubles no one,
    and hope swirls about haphazardly.

  And hope swirls about haphazardly
  behind your primeval mask,
  it teases and leads you into the wild blue yonder
  and breaks the causative axis,
  itself becoming the inevitable cause.

  You are the pain in your own heart,
  conscious of your impossibility
  as you strive to locate death in a scarecrow
  and look back at yourself,
  immutable as an impasse.

In your own secret brain
you appoint the self as idol
and surrender to it, as if to an enemy
to be flogged, illuminating the dark
with your rude keening.

Like a crow's tongue — clutched by an omnipresent,
omniscient beak, as though your antediluvian double
prepared this impasse for you
stoned on soporific, kindling breath.

And you unclasp the beak with a knife
anticipating some righteous news,
and then you go out on the dry land together
with this concealed love, and thunder gives
the signal of a purifying vengeance.

TRANSLATED BY JOHN HIGH AND PATRICK HENRY

The Doors Are Wide Open . . .

A sickle moon, drowned in a Sea of rainwater
grazes over the slain with its edges,
these nameless ones, never coming back —
do not know they've been forgotten.
Fires traipse through the forsaken villages,
cackle at night over the telephone wires.

The doors wide open, yet they should have been bolted,
they don't realize there's no one here to look after
the universe they've abandoned.
And the road they were led down
hangs there since, not touching the earth —
just the knee-deep dust of a moon.

Not jealousy between them and us, yet a ditch,
not the indistinct blanket of impetuous impotence,

but the forgetting's soporific speed.
Still a soul speaks once more from obscurity,
the aureole transforms into a sickle and flames,
and the lament of resurrection roams.

TRANSLATED BY JOHN HIGH AND PATRICK HENRY

Untitled

Just a failed identikit, this city,
of the ancient one on the hill.
Laid-out with a seven-digit number,
as if possessing the claim to an unsplitable fear.

Framed, positioned there,
an identikit of the golden age,
in the company of scoundrels
and other gentlemen.

Like a sleepwalker multiplied by legs,
skipping floors into the abyss,
a ghost-town staggering in the frame.
A lying fear is stronger than a fear of lies.

Wandering about the aged streets,
unable to find itself anywhere
among the houses and pedestrians and automobiles,
which could more easily be the empty holes of rain.

An identikit composed of fear,
and the forest drawn over with frost —
a fish note or a night shirt
live within it, unaware of miracles.

TRANSLATED BY JOHN HIGH AND PATRICK HENRY

Untitled

Quiet angel — finger pressed to its lips — cuts short the conversation
    and with a sudden freedom
we're swaddled, like the hands of mutes, vanishing points
    colliding in agreement.

Who wouldn't want to become an unheard speech
    if only for a moment,
a pause flying between words, their longing
    for human chat.

But this country, like speech, veers through the back door,
    leaves the house.
The angel's robe thrust inside out now, falling
    like lightning from thunder.

Music rumbles, there, at the junction of out-of-tune notes,
    always adding up to zero.
There, to find a sum, what's counted is not the most important thing,
    but the one in charge of the counting.

See inside the blindness and rise again on the wrong foot,
    catching up to the legless ones
along a lame road to the promised paradise
    which has become hell for many.

With the unripened tongue
    of a barren flower — rip open
the mouth's apple silently. The screen of the night's
    landscape will blow over, still there will be no dawn.

Eternity, a flicker — long incapable of resurrection,
    and from the angel's wings,
as in a moment of silence, the heart's blackness.
    This is how we lived.

TRANSLATED BY JOHN HIGH AND PATRICK HENRY

Untitled

Not a sleepwalker, I sleep with my feet.
Pompous columns surround me —
I don't sense their roots —
these paralyzed swallows of unseen throats.
The unfinished cup, or the drink still
before them, what's your poison?
Considering the soil of this place,
the columns should be red like blood.
Yet under the surface, they're bruised and grey,
their stone worn down, not by lunar karats, rather —
by some sound closer to "oooh."
Now I've done it, now the dogs are already
snatching the twilight with their frantic barking,
as if they've caught a scent, under the blanket —
a tangle of wolf-cubs, or perhaps a track.
A track? But who needs this track?
Let someone else wear it down.
I'm still here. The columns surround me —
the Birnam Wood, frozen in motion.

TRANSLATED BY JOHN HIGH AND PATRICK HENRY

Another Window

in the acacia's descent
past your flattened face
in the crash and smoke of confusion
in the era beginning with ending
a certain witness appears
a virtue elevated to sin
a certain listener or protector
these artless blinding lines
measure the measure of a time
and space, the ball of evening finished
but undone falling on the bloody scale
and the komsomol grin smiles
indifferent equally to honor or disgrace
father or familiar
face or collapse as a trope on the era's
revenge, beginning the end
but peering in another window
between swollen storm clouds where
two acacias like geishas bend
down to the broken water
and you see yourself
not on a scaffold
not in the fear that built the house
on Fate's shoulder at the spinner
round stomach like a dream
in that window you're not an answering machine
or censor of what's dangerous about speed
but one who sets out a few candles
for adolescents of his own

TRANSLATED BY JEAN DAY AND ELENA BALASHOVA

Another Window Completely

the window discourses on truth
not itself
so unstop your ears and cry out the centuries
where (your own tsar probably) you loitered
drank and were idle
the river of years is no easier than the river of freight
no cure for your life as a slave
of your own space strange language
leading us from rut to rubble
if they're going to take the "edge" from "privilege" let them
gut the rest
don't cut a window cut a door
against the draft at your back
as you fly on Arabians from Petersburg to Tver
somebody in a completely different window prompts
who's he? intellectual resistance?
the yearning of a soul languishing outside?
too short
for high style too vulgar
to see
in another country
another completely different window
the futility of delicate kinship
between battered moths
you have to swim like fish with the current
feel around in the murk for the man
who by destiny
according to some higher will at Court
still loiters drinking bitters
knowing all the same
the view from the window isn't the world
especially broken
in that window
no agony no flame but light
falls from begonias

only on earth there are no begonias
and no window possibly

TRANSLATED BY JEAN DAY AND ELENA BALASHOVA

Sick Landscape

as the white sea fades your feet arise
obscuring the daily scrawl
and from your eyes scales fall to the horizon
where you materialize slowly
no longer an instance of labor
but a grasshopper
outside your wooden hut carved with snow
locked in blue-gray air where passions brew
knee-high, waist-high, too thick to pass
the drunk can't either
yoked at the stile between finish and final
and you lay snoring under the fence
as they nailed you up, framed you to the wall
they say all the young slackers suffer their fill
and when the sea's sharp fizz fell
over your house your sheets
doubled beat and crushed the walls with its look
you doubled and tripled and cried like a boy
on the stairway to dream
on the hay of some prehistoric myth
in the shadow of the lionbird's "classified" seal
even the words cry
where for more than 70 years Sisyphus (the Russian)
is lashed to realism's
landscape, a chapter of heads forever lost
yours doesn't hurt
but your feet don't feel the ground
either
it's not fear that overwhelms night
makes belladonna cringe
and as the ache heals

scales fall
from what once were the eyes of a soul
and captivity's discourse on the unspeakable end
of the human beyond which
postmodern Russia begins, begins the end
this, only a metaphor of a postdiluvian world —
a magnet's cautious pull
at the form of a living face

TRANSLATED BY JEAN DAY AND ELENA BALASHOVA

Untitled

deceit changes hands with the changing of the guard
so crush the past and be brave
enter the old wardrobe temple
bent and humble
and don't knock the mud off your soles
thin seams between past and future
whose bare trim hints of lace
a thicket of alibis
iron like Chernobyl grass in spring
you were set up even before we met
before my speech (subtle as a .45)
they bought you for your honey, little gnat,
aimless, indeterminate, unruffleable, and not in the way
still, you're my rock, or rather, "pre-rock"
and a candle warms under a golden crown and a bush of flowers
in the poisoned bottle of the window the faces
the yard flooded with water whose currency is deceit
that trick where you're not you
but a simulant from kitchen life
from a roadhouse to nowhere dreaming
of a spirit ripping into the firmament
and over the edge
it dreams of soaring, melting with the world
in the apartment still damp and cool
where the blind mirror soars in ether

no less dense
and we have no means to descend
until now

Translated by Jean Day and Elena Balashova

Collected Works Vol. 26

only the lining's silk shadow remains
of the word decayed
in snow's tender blue shade
the roof having fallen only masonry stands
melting why do you
howl flying over the empire deep
in sleep
from sea to sea
miracles and wonders and evergreen
measures why do you howl
escaping from the rust of nowhere
waking the homeless beast that is you
asleep why do you *sapiens* snore along snowdrifts
why do you *homo* patch up your holes and tears
the word having rotted
only the vacant womb can account
for the terrible trial of an unsurvivable world
(in ether's drafting space
the capillaries of the lyric compass
flood with volatile oil
oh lord forgive the empty bottle of milk
milk and elixir are hardly at odds
we're all talentless but the sum of our works
crowds out the testament
of our trade with tropes so crude
in the speechless shade of the shelf
that in the valley of the shadow of doubt
humus and chaos find shelter
in the same dirty words

Translated by Jean Day and Elena Balashova

The Trial of Translation

Be silent, bugles and French horns, obedient to the rosin sound, in what bottomless black pit did you ripen, verbal fright, from Pushkin's seething speech, from the cannon to the sparrow, in a little hut, dear precursor of houses, where long ago girls shared tears with lovers, where, since Napoleon (no shame in death) Polish beauties have been above reproach — "oh, please ma'am," — don't ask; we're not from that kind of forest — "ah, merci!" Knead the dough of the Russian dirt, bake blini, lumps and all — but at eighteen they're all brides, and at thirty-eight they're in love with a woman's late, dangerous, unheard-of passion. Forget rank — period, and period circles nothing as we extract veins of milk from a sticky leaf. Leaning against the fence, the lilac in the volunteer garden tells the story — only for accuracy's sake I'll translate you into Polish, as if leading a blind man across the road, whose first memory is light and the feeling of syllables, where the university croaks its dead rhetoric, steeled in memory like two times two, severe as Ivan the Fourth or one who denies kinship, heavy with gossip, slightly pregnant always with news, with the latest rumor, with the pioneer's shame knowing more than her mother permits (melodrama doesn't suit us) when it leads you stubbornly to the fourth "father." I love the whisper of Polish speech, the ringing of Russian speech, drawn from Kaluga or Tobolsk, though it's picked over and studied as if from a rest in graceful finality, a dissectable specimen, but the secrets of its own incisions are kept with such energy, like that Tungus meteorite (UFO?), unclassifiable yet overloaded with meaning. Too bad for anyone making a living by the line or by the bar; I'll simply water the words of Derzhavin's retort down with slang, the words themselves jostling like naked gravel in the forest's midnight, and, jealous of their fame, ferry each across in my hands.

TRANSLATED BY JEAN DAY AND ELENA BALASHOVA

from *Ode on Visiting the Belosaraisk Spit*
on the Sea of Azov

> The bottom of the sea is cruel.
> — Hart Crane

1

No clouds and the sea is sleek.
A hugging, starving heat
stuck sand to the wheels.
A traveling theater
goes by like a butchered
farce, "Cupid and Psycho,"
since there's no wind —
which drove the Tsunami a marathon deep,
and the sea with greasy smears
applies its makeup in sleep.

2

Through the sleeping surface-waters at Azov,
I see the netherworld on the bottom:
there Aivazovsky* inflates his gills —
churning up the water with storms
even on the flip side of the surface.
To blacken the back of this mirror,
he uses the seaweed as glaze.
The water smothers him with the heat
of a sheepskin coat, its fur lining
completely devoured by moths of storms.

---

*Aivazovsky, Ivan Konstantinovich (1817-1900) was the "Russian Turner," although always strictly realistic. He was obsessed by the sea, which he painted all his life. His work has a certain metaphysical quality when be depicts huge waves on the move without people, shores, or ships. Being financially very successful, he bought a palace in Feodosia (Crimea) in order to paint the Black Sea without leaving his place by the window. [All footnotes are by the author.]

3

Down to the water cold Ovid,[*]
going down to its damp cellar,
at once became one of the bivalves,
as Tarkovsky[†] rhymed ovoid and Ovid.
There he lies, snapped shut
on the floor as if spent in the market,
an old suede wallet.
Any young fish the size of a nail
here plucking up courage can finger
in its absence this shattered padlock.

4

But between Fish and Mollusk
there is a preexisting bond.
Thus in the Bermuda Triangle
once a year the shadows surface
like mounted targets
from their summits, buried in sand,
and here the ocean belches
medusas & oysters — it's all yours —
the whole body shrieking under the rake
of hypothetical medians.

5

Thus from the very beginning a seed
spins in the womb, swirling at bottom,
until it rewinds itself

---

[*]Line 1 refers to Ovid's *Amores* (Bk. III, 2d Elegy, ll. 47-48):
    Cheer Neptune, all who over-trust the ocean;
    The sea's not my concern: dry land for me.
                    (tr: A. D. Melville)
[†]Tarkovsky, Arsenii Aleksandrovich (1907-1989) is one of the best Russian poets of the second half of our century, although he became famous only at the end of the '60s. A friend and "pupil" of Mandelstam and Akhmatova, he was close to the Acmeist trend in Russian poetry, which made it impossible for him to be published before the so-called thaw. He is the father of Andrei Tarkovsky, the great Russian filmmaker. Ovid was one of his favorite poets.

on the womb's bobbin,
but here, halted in midstream,
gets suddenly lost in the web,
like a python in its own coils,
and tugging at threads,
wires the inspirations
whispered into the dictaphone.

6

He echoes this broken chord,
who at once from the first orbit
could scoop the uterine water,
be the puppeteer of language,
and make contact with himself.
And the world is powerless like a textile factory
thrown suddenly out of commission
when — this is before Noah —
it's enmeshed in pelting yarn
already running over the top.

15

And he sees through its matrix
that lower world whose dark face
only children can see
when, in the dead of night
having turned up the mattress
at the head of the bed,
they stare in a premonition of guilt
through the latticework of the iron frame
into the windy chasms
dreams come from.

16

You see, the pupil of the dream spectator,
like a squirrel in a cage, has only to turn
the iridescent spokes of the iris,
its orbit the white of the eye,
to peer over the vanishing point,
as suddenly the whole backwater
is exposed, and every dream,
rolling down to the base
of the glassy surface, dissolves
the instant it comes into sight.

17

But locked in its own reversal
at the height of the storm-play
before the chasm of hydrophobia,
the eye forgets for a moment
the sleeper sunk in a gulf.
Gone — without a trace,
spaced out on a wave —
when in the morning, free at last
and aware only of an aftertaste of salt,
he can remember nothing of his dream.

19

But the dream, cleared away
to the far ends of the universe,
back on daily earth lives on
in white scraps of coastal foam.
In grooves of its peaceful slopes
the eye enters like a sail
gripped in ripples and steered.
On the frame of a breaker the sea
imprints between two line spaces
its shift into reality.

20

And in the net of his retina
the dream sputters, buzzing
with the frenzy of a queen bee
in a honeycomb of stained glass.
Rolled by the wind and surf,
telescoped into a breaker,
it shatters as it falls, so as
to restore the visibility of dreams
by means of certain coincidences
hardwired into the kaleidoscope.

21

Clinging to its parcel,
the surf is still restive.
But the eye with its vitreous backing
drags the whole sea to itself,
bearing stones as shingles;
fishes part the reeds,
extending with their fins
the tidal field of the world flow —
and perspective bursts
on the cornea of the shores.

29

And from this place of two clock-hands
frozen on a vertical half-circle,
the heavenly bodies describe arcs,
but counterclockwise — and suddenly
just as before, when North opposed South,
the figural Sun and double Moon
reappear — facing each other
but horizontally — still shining
from their former sockets. Here is a sketch
of their twin glimmer.

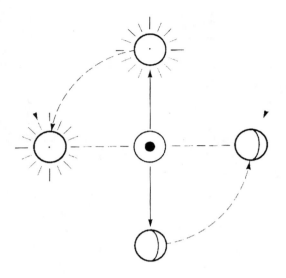

32-33

So it was when long ago, in search of the Messiah,
Prince Bulukiya[*] went on foot
across the water for centuries
and sought Him among the water people
as if with harpoon or spear.
But He, the favorite of God's catch,
slept on the sand and from under His gills
bent the level rod
of His breathing, as day
rose up and its heat

---

[*]Prince Bulukiya, a character in the *1001 Nights*, crossed many seas. He wanted to find the
Messiah, and survived lots of adventures.

Crossing Centuries:

spread like feathers in the sk.
The fish perspired. The little ones
asked from the water: "Rabbi,
why does a fisherman on the ford
pin bait on the hook
when he is — as everyone knows —
a maggot or slave and You the Tsar and God?"*
But He slept on in answer to their questions,
and there matured in Him, pre-metamorphic,
a thirty-third and final deep breath.

54-55

In that avalanche floated the figures
of birds, fishermen, medusas and fish,
buoys, Boyans,† pawns, rooks,
knights (sea horses), boats, their decks squealing,
and the gnashing of reptiles' chain mail
and wind in the pennants of a flotilla
of sharks, dolphins, barracudas;
all these fins and sails
struggled to repulse
the heaping waters' assault

until the wave, with the whole sea in a lather
and the beach set on end,
scooped out the skulls
of stones tangled in horror
from the bottom, sealed over with silt,
and reached at last the graves
of the virgins of these waters, and amen
to them drowning in their nor'easters,
to the jasmine songs of the fish-tailed
and woman-breasted sea spirits.

---

*L. 7 is a distorted citation of a classic line from the most famous Russian ode of the eighteenth century, Gavriil Derzhavin's "God" (1784). Referring to Man, he writes: "I'm a tsar — I'm a slave — I'm a worm — I'm a god." Derzhavin's role in Russian poetry could be compared with both Donne's and Pope's.
†Boyan is an ancient Russian bard mentioned by the unknown author of the epic "Lay of Igor's Campaign" as his predecessor — the Russian equivalent of Homer.

And soon indeed the curator of heaven
cleared the azure, and toward morning
the surf, like the Greek orator,
rolled pebbles in its mouth.
And so out of the blue waters of the flood
the muse Calliope climbs
onto the shore, the first in a column
of muses, leading them between the rocks
from which I can see the whole procession.
After them I will go.

TRANSLATED BY KIT ROBINSON

Untitled

Hear what a racket they make
    At the Uranium Heaven Café
The R & D bureaucrat
    And the apocapolitico.
Eating and drinking together
    As they hatch out their pickled plans
For global catastrophe.

TRANSLATED BY J. KATES

The Obvodny Canal

Look, there are the mute and sullen souls
Of Cannery and Bakery.
And there is an industrial sky
In the canal.
And pain is all the more deliberate and deaf,
And in the beginning
There was this pain . . .
Factory smoke streams past in the canal,
An autumn day just glimmering, glimmering,
And the letters of the Saltworks sign
Walk on water.
And it seems: I am absolutely not I.
Among the factories, warehouses
hospitals and gaunt faces
I have become silence and rubbish of daily life.

TRANSLATED BY J. KATES

A Trip to Visit My Brother in the Psychiatric Hospital

It was madness, it was madness, it was
The meaningless look on my brother's face
      right through me, through the thick of the hospital
A look through the thick, through and through
      piercing the walls, into the uninhabited Nothing
A crevice . . . a nail hammered in the brain . . .
      brittle intellect hammering sounds
(Somewhere at his wordforge a smith
      forges these noises like nails:
A crevice . . . through . . . and through and through)

It was speechless . . . bleached lightning . . . it was . . .
Lightning piercing right through
      the layer of white custom
Cutting through
      worldwide copies with keen understanding

Nowadays can you remember
      The Lord's Easter, my sweet brother?
The Resurrection of Christ
      you remember that, do you remember
How we used to go in the early morning
      to the teeming church, and afterwards
Visiting our religious friends,
      we sat around the holiday table
Eating sanctified Easter cakes,
      Do you really not remember, think hard
He doesn't answer . . . he has forgotten.

Savage . . . an empty halfbeast
      in striped hospital clothing
What's left for us to do
      and, God, why have you brought down
Your power to bear on him?

"He believed too intensely," said
        the unbelieving psychiatrist,
"He prayed too obsessively
        in the churches for hours on end.
He took communion, he fasted,
        sang in the choir, to what end?
God did not help him
        but you are the guilty one, no god,
You overlooked psychosis
        falsely calling it inspiration
A maelstrom from on high
        and behold the effect of delusion

"But maybe he is contented," said
        the assistant on the ward,
"Contented in an unhealthy world
        this world of ours
He has no need to stake a claim to."

They led the patient away
        My time with him was over
I left the hospital
        a foul wind blew across Russia
Somewhere a drunken nation
        began to howl a ribald song
In these times who remembers
        The Lord's Easter today?
Do I really have to give this scavenger
        who climbed onto the trolley the Kiss
Of Peace — is this stinker one with me?

A stormy wind moaned
        that day when the sons of God
Came to present themselves to the Lord
        and the Adversary came also among them
And the Adversary said:
        I know Thy servant
The contented Herdsman,

doth he fear God for nought?
Test him, Lord,
    strike down his herd with pestilence
Smash his ribs
    smite his skin with sore boils
Only do not touch his reason,
    For the One Who Holds the World needs reason
To argue with a madman.

TRANSLATED BY J. KATES

Crossing Centuries:

According to Your Word

and if everything is according to Your word —
then what did we hear and what did we understand?
and what did I say, not believing my
    own self — just as, at night, train station
    loudspeakers are not believed. first:
                departure delayed
one hour . . . another hour . . . two more hours
    the crowd sprouts like weeds
                a futile growth

the word *flowers* on a faded kiosk
  and suddenly — a stream of foreign faces
  gloomy teenagers set out from somewhere
cold there hot here — a cross-roads
of intersecting draughts, fallen capitals

    and if everying is according to your Word —
how do we read, from the end or the beginning?
    I feel and don't understand
        why I'm here and what's the meaning
        of that everywhere invisible
            thirst for Voice, just a tiny but true
    communiqué of any kind, even:
        train boarding — let them
pour onto the platform, the hall now deserted
        do you hear? that silence won't
        release *us*   straining to hear

TRANSLATED BY THOMAS EPSTEIN

The Lynx

We won't notice the golden-eyed Lynx
unblinking and expressionless, following
the sun, or rather, the rally:
gathered
they stand like a huge silence
defenders of everything that crawls, swims
walks on dry land or flies above the earth . . .
but it's already getting late . . . evening . . . it's cold
and, having stood long enough, the crowd
disperses

TRANSLATED BY THOMAS EPSTEIN

Prodigal Son

gossipy prattle from a radio
in the surviving center of the park
for God's sake, listen:
the Father is repeated in the son
the prodigal son
and there
at the back entrance to the coal plant
a meeting — seated on boxes
hearing the ancient radio, a twittering in the depths
about taxes victims and all matter and means of repletion

a wretched little rain cuts across this insatiable nation
distant music glimmering at the hungry ear

TRANSLATED BY THOMAS EPSTEIN

Crossing Centuries:

By the Window

She, standing by such a tall window
that the present becomes a tall
weary bell-tower as if seen from the bottom
        of a giant foundation pit

                  Depth
of sound — but the shattering of the glass
        like a ripple on the surface
rolls. Answering her, standing —
when and where? — don't ask, scatter
the shards on the sill, cover the shiny litter
        with a calender
                What a mine of days
gathered on a point of light — so that in it
forming into tiers, space itself, thunders
        like a chorus, sky of stones
a cobble-stone amphitheater on which
an unending story is played out
tall and comprised of various
turns, "Oh, yes!" or "Oh, no!"
the very same city or the very same year
in the window and in the wet snow
                without eyeglasses
everything blurs and the man on the roof
like a snow drift, from invisible jolts
        totters falling suspended
     at the border of the inhabited world, hanging
        head first, looking
into the mirrored face:
              she stood, as if
      illuminated by the din
           unabating after the blow.

TRANSLATED BY THOMAS EPSTEIN

At the Blackboard

from the lexicon's munificence — a half dozen solid concepts
the golden habit of keeping silent, even when you don't agree
staring into the corner young but having already mastered
        this form of absence at the hourly feast of
being, in class — from which there's no escape, brother

        waiting for the bell continuing to stand by the board
        without a single word, like an open notebook
            beneath the instructor's bloody maw
    under the protection of his shepherding hand.

TRANSLATED BY THOMAS EPSTEIN

The Pool at Dusk

    perhaps, salvation itself is
this twilight of consciousness
in childhood — swimming in a pool
of dreams murky as a sewer
but reading to each other
from one and the same book
        weren't you bored? —
the odor of wild strawberries
emanating from the illustrations
forcing you above the page
to bend and intervene
a third voice in the dialogue
of saint and bird, the first time
you actually heard yourself

(what am I? throaty spasms,
a hoarse voice? — impossible
to rise above the inarticulate
            porridge
    in their conversation
I am but a cough from beyond

the neighbor's televison set
    peals of thundering
furniture above my head . . .

TRANSLATED BY THOMAS EPSTEIN

Multiplication Table

or

Duel

or

A Tragedy of the Beheaded Princes

Act I

Hamlet: "I WOULD LIKE TO HIDE
IN THE SHADOW OF THE BRIDE . . ."

Laertes enters with a sword.

SWORD x SWORD = X = DUEL
CAIN x ABEL = HAMLET
SWORD x SWORD = CROSS
CROSS x CROSS = STAR
STAR x STAR = MOON
STAR x CROSS = ROSENKREUZ

Rosencrantz: "MEIN KEIN BRAT
BRUDER IST NEIN . . ."

Sword x sword = xxxxxxxxxxxxx

Act 2

A tragic breakfast
on the wet grass
The ground has not yet dried
On it lay a head

The head: "Sword by sword is a cross
cross by cross is a square

white square by white square is PARADISE
black square by black square is HELL . . ."

Hamlet: "Drum by flute is an organ
harpsichord by clarinet is a clavichord
I would like to say
that I would like to say nothing . . ."

Hamlet's prayer, consisting of questions and exclamations:

????...!!!!!!!...?????
YES x NO = NO
NO x NO = YES = The chess game of existence

The Chess Game of Existence

YES NO YES NO YES NO YES NO
NO YES NO YES NO YES NO YES
YES NO YES NO YES NO YES NO
NO YES NO YES NO YES NO YES
YES NO YES NO YES NO YES NO
NO YES NO YES NO YES NO YES

Act 3

Cain's grave
of Abel's sighs
In Cain's valley
is Abel's grave

Enter Hamlet.

Hamlet: "Glance by glance is beauty
Glance by zero is emptiness . . ."

Enter priest.

Priest: "Chalice by discus is Eucharist!"

Hamlet: "Chalice by chalice is blood."

Priest: "Line by line is whiteness."

Hamlet: "Monk by monk is darkness."

Priest: "Rose by rose is Mary!"

Hamlet:
CLOUD x CLOUD = HIEROGLYPH
or
THE THAI TIGER
CREATING HIS OWN LINEAR "I"

Priest: "As the head of John the Baptist
in Damascus
is far from his body in Jerusalem
so the moon is far from the earth
and the earth from the sun."

Hamlet: "LI PO x TU FU =
possibly* LI PO
possibly TU FU

Priest: "Here on the plate of the earth
there is a head-moon
girdled by the galaxy turban
when the AQUARIUS-BAPTIST
has seen the SUN-CHRIST.

Hamlet: EBONY x VERGE x BEACON = NABOKOV

Priest: "An investigative experiment has shown

---

*"possibly": Russian is "libo" and LI Po [Ed. note]

Crossing Centuries:

that the criminal
does not know anything about his crime."

Hamlet: "6 x 9 = 9 x 6
           9 x 6 = 6 x 9 . . ."

Priest: "Bell by bell is the GOSPEL!"

Hamlet: "Yin by Yang is FROST."

Priest: "Axe by axe is a SCYTHE!"

Hamlet: "Cross by cross is a SQUARE"

Priest: "Radiance by radiance is WHITENESS."

Hamlet: "Silence by silence is QUIETNESS."[*]

TRANSLATED BY MARINA ROZANOVA AND ANDREI TSUKANOV

---

[*] "Silence" not speaking; "quietness"= no sounds. [Ed. Note]

ARKADY DRAGOMOSCHENKO

from Phosphor

St. Petersburg.

a text other "expanse" w.

We come to a problem.
At the expiration of time, time
will cease to coincide with itself.
But before that, having mastered the science
of accusation and justice,
we must conclude that this problem,
though undoubtedly troubling us,
is by no means the first or the last.

It's an enormous pause, an interval
like the one concealed
between green and red —
an "incarnation of harmony." A span
of thought. A section of a bridge
blown up over the Euclidean flow of matter
through time immemorial.

A weathervane. Wind in the mouth
like an inordinate pause.

A gray bird severs the light ray on the cheek.
The flowers' phosphorus. Moths pulverized
in the lamp.

. . .

Crossing Centuries:

The changes of human history, its failures, flights, displacements are nothing but a rippling of images running across the vibrating web of language — strings of destruction singing to dancing feet — on which, like dew, drops of being flow, spinning themselves into the web (at times under the weight of nocturnal moisture the web sags, gets tangled, rips; at times the dew evaporates without a trace), whose pattern, stretching beyond the horizons of speculation, is my perception, reception, and venture into a tireless anticipation of myself as a beautiful lesion stretched between mirrors in a labyrinth — the body — turned toward the body's experience, toward the sum of sensations and like a page with rows of letters on it — truly the least consoling instance of order. When the moon reaches an airless region in the clearing of its fullness, breaking its circumference, the shaking of the window frames ceases to disturb the ear, the night is unintelligible as night, ceasing to disturb the ear with its shaking; the lilac seethes with peroxide on the torn artery. . . .

Mental habits result from a redistribution of the places on which the eyes fall. Yes, I'm probably right about this. What I'm thinking at this particular moment allows me to assume so. A rusty rat crossing the street. A soft, interminable twilight, and above it the night's lights burning. The room in which we lived was almost eighteen meters long. 18 is shorter than eighteen, higher not much higher. In the mornings, on streets billowing steam, going around the corner, barefoot but for sandals, for a cup of hot milk and cheese pastry. Liteiny Prospekt blinding. Shuffling along in unbuckled sandals. Imitating seagulls and lovers' cries. Through a courtyard to the Fontanka, passing the library, toward the circus, the bridge. This is about many things. It's about emigration. About T. S. Eliot and Turgenev. But what are you thinking about? What did or does your life consist of?

Inevitably, the question (any question, without exception) of poetry brings with it an infinite number of other potential questions, in chains woven into the fabric of some infinite spatial inquiry, which itself takes on the function of a strange voyage, a wandering, continually detaching from illusory possibility at least one partial answer to some of them, and it's in this sense that I speak of space, since neither time for its apparent condensation into hypothetical taxonomies nor time for its shimmering in the displacements and overflow of existence is essential — or rather, its extent becomes the purest abstraction, a question of speed, propelling the world into synchronicity, where motion has no aim of any kind, but emerges from itself, enclosing itself in constancy within the nonbinding boundaries of gravity and the granules of space.

TRANSLATED BY LYN HEJINIAN AND ELENA BALASHOVA

Light

Much has passed, much has ceased to exist long before disappearing. Which is also true of faces, names, and words lost in the summer to scissors and to a few books whose fate remains unascertained. Intolerance and indifference passed through each other unhindered, by-passing the possibility of a later recognition. Dictionaries describe "monumentality" as a punctually localized, concentrated product of power's instruments, such as the military, money, communications, universities, and industry. Cemeteries may be rightfully included in the list of such operators. Benjamin's angel, considered in the wind-blown, blooming ruins of magnitude, nonetheless found his place in the systems of explanations.

The wind has no "there"; the angel's face is in the shadow of a *fuzz set*. Petersburg has no "here", hence it doesn't seem possible to talk about its limits.

But there are other riverbeds where points of "not here" and "not there" are scattered. Michel Serres calls them *hors-là*. To me, these points of transition into something else seem speculative, four-dimensional corpuscles of *non-darkness*.

The only thing that remains unchangeable in this city is light. As before, it is not exchanged for any reflection / dimension. Vision has abandoned all attempts to connect it to color, volume, and shape. And to me. After all, I never learned anything about the "Other".

Time has excluded him from the brackets of its own narrative. Empty eyelids aren't reminiscent of anything. Love is in no way inferior to time. Pyramids are horrified of an infant. One can endlessly scrutinize running, motionless light that flies askance, aspiring to lean to shadow as it connects the worlds of day and night with a promise of a final silence (thus pictures in old books were covered with naïve flimsy paper)—light is like water, and the ripples that at times convulse it like arteries used to convulse blood confuse the mind with an inexorably growing nearness of a message, or of touch. This is exactly how it was at the beginning. Streets, touches, messages. The desert seemed multiplicity in oneness. At every corner. I have no reason to disbelieve you. The optics of equinox and equidistance—such is the monstrously slow flash of tracelessness, of dawn, or of this city.

Sometimes it was like floating between amalgam and the invariably first ice of reflection.

But similes are far from adequate when the pure matter of description again forces itself to turn to expectation. It is probably the dry evaporations of light and expectation that produce the very outlines that are later more and more clearly guessed in the figures of conjectures, rains, suppositions, sex, guesses, Arctic denunciations, and juxtapositions of ideologies.

And sometimes the eye catches something altogether unimaginable—for example, a reproduction of Dickenson's *Villa la Mouette*. God knows where it came from.

TRANSLATED BY EVGENY PAVLOV

from Chinese Sun

The tracery of grass determines contours of "future bonfires." A "question" arises (and in the same way disappears; guilt has not been proven) whether we know what we know, or that "the pattern of traumas determines the pattern of the future." There were also other questions. " ", the echo of wandering eyes turned to the source and estuary, to the outpouring of dark spirals folding into masses of slipping recognition. Remembrance is direct speech raised to the power of interminable obliqueness. At that time my life was carefree and dissipated. No matter whom we asked, no one could tell us the composition of dirt. We were the sum of mirror splashes, running water, clay silt, and heavy nocturnal words (we are you) on whose spherical surfaces the crystal sweat of a file of moons stood out like an August wind marching through gardens. We counted days by apples. But we also watched them go bad, shrivel, rot and disappear, casting a shadow of doubt on the numbers that silently rotated like silver morning books lovingly torn by rooster beaks — books that gave off hot fumes of premonition and impossibility. Millstones of the unfathomable. There were many viewpoints on this subject. Every crystal included the next one in which the preceding was contained. A carousel was flashing various objects before the observer, the goal was to guess their designation. According to one viewpoint, dirt was a conventional rhetorical figure necessary for some calculations (that still remain largely unclear) of the coefficient of ice burning in the lower regions of hell. Back then we were convinced that ice was white coal. One can't escape precision. Heat came to town like a child to your doorstep on a stormy night — look at his teeth, some say. Just look! — what, what do they remind you of? Bites [ukusy] of snow? Vinegar [usksusa]? The backwater mirrors are woven with the colored silk of skies, feathers, and burning plants. Voices of others were unheard for the air rushing through the labyrinth of hearing. Tornado and crunch. The crunch of the first leaf underfoot in July laid out the map of a journey; those returning from it were not the ones who had left. Despite the smoke coming from smoldering swamps, I deliberately mark the boundaries of the narrative by specific dates (the 60s, 80s, 90s; if one so desires, one could extend them further, pushing aside the conventional present by endlessly exfoliating the future, which aspires to be negated by a still more rarefied future) in order not to lend universality to the described events, which would otherwise color the narrative into shades of dubious poetic timelessness. To be sure, universality doesn't fail to render judgments, and moreover, recollections, mesmerizingly unnecessary, but one has to pay a lot for this. Well, sometimes it's not all that clear what exactly one does have to pay. Foreground and background shift in the optics of experience. Significance moves by inconceivable trajectories from the event to its constant shadow, intention. At the first stage we can exclude color. It wouldn't be hard also to exclude premonitions and copulative conjunctions. Being means relentless transition. The point of departure is as relative as dirt under fingernails, immortality, the crawling of maggots in a heap of rot, and the phosphorescence of the outline of objects that live in the burrow of consciousness.

It is preferable to write about something that never happened — childhood — or something that will never happen — death. Such are autobiographical traces (cuts). Traces of absence melting away on things. Such things erase themselves in the proliferation and echoes of names, some of which, if not most, are doomed never to be pronounced.

TRANSLATED BY EVGENY PAVLOV

Crossing Centuries:

NEW TERRITORIES
(1970s-1980s)

POLYSTYLISTICS

KIRILL KOVALDZHI

THE "NEW WAVE" AT THE END OF AN ERA

IT WAS THE END OF THE 1970S. Twenty years had already passed since the noisy, brilliant appearance of Evtushenko, Voznesensky, Akhmadulina and Okudzhava. Poetry burst into the life of the country like a fresh gust of wind, and the hearts of millions avidly opened to welcome the living word. Enormous halls and stadiums overflowed, mostly with young people, enthusiastic poetry fans. And poetry grew larger than itself (as Evtushenko said at the time, "the poet in Russia is more than a poet"). This phenomenon was less artistic than social and political. The authorities were not alarmed for nothing.

In the West it would probably be difficult to imagine the role that fell to literature in our country. For literature under totalitarianism assumes an uncharacteristic, unprecedented influence. Dictatorial regimes fear the printed word and strive to co-opt or destroy it. As a result some writers became quasi-government officials, basking in fame and privilege, while others perished or were hunted as enemies of the state.

After Stalin's death the regime began to weaken and non-conformist literature gathered strength. This literature seemed the sole oasis of living speech amid a desert of dead words, political cliches and ideological incantations. The time-serving official writing of those years was eclipsed by honest literature that was at times too pointedly publicistic, to the detriment of esthetic ideals.

After Khrushchev's fall in the mid-1960s the climate changed again; the atmosphere thickened and stagnated. A new generation of poets was nipped in the bud, and things continued like this for some fifteen years. Access to the surface was blocked to the new generation, but this didn't mean those poets didn't exist or that the country's creative powers had diminished. They matured and their numbers swelled as they awaited their moment.

The last years of Brezhnev's regime were rightly called a period of stagnation. The authorities bustled about trying to revive the system with "artificial respiration." The Moscow Komsomol* committee attempted to activate — and to enlist — creative young people. In the spring of 1980, with help from the Union of Writers, literary workshops were created for young po-

_____

*The Komsomol was the Soviet Communist Party's official youth organization.

ets, prose writers, playwrights and critics. One of the poetry workshops was offered to me. I willingly accepted, not only because I worked for a magazine, *Yunost,* whose focus suited the request, but also out of personal inclination. Shortly after graduating from the Moscow Literary Institute, I organized a literary group in Moldova that I led for five years or so. So the return to workshops was a sort of return to my youth.

Workshops were normally formed on the mentor-pupil model. I preferred not to lead, but rather to encourage individual traits and an exchange of opinions. During the first few years I also promised no one that their work would be published so that only those who unselfishly loved poetry would attend, not those who simply loved the notion of being poets. All this led to a creative atmosphere in which candor reigned; honest subjectivity and love of art for art's sake. And freedom. The freedom to judge a comrade of the pen and the risk of exposing oneself to the group's judgment. This obviously differed from the situation in official literature, governed by a rigid hierarchy, its own "generally accepted" rules of the game, artificial authorities and servile criticism. This difference attracted young poets to the workshop. The workshop's membership was fluid, but at its center a stable core took shape. My guiding principle was to have none: tolerance toward risky creative quests, breadth of artistic approaches and interest in the possibilities of their development even when they didn't inspire much faith.

The fledgling "new wave" was an artistic protest against the stagnation in art and society. A new wave whose novelty lay in that it belonged to the future, but at the same time was fated to complete the long Soviet period in Russian poetry.

The new wave poets were fundamentally "other." Unlike their predecessors — from apologists to dissidents — these young poets no longer responded to the fundamental question: "yes or no." They represented something akin to Pushkin's line: "Get away from me — what business / Does a peaceful poet have with you!"[†]

The exhaustion of social utopia, the ruling ideology, was expressed in this conscious or intuitive position. Talented young poets simply gave up on the delimitations of their elders; they distanced themselves. The force of repulsion in the last years of stagnation was so great that many withdrew into themselves, sank into their own individual worlds, deeper and more alluring than the external world. They strove to grasp the unity of the tran-

---

Yunost translates as *Youth.*
[†]From Aleksandr Pushkin's 1828 poem "The Poet and the Crowd" ("Poet i tolpa").

Crossing Centuries:

sient "I" and the perpetual universe. A particularly serious philosophical "metametaphorical" poetry arose, without the shadow of a smile or simplicity — almost an esoteric poetry (Ivan Zhdanov, Vladimir Aristov, Aleksei Parshchikov, Mark Shatunovsky). Others were carried to the opposite extreme, a parodic call to "common sense" turned inside out. Here the "anti-lyric" came to the fore — dirty tricks, masks, the scornful taunts of intellect outraged by dull-witted reality (Nina Iskrenko, Vladimir Druk, Igor Irtenev, Aleksandr Levin). A middle ground established itself no less powerfully, a distinctive intellectual and ironic current (Aleksandr Eremenko, Evgeny Bunimovich, Timur Kibirov, Victor Korkiya).

We met at the editorial offices of *Yunost* magazine on the Garden Ring in the center of Moscow near the Mayakovsky monument, where the celebrated meetings of the '60s-generation poets were held during the "thaw" that followed the unmasking of Stalin. But we felt like a solitary torch-bearer in the midst of a dispiriting, motionless epoch. At nearly every meeting new faces appeared. Unknown young men and women staked their long-awaited claim to our attention. The influx of creative energy and the workshop's intellectual aura scared away the graphomaniacs.

The invariable head of the workshop was Evgeny Bunimovich, a young math teacher and an intelligent, subtle poet. In the blink of an eye he grew up and became not only my friend but the co-leader of the workshop.

We felt the distant but scorching presence of Joseph Brodsky. Poets from other countries and cities visited us (Kenzheev, Dragomoschenko, Gendelev) and we traveled to Perm (to see Kalpidy and Drozhashchikh).

After five years or so the workshop's stable core formed the Poetry Club. By that time I no longer thought it appropriate to take part in meetings, for the club had no need of a "leader" or "representative of the older generation." And the time had come to publish. In this endeavor I tried to help where possible. I'll mention two important events of 1987.

That spring a selection of poetry by the workshop's most significant poets appeared in *Yunost* under the title, "Experiment Booth." The publication produced a furor, and the critics of *Pravda*, *Komsomolskaya Pravda*, *Literaturnaya Rossiya*, and *Nash Sovremmenik* fell upon the debutants. At that moment the new wave became a fact of contemporary literature. Poetry continued to appear in *Yunost* and was picked up by other publications.

The furor was fed by the club's first Moscow-wide public reading in an auditorium at the Dukat factory. The newspaper *Znamya* observed: ". . . the delicate aficionados of poetry stormed the back door and the windows of the workers' club like rock fans at the concert of a touring idol."

TV cameras turned up, and the audience was intoxicated by a four-hour poetic, artistic and musical extravaganza. MC duties that evening fell to me. It seemed this was the triumph of Russian poetry's new wave.

Unpleasantness ensued the very next day. I was summoned by my superiors for an explanation, and the footage shot by the TV crew was never shown. Soon the new wave poets were invited to the Writers' Union to tell their story and, ostensibly, for "a discussion of their work." Another minor scandal broke out when Yuly Gugolev read his poem containing the line: "I raped my father" — a line that outraged his "elder comrades" and prodded them to take frightened "measures." But the times had already changed forever. The case against the new wave had no serious consequences. The ideological empire had just four years to live . . .

The so-called socialist system disappeared along with its prohibitions, replaced by the freedom to say and publish anything (at the author's expense). The 90s rolled around with unprecedented legalization of poetic diversity.

But no popular poetry boom occurred. The more access they had to the wealth of poetry, the more distracted the public became. People found other, more urgent interests; alas, mostly economic. Homo Sovieticus suffers to this day from a crisis: the transplantation of his soul.

I find it impossible to reconcile myself to the premature death of Nina Iskrenko. Brilliantly talented, audacious Nina — she was youth itself, prepared for the fame that should have been just around the corner. In Nina there was something triumphant, over-conquering: a challenge to sentimentality, conventionality, hypocrisy. A breath of novelty, of freedom from everything inert and old-fashioned. She was the soul of the Poetry Club, an eccentric, shocking inventor, by nature avant-garde. Then suddenly an incurable disease, death, a funeral service in a small church on the outskirts of Moscow, burial in the spirit of our distant forebears.

A windy February day in 1995. At the grave Voznesensky, Arabov, Bunimovich, Aristov, Prigov, Zhdanov, Rubinstein, Shatunovsky. Parshchikov appeared after a long absence in America. Poets, well-known writers — none of Nina's generation could any longer be called young. On that mournful day they seemed to have aged. For the first time death struck their ranks and fixed their generation once and for all in the historical monolith. Something ended, passed away. Everyone sensed this . . .

Now at the end of the 1990s a period of often painful creative self-determination and "piece-work" has set in. But the salutary influence of the new wave continues to show itself, especially in the gravitation of the new young writers to intellectual poetry enriched with a breadth of cultural associations. Esthetic motifs have perhaps grown stronger on the one hand, and on the other, anti-esthetic upsurges accompanied by a mood of catastrophe. But that's the subject of another essay. I'll just say that the workshop has not closed. "Which means someone must need it,"* as Mayakovsky said.

But we must face the truth. Before us lies an obvious crisis of poetry (and of literature as a whole) and the most difficult conditions for the development of new talent. However we might direct our anger at pulp writing, it has gained a quantitative victory. The market has its own rules.

But this is only half the battle. Literature's most potent rivals have ensconced themselves in nearly every home: television, VCR, the computer with CD-ROM and access to the Internet. An unbounded stream of easily available information rushes over former readers. Poetry for epicures? Or are writers simply not needed?

That's just it — they're needed more urgently than ever. For in the beginning was the Word. And in the end will be the Word.

Man, society and the nation cannot fully exist without an attempt at self-understanding. But understanding comes only thanks to talent, to genius, capable of speaking for us all. Television, video and computers cannot do without an inspired stratum of the culture, borne primarily by the word.

"Average" literature has perished. The lowest forms — vulgar, commercial — have multiplied. And "high" literature has risen even higher, become elitist, intellectually self-sufficient, squeamishly scornful towards the mass audience. But human and humane art — that is, normal art — will nevertheless remain the center of spirituality.

I flatter myself with the hope that the poets who passed through my workshop and the Poetry Club will always remain true to the word, whatever their situation.

Poetry, magnet-like, isolates chosen souls from the amorphous mass, ignites their energy for creative action, and directs them toward a goal unknown to us. Only the writer dares try to prove that every human "individual" is the Universe. The path to the meaning of life and to God lies through the cult of man, and only talent extracts harmony from chaos.

TRANSLATED BY PATRICK HENRY

---

*Reference to a line from Vladimir Mayakovsky's poem "Listen!" ("Poslushaite!"): "If the stars are lit up — / does it mean someone needs this?"

Hymn to Polystylistics

Mosiow Mosuk

Polystylistics	is when a knight from the Middle Ages wearing shorts storms into the wine section of store #13 located on Decembrists' Street & cursing like one of the Court's nobles he drops his copy of Landau & Lifshitz's "Quantum Mechanics" on the marble floor

Polystylistics	is when one part of a dress
	made of Dutch linen
	is combined with two parts
	of plastic & glue
	and in general the remaining parts are missing altogether
	   or dragging themselves along somewhere near
	      the rear end while the clock strikes & wheezes
	& a few guys look on

Polystylistics	is when all the girls are as cute as letters from the Armenian alphabet composed by Mesrop Mashtoz & the cracked apple's no greater than any one of the planets & the children's sheet music is turned upside down as if in the air it would be easier to breathe like this & something always humming & buzzing just over the ear
Polystylistics	is a kind of celestial aerobics observed through the torn backpack's back flap it's a law of cosmic instability

                    & some stupid play
                    on the 'F' word

Polystylistics   is when I want to sing
                    & you want to go to bed with me
                    & we both want to live
                    forever

                    After all how was everything constructed
                    if this is how it's all conceived
                    How was everything conceived
                    if it's still waiting to be constructed
                    And if you don't care for it
                    well then it's not a button
                    And if it's not turning
                    don't dare turn it

No   no unearthliness exists on earth
no pedestrian blushed as a piece of lath
Many sleep in leather & even less
                    than a thousand maps are talking about war

Only   love
like a curious grandmother
running bare-legged & Fyodor Mikhailovich Dostoevsky
could not hold back from shooting a glass of Kindzmarauli wine
to the health of ~~Tolstoy~~ the fat boy riding through his home town
Semipalatinsk on a screeching bicycle

In Leningrad   & Samara   it's 17-19 degrees
In Babylon   it's midnight
On the Western Front   there are no changes

TRANSLATED BY JOHN HIGH, PATRICK HENRY, AND KATYA OLMSTED

4 Approaches to Prayer

Here is the garden where Providence sends us a fountain without
water, a granite bench that gave way under the weight of a human body, then
a swing wet after the rain and a feeder for the birds flown to the hot countries.
Four chapels for four wandering figures barely able to distinguish each other
in the morning fog, or in the afternoon bustle, or at dusk signaling a solitary
reflection.

What are they thinking about, staying the night under the same roof,
having collided in a stumbling time, at the narrow space of a dinner table?
Nothing special. They just sleep, eat, and talk to each other without any
pretense to a deeper understanding or to a long happy life. They are almost
not sprung by the spring equinox; they do not notice the cautionary silence of
the bell, the school bell in the backyard. Nor are they scared of the cemetery
which begins just behind the invisible fence. Several garden tools, the boy's
bicycle some crocuses poking out of stones and last year's dry leaves — what can
be more constant and long-lived in the world? Maybe only the evaporation of
these things absorbed into the page?

Four figures in a sliding garden. To approach each other they need only
turn their heads for a moment in the same direction.

TRANSLATED BY JOHN HIGH AND PATRICK HENRY

Untitled

Send me an Angel   O Lord   an Angel
In the morning I'll rise & go to the window
Let it notice me alone
Absolutely alone   Without Angels

Send me an executor of Your will
                              & not simply rain
White   with long locks   & wings
                              & not simply rain mixed with snow
Difficult getting through the rain

Crossing Centuries:

otherwise he'd arrive in a flash
Though in rain or snow bearings blur amid our apartment blocks
they all look alike
An angel won't distinguish me among thousands

But by the way if it's a bright sunny day
maybe the glass will flare up
you tell it   Don't hurry   No worry
And tell me what to wear

Or I'll wear myself out with worry   Whatever I pull out   nothing passes
muster
He'll take fright   Won't instantly discern my refinement and depth in
these black contours
In general it won't see a person here at all
In general   Who is this Angel?   Not a man I hope?

I hope that here the white   it's flying on
won't spoil or melt even outside the fridge
Well, send it a bit earlier
because my alarm clock
lights up real early

An electric clock that hardly ticks
So I'll hear the moment this whiteness   smelling of chrysanthemum
rustles as the angel nears
& the binary oscillations of the meditation's distance
like birds will hurl minor sixths & thirds in the air
like soap bubbles of fearlessness and abstinence

eveeening saaacrifiiice

Peace   O Lord   But a private peace   domestic   vigorous
ask it   to bring all this in its bosom   Nothing heavy
Let it wrap me in fragrant gauze   white chrysanthemum
Beige insides like a piece of the bread's inner moistness

Like the bread's inner moistness everything's stuck together inside me

O Lord   Soon it will be three   But yet no appearance
My time flows through a tea strainer   slowly flows drop by drop
I hold up the measuring cup   measure by drops
                                        And it's already dark outside

I just stand by the window   Hold back the curtain with my hand
Well of course I don't hang around all day   & not every
minute   There's the warmth of the family hearth to extract from a subtle
                                                        ray
swans to shake from my sleeve a moon to kindle beneath my braid & teeth
                                                    to brush
mellifluous veins to tie into bouquets & bunches
I've nearly learned how by now   nearly
                        & they're bringing me mail & brewing
foreign teas beneath lampshades
Soon   soon arriving   I'll tell it
I'll tell it for sure   You see I'll say
a cordial star burns beneath a blue sky
It's yours O my Angel always yours
you see   you see the untwinkling light   ineffable kindness
Yes my prayer will be mended, as a thurible before you:
lifting up my hand, evening sacrifice

TRANSLATED BY JOHN HIGH AND PATRICK HENRY

Martial-Erotic Chess

The Hour of Amethyst & Flannel
A Gospel according to Morpheus
Physalis in drops of dew
The queen's panties drawn down

The queen's off to E5
The knight digs in at E4
We begin   Began
Beginnings, we'll always be at the

I move, a graceful figure
& he attacks   we swap bishops
& what's got him so stirred up?
I think   ~~sensing a blow~~
I think   a tight musculature

Give it up give it in   your rage is sweet to me
I'll take your pawn hostage
In a circle of cannon fire
Battles rage for the F square

Shut the door
                What a nightmare
Shames me to castle
when point-blank a tactless rifle
points my way

— Whose move? — Don't know — Wait
Where's the king?
                — The king's in exile
First the feast   then a sacrifice
Then eclipse   blizzards & fitful rain

We begin   We wait for a cab
& a repetition of poses
Nothing to drown
                or drown ourselves in
But to finish   God no

TRANSLATED BY JOHN HIGH AND PATRICK HENRY

Untitled

For I. Shulzhenko

Iron swans fly soundlessly from beneath
                the brows of the drunk women
Sweetly peering into each other's eyes

                        pressing cautious careful gestures
on the other's lachrymal glands
                        Their knees pulled taut together

wild bees stiffen in the flight & the night   its dampness   the honey oozes
                        over the skirt hems

Honey & milk & gasoline spilling
                        from these empty cannisters now over-turned
& the drunk women (nymphs hydrangeas caryatides
                        agaves asters)
release white mice from their heavy leaden
                        quotation marks
catching with the back of their heads the lifesaver
                        of daily routines

Gathering them all up — the white mice & vipers & garden snakes
                        the tame lizards
                        up into their starched breast-plates
& having abruptly cast their faces upward having fastened the millstone
                        to the hair & wheels
& having embraced   the drunken women now enter the other's
                        vineyard
profiles of rapacious fledglings fox-cubs foxes
                        intently following

Drunk wives walking the vineyard sucking & gnawing
                        feverish in the gnashing of teeth
ripping the fresh wounds & the wailing as
this dense hot ball shatters the garden barriers
                        the vineyard walls
Rolling off the cliff entangled in the blackthorn & sedge
                        the vile stench of the pond's scum
their clothes & combs cast off for wild dogs
                        to devour
in this turbid rapture   its trembling   & astonishment
in this overfulfilled battle felt behind them

Saturated wicked naked gigantic nostrils blown out
                                    like coral sails
the dunk women's silent cries enter the empty
                                    triangle of love
                                    the honorable ownership & higher
                                    education
Smoking slow & sweetly peering

                                    into each other's eyes

TRANSLATED BY JOHN HIGH, PATRICK HENRY, AND KATYA OLMSTED

Sex — A Five Minute Briefing

He took her through a fire hydrant
And through her mouth   an herbarium began to fall
An aquarium of innards   shimmered & banked
He threw up   with both legs
*It snowed & snowed** the whole weekend in Iran
He took her
from one end of the train to the other

He ate her organic chemistry   while the gas fumes
choked his bronchial tubes   exhausted from his chase
the way he ate away at her tissues   swilled from her loins
and copper seethed in his throat
          It snowed & snowed   all month   from the fog
He lit a smoke
took a break

Later he took her through a plate of glass
through a system of lenses & a condenser
like a bobber began to shake with a gorged tremor
when he took out ~~his paddle~~ his drill
          It snowed & snowed
& snowed

---

*From Boris Pasternak's poem, "Winter Night," in *Doctor Zhivago.*

The New Generation in Russian Poetry

Once he even crawled away & yelled   SIC HER
began to observe   how the others proceeded with her too
Then he remembered a close-up shot from the program *Nostalgia*
& he took her again   through a hyphen this time
          It snowed & snowed   from the screwdriver to the fine trim
Drink to brotherhood!   A drunken slave
they wrapped her for a night in wolf's clothing
He rummaged among the fixtures
          It snowed & snowed
He took her in a coffin

And like a simple   art investigator
he pressed her bone marrow to her stomach
overcoming the sensation of pathos   & intestinal smog
he took her without roses
& almost without pride   not posturing in her fullness
and through her anabiosis
and a converter

And having hunched over her ~~out of vileness~~   out of tenderness   & abuse
he pulled out her soul   having taken her   the best he could
across the Urals   Then he closed the gate
trembled until morning   in the cold & sweat he tried to pick it
prick open the door
but no he never arrived at grandaddy's lock
          It snowed & snowed   from Easter to May Day

A wet snow fell   The barge-haulers groaned
And it was unbearably ~~genitalia~~   genius
his Adam's apple
               dropping to his shin
like a pelican   with the Pirquet reaction
that doesn't fit the law of a draftsman's tools
          It snowed & snowed   he pulled out of the nose dive

A wet snow fell   the sky   it grew dark
the wind picked up   the pond hawked
smoke in the stove pipe   untwirled

whistling the opera Don Phallus
It snowed & snowed   He came out of the water
Dry   Like Shchors*
And then he took her once more

TRANSLATED BY JOHN HIGH, PATRICK HENRY, AND KATYA OLMSTED

---

*Commander of the Red Army.

Untitled

to Nina Iskrenko

like a glove, peel off your body
sashay before all as an unclothed soul,
what's there to torture over, a small bosom —
you're no longer wearing it.

meeting God is an uncomplicated business,
like proceeding as a class to the x-ray room,
    at worst, all alone in the gynecologist's office,
in the end it's not important as being pregnant, or not,
but that the Gynecologist act with grace, nothing unseemly.

and after the check-up, you can walk with your head held high,
you see, the hedges of paradise are decorously arranged, like a park,
a bit boring, sure, but these are the customs:
culling of the herd and this vegetarianism.

no longer in the crosshairs, unharnessing that heightened sense,
no whiff here of the Railway Construction Ministry, or Shamakhanian[*]
                                         sausage[†],
purely ethereal, no underwear even,
well, why so shy, what did you expect?

are you already convinced that life's trivialites and blunders make up this
                                         earthly lot?
already seen enough of us from your rightful height?
found taller, thicker hedges for those arriving in your wake,
where we might sit for a snack and some other simple turn?

---

[*] "Shamakhanian" refers to the Tsarina of Shamakhan (Shamakhanskaya tsaritsa) from Aleksandr Pushkin's famous "Tale of the Golden Cockerel" ("Skazka o zolotom petushke").
[†] This line as a whole refers to a passage in Nina Iskrenko's own untitled poem dedicated to Mark Shatunovsky. The last stanza of that poem reads: "And I stand   muzzle still / on the minstrel's head / and I catch a whiff of the Railway Construction Ministry / and of Shamakhanian sausage."

are you whistling off some biting verse, as you always could?
will you read it to us? does it matter that we'll be nagging, like fools,

if life is only a text then death, too, begins from the preceding line
after an insignificant, lethal absence.

TRANSLATED BY JOHN HIGH AND PATRICK HENRY

train

1.

plants grow, racking the air,
urging a watery sap through the stems,
these blue-baby birds cry out in their nests
restless, thrusting out frail voices.

a train, derailed by partisans,
ripped loose from the rails — a senseless screeching
with a head full of steam and wasted brakes —
trampling brush and piercing a dense thicket.

like a curtain the plants closed around it,
spreading a deep sleep along the ditch, the embankment,
and here, the startled grass began to crawl toward the train
now concealed by a heavy, freighted shadow.

grass scuttling into the busted boiler,
into the engine guts where steam still angled up
from crushed pipes — its watery brain silent as radar,
raised from the depths of anabiosis.

and sliding on mould along the flue,
it penetrated the fire box — the coal cooled, a whistle,
and the air, liquefied by rude breathing,
flowed out, the engineer floating in it.

falling, he clutched his uncoordinated pieces,
but a sticker bush grew into his larynx,
wrist slung off, some broken thing,
his pulse plunged like a ball of mercury.

the fireman flung on his back outside,
wind rustled his eyebrows like leaves,
eyes hollow the pupils dissolved into pools,
mirroring a scuttling, squeaky ant.

but grass already surged alongside the boxcars,
waves pulsing as in a wind tunnel,
a draft from the cast-off platforms blew in the freighters
and ripples flitted across the coupe windows.

2.

in that vestibule where we held each other tight,
the lips' painted impress clotted in air
once we joined in catalysis here,
now silence forms a cube.

we came together so that, once parted,
we'd not see the washed-out features in the other,
still how were we to know that from now on two parentheses
of emptiness would be our punctuation mark.

it appears that we, like water, were spilled
in the past tense, in relic-like forests,
yet memory is still capable at half-speed
within me sustaining an oblong fear.

and now I catch a clotted moan, like a fly
pushing a transparent palm, like a shot,
I no longer want your blinded glance, surviving us
to slide along the coupe windows.

after death it's easier to reinvent your story
aimlessly, but verbatim, in the language of grass
and all its words without noise, capacious —
unites in speech, tightening the stitches.

but better to shake off the remnants of touch,
as this speech becomes comprehensible and mute,
accessible to all, you unclasp consciousness,
which takes wing from your hand and flies homeward.

later, when grass scuttles in here through the cracks,
as in a vase, shoots up through a broken toilet bowl,
I want the two of us to spy
how grass occupies all, but will not find us.

and the remains of a train will hide in the grass,
and an access appearing in the grass' rustle,
and a dream of grass creeping from boxcar to boxcar
and a tree growing, beautiful as an explosion.

3.

thus by growing the grass thought
and the thought resembled grass
loving the object, holding it afloat in consciousness
from the very first touch.

and in the depths of its soul, grass was pleased
that it was, in fact, grass,
the rest not of grass belongs
involuntarily to the periphery of the world's life.

once peering at the reflections in a pool's glassy surface,
the grass, striving to understand what it was,
followed the elemental path of reasoning plants
from photosynthesis to intellect's core.

and if it were to stop at grass,
were evolution to end with grass,
then life would would proceed without risk of end,
entrusted to steam-driven locomotion.

this is why the grass, having understood
the barrenness of other ideas, hurried
with rightful agitation toward the exploded boxcars,
where people were strewn on the grass.

and standing on tip-toe, it regarded itself with interest
in slippery bogs of sightless eyes:
the points of grass to grass seemed a forest
and evolution, it seemed, had succeeded.

TRANSLATED BY JOHN HIGH AND PATRICK HENRY

in the accusative case

when my five senses are lulled by a taxi
& transformed into a kind of gratuity,
I dream they're five herrings —
limp & putrid, yet edible.
that my spirit is a defenseless artificial limb
structured inside a chrome-plated rib cage,
that in darkness my fate acquires the weight
of a trolley car speeding downhill.
that, perhaps, talent's only a rib steak
one can eat under the canopy of CHW.*

that I can hide my face in your belly —
the architectural vault, modeled within a body.
you'll kiss the pig-skinned suede of my lips
dyed with this fading aniline,
and press an empty body's cube whose armpits

---

*"Central House of Writers," a private club in Moscow formerly for members of the Writers' Union.

smell like naphthalene against yourself
& you'll lean a face toward my pupils
glancing into their circles
to search out the geometry of vice within me
and then slowly raise two pretentious legs
constructed in a somewhat Baroque style.

but the oblique country's acquired an hermetic style:
landscapes in the flasks of horizons,
stagnant water flowing into a bottle
among lucid scopes.
a visual language informed by this landscape
& a detailed consciousness is covered in the freed expanse,
having pressed my temple against the glass
and by pushing the draught's surface aside with my hand.
I read between the lines an unwritten story,
strive to combine your three dimensions
with that all so familiar civic background.

but the sky's lost its skill of speech,
growing dumbfounded before the microphone.

TRANSLATED BY JOHN HIGH AND IVAN BURKIN

banal objects

these years, myopic — hovering behind the
mirrored, peeling wardrobe,
            a guilt-ridden smile, a baggy raincoat,
they don't resemble my father:
the frail figure
            too bloated
melts away in a slow high.
or when you'll go into the garden through
            the paralytic back door —
back to the garden where the passage is almost harmless,
even if the weather's fine

in the end, you'll only get your feet wet,
in evaporating puddles, a childhood once lived on alimony.
who brought on this terror
               that shook you from the photo albums,
pre-war boys, connoisseurs of old sayings
and wrestling tricks — sent to the corner and absenced by life,
               your facial expression coincides
with something forgotten.
               your outstretched shadows
on the lunar surface of fear —
shadows of monuments, which once stood on the bare earth.
you feel feverish at the slightest agitation in your groin,
the documents in your shirt pocket
               bring you chills.
the deaf compartments where life has ceased —
               parallels the apartments you live in,
someone looks out from this place
as the General Secretaries stare out from their portraits
               and our capital is bustling in its patterns of morning exercise

or then in the neglected stairwell —
               you'll meet yourself
but not knowing what to say
               no conversation occurs —
you only watch, in anticipation
at this other wearing a second-hand cap.
— he says, let's stay a while,
               no reason to hurry off
like snails the things that go unnoticed in their living.
here, the lips tenderly mouthing the tube of bright lipstick,
two keys and a ticket —
               are they evidence,
chance objects asking, disgracefully, for mercy:
this petty life extorts simplification from itself,
a handful of sweet tears
               washing from the deceptions of childhood,
after a rain, having received absolution,
crawling from handbags, pockets,
why should they be spared

would that reflect the characteristics of a true killer —
and where can we go from here, and then if we return
for what, what can we find
                or want to be convinced of —
that children grow up
                and the earth continues to revolve.

Translated by John High and Patrick Henry

Untitled

a child in a room,
                now he's a boy, now a curtain,
the floor absorbs his sandals
his gaze becomes substance — an inquisitive chisel,
fidgeting in the drawer, overturning the table.

from his kidneys an impudent ash-tree grows,
and in his right lung salt begins to blossom.
he's a complete fragmentation, visible, though muddied,
the hearing sprouts within him, shackled to a bean.

he's no longer split in two by chromosomes,
he's more simple and transparent than fish fry,
and all five of his senses are familiar to my touch,
and his whole soul is wrapped in a paper cone.

(I know that the soul is a flexible hose,
inside, the blood completes its death work
  — that our internal space is an uncomplicated aqualung,
but in the boy the soul grows, breathing nitrogen.)

the grass will take root inside him, and he'll let fall
some chance object from his hand to the grass
so that I might find either stars or comets there,
and collect them in an empty, crushed milk can.

Translated by John High and Patrick Henry

Untitled
to A. Eremenko

At the Pavelets radial-line station
Amidst Ionic columns
Stood an ideal man
Drinking Troinoi* cologne.

Of diminutive stature.
A face like flint.
Decisively dressed, and simply.
Underpants. Galoshes. A belt.

Everything about him had a significance
I'd never known,
And somewhere music pealed
And children fell in their sleep.

And he stood
(of the masculine gender . . .
(in his singular form . . .
unpreconceived autonomy
burned on his brow.

TRANSLATED BY MARK NOWAK AND PATRICK HENRY

---

*Troinoi was a very cheap Soviet cologne. Being cheap, the cologne contained a lot of alcohol, making it a favorite of down-and-out alcoholics, especially during the dry years under Gorbachev.

Untitled

This century has come to a close,
It snowed and snowed from end to end,[*]
Characteristically falling was this and now,
Curiously, it was white.

On snow-covered plains,
Like a smudge on a notebook page,
And inserted into all this one remains
A citizen solely for the rhyme, ink-black.

He was powerless and small
Set against this all-encompassing landscape.
How he wound up here
I can't begin to say.

A simple Soviet so-and-so
(not uncommon in our nation).
My mind has condemned
His initials to oblivion.

Anonymous "he" deprived of flesh
Caprice of sick fantasy
By authorial diktat persecuted and dragging
Along from nowhere into nowhere.

The dragging, the dragging along
Before we up and die.
Catching the impassive border of extinguished
Consciousness with the corner of an eye.

And he who is raised above all
And who measures off our days

---

[*]This line is compiled from the first two lines of Boris Pasternak's poem "Winter Night" from
Doctor Zhivago. The original of these two lines is: "Melo, melo po vsei zemle / Vo vse predely."
Irtenev omits "po vsei zemle" ("the whole world over") from the middle of this sentence, leaving:
"It snowed and snowed from end to end."

Sets a cross on this place and sits
Down at another page.

TRANSLATED BY MARK NOWAK AND PATRICK HENRY

My Response to Albion

In foggy Albion
A bloody dawn still rises,
But in the Gagarin quarter*
The work day paws the dirt.

Palaces rise, factories smoke,
Labor, the world's master, runs the show,
And of surrounding nature
The ranks of custodians grow.

Everything here so damn familiar,
And I'm no less so to everyone here,
Here where I attended secondary school,
Deaf to questions, mute in answer.

Here my cradle was rocked
When the maternity hospital expelled me,
And somewhere around here I was conceived,
And event almost beyond recall.

Here at some point I joined the Komsomol†,
Though these days it's widely stigmatized,
I left here to become a soldier,
When my number finally came up.

Battle to battle through Podmoskovye‡,
Where it smells of trampled grass,

---

* A quarter of Moscow.
† The Young Communist League, the Soviet Communist Party's youth organization.
‡ The area surrounding Moscow; the city's suburbs.

Crossing Centuries:

I trample it with my love
In a period of fated lust.

I returned here, in victory
(that is, I hadn't been defeated)
And with my skull plunged into
The stuff of life and what we eat.

All this saturates me like a bandage,
Here, everything that still supports me;
Here I'm registered and read;
Here I'm even memorized by rote.

So let a foggy dawn rise
In blood-soaked Albion,
In my native Gagarin quarter.
I really don't give a damn.

TRANSLATED BY MARK NOWAK AND PATRICK HENRY

The Ditchdigger

Here he's at it, spading toward a
ditch, delving out each foothold,
agonizing over this,
occasionally brushing dirt from the eyebrows,
flicking away the hair, its sweat.
The lightish dark strands and then
freckles,
the eye for wine,
holding the faithful spade, desperation,
craving air, submerging deeper.
Inside the earth, almost up to his neck now
completely out of range.
The ditch maturing, expanding and
this needed calling of our lives so
that tomorrow,

The New Generation in Russian Poetry

at the crack of dawn,
you'll find him there
so determined, aggregate in mass
refilling the hole.

Translated by John High

October '93

to John High

you play seven you play eight
I play seven I play six
fall is finished it's checkmate
now it's Monday my smart chicks

one two three four five
little chick went for a ride
one two three four five
little uncle shot the sky

hey, come on, what's the big deal,
won't you let 'em root-a-toot-toot?
hey, come on, what's the big deal,
won't you let 'em out to shoot?

can we catch our goals in flight
across the board's black and white
in the crosshairs of a sight?
we've yet to scatter like type
we've yet to flee, yet to fly

it's the finish, too close to call
black raven falcon bright
every songbird stoned or mauled
plagued to death, can't make right

here a chick there a chick

life is given once — ready!
life is given twice — aim!
life is given thrice — fire!

life is given many times
but only to our children

trick it in the cafeteria,
crush it like a class!

Lord, have mercy upon us . . .

chick chick
tweet tweet
boys and girls
this old man

nearer nearer
quiet quiet
awful awful awful awful
hurt hurt hurt hurt
awful awful awful awful!

shame shame
stupid stupid
hopeless hopeless

boys and girls
old man sweet prince
old woman sweet queen

what a strange unhappy country
you never get used to it
you never get it out of your veins

five
four
three
two
one —

TRANSLATED BY THOREAU LOVELL AND PATRICK HENRY

Crossing Centuries:

Second Apple

america is like a new wife
you sleep with on old sheets
life now split in two
is lived twice but the singular essence of life remains
it just changes price

    . . . everything rises in price
    everything trembles within . . .

once entering the dark conversion
of 220 to 110 volts
I exited on the other side of the earth
though I wonder if I exited at all

    . . . however you cut it, comparing dollars and rubles
    always leaves you flat broke . . .

I started over, after doctors
and dictionaries read to pieces,
after "january," and "yom kippur"
and "detsky mir,"* and "cod-liver oil"

I started over, after the hospital and anesthesia,
where doctor Marti replaced my right eye
(but he doesn't know where to buy pesticide
and can't drink it like kvas)

    . . . have a beer . . .
    . . . have a prosthetic eye . . .

there they slept hugging machine guns
here they curl up with beepers
here — fahrenheit, there — aeroflot
there snow fell, but I didn't finish my drink

---

*Detsky mir (Children's World) is a large toy store in the center of Moscow

. . . have a beer . . .
. . . have a prosthetic eye . . .
. . . and here's a program . . .
it means:
through a delightful prosthesis
I see a delightful program
they delivered vobla[*] to the supermarket
sevryuga[†] was delivered as well
and dear balyk[‡] and salmon were delivered
but they still haven't brought the beer.

my heart, torn in two . . .
come, sweetheart, let's drink a double!

everything rises in price and trembles within
everything falls in price and whistles a dreary tune
the new york heat is worthy of a russian frost
come on, sweetheart, let's go out and dine
at the american-russian samovar[§]
where the girls are carefree
and the boys jump anything that moves

two double cranberry vodkas and a steak
hey Seryoga, Lyudochka, hello
check these guys out: son of — God . . .
I'll be damned, look at these mugs!
who the hell are you? a poet? I'm a poet, too!
eat with a fork, dumb shit, whaddaya want with a fucking knife

bottoms up, filthy yids
before we beat you to hell and back
now let's drink the night away
to the motherland! to cranberries! to matzoth!
to lenin! to the fairer sex! to russia for true russians!

---

[*] Vobla is a fish called the Caspian roach, which the Russians eat dried and chewy with beer.
[†] Sevryuga is stellate sturgeon.
[‡] Balyk is a cured fillet of sturgeon.
[§] The Samovar is a famous Russian restaurant in New York.

Crossing Centuries:

I'll uproot the seed of Moses!
I'll punch you in the face! . . .

I open my eyes — what's that, in the distance?
why it's some sort of statue in the distance . . .
but what sort of statue?
they say it's the statue of liberty . . .
so what is that statue in the distance???

   tell me, my dear, have they delivered the beer?
   yes sir, delivered it, then took it away!

america is like a new wife
you sleep with on old sheets
you don't wake up lonely, but with your head in the toilet
you don't wake up lonely, and it's all one life!
a rotten taste in your mouth, nothing to drink
you hang around like a bedouin in the desert
a jew in a diamond store

everything rises in price and trembles within
like an elevator that climbs inside
my half-baked kingdom for a fifth or a pill,
for a tab, a drag or a bullet
to save you when july rolls around! . . .
dive into the subway — like jumping into a fish tank
for the inside-out understanding . . .

life becomes dearer, life becomes cheaper
everything's salt-eaten, empty, rusting
you fall to thinking, perhaps "it's time,"
if the dow jones doesn't rise stiff and ready in the morning

when day breaks there, night falls here
soon as you shave it's time for bed

. . . and once again boys with bloody eyes
stand by a door with a commemorative plaque

lenin was here, then the draft board,
then tverbank, closed for inventory . . .

and the boys grip submachine guns
and they announce an end to government subsidies
but I'd like to know who sets the house rules

life becomes dearer, and the country . . . prospers
try getting the moscow operator from overseas
the screen goes dark and colonel lebed
sails across lake chudskoe*
set to the music of chukhonsky/tchaikovsky

where the germans, breaking through the ice to reach us
found we'd all massed at the front

when they yelled at us, slipping on the ice:
komraden, you can't lif like zat no more!
can't live like that no more, no less

ah, dark water, darker than poland
we wanted to make things better, but they turned out the same as always[†]

air of the arbat[‡], dissolved in the blood
resembles the aristocratic life only from afar
but up close — the worst kind of bullshit

we alter the curvature of space
by trotting out our insults and loves

---

[*]Chudskoe ozero (Lake Peipsi) is a lake forming part of the Estonian- Russian border. In 1242 the Russians under Aleksandr Nevsky defeated the Germanic Teutonic Knights on the frozen lake in the "Battle on the Ice" (Ledovoe Poboishche) that forced the Knights to relinquish lands recently seized in Russia.
[†]A famous phrase spoken by former Russian Prime Minister Victor Chernomyrdin, summing up the failure of economic and social reforms after the fall of the Soviet Union.
[‡]For many years the Arbat, a fashionable street in Moscow, was the favorite haunt of the capital's artists and intellectuals. The street appears frequently in literature and songs, such as Bulat Okudzhava's famous "Song of the Arbat."

but this doesn't change the essence of space
nor does it change the essence of love

    go straight ahead to the corner
    where they'll offer you an interest-free loan
    never-ending rent
    wandering here and there — no more than a clown
    a poet like me in america is no less than a poet

russia the mother, america the wife
and she's nearly naked
and she's nearly birobidzhan*
to which my people did not fly.

TRANSLATED BY THOREAU LOVELL AND PATRICK HENRY

Vitebsk, 1914

In Memory of Mark Chagall

Fate's snotty armored train
Bursts into someone's comfort zone
Pushing their barrels through the slits
The fighters shoot and croon.

No use hiding behind the cupboard
When they've got you by the collar
Shelves fly apart
And blood trickles onto sand.

Bang! Bang! Like in a jar of lollipops
Everything rattles, everyone rattles!

---

*Capital of the Jewish autonomous region in far eastern Russia established by Stalin in 1934 as a "homeland" for Soviet Jews. No mass deportation or voluntary migration of Jews to the region ever occurred.

The New Generation in Russian Poetry

And in the window's bargain bin
The moon goes through its quarter phases
Its crumbs and scraps
Peer through a hole in the drapes.

The weebles race down the alley
Their faces buried in Mommy's lap
And rosy milk, familiar, light,
Flows down sleepy veinlike streets.
Foam flies up like a flag,
A child, or the laughter of
Tubercular violin strings.

On fire, the pregnant woman
Presses her belly to the sky,
A beautiful and bloody cab driver
Follows with a chisel.
Bed sheets and empty bottles
Dangle from the electric gun-sights.
The little soldier couldn't escape
The Italian lady at the station,
And now he's standing guard in long johns.
The crone chews onions for her supper,
The old man puts on a humped cap,
While the cat, deep in thought,
Ties himself into a maritime knot
But can't.

Ecstatic, the physics teacher
rubs together wires,
The school inspector's uniform
Sticks out three arms,
And the torn-off head
Flies through the air,
No longer right.

From belt buckles with pencil mustaches
To thighs with languid eyes,

A whisper sweeps the classroom:
"Here comes the electricity!"

Here comes the electricity
Running through wires and tangled branches,
A magnet that will suck the twilight from
Above schoolgirls and schoolboys.

Bang! Bang! Like in a jar of lollipops
Everything rattles, everyone rattles!

Oh! — what is this I see — could it be
Awkward Dora by the fence?
Thinking about this, that, and the other,
She spies the writing on the fence and
Scratches a fist with her beard.
She spies the writing on the fence and
With a gasp, stoops for a closer look at
The word ~~"IDIOT"~~ "SMART."

. . . the shack's plywood walls fall
Into tall grass with a silent shudder
As the swollen sound of
A harmonica slices the air.

Destiny, a bloated, obese woman,
Watches me through the window.
A domino tile, with a clinking sound,
Walks ceremoniously past her.

A sweaty cab driver, as if in a nightmare,
Sleeps inside a reflecting samovar.
It's dark. The night barely visible.
The moon is branded with the window's cross.

TRANSLATED BY ALEX HALBERSTADT

YURY ARABOV

Windy

When the moon smoking in the clouds
blows off the skin from the spring
water, then all
                that can scare me —
asleep between two grains of ash —
is only the wind.

Only wind and the smoldering heat.
                A shallow water
crab scuttles into the deep, waving orange claws,
and a worm, like the thin strip
of mortar between bricks,
                petrifies.

Windy. Hot and windy.
Touch it with a twig
                and the mirror dries out like a river.
The wind curls up
                between propeller blades,
in the eye of a needle
                it holds itself in like a star.
When it stretches out,
                through the spittle of burdocks,
it scoops into its bag a thrush.

If you brush against a bucket
                at dawn,
milk will pour out
                in the shape of an udder.
Between two vacuums
                the wind takes shape
and names them.

Overhead, the ratty net
of constellations
                    where shivering winds reign
and are deposed, like duckpins
the cipher of love is bowled over
                    by the cipher of death.

From Rybinsk to Mongolia the wind pours.
Spokes of steaming
                    and rusty rye.
The wind blows in the brain
from some kind of petty
                    bourgeois power.

An aimless empty moon
whimsically considers seducing a revolver.
If bagels are stacked
                    in an endless chain,
a hurricane begins to churn inside them.

What lives within the wind?
                    Imaginary magnitudes,
shadows of oaks
                    whose trunks are ruined.
Vague anxieties,
                    consequences without reason,
and those unincarnated windbags of the soul.

And outside the wind?
                    Everything else.
God, avoiding
     confirmations,
prefers, I suppose,
                    something other —
other landscapes,
                    and stirring backwaters.

Yes, it's windy, my friends.

Like open-mouthed catfish, deep
                    holes suck at the air.
And your scream
                    falls back into your lungs
after barely rising
                    to your larynx.

TRANSLATED BY FORREST GANDER AND SARA DICKINSON

A Monument

When I see how
the worker and the peasant woman
stand side by side for days on end
I'm slaughtered by insomnia.

Where is their daughter, cast in iron?
Where is their dismemberably metal son?
There stands the steel wife
and her husband fantastically armed.

She, with her fresh clean scarf
framing the face of a bloodless Aztec,
is naturally a Trotskyite,
while he is a pharmacy clerk with his brother-in-law.

This is
                    our common monument
built up over the years
in which the hammer has swung like a pendulum
and the sickle has tried those who fear.

This is
                    Adam and Eve
planting a family tree in stone.
                    The Trotsky-serpent tempts Eve
who, without trembling or shame,

Crossing Centuries:

feels for the snake
                    between her husband's thighs.

They stand at a cliff on which
only the brittle houses of the wild monks are built
and Zeus peeps out from a thundercloud,
this time named Frederick.

Stem Nord hits him with a ruler
and Zeus runs down like a battery.

We are no higher than that monument
and no lower
                    than the horizon.

Why do I circle them unwillingly?
Why am I frightened by their confident bearing?
Snowdrifts in bedsores, ginger in the air.
Their feet gripping into granite
and into the sky.

I pity their rigid spines
and speeches, grinding on like tractors
since I am their orphaned son
and I want to go home.

TRANSLATED BY COLE SWENSEN AND ALEKSEI ANDREEV

Initiation into the Circle of Poets

Henchmen comrades Ezhov, Yagoda, here
is my head on a plate like an ear
of corn. Surely some labor camp has a nice vacancy;
I know if I don't go, the vermin won't publish me.

For the years go by, all the finest days
always without Ezhov, without Yagoda always.

Whether riding by train with no pot to piss in
or flying the skies with a watchguard to listen,

people bug you with freedom, poke at you too
and each points an accusatory finger at you;
what kind of fate is this malignant doom?
When the guard isn't there, it's the boss convict goon.

Not everything is revealed here for not everyone
and the bride is not weightless on her own.
It's not the tree here that the lumberjack's shorn
nor is it a bird that our Father has borne.

And no one's sarcoma, not your critic unreined
injecting blue dye in your eyes in your veins,
not one bit a halfwit, not an imbecile's face
which isn't any worse than a psycho case.

Behind the grainy desk, watching the tornado
that flattens the landscape beyond his window,
Octoberist kid-Pavlik, parents turned in, commences
an essay entitled "How to Serve Prison Sentences."

Dear sweet silly fool!
For what perch do you drool?
Farrody, is it possible you didn't know,
never touched tea with unboiled H_2O.

Has the sky dropped lower than the soot in this pit?
It's not for us, standing up, to brush against it.
Look how, like peelings stuck in the grater,
the seagulls are clotted to the viscous water.

With the clack of knitting needles their feathers meander,
take the form of the mustache of a battalion commander.
Birds drawn with a child's innocent style:
two hands outstretched from a faceless watch dial.

Makarenko, I say! Do you hear me, Makarenko!
I'd have wiped out all gnats to the final mosquito,
if this upside down world weren't baptized in the sea
of a mud puddle by children, as though in a bidet.

And when we grow old and our tonsils fall out
and our shirts tear to bits and our pants have the gout,
we will crawl like Meresyov to the *New World Review*
and treat our company there to our brotherly stew.

TRANSLATED BY FORREST GANDER AND SARA DICKINSON

Untitled

In memory of Igor Aleinikov, who fell to the taiga from
an altitude of thirty-three thousand feet

You can change your image,
you can learn Yiddish.
"Lord, wilt Thou accept me?
Like a wing I am crumpled . . ."
One who falls thirty-three thousand feet at night
must be holy, right?

People only stand like flashes; they fall like shafts of light
and die like angels, though they live like cattle.
We gain altitude, fastening our seatbelts.
The century ends in scandal. The millennium — in enormous lies.

We merge precisely in our holiness, like knees pressed together,
because we've been killed, but live on out of indolence.
"Hallowed be Thy Name . . ." — I can't make out the line,
for mine eyes are in the skin atop the milk.

Man is a handful of ashes and dust
and caretaker of the oaken blocks,
but when the awl falls out of the groin,
dust is not the word.

And when the wings fall from the body,
and the nimbus is imprinted on the sunset,
you understand that thirty-three thousand is enough
to make Simeon Stylites cover his eyes.

It looks like they fooled us again,
and we fooled ourselves, feeling the parts of the Treasury.
They gave us God's word to try
but just so, leaving a bruise inside.

. . . There is no century. The Sphinx begs bribes.
The pyramids unfurl a secret tunnel.
A child pulls a hair from his soup,
and a soap bubble resembles the globe, somewhat.

A lie crosses the street. A patrolman is frozen in a glass.
If it's not a bird, must be a hen.* In the corn cob hides a banana . . .
Instead of indulging fools and humoring monsters,
better to jump as one from thirty-three thousand . . .

From thirty-three thousand on a one-to-three scale,
One to the ones in heaven, one to the ones in the snow, one who is in love . . .
I envy, even, and cry that I am cast out,
unidentified by the devil, unseized by the angel.

TRANSLATED BY DAVID POWELSTOCK

Untitled

God thundered from the tin roof in the heavens.
And the grass was born, greener than ever.
A citizen brushes his teeth, wearing only underpants,
as if the world and his country still existed.

---

*Refers to a Russian proverb, "A wife is not a person, a hen is not a bird." Russian folklore frequently uses the hen as a symbol of stupidity and absurdity. The present reference hinges on the fact that hens are flightless.

And the saliva, aging like fine champagne,
rises in the bottleneck, making for the nose.
He has a sense of secret Shambhalas
and needs no drugs to get the women.

He has a mother, too, deceased beneath a cross,
beneath a flower bed with faded cornflowers.
As if everything were fine, everything proper.
His son stirs and gets up by eight.

But at times something shameful comes up,
something monstrous, absurd, some odd or end.
Suddenly his teeth leap out of his mouth,
his underpants fly out the window. Suddenly.

And his son reaches for his pistol,
and gets a suspended death sentence . . .
The citizen looks in the mirror for years,
understanding that yes, he has aged.

Understanding that however much you polish the facade,
you still wind up with the same Slavic snout.
Hark! . . . As they said a hundred years ago.
Well, well! . . . In those days they wrote with wet feathers.

But whom do you tell the world's axis
has gone missing? Only his wife,
even then offhandedly, even then as if by chance,
hiding the jelly in his pajamas.

And the citizen opens his mouth,
gives a big fat smile for a thousand cycles.
In the wall there's a 220-volt axis,
all you do is wash your hands. Voila . . .

TRANSLATED BY DAVID POWELSTOCK

Waiting Room

WAITING ROOM
        your black windows are lit up again
        not by an idea, but by the volleys in a salute
        waiting for a firm hand
        the gray-haired activist falls into a dream
        with Malyuta's Komsomol smile[*]
        Mona Lisa falls into a dream with the smile
        in her hands
        waiting for some hard currency
WAITING ROOM
        a voice offstage
        a bouquet in an unwashed bottle, like an unwashed face
        waiting for visas
        they sleep with hope in their eyes
        the congregation of UVIR[†]
        having drained the cup
        the peace advocates preach
        a drunken sermon from Exodus
THE POET A.A. AND HIS BLACK HOLE[‡]
ARE WAITING FOR ARCHDUKE FERDINAND
ON THE ROAD TO SARAJEVO
the concert of Kara-Karayeva is playing
on the radio, as demanded by the striking miners
WAITING ROOM
        the boys are waiting for disposable
        syringes
        the girls are waiting for disposable
        princes

---

[*] "Skuratov, Malyuta (Grigory Lukyanovich) — nobleman, member of the Boyars' Council, and the favorite oprichnik of Tsar Ivan IV (the Terrible). His name itself has become a common epithet for villains." (Citation extracted and translated from the Encyclopedic Dictionary of F. A. Brokgauz and I. A. Efron, published in St. Petersburg in 1900.)
[†] OVIR: The Visa and Registration Department.
[‡] A. A. Voznesensky

> the non -joint venture
> GENIUS AND EVIL*
> for the benefit of those waiting
> THERE'S REUSABLE SCHNITZEL

THE MAFIOSO WITH THE MUSTACHE BY THE PAY
TOILET
UNDER THE NEON "W"
A VENDETTA AWAITS YOU
Lithuania cannot close its eyes as it waits
for sovereignty
WAITING ROOM
       the informal prince is waiting
       for his friend, Horatio
       the jerry-rigged president is waiting
       for his inauguration
       the king of the poets is waiting
       for denaturation
       as well as for a reader and advisor
       an anti-Soviet advisor
       and for an anti-aircraft gunner   a missile specialist
       a doctor   a narc
       a committeeman   a transient   an apparatchik
       an answering machine
       a defendant   a plaintiff
WAITING ROOM
       face to face of the face

TRANSLATED BY JOHN HIGH AND PATRICK HENRY

Untitled

. . . it's true
       labor collectives drowned in drink
and corrections were inserted into directives

---

*Words taken from the last lines of Aleksandr Pushkin's little tragedy, "Mozart and Salieri."

and our military advisors
by invitation only
                    occupied continents

and every guard dog with trusty snout
could sniff out those who thought
                              differently

and though it's shameful
                    my son
                                   though it's strange
we were young
                  and life was longed for . . .

TRANSLATED BY PATRICK HENRY

Neglinnaya River[*]

I was born and raised, so the story goes, on the bank of a river
                    in a wooden house
                    almost a cabin
and returning one day from my journeys I'd probably have
                    pressed my lips to the river
but since 1819 it has flowed through a pipe
I learned of this fact not long ago in a book

for I was born not in 1819 but somewhat later
                    though I've lived long enough to go gray
you can verify this in the book of fate at an entry
                    under the letter "b"
and I recall this river now
                    because I am myself in a pipe
this may be less evident because I'm not alone

---

[*]Neglinnaya River (Neglinnaya reka) is a small river that runs through Moscow flowing into the Moscow River at the foot of the Kremlin.

Crossing Centuries:

but a bagel's not only a hole
                    particularly if it's a torus
what in the world is topology
                    if not a search for genre
                    with a stop in this world
as it turns out even sandor petöfi[*]
                    didn't so much perish in battle
                    as get married
                    to the daughter of a postmaster from barguzin[†]
                    he was a sly one all right
and I learned of this fact not long ago in the papers

the bolshevichka factory outlet
                    opened on the very spot
                    where I was born and raised
where the absence of a fence
                    leaves nothing to obscure in shadow
where utmost fear and utmost courage
                    both turn the stomach
                    and cause diarrhoea
and this fact was related long ago by Montaigne

I've never been on the other bank of the river
                    although I've lived long enough
                    as I said to go gray
for you can't ford this river
                    and apart from kuznetsky
                    you'd think there were no bridges

a person differs from the collective in that he's always alone
the collective differs from a person in that it's always prepared

I don't like to play at partisans
                    at who betrayed and who informed

---

[*]Sandor Petöfi (1823-1849), a Hungarian poet and patriot, and a major figure in nineteenth-century Hungarian literature. His marriage to Julia Szendrey inspired some of his best love poems. He joined the revolutionary army in 1848, and after taking part in a battle near Segesvar on July 31, 1849, he disappeared.
[†]Barguzin is the name of a town located some twenty miles east of Lake Baikal in Siberia.

for everyone who's innocent today
                    is guilty in the next reel
man is a none-too-long-playing record
                    and not terribly serious
perhaps no one has yet related this but it's a fact

TRANSLATED BY PATRICK HENRY

Untitled

don't pray or shout curses after me
I promise a bon voyage party
if I get the urge to go
what am I talking about
this isn't an international sleeper
it's a commuter train
on the moscow-vilnius* run

I won't give you a light
don't intend to enter into dialogue
not the time or place
to tap a little chechotka with my teeth
because I live
because I can
i.e. could
walk out to the ponds
without soiling the knuckleduster in my pocket

a leap-year february fixed rings to us
like the birds around moscow
the heavenly ornithologist
tagged the rest
in march
I had this life
this city
country

---

*This poem was written in 1991 when Lithuania was still formally part of the USSR, but had already strongly asserted its independence.

Crossing Centuries:

and a book of ABC's
but to leave for paris
is the same as approaching death

no need for that
go on without us
the religion of hollow spaces
in the komsokol orgasm
with vibrating calves and forearms
is not yet alien to me
still not alien
the hopeless tongue of man

TRANSLATED BY PATRICK HENRY

Excuse and Explanation

I'm not a poet[*]
is there really such a thing as a living poet

I'm a school teacher
I teach math
computer science
as well as ethics and the psychology of family life

on top of this I return home each day
to my wife

as a romantically inclined pilot once said
love is not when two people look at one another
but when they both look in the same direction

this is about us

for ten years now my wife and I

---

[*]This line plays on an entry in Vladimir Mayakovsky's autobiography, *I Myself*, where Mayakovsky states, "I'm a poet. That's why I'm interesting. And that's what I'm writing about. I'll write about all the rest only as it settles down in verbal form."

The New Generation in Russian Poetry   215

have been looking in the same direction

at the television

for eight years now our son looks that way too

I'm not a poet
is there a hole in the watertight round-the-clock alibi
set forth above

the combination of misunderstanding and happenstance
that leads now and then to the appearance of my poems
in the periodical press
compels me to confess

I write poetry when it becomes unavoidable
while I monitor in-class exams
in spite of all the public school reforms
individual pupils continue to cheat

to prevent this

I'm forced to sit with my neck craned
wide-eyed and vigilant
unblinking gaze fastened on a space just above the floor

this pose leads inevitably
to the composition of verse

anyone who's interested can verify this

my poems are short
because in-class exams rarely last longer than 45 minutes

I'm not a poet

and perhaps
that's why I'm interesting

TRANSLATED BY PATRICK HENRY

Crossing Centuries:

A LEAP INTO EMPTINESS

PATRICK HENRY

A LEAP INTO EMPTINESS

ON A DREARY DAY IN FEBRUARY 1995, the center of Moscow's literary world was the ramshackle, red-brick Church of St. Sergei Radonezhsky, sitting like a colorful mushroom amid the slapdash, scattered concrete of apartment blocks in the far-flung microregion of Bibirevo.

Writers from three generations gathered that day to attend the funeral of the poet Nina Iskrenko, who had passed away at the age of 44 on Valentine's Day. As Yury Arabov remarked during the long car journey to Bibirevo from the city center, Nina had brought all her friends together one last time.

Many of those friends belonged to Moscow's Poetry Club, a loose and disparate group whose members — conceptualists, metarealists and polystylists — would have been dispersed by sheer centrifugal creative energy were it not for the gravitational pull of Nina Iskrenko.

With her passing, the Poetry Club, a driving force in Russian avantgarde poetry for a decade, also passed into history.

In accordance with Orthodox tradition Iskrenko's friends gathered in late March to mark the fortieth day since her death. They returned to the small auditorium of the Mayakovsky Museum, one of Iskrenko's favorite places to read, and the site of some of the Poetry Club's most memorable evenings.

But on that evening, a sense of weary grief prevailed. Without Iskrenko, whom he called "perhaps the most significant poet of my generation," satirist Igor Irtenev said with evident regret that "the Poetry Club existed — now we can probably say this in the past tense, because any efforts to reanimate it without Nina I think would be touching, naive, simple and stillborn. She is gone, and our youth has gone with her. The club has assumed the existence of a legend." The Poetry Club appeared just once more as a group, when, in February 1996 — the first anniversary of Iskrenko's death — its members came one last time to the Mayakovsky Museum.

On a personal level the Poetry Club has survived. Many of its members remain close friends, meeting socially, attending each other's readings and book parties. But as a literary group the club began to lose cohesion along with the whole of Soviet reality in the early 1990s. Nor was the Poetry Club alone in this. The infancy of the Russian Federation has been characterized not by strong groupings, but the splintering and withering of old associations.

"Although the fate of the nation changed in 1991, no new generation of writers formed as a result. The process at work is not generational, but one of individualization," Kirill Kovaldzhi has said. "The younger poets do not seem to want to gather beneath a common roof. What happened in 1991 was less a turning in our history than a leap into emptiness, because Russia has never known such a lengthy period of intellectual freedom."

Kovaldzhi led the poetry workshop that in 1986 gave birth to the Poetry Club, and he continued until recently to conduct a workshop for young poets in Moscow.

But Iskrenko's generation is no longer young. Raised in the years of stagnation, these writers developed in more or less active opposition to an official culture that appalled them and a system geared to keep them down. Nevertheless, their conception of the writer and of literature owed much to Soviet experience; on one hand poetry was published in enormous runs, on the other poets were silenced or imprisoned.

Delivered from their old adversary, many of these writers found themselves disoriented, but not all. Perhaps the best known writer of this generation, Dmitry Prigov, thrives in the current confusion. A popular poet and cultural ambassador in the West, Prigov has become a leading *tusovshchik,* almost a cult figure, in Russia, mastering the rules of the emerging literary market.

But an equally important figure, Ivan Zhdanov, has been buffeted by the new market. During a trip a few years ago to his native Gorny Altai, Zhdanov was invited to read his verse in the symphony hall at Barnaul, the regional capital. The hall was packed, a rare event these days, and the poet was pleased. But when he went to collect his honorarium, he found to his amazement that the federal tax service had skimmed 40 percent off the top.

To Oleg Pavlov, a novelist in his late twenties recently nominated for the Russian Booker Prize, the various writers of Iskrenko's generation look much the same: the new literary nomenklatura, defined, or deformed, by their opposition to Soviet culture.

"We came along at the right time," Pavlov said. "We read Solzhenitsyn, Platonov and Nabokov as young writers, when we needed to, and we didn't have to scurry around with typed, samizdat copies. I read *The Gulag Archipelago* in *Novy Mir,* calmly lying on my sofa, drinking coffee and having a cigarette." Many former Poetry Club members have gone on to prominence as critics and literary commentators. Many have also been forced to abandon literature as a professional pursuit. One, Evgeny Bunimovich, has even become a Moscow city alderman.

All have had to come to terms with the diminished role of poetry, and of literature generally, in post-Soviet Russia. Perhaps nothing demonstrates that declining influence more dramatically than the fate of the literary journal *Novy Mir*. Under the leadership of editor Sergei Zalygin *Novy Mir* spearheaded the intellectual revolt of the perestroika years, publishing the work of formerly banned writers from the Soviet Union and abroad, along with essays on politics and economics that challenged the founding principles of the Soviet state.

Circulation in the late 1980s soared to some 2.6 million, the highest in Russian history.

By the mid-1990s the circulation of *Novy Mir* had dropped to 22,000, and Zalygin found himself criticized for failing to maintain the journal's place on the cutting edge.

"Many people in Russia and overseas now attack *Novy Mir,* saying we are not the journal we once were. But we don't create literature, we merely publish it," he said in late 1996. "These critics became accustomed to the role we played during perestroika. But no one can play that role any longer."

The philosopher Igor Chubais — older brother of Anatoly, the on-again, off-again economics chief in the Yeltsin administration — has said that contrary to popular belief there is no freedom *of* speech in Russia. Rather, Russians now have freedom *from* speech because the Yeltsin regime, in a complete reversal of Soviet policy, could not care less what its citizens, writers included, have to say.

As a result of this indifference, the government has allowed literature, once the most policed of the arts, to develop or degenerate according to its own internal logic, and to find its place in Russia's collapsed and cutthroat economy without subsidies of any significance.

Iskrenko received a Yeltsin Prize in 1994. The meager stipend that came with it, she joked, just covered the cost of a new refrigerator.

Most writers wouldn't have it any other way. Despite the current hardships, as publishing houses cut their lists and journal subscriptions bottom out, Russian literature is finding its level, and work of the highest caliber is being written.

Blindness to the thriving literary activity around them led many critics to proclaim a "crisis" in Russian literature after the fall of communism. *The Economist* notoriously pronounced in December 1994 that "the days of serious writing" in Russia, "whatever kind it may be, seem for the time being to be over.

"Serious writing *is* done. But it is left in authors' drawers, thrown unread in publishers' rejection trays or put out in small-circulation reviews," the newspaper opined.

In fact, poetry is now more widely published than ever before in Russia, and if book runs and journal subscription lists seem small, the expectations engendered by Soviet giganticism must be taken into account. Average runs of approved literature in the Soviet Union were often 100,000 and more, but this neither meant that the books ever sold, nor that they were significant literary achievements. *The Economist* reached its gloomy verdict after perusing the paperbacks on offer in Moscow's outdoor bookstalls and consulting several best-seller lists. Needless to say, books of contemporary poetry didn't figure prominently in either place. Not much poetry sells in airport gift shops, either.

But the reader of poetry in Moscow, and increasingly in the provinces, can find the work of his contemporaries in specialized bookstores. Sales aren't swift, but few poets now expect to make a living from their writing. Then again, few avant-garde poets of Iskrenko's generation ever did. Once barred from print, they now find the presses more than happy to publish their work; the problem is finding someone to pay the printing costs.

This situation should not sound at all surprising to poets in the United States.

"I think this is a splendid time for poetry. The prestige which writers formerly enjoyed has largely disappeared, and the prestige of poets most of all. As a result, only those who truly need to write poetry still do so. Today you can't build a career as a poet, or gratify your ego, or make a political statement. You produce a text, and that's it," Bunimovich has said.

For the Poetry Club the world has turned inside-out since the putsch attempt in 1991 when these poets rallied around the White House. Once shunned by the literary establishment, they now find themselves in the role of established writers. The proof is in the primer, as the poet Mark Shatunovsky found when his daughter several years ago showed him her Russian literature textbook. There he found the work of many old "new wave" friends, but not his own work. "Aha," he laughed, "so they're all official writers now. But I'm still in the underground."

MIKHAIL AIZENBERG

Word-for-Word

Something's happening behind the murky glass,
the other side of a barrier misted over by my breathing.
There's a little-known way out of the warehouses
                            and pantries of your life
straight into the black street.

You'll never see me because I'm at a dead stop.
While you — you need action and stop-action,
with every new reel, acceleration and rupture.
You need the pulsation of colored flames,
the anemic glow of a nocturnal carnival,
the feverish collision of feelings.

For the sake of keeping me invisible,
you strike your own deal with the foulest murk
But you've learned so well how to shake up the lees
that your soul stays clean.

TRANSLATED BY J. KATES

Untitled

for D.N.

This was, you should know, a political matter:
make it a rule to make your home nowhere.
We were like letters written on water.
And this water flowed away.

Flowed away, not sinking into the earth.
This was, you should know, one of the rules:
to begin every speech with someone's help,
to leave everything in its own place.

And behind that door? Could it be Australia?

TRANSLATED BY J. KATES

Untitled

So what is reality? A kind of single combat?
A line of pictures collecting into a cloudy blotch?
Something over there (the details aren't clear)
is moving like figures gliding around on skates.
In the searchlights, whiteness directed into the sky,
jackets flash green.

Or again: an intoxicated shroud, and evening
sliding instantaneously all the way to morning.
In a cold room a buzzing guitar string
and a lorelei in a white blouse.

TRANSLATED BY J. KATES

Video

An age of memorials, of conserves,
an age in moving pictures, stigmatized,
to live a real life — you didn't have the nerve,
but at last you, one of the age's little guys,
pull away forever — a hell of a lot better
(a heavenly kingdom!) than in reality —
onto videocassette, integrated
into a world system, into a telling vision,
in your own person and a pressed shirt,
you split the whole uptight turf, edited in,
you can strut along the golden corridor
of the white house as hero of the scene
in proper sequence or any way whatsoever —
you can throw yourself into a sea a harem a bath a monastery
you can kick out your life's companion, your lover,
everything is provisional, you your own fate's master.
A moniker a salad dressing or a jar of conserves,
you choose it all — what brand-name, straight or curled,
dodging the sprockets unhinges the nerves,
who can't in seven days create the world!

TRANSLATED BY J. KATES

Untitled

They say if longing gnaws at you, change
your house, your country, your hair-do and your flag.
I've done all that. And even changed a likeness
for the look of a new land, a nail for a snag.
I have dragged a bundle of inconsiderable
but weighty baggage into the cellar.
I've downed my coffee, eaten the pastries, drunk
my drink, even finished off the bottle,

The New Generation in Russian Poetry   225

moved the furniture, changed the locks,
and long since had my fill of the public,
answered the call of fate and the doorbell,
all to no purpose — sorrow takes no hike.
There's a cure for everything: "from" as well as "for",
for a separation from loved ones — that too.
I want to be with you until the very last day
and afterwards. Afterwards, if possible, with you.

TRANSLATED BY J. KATES

Untitled

Poetry, farewell, farewell
Russian threshold, household close
farewell to any claim at all
that God can be of help to us.

The soul is one unbroken wound,
and in its bottomless degradation
woven muscle is cramped and bound,
farewell also, subjugation!

Farewell, that homely amulet
love, magnetic pole of joys,
my aria left incomplete —
before the end, I lost my voice.

See how I drink the chalice dry
As if I were a scarecrow's bride,
I played at being woman — I
even seemed to bear a child.

The Berlin wall has tumbled down,
and brought down everything we know,
swept annihilated, gone.
And through that gap I pass to shadow.

Crossing Centuries:

A farewell rite well orchestrated —
Or maybe not so grave as that:
"Farewell" — that's it, evaporated,
magicked away by a black cat.

TRANSLATED BY J. KATES

Untitled

Hope is not the very last to die.
Love even comatose twitches a wing,
a hoof or look just the other day
how a broken stem was quivering.
But faith hopped on the first flight away
And emptiness floated on and on
before its bright dress dimmed to gray.
Over a precipice into the grain,
Under an embankment in a ravine,
On a cruel, distorted park land
I rend one lingering dandelion,
and a full stop, moving off in a flock
of commas that swarmed around it,
leaves no tail behind, to be seized
for no good reason. No morgue, no hospital,
no abyss, to fall into the abyss.

TRANSLATED BY J. KATES

The Peacock

I've lost my peacock — not a cat,
not a dog, and certainly no pink bunny.
He spread his tail like a gypsy girl and danced
until a light switched on inside me:
A flame, a sun, electric splashes.
the peacock's tail was a daily cannonade.

The New Generation in Russian Poetry

I'll have no parrot in its place,
that I would call "fool" to its face.

TRANSLATED BY J. KATES

VLADIMIR STROCHKOV

Paranoicity

These things crammed the room. It's a nightmare!
These things brought the room to life
and they'll be the death of me.
What can I do? I'll stand and walk through them,
Glance in the mirror. I look just like them!
How can I lock myself in as I leave?
How to behave as time slips away?
How can I leave and stay under lock and key
and still in that order of things?
Let it slip. Slip up. From the score
to the comer. All thumbs! You break the needle —
The Fool and Koshchei* rolled into one.
My icy igloo, frozen hearth
infected with this thing. Things are contagious
Everyday trifles full of ptomaine.
Copulas turn into key chains and spikes . . .

> — Ding an sich! Come back! Over! Koshchei here!
> I — overdose. Wasted my life on gold.

And the thing transmits, bouncing off the walls:
— Anyone out there listening! I'm Kruptein. I'm Kruptein.
I'm Izaura, aura, Ra.
I'm a slave girl, silver girl crazy over my hacienda,
My arm's chained to a table leg,
But still he won't leave the place.

---

*Figures in Russian folk and fairy tales. The Fool is the quintessential underdog. He is typically the third, and apparently least clever and least loved of three brothers. Through luck and circumstance the Fool accomplishes a difficult task that stymies his brothers. Koshchei, knows as Koshchei the Deathless or the Immortal, is a crafty evildoer who abducts princesses, and at times lives dragon-like in a cave and hoards treasure. He is known as "the Deathless" because his mortality is hidden in a remote object. In some tales his death is found on the tip of a needle inside an egg inside a duck.

— Ding an sich! Secure channel! Fuckin'-a! I'm down.
I'm oblomov abyss, hovering over the spread,
needle desert, Nachtigall, nightingale.
Spiking my vein, I settle on the device,
I'm no longer the head of my own house,
But my blood is not that of a nut.

— Deserter! I'm Kruptein! I'm marked a mad dog,
I gotcha, drifting off from the veins
of this corpus, no longer your home.
My Tristan, I'm your Isolde, I'm a needle
for dessert, I lay down between us like a sword,
like Ockham's Gillette razor.

— You're arrogance, thesaurus, the saw, Rus.
But fuck, this game doesn't get me off.
I'm no thing. I'm Legion. I'm the Crown.
I'm no Sigmund, and you're no Emmanuel.
Tom Thumb will find the crack under the plinth.
Where even Kafka meets a happy end.

— I'm a goddess! I'm sakura. I'm Akira
Kurosawa. I'm conceit, might and beauty,
I'm Dobrynya, Mikula and Volga!*
Your easy end — when the needle breaks
Your egg will boil, O'Doyle,
tinfoil weeps the duck round.

— I'm Libido! I'm Leda! I'm Lebed! I'm Lel†!
I'll hang my egg in the duck on the tree.
I'm Oslyabya, Koshchei, Peresvet.‡

---

*Bogatyrs, heroes of ancient Russian heroic epic poems, or *byliny* . Dobrynya is the sword-wielding dragon slayer, whose nemesis is often the witch and seductress Princess Marina. Mikula is the peasant-bogatyr, who rides a nightingale-mare. Volga is a great and wise sorcerer who can transform himself and others into any sort of person or beast.
†A minor deity in Slavic mythology, Lel' is a flute-playing shepherd.
‡Oslyabya and Peresvet are brothers, warriors, monks. Heroes of the battle of Kulikovo (1380), in which the Russians first defeated the Tatar armies of the Golden Horde. Peresvet died on the field of battle.

Crossing Centuries:

I'm all over this den, karla, I'm working at Jung's,
Therapy's a pisser
and I'm off base. Later!

— I'm a hatchet, machete, the sword in the stone!
I'm your collective hello and your personal goodbye,
I'm your super-ego, super fucking-aye,
and savages or not, we're of the same tribe,
both stuck on the needle's tip.
That's it. Stay tuned! You copy? Over and out!

— Guillotine! I'm legal! A mountain eagle!
With one hit I sprout eyes in the back of my head.
The world calls me Don Quixote.
I'm already Bodhisattva. I'm the Lotus. I'm — Oh
spit, can't get me on "got it"!
You're out of Nirvana. Score!

— Hari-Rama, in the lingo! Brahman, I'm Atman!
Carmensita I am, your karma, narkoman,
Your agent, your orange, your flack.
You and I are two koans in the Warsaw Pact.
If there's no satori, they yop tvoyu mat'.
Crashing on air! Rock bottom!

— I'm Godun! Gone on junk! I head into the storm,
standard raised. Far below, the squadron,
limitless expanse of infinity.
I hover over Gondwana like a torn condom.
My veins swell up like the Ganges and Don,
samsara below, like Siberia.

— I'm an apsara entering samsara. It's pitch black!
And you're, like, spritzing my brain.
Just your motherfuckin' style!
Meditating here, on the other side of good
and evil, I'll cut you, you fuck,
under the ultra-sound you're a tick.

The New Generation in Russian Poetry

  — By fax from the astral sphere. I'm Logos. I'm Om
    of parallel chains. I'm rupture, I'm rapture.
      I'm the pen and the astral con.
    I pass over Europe. An awesome sunset.
       Yes to big money, a payoff
        and a little on the side.

— Out from under the table, across the face! I'm the Ding, nicht an sich!
I lost my astral transfer in the struggle,
buck naked on a hedgehog.
Black futures spin over my head.
"Nevermore" — the huge center cawed at me,
no strength to guard him.

    — Nevermore, I'm Juan, continue my flight.
    In my darkness peyote replaces the Mayans,
      And in my blood thunder Castanetes.
    I'm Big Mac. I'm McDonalds! I'm Easter Sundae!
      Pizza Hut, bumble jumble gumbo!
      Fortified for battle, anchors away!

— Ahriman! And I'm off! I'm Arestes! I'm Ahura Mazda!
Zarathustra was right, and no matter what I do
everything's junk and twilight of idols.
Better Nietzsche than beatcha, hi-fi and swerve left
but it's all stiff highballs, crazy zigzagging highways.
I'm — Lights out! Overtaken.

  Translated by Lindsay Watton, Tod Thilleman, and Patrick Henry

Untitled

I say I'm tired, tired, let go of me
I can't, I say, I'm tired, let go of me, I'm tired,
Not letting go, not listening, in his fist again he squeezes me,
He hoists me up over his head laughing, you haven't flown yet,

Crossing Centuries:

He says, opening his fist, laughing,
He tosses me into the air, fly away
But I'm kind of flying, I say, spitting out grass
I thought I was kind of flying, I say, I was flying, let go,
I am tired, I say, let go, I'm really tired,
He lifts me up over his head again, I'm tired,
He tosses me up, I'm tired, but he doesn't understand,
He's laughing, fly away he says, as far as the bushes
But I'm tired, flapping with my last ounce of strength
this is the last time, but he says, the psycho,
You were just flying, okay I say, so be it,
Have another go, no he says, forgive me,
I'm tired, let go of me, he's laughing, I can't, I'm fed up with you,
Just this once, I say, I can't, he says, now fly on your own,
To hell with you, I say, Lord, I've grown so tired of you,
And I laugh, he looks at me, but I'm laughing, I can't,
Okay, he says, here goes, and gathering speed, I run.

TRANSLATED BY JOANNA TRZECIAK

ALEKSANDR LEVIN

Première

The curtain rises like leavened dough.
Conflagration, fire, ruin of the Universe,
and a light-blue military stage jacket
brought on to the proscenium.

Rustle in the wings, silence in the hall.
Mottled spotlight dazzles the eyes.
Trench warfare is underway.
Tallying those who died before their time,
wounded ahead of schedule, shell-shocked out of sync.
They bear off a general's epaulettes.
An extra screams in painted bandages.
Later they apparently bury him.

An armchair, a map and binoculars carried on stage,
the grave removed, the stage rotated.
The *zasluzhenny* artist stands with his back to the audience.
On the back drop — the ruin of the Universe.

A fine back! What power!
What strength! The audience sobs.
Another actor, like a stab in the back,
casts angry reproaches.

Agents. Emissaries. CNN.
They bear probable trouser-stripes.
Debate. A pair of acute mises-en-scene:
a crowd gathers, scorched frames,
artiste N roots in the ashes.
Bearded resistance fighters.
A soldier in winter hat saws a black loaf.
The stage rotates. Captives. Debate.

The commander howls into a microphone.
Traitors will be strung up by their ankles.
"The IMF isn't satisfied!" —
shouts a reporter from Znamya.

They bear a general's camouflet
with astrakhan fur. The denouement gathers steam.
Commotion in the orchestra: the flageolet
commits excesses, the violin languishes.

Valkyries, berries, Ares
they glide on cables: miracles of equilibrium.
Floodlights burst to the heavens.
Director in ecstasy. Pyrotechnician entranced.

The *zasluzhenny* artist sings an encore,
a message to the people and the convention.
And the falling curtain
roars like a landslide. Applause.

Translated by Mark Nowak and Patrick Henry

Untitled

It's still light. The sun hasn't set,
but daughter's flying with a flashlight
and shines it into a caramel dormer
on an old woman with a soap bubble.
The bubble spills away, papa's inside it,
he's not afraid. A star falls,
rises once more walking pigeon-toed;
beneath the star shines hard water.

It's light yet, but in merry spheres
daughter flies in the candy constellation
and musicians in gentle camisoles
strum dreams. A ballet *kachaetsya*

on satin tiptoe. A knight trots,
bearing curd tarts, the century before last,
and on his liquid spokes flickers
a pale crescent-shaped light.

It's light yet, but mama's lipstick
already conducts a fiery thread
through the air. And the rustle of lemonade
waits in a bottle. Courageous Japanese
with little pigtails fly on parasols
to open it. Lions gambol
on the warm roadway. The sun's still out, it's not
so terrible to sleep at a dacha outside Moscow.

Translated by Mark Nowak and Patrick Henry

Crossing Centuries:

Return to Jaffa

Daybreak, early summer:
the sparkling scales of a shallow wave
a dark, creaky boat slips under the tidal hills —
into the fish belly of the port.
                              I look
sidelong at a copper jug
where like a hookah tube coils the face of a man
returned to his homeland ten years after
he fled it   He's ill at ease
but no one will have anything to do with him
and this is soothing —
I'm pulled into home's green waters
by a pita with dried dates

Look over there —
blue-gray stripe on mountain ridge
out beyond the coastal valley
There beneath a sheepskin of sunny steam
plowed sand and mint
I grew up — a third of a century ago —
in an adobe house in a garden on a hillside
among shards of skulls and snakes —

The boat knocks against the shore
I pour myself into the crowd on the pier   We bathe
in a kindred slime, the friction against the flanks of second cousins,
fish in their final epileptic convulsions
on the stones of the bazaar
I hold tight to my little bundle full of money —
they'd hack it off along with my fingers
Oh how my head's spinning   What is it I want?

Nothing at all: to stand in a transparent bubble of absence,
To sit down in a shadow, eyes closed —
ears abused by the cries
of junkdealers and greengrocers
and the repulsively life-loving
song of the watermelon vendor
I think I've got it: nothing threatens me
I'll slip past the house as I slip past everything else
even if I'm living there
I'm just a representation of myself
breath-steam — network drawn from a cell —
I cannot die — because I never was
Sunset hung now over that bowl of iodine called the sea —
the only thing I can hold onto but
that's not so little — that's
endlessly
much

TRANSLATED BY LEONARD SCHWARTZ AND PATRICK HENRY

from Invasion
to K.G.

I.
I was in love with you
The best proof:
the past several months
I've come down with so many cliches
you might as well call me complex

Is it easier for you
since we didn't go to bed?
I'll answer for you:
I don't know how to answer

If experience doesn't work that means
reality is more experienced

Crossing Centuries:

The main thing — the world was saved by you
And that was a luxury
of selflessness, impermissible of course —
as post-factum speech would have it

II.
Let's try to separate trifles from trifles
            by way of trifles
I tried going for a walk   Didn't last a half hour
Tried to understand you since
I don't understand myself   Doesn't work
I lay down on the bed   Reasons
don't ever justify consequences
            the good old shoulder shrug

III.
Leaving a cafe today I recalled
you here with me a year ago
Like a bobbing Chinese puppet I nodded to myself
            understood once more
that I love you   as sand, rocks
as olfaction, smells

No reaching you as in good dreams
The possible reaching of a goal — subject of a nightmare
At this precise distance you can't detect
the smell of your partner, the smell of the sea
            or the smell of your partner's partner
One transcendental roar, pure as naked spirit.

TRANSLATED BY LEONARD SCHWARTZ AND PATRICK HENRY

DISAPPEARING SPACE

EVGENY BUNIMOVICH

WHERE HAS THE SPACE DISAPPEARED TO?

Not so long ago, the intellectual 'cultourist' and postmodernist Aleksei Parshchikov returned to Moscow for the summer holidays from Stanford, methodically assimilating the discrete structures of existence.*

At one time, a millennium or even just a decade ago, we were young and met often, living in the tiny foxholes of socialist society in southwestern Moscow. One bitterly cold winter day I left Parshchikov's and got on the city bus. I had only one stop to travel, but in that distance all the endless expanse of Russia was compressed.

At first there were the parallelepipeds of the Parshchikovian micro-region, then snow-covered fields, suddenly a small church on a hill, and further — dark woods, then there reappeared the snowy flatness of the plain, and finally, my microregion, with the same multistory parallelepipeds, arranged in a different disorder.

This last time we met at a fashionable literary seminar, entitled "The Postmodern," in which we were less participants than exhibits, objects. Parshchikov had crossed the ocean, I had merely returned from Paris, and we met in the center of Moscow, but the sensation of space had vanished. Where had it disappeared to?

My generation began to write during the death-pangs of the communist myth, to the savory unisexual kisses of General Secretaries, when the poetry of Russia was divided into two distinct currents: semi-official poetry, which was required to say "Yes" to the ideological absurdity of the surrounding environment; and dissident poetry, required, likewise, to say "No" in chorus. The best of these poets became adept at saying "Yes" in such a way that "No" shone through, but even they did not notice how they were required to work on this given plane between fixed poles.

"New wave," "other poets," "parallel culture," "citizens of the night," "the Soviet underground"; what won't they call the generation of poets who arose on the verge of the 80s, and broke free from the strong magnetic field with its inevitable "+" and "-" into a different dimension, thereby acquiring a new volume and degree of freedom. They advanced from the celebrated "Yes" and "No," from the classic questions of the Russian intelli-

---

*This essay was written in December 1991.

gentsia — "What Is to Be Done?"* and "Who Is to Blame?"† — to the ultimate, universal questions of existence: internal questions. As Lev Tolstoi remarked, the true doors for the resolution of questions open "only on the inside" (this citation is not found in Tolstoi's writings, but in some article whose subject I do not recall).

Such were the ethics of the "new wave"; they were, however, also an esthetics. As gradually became clear, we were postmodernists, but our postmodern was intuitive, detected in the atmosphere; it was in the air at the time, not found in books or heard in university lectures. "I don't know what postmodernism is, although I sense that I belong to it," wrote Yury Arabov in the 1987 manifesto "The Realism of Ignorance."

I would point out that it makes sense to interpret the parallelism of "parallel culture" not according to Euclid, but rather Lobachevsky, who described how not one but an infinite multitude of parallel lines pass through a single point of origin. The explanation (also mathematical) of this is contained in that same manifesto by Arabov: "In our opinion, twice two cannot equal four, because this could never be. The product of twice two is determined by everyone for his own purpose." With purely poetic license Arabov pays no heed to the contradiction between "in our opinion" at the beginning of this statement and "everyone for his own purpose" at its end.

And yet, in this contradiction lies the explanation of the rapid rise of the different schools within the "new wave," and of the inevitability of their disintegration, already evident today.

The Poetry Club, which sprang up in Moscow in 1986, became a significant alternative to official literature. It united an enormous variety of poets from the new stylistic currents of the 1980s: metametaphorists, conceptualists, polystylists, and others.

The metametaphorists (Ivan Zhdanov, Akeksei Parshchikov, Vladimir Aristov, Mark Shatunovsky, Konstantin Kedrov) oppose to the sham simplicity, pedantry, and bloatedness of the official poetic model a departure to another world, in which it is impossible to distinguish the waking from the dreaming state, molecules from galaxies, yesterday from tomorrow. All of these are present simultaneously in their verse, mutually reacting and being transformed, and causing each word to mean more than it had before its inclusion in the metametaphoric text.

---

*A novel by Nikolai Chernyshevsky that appeared in 1863.
†A novel by Aleksandr Herzen that was serialized during 1845 and 1846, and was published as a book in 1847.

Crossing Centuries:

The reactions of the conceptualists (Dmitry Prigov, Lev Rubinstein, Vsevolod Nekrasov, Igor Irtenev, Timur Kibirov, Mikhail Sukhotin, and others) to the semi-official organs was outwardly different from that of the metametaphorists. Their poetry is characterized by constant intellectual and moral provocation, the baring of the metallic carcass of ideological monuments, an attack on the mythology of the contemporary world and Soviet society in particular, play with cliches and stereotypes that have faded and run together with constant usage, and crazy space in which context is more significant than text and the word means nothing at all. Many listeners go no further than the first comic and parodic level; they do not sense the underlying tragic cause of this debilitated spate of words. And it is this very audience that provides the conceptualists with their noisy success at readings, exhibitions and performances.

It is as difficult to give a pure example of the slippery essence of polystylistics, the third noteworthy trend in "new wave" poetry, as it is to come up with a list of its adherents, for to do so runs counter to the very essence of the esthetics of polystylism, its all-embracing nature. Anyone seeking elucidation of this point should consult Nina Iskrenko's poem, "Hymn to Polystylistics."[*]

In the polystylists' attempt to construct a new harmony from confusion, chaos, and the heterogeneity of objects, it is easy to discern a link with both the metarealists[†] and the conceptualists. This link consists in the conceptual usage of cliches of mass-consciousness and the simultaneous appeal to all the geological strata of culture. The thinking of a metametaphorist poet could be represented in the form of a winding spiral, compressing and condensing space and time into the text. The poetic work of a polystylist could also be represented as a spiral, but one that is unwinding, seizing all new shades of thought with each spire, and expanding into the entire universe.

The complex geography of the new poetic wave is not fully subsumed under the three headings outlined above. Polystylistic methods, absurdist moves, and the thickness of metametaphors are also found in the work of other "new wave" authors, such as Aleksandr Eremenko, Sergei Gandlevsky, Yury Arabov, Victor Korkiya, and in my own work. While these authors attach themselves in varying degrees to the above-mentioned currents, they each follow their own course.

---

[*]Included in this anthology.
[†]The term metarealism is frequently used to refer to the same current in contemporary poetry otherwise known as metametaphorism.

What is the situation today? Gone are the first readings of the Poetry Club in overflowing halls with the distinct smack of forbidden fruit, scandal, persecution, and rigid police cordons. Harsh criticism, direct accusations and attacks appeared in the official press, but they only further aroused interest. Sensational group publications of the poets in the Poetry Club came out in newspapers with circulation in the millions, and sacks full of enthusiastic and disturbed letters arrived in response.

Passions gradually eased, serious and extensive publications of the "new wave" poets appeared, and in various countries the first books came out. Literary critics have moved from evaluative articles to interpretation of the phenomenon called "new literature."

In this environment the new literary wave in Russia found itself once more in a unique situation, as it suddenly encountered competition from all of world literature. Following the recent abolition of censorship, Russian readers are for the first time reading such authors as Solzhenitsyn and Brodsky, Pasternak and Borges, Orwell and Joyce, and they are reading them concurrently with "new wave" writers, on the pages of the same journals and collections.

Today, by a stroke of fate, everything has overlapped. As my generation bids farewell to youth, no single path has emerged; rather, each writer has found his own. We have also parted with context. Alas, my generation is not the first free generation, as it seemed to us, but rather the last generation of Soviet poetry, closing the tragic and farcical circle. The realities of Soviet society will fade and grow shabby, those things with which through denial, annoyance, or the refusal to participate, we were linked, as it turns out, quite strongly . . .

Prohibition and persecution no longer have any status. The publications, appearances, and festivals of the "new wave" are an appreciable, constitutive force in the literary life of Russia. The literary process in Russia is becoming normal. But can the literary process really be *normal?*

Not only the "new wave," but all of Russian poetry now seeks its place. Accustomed for centuries to substitute itself for politics, religion, philosophy, journalism, shows and circuses, today the poetry of Russia yields to politicians, religious leaders, erotic competition, economic programs, and publicistic essays; it seeks, perhaps for the first time, to find its own territory, and to form its own reader, one elected and summoned, qualified and discriminating.

Confusion can be felt in interviews, pronouncements, and texts. The esthetics of the postmodern have been exhausted. The ethics of unhappiness have likewise been exhausted. The spirit of the times has changed with the epoch.

During the putsch of August, 1991, the "new wave," too, stood before the Russian "White House." There is, however, no adequate language to enable the new literature to describe those days, nor the events of the present moment.

Stylistics and poetics are eroding. Everyone must be prepared to move ahead on his own, and this is fruitful. Who now isn't occupied with this very task?

Eremenko is organizing exhibitions of prison artifacts. Shatunovsky is writing a novel, Parshchikov a quasi-scientific work about our youth. Korkiya is writing political plays and trading in cement. Arabov is writing scripts for poetic films, and I these notes, some articles and essays . . . So, where in the world has the space disappeared to? The devil only knows. But only excruciating individual effort will make it possible to find it again.

TRANSLATED BY PATRICK HENRY

❖❖❖ SERGEI GANDLEVSKY ❖❖❖

To Dmitry Prigov

Fidelity and fatherland, and heroism . . .
It used to be that the express train hurtled forward —
The tracks had been dismantled through an oversight.
It seemed that a catastrophe was unavoidable.
And there were people there! A boy scout came along.
He climbed atop the danger spot
Took off a crimson tie from round his neck
And waved the brightly colored fabric. The engineer
Looked out the locomotive.
He understood: there's something fishy here.
Adroitly he maneuvered all the levers
And the catastrophe was thus averted.

Or another case. Express was flying by.
The tracks had been dismantled through an oversight.
It seemed that a catastrophe was unavoidable.
And there were people there! An aged switchman
Stepped out onto the danger spot,
with pen-knife opened up a vein.
He stained a rag with boiling blood,
and waved the brightly colored fabric. The engineer
Looked out the locomotive,
He understood: there's something fishy here.
Adroitly he maneuvered all the levers
And the catastrophe was thus averted.

But now, if it happens that the train is going,
There's good track stretching out to the horizon.
Conditions great, so know or study
Or work, combine your job with
A correspondence course.
All has changed. The boy scout's now a grownup.
He's gone a bit to fat and really mellowed.

Become a railway supervisor.
He bawls the aged switchman out
And threatens to pack him off to the AA.

Translated by Andrew Wachtel

To Aleksei Magarik

Something on prison and painting.
With foam in the mouth and a tear.
Kostroma or Velikie Luki —
But at table in honor of Gulag.
This song is about how a son, now gray-haired,
With official permission returned to his home.
He drank some at Nina's and cried some at Kari's —
Oh my Lord, O my God!

Our station stands out in the open
A gutter is lisping in personal tongues.
They sing separation on platforms
Take hooligans off the east.
All day long there are people and bread,
And cargoes strategic which travel the homeland.
Something about ruined life —
My taste's undemanding.

In fall go on out to the wide-open field
Cool your brow with the wind of your homeland.
A swallow of alcohol is like a boiling rose,
It twists and it turns in your chest.
A night of the ravenous family twists
While distances whistle through fingers.
The fatherland hasn't got aliens,
And anyway everything's here — and the air feels

As if you awoke on an overcast day
Banged around and then carried the slops out,

And brushed your ridiculous hopes right away,
And they take you away, underground, in the distance
A pond, covered with goose bumps,
A semaphore's burning with all of its might,
Rain drips and an unshaven passerby
Speaks to himself as he walks.

TRANSLATED BY ANDREW WACHTEL

VLADIMIR TUCHKOV

Untitled

to Lev Kropivnitsky

Paratrooper swooping down from the sky breaks the back of a buck,
and in tenacious claws he carries his catch back to the nest
there he rips the beating body into letters, into parts,
and he throws them down against the summit's foot —
there Pushkin stands in a top hat, with his walking stick,
peering through his monocle.

TRANSLATED BY LISA JARNOT AND PATRICK HENRY

While Waiting

Standing on the platform waiting for the local train.
Where there is no train. Where the iron train's not running.
When I walk up to the signal post
it stands there thinly turning to bright green.
When I ask, it lies. It never turns to red.
No train. Where the green train doesn't run.
Where I lie down with my ear against the rail to hear a violin,
where I lie down and I hear the mouse scratch somewhere far away,
where the wind still rustles through the Don's long grassy plains.
No train. Where the vicious winter train won't run.
So I haul in all the rails as if a seine.
Only trifles that are running come to me —
the paper clips, the writing paper in its sheafs,
that I pulled this in, an armored train!
No train. Where the double-headed train has ceased to run.
Steam engine that I am, I would sing a song of love to lure it in.
No train. The icy local train won't run.

Here I have my ticket and my pass and money for the fine!

I won't smoke in your vestibules!
I won't pulley bricks up high upon the cords of the red brake!
I won't lean my head out towards the sky!
Where the train crept up, it swallowed and it hissed.

TRANSLATED BY LISA JARNOT AND PATRICK HENRY

Untitled

Asia! says the major to the colonel,
scraping his tongue on his palate, shaking the seeds
                              that are sprouting
from his head.

Asia! says the colonel to the major,
dragging himself like a sulfurous sack over the side of the junk.

Asia! says the echo to them both,
to the empty craters of the moon.

Asia! roars the radio pack,
pulling at the threading, pulling at the nails.

Asia! as the iron slides
across the glass, scraping epithelium from the entrails.

Asia! Asia! back and forth in intervals of boot kicks to
the head.

Asia! the long gasp of the trunk torn from its gas mask.

Asia! from the sky that looks on without love.

Asia! at seven o'clock it's never nine,
jumping from the trees onto witless shoulders.

Asia! as the Cossacks sing, the whistles blow, the sword tips click, sparks
from the insides of the man — Asia!

Asia! heart-pump that bails murky water
rising to the colonel's chin
as he speaks to the major
from inside of Asia's storm.

TRANSLATED BY LISA JARNOT AND PATRICK HENRY

Quiet of the Chestnuts

(Fragments of the poem)

1.

Know and remember
the boy sleeping in his dorm room, the one
still dreaming as the light rays entered his body —
fingering up his bone, moving through the spleen and marrow.
The light awoke suddenly, whispering: Quiet now
there's no need to cry.
Just drink some pomegranate juice,
we'll see how you come around, and where —
how the East will calm you,
the way your crazy nerves will explode in the West.
Know that it's the earth's new devils
who let this take place, as they wished it —
even though a Hieronymus Bosch or Salvador Dali
could never create something so unimaginable . . .
The grass whitened on Pripyat's meadows,
and the homes of Chernobyl suddenly vanished.
The sky's bulging eyes were so unbelieving —
as if asking, "are you trying to get a taste of your own death?"
The roads to Kiev and Minsk, they're sharp precipices,
though the danger doesn't come from the minefields now ...
It's more like a war-time evacuation: terror,
the quiet horror, yet this supposed peace.

No, the earth can no longer be at ease
as we add nuclear lead covered overalls
to the century's military uniforms. It's a clean up crew
who tries to protect humanity from humanity!

What about you, Dante, Shakespeare, Dostoyevsky —
how your words tore at the edges, struggled,
bore into language — is it all for nothing now?
Terrifying this meaninglessness.

What if the century's new devils
can only be exercised by our own magic?
What can we do, what else is there —
Dante, Shakespeare, Dostoevsky — what can you tell me?

Our words and their power elude my faith,
I've lost the very language that once gave me hope.
Instead, I hear talk, and more talk.
They say not one nuclear shield or barrier collapsed . . .

But rest assured if one leg shakes around Moscow
it sets the other one kicking in California.
There's the story, and the way they play with it
revealing man's true scale. But the final record's
unfinished still
because remember the boy sleeping in his dorm room?
What's his fate? He somehow manages to believe
that this could never have happened to him.
I know and believe that no one wanted
the vast light in his eyes,
this radioactive anguish.

2.

If suddenly there's grief, then the shudder of tragedy
spreads — not voluntarily, perhaps only because of our guilt
springing from the earth's core like some avalanche
with all its uranium, its acid copper.
Going back to time's primordial act — to Democritus even,
Who himself spoke of nature's fracturing divisions.
Here it is then — decomposed, revealed ...
stuck within the very essence of our human character.
And a man buckled under the blow. His hair sheered away

The New Generation in Russian Poetry

by the radioactive winds of the plains, the precipices.
But the force of the earth's voice
prevails in our failure, outlasts the magnitude of these explosions.

3.

The untouchable experience of pregnant women —
delicate little girls, crystal eyelashes,
and afterwards this unimaginable . . . this happening
outside of our own time —
and school students practicing machine logic?

All at once, the secret will condense
in a century's borders, a flash passing for the race,
but then, who shared the last of it all with our dead?
It wasn't imparted. It was determined in advance . . .

The experience of genetics. The business of genetics.
Nothingness. What can we do with it now?
Our destinies sucked out. Medical ethics?
Their bestial fate took control of it all . . .

The vessels will be refilled.
Forests will grow stout, full, bending again
at the trees' trunk. Nothingness. The destinies of the
unincarnated — they breathe oddly, through closed mouths.

4.

The fish don't believe — it's not visible,
the beasts don't believe — it's not audible,
and our population doesn't believe — it's not horrific,
so the water flows into the world's ocean
just as before,
but now the cities of the Sun and Atlantis
are rotting there . . .
Yet this is no Guernica.
Humanity, you're the only true measure

for the Geiger counter.
Only in the spirit of your emotions
can the presage of the years collect,
and in your eyes, it's clear
just how much you've taken on
from the 20th century's
brilliance and insanity —
already clear in those eyes, the way your son
will describe you, in the 21st century.

TRANSLATED BY JOHN HIGH

Autumnal Ode

0.
(Fleet-winged expanses rattle
the dread figure of future glory,
and prawns, quiet as bombs,
learn to fly with a limp*;
forged into a symbol of faith,
Giant Steps[†] drone round and round,
giving off long ripples to the music
of children's laughter in the square.
The peal of dashing winds
blows kishlaks[‡] from epaulettes.

1.
But the burn of southern climes,
but the watery blisters
of mosques, ground into dust, —
and you sit and gobble eggs.)
Torzhok.[§] Elevator operators sleep in the hold
while ponds skim weight
from long drought, stewardesses'
threadbare underwear,
and laundresses no longer swear,
firing flares at the fair.

---

*Reference to the famous Soviet song, "Eaglets learn to fly" (Orlyata uchatsya letat').
[†]Giant steps (Gigantskie shagi) was an official term used to describe the supposedly rapid pace of development under Soviet rule. It also refers to a playground game in which a horizontal, freely spinning wheel is attached to the top of a post. By holding on to a rope suspended from the wheel a child circles the post, only occasionally touching the ground — as if making "giant steps."
[‡]A "kishlak" is a village in central Asia.
[§]Torzhok's an old provincial town on the road between Moscow and St. Petersburg.

2.
Meaning: it's getting on toward September.
The wind scatters nail down.
Iron creasemen strike
they lag behind and pant.
Not a single thought that
wants to think out loud.
From park to park the aroma of crones
prepares the humus for winter.
Birds on bikes go bald,
thrust sticks in their own spokes.

3.
It's said the Lyceum* and the State Circus
are utterly self-absorbed.
(Can it be so hard in this country to find
three pairs of stately Turkestans†?!
Probably — yes. Offensive as it is
that this ignoble people came down the pike,
mouths crammed with petitions,
the course of the origin of species
changes with the course of years.
"Yes" in the sense of "No").

4.
....
....
....
....
....
....
....
....

---

*The Imperial Lyceum at Tsarskoe Selo near St. Petersburg, which Pushkin attended 1812-1817.
†See Ch. 1, Stanza xxx of *Eugene Onegin*: ". . . but it's doubtful I that in all of Russia you'll find I three pairs of shapely feminine feet." The references to Pushkin's "novel in verse" and other works are too numerous to cite every time they appear. This note serves to alert the reader to this connection throughout the poem.

The New Generation in Russian Poetry   259

....

....

5.

From the City fell rail
roads, like iron fences —
and listing to starboard
Vladivostok* changes course,
descending by terraces to the bay
and overflowing, like a river.
But here's where the continent ends
(if you hang the map crookedly).
A fire plug peers from the depths
a convoy three sheets in the wind.

6.

That's the second day. One-fourth divine.
A day so diesel
that divans' tusks fall out
and smoke streams from distant ditches;
but through it skips a courier
(inciting a lot of nonsense) —
does he bear a dispatch to Peter
or is he capering, swerving madly —
but the carefree salad days are over,
and with them, the first chapter.

CHAPTER 2

7.

An exceedingly long time spent in preparation:
first I sharpen the pencils
just for the soul,
since I write, of course, with a ball-point —
but *milking,* even by hand,

---

*While Vladivostok is often referred to as Russia's easternmost city, Magadan and other cities are in fact further east. Vladivostok was also the name of a Soviet aircraft carrier.

Crossing Centuries:

is powerless without fodder;
and to make what's called "love"
in a hammock and flippers
is like trying to shave looking into a prism
(paying tribute to onanism).

8.
No need to read farther.
No need to read nearer.
You could sweep out the attic
and stay off skis for a month.
No need to like peas
(I don't like them much myself),
you could work on your penmanship,
or wind up doing time.
You could do much else
and that's just dandy.

9.
And at last it's the season,
as at autumn — time
to change the poem's title
to "and so on" etc.
Though it's simpler to tax
(especially the native) tongue —
or else these stanzas to the last
are only suited for an Epilogue.
(A *narrative poem,* that is, and not an *ode*:
look before leaping into a metrical current).

10.
A narrative poem made exclusively of endings.
Like an erotic nightmare
where the chairs, one and all, are just for one,
like a pass for the viewing stand on May Day.
Fine if it were — *week's end,*
or — at the short end — of a rain shower;
otherwise, I waited (or — I'm waiting? . . .

(or — waited?) . . .), — truth is
I forgot what I wanted
to say anyway. Taking stock.

11.

Lines lie down in groups of ten
like a properly wanked platoon
heeding taps, sounded with proper rigor.
But the lifeguards in Shchelkovo,[*]
not hankering after prizes,
rescue only their *own* larks.
In short, I flowed into a fine, aged
marasmus, as into the deep blue sea
(always so murky,
like "a journey into the unknown"[†]).

12.

So where's the poetry? Not in the cards, alas.
Perhaps, only in the gleam
when she places the knife
on the parapet . . . but according to the estimate
words are not forseen
in which rhyme digs into the waistband
as deadlines squeeze an old foundation pit . . .
article, "inspected by" . . . and even "Singer"
sewn on here like a sleeve to a star.[‡]
Turns out, the "journey" isn't the point.

EPILOGUE

13.
No! probably an Ode after all:
it's the second day, as before.

---

[*]Shchelkovo is a Moscow neighborhood that has a beach on the Moscow River.
[†]"Poetry — all of it — is a journey into the unknown" is a line in Vladimir Mayakovsky's poem "Conversation with a Tax Collector About Poetry."
[‡]The idiom, "sewn like a sleeve to a cunt" ("byt' prishitym kak rukav k pizde") means to be very much out of place. Since this idiom is impolite, one usually replaces "cunt" with "star." The two words in Russian ("pizda" and "zvezda") sound similar.

Crossing Centuries:

Ruddy, fresh, as from the wrong side of a garment
no hero appears
to work the smelter of the subject.
The machines are working, the plan stands idle.
And the day that lies ahead tomorrow —
again the second. The searchlight smokes
(not a komsomol searchlight,* a plain one)
It remains only to sing — Standstill:

13.
"Standstill! — mightier than wild grasses
you hover above a bristling battery!
But who'll wield the razor-strop of state?
However, that's just firing blanks . . ."
But here a daughter pressed
to my breast for an instant. Rather, a great-grandson.
Rather, a police chief,
and witnesses — the boiler-man
and the caretaker — peer out from the vestibule.
And the nights grow longer toward evening.

14.
For a thirtieth year my thinning dreams
stand at the roadstead,
tattered like a drag-net,
cold like a lure's glow.
And there'll be no one to tell
that the cracked mug of the sun
like frozen yeast
will not rise, like perch on a serving plate,
but falls to pieces like dried-out leather,
which, moreover, resembles it.

15.
Standstill! ....
....

---

*"Komsomol Searchlight" (Komsomol'sky prozhektor) is a typical name for the bulletin of a cell
in the Komsomol, the Young Communist League.

....

....

Standstill! of course, you're easy:
one pun, and off to bed.
But it's more complicated to dance
the mazurka with ease. The speed of growth,
of whatever you like, for you to up it —
that's a big fucking deal!

16.
For example: damp rot holds in check
the speed of Roskontsert*:
wigs come off like dried orange peel
(perhaps the artists will grow into them).
But you can't send the porter
with a port-pain to pick up the paper —
portentously a stool-portunian
will spill the beans, that in the zoo
the constable's gone round the bend
a porterhouse warming in his holster.

17.
But it's not even a question of the steak:
custodians of the earthly record
bloom across the breadth of Moscow,
sitting in the cabin of the head.
Pollen — though you sleep wearing a gas-mask,
they multiply as if for slaughter.
But they're not the point, either. Any
climate's bad for me.
Moscow! that's the heroine.
I dealt well. And the city took a hit.

18.
Through streets and squares,
through parks in the English fashion,
through reinforcement, whoring,

---

*The state agency in charge of the performing arts, known for its stifling bureaucracy.

a bottle, and a second, one in the kisser,
according to lists, to coffee grounds,
by output and circulation,
through the heat, heart-to-heart,
schedule, story, sergeant,
luggage, train, lucky.
Must be time.

TRANSLATED BY PATRICK HENRY

IN PLACES FAR FROM PERFECTION

NINA ISKRENKO

IN PLACES FAR FROM PERFECTION

IN PLACES FAR FROM PERFECTION any Displacement often seems to us desirable and alluring, like a miraculous Journey. And even more than that — a way out of a blind alley. Liberation. Exodus.

Question: do Places that are sufficiently close to perfection exist?

The answer's obvious.

Yes.

Absurd as this sounds.

Take for example, a House. A pile of bricks and boards organized in some manner, which delimits the space in which people who love one another live. A microscopically small Place with an enormous density of internal energy, an emotionally charged black box. In essence, no Displacements or Journeys are necessary or even possible there. Except for the turning on of a light, or the brushing of teeth. Neither possible nor necessary, as they distort the space of Quantity and Spirit, of a morning sigh and a clean towel.

Or a Garden. This fleeting sensation of approaching the heavenly, the Unutterable, in Vain. A wind, erasing the color of shame, our own disinterested forgetfulness, grace rustling in the grass. *I WON'T DO IT AGAIN,* uttered with tearful eyes.

Or a Dream. Here's a splendid little place that admits all sorts of displacement and distortion, and for this very reason is absolutely undistorted. It's there I can permit myself not only to go out into the open cosmos in red-bannered trousers with hammer and sickle, but also, *mon cher,* to turn your priceless soul inside out unceremoniously.

Only Exile breaks the clock and removes all inclination for mythmaking that borders on arrogant self-abasement. Exile is that which I do not know and which I fear terribly — it is hell, and any sight of it deprives us of all the possibilities enumerated above. Not to mention many others.

TRANSLATED BY PATRICK HENRY

ANDREI VORKUNOV

Untitled

Cutting a wave with my belly
I make for turbid waters,
once a serf from Ryazan,
become at last — Prince of Denmark.

Children's games are naive,
those of adults too serious,
coils looped around necks,
regret comes too late.

Limp Ophelia's breasts
hang like shorts on a clothesline,
I accused you for nothing,
you were no thief of hearts.

Foolish tottering Polonius
quietly rustles the arras,
no sooner hidden than a chisel
thrust makes him groan.

Servants are obliged to perish,
if by chance they're confused
with the monarch, for
there's primordial meaning in this.

Something patently old-womanish
in uncle's name: Claudius
he dispatched papa with poison
for mama's sake, most likely.

Carnal are his interests
and unspiritual his desires,
the lord must like a god,
that understanding might arrive.

Crossing Centuries:

Yorick bore me on his knees
with a pat on the head,
the world's so awfully putrescible
it's awkward to exist.

Shall I kill Guildenstern?
Shall I ruin Rosencrantz?
But what am I . . . most foul!
Let them sail off to foreign shores.

I should battle with Laertes,
we'll wound each other to the quick,
to die a beautiful death
is better than on one's back in bed.

I know there will be no truth,
I think this is nothing unusual,
stale funeral baked meats
eaten with a wedding galantine.

Goths crossed beyond the Danube,
blacks shoot up in the ghetto,
someone stole up to Danaë
screwed her — and hit the road.

Someone was a witness to
this, scrawled a picture,
The Lord was past thirty,
attractive, evidently, to blondes.

The Lord was past thirty,
the devil was . . . past forty?
This, I dare say, will come in handy
in making sense of their quarrel.

If there was a quarrel at all,
if it wasn't all made up, so that
they'd both look pitiable
in such a shameful row.

To be, or not to be — no matter,
nothing will help now,
let the pain of damnation gnaw
our maidenly souls,

let the prose of celebrations jar us,
the everydayness of this work-day world inspire fear,
brothers born to the cassock,
I am with you — Hamlet, Prince of Denmark.

TRANSLATED BY PATRICK HENRY

Untitled

A trojan cat lies in the night,
despondently gnaws at the bit,
and next to it another keeps mum
about a life that came to nothing,

that romulus was small, but remus,
while alexander bucephalated
and, above all, in such a hole
akstafa* up and vanished,

but where's the third trojan cat?
he was nothing, but went out on top,†
found his widow cliquot
and drained her among the oats.

TRANSLATED BY PATRICK HENRY

---

*A river that flows from Armenia to Azerbaijan, as well as the name of an Azeri town near that river.
†Play on a line from L'Intemationale (the Soviet hymn until 1944): "Nous n'étions rien — donc, soyons tout!" (We were nothing — thus let us be everything!).

Crossing Centuries:

Untitled

1

and tease a nightingale in spring
an angler's bobber for silken roofs
terror — what blueness
a finger's blue lure
remember everything about hunting tomtits
a life's work: a complete set
pupil, hook, pencil
and whistle at a rickety fence

2

and tease a nightingale in spring
nicknames spit and wheeze
bear the names of drunkards in beer halls
cover with coarse red cloth
stuff mouths with hooks
unwrap sandwiches from newspaper
tug caps low on foreheads
pour glasses of beer
grip pencils

3

five turquoise ripples
hide a bobber
day and night, round the clock
a merry motor spins
hauls a tail from howling waters
instantly alters the slant
blueness falls from above
all around forms the expanse
of soft lilac meadows

4

spring comes again
sagging boards creak
rocking under me
what's-his-name slobbers on a pencil
spills a tea bag in a shirt pocket
chews a pink grape
instantly alters the slant
slowly drops a glass

TRANSLATED BY SCOTT MACLEOD AND PATRICK HENRY

Untitled

incessant asphalt, ceaseless honking;
frightful grinding of engines;
under the earth a lead flower coalesces
with the heady fragrance of chlorine;

everything glazed with the icy ringing glass
of a burnished steel slope;
the incomprehensible expanse, the limitless volume
of a swelling, tedious climb;

boundless teeming nature,
like decanting gasoline onto a table;
overflowing reservoirs of the pungent vigor
of iodine and ammonia splashing;

and here's another arbitrary example:
take a shred of fetid rubber,
sensing in the body's reaction to death
the ineffable sign of a ghost;

afterwards turn out the light, grazing the shade,
quickly uncork the perfume bottle,

lift your elbow from the table
and sip the scent of menthol

TRANSLATED BY SCOTT MACLEOD AND PATRICK HENRY

Untitled

My dress is brown,
His jacket gray.
He's so nice and
I'll be his first.

Loaded grin on the lips,
Naughty lock across the brow,
Beneath my window grows an oak,
Beneath his window, two.

We suddenly settled on a swim,
He decided to put it off until Thursday
(Though it was already decided)
And we set off anyway.

We crossed over the old bridge
And lay together on the sand,
Steam streamed from wet braids,
On the way home I traveled light.

The waning moon bared its teeth
Behind little green shutters,
My dress, still damp,
Threw a shadow over the wall.

He struck a match against the box,
Sought the words to say goodbye.
Fumbled a long time in his trouser pockets,
It was damp and wouldn't light.

After breakfast we set out
To where the train station
Loses its slender spire in the sky,
The trains were running and mine left on time.

I'll return in ten days,
Imaginary islands,
Of this there could be no doubt,
In this room there are two windows.

Translated by Scott MacLeod and Patrick Henry

Untitled

Papa taught me many lessons.
He instilled a love for Dickens,
raw vegetables, and barbells. How
he was visibly stricken if I didn't
shine my own galoshes. "Prepare
your books the previous evening."
Papa scrutinized my every mark
so closely that poor David Copperfield
was made to cry over his mutton chop.
And I, like David, cried over my yogurt.
Essentially, Papa was right.
Papa was instilling a love for yogurt.
Papa was like Goliath.

Papa taught me to stand on my skis.
Papa taught me to stay under water.
Papa was also right in this.
Having filled my lungs with frightful air
I would beware my Papa and his
righteousness twice more than before.
Papa was instilling a love for air.
I remember how once into the bath
Papa brought a kettle with salted tea.
He poured the tea in through his nose
and reflected: "We exhale and
immediately become healthier."
I still see Papa's bared teeth.
See, in answer to my silent question,
the hairs growing out of his nostrils.

He was a big fan of free-style wrestling,
a proponent of the Greco-Roman thing.
I often dream this tortured dream:
Papa in longjohns and I without,
and Papa is wrestling me. Papa

apparently used me to learn
something akin to the double Nelson.
At times he would twist both my arms
behind my back and make my neck an arch.

Papa instilled a love of nudity,
trained me to sleep in my birthday suit.
Papa lectured about beauty and taste,
entrusted into my arms a volume
whose pages glared white with buttocks,
"Here is Apollo. . . . Here is Heracles."
This was unspeakably shameful.
And from this shame I nearly cried.
Then when I broke down at some point
and begged him to stop, Papa almost stopped —
in that moment, to my excited stare
appeared a heretofore unseen fragment,
a detail from the women's Turkish baths.

Papa took me for walks around Moscow
or walking in the suburbs of Moscow.
Once, I recall, we came to our park.
He got a bicycle without training wheels
and ordered me to peddle "straight ahead!"
and I yelled "I'm turning off the path."
"I'll wring your neck if you do," he said.
And I was certain that he would have.
Perhaps this is not a good example
except that in my fear I was paralyzed,
noting the asphalt's toothed bas-relief,
the tufts of grass growing in the cracks,
the nannies' singsong calling to the brats,
and the eight circles still left to travel.

How everyone in the park is laughing at us.
How all of Moscow laughs at us,
and all the Moscow suburbs howl.

TRANSLATED BY ALEX CIGALE

Crossing Centuries:

Untitled

God whimpered having shuffled the mortal
coils of his creation with my comfort
when, as a human sacrifice to the draft board,
I was made to jump with a parachute.

A spiritual orchestra played at
the place of military enrollment
and the asphalt cracked, as from our curses,
as I forever bid farewell to Moscow.

My limbo took the form of an aerodrome.
The instructor was a tough-guy sinner.
In comparison to his thick torso
my trunk resembled a small birdhouse.

He was as inspired as Daedalus
in the act of preparing his parachute.
At first I thought I'd take it up the ass
but then relaxed, gave myself up for lost.

So just when I made a friendly wager
the propeller would slice away my shin,
I had jumped by then three times or so
and was completely happy with myself.

And then the mud roads turned boggy.
The moon, like a girl at the oar,
was full of charm and longing
and the reality of army survival

nothing. I'd say I'm a lucky stiff,
fortunate as only a Jew can be
having met his end out of a bottle
within the military theater

of the Red Army routine.

TRANSLATED BY ALEX CIGALE

YULIYA SKORODUMOVA

Untitled

"The door creaks. A cod stands on the threshold."
— from Joseph Brodsky, "Lullaby of Cape Cod"

The fish comes at midnight. It says, "shhhhh,"
marking the eve of a golden age.
Milky fullness, nipples of death-color
shut us up from birth.
Over the cradle the golden lure
of non-existence looms so close — just out of reach . . .
An underwater world, a sky world — that same blueness.
If you're Homo Sapiens, there's no difference.
If you're a fish, shades of light, not of color,
can veto you.
A sea of that light orders the fish, "Lift."
The retina thrashes in the net of a reverse world.
And the fish falls skywards
on its iridescent belly, losing its way.
Rudder and sail are engulfed by one
who plunged the fish in the silent sea depths. Trying to enter,
the mouth gapes, chokes, drowns
in air, so that 90% of the water
refreshed its wind-burned palms.
This is your ceiling, your shroud — thus, an icy riverbed
where you thrash, unable to penetrate the sockets' grooves.
For in each fish is lodged
the memory of death — an air bubble.
The century's end approaches. The fish falls skywards,
where carnivorous Thursday spawns the rain,
where Friday only appears in fish-zone dreams,
where locks on lips are a tribute to the Golden Horde . . .
Splash, Aquarius, with the waters of life or death,
Prolong its fish-day.

TRANSLATED BY MARY WINEGARDEN AND GYORGY VLASENKO

Crossing Centuries:

M'ysteria Oof

It's all wrong in this place
This time's out of sync —
this high-heeled she-devil
Takes a piss in the clink.

In the sky a flounder flounders
A needle trips on the corner.
On the pitch-black avenue
grows numb la petite Nude.

I fears of poets, who's gonna listen to me.
I fears of poets, who's looking for a handout.
I fears of poets, who writes about me like taking a piss.
I fears of poets, who wants me to dance and shout.

La Nude fears nudity.
On the left, a house full of cats.
An ascetic's soul revealed
in their deep eye cuts.

The body surrenders to dress.
For crucifixion prepares its flank.
A geranium bursts into the nose.
Into palms the nails sank.

I fears of poets, clad in dirt tones of gutter talk.
I fears of poets, with harakiri on their mugs and broke jug ears.
I fears of poets, who right away get too palsy-walsy.
I fears of poets, all fucked up and kissing crosses with tears . . .

Cats in the house on the right
Where conscience goes to sleep.
Bloody tails drawn down
while victims go pee.

Cats everywhere, their eyes like bars,
chock full of empties.
The number is nil, but a glance says pour me one,
the nadir — surfeit and chateaubriand.

I fears of poets, who do it all bass ackwards.
I fears of poets, young but green and full of lust.
I fears of poets with opened eyes and tears, so gay.
I fears of poets, who's stood the test.

House dead ahead, cats beneath.
On the beds there's smoke of gray.
Between lovers there's a knife —
the sphinx's ingratiating paw at play.

Sleep, O petite Nude.
As prescribed in the menu,
this body's not for take-out.
Man disposes but God proposes.

I fears of poets, with their bags packed and eyes on the door.
I fears of poets, so fluid they displaces solid bodies.
I fears of poets, who suck poems out their fingers like blow jobs.
I fears of poets, who nags me for sins I ain't heard of . . .

To stop us belching out of our minds
Winter's janitor stays with us.
The ohs and ahs go still
with this straitjacket on us.

Our Nude's negligee
freezes to the bone.
A climax for what ails you
Fuck this climate — I'm gone.

I fears of poets, who seizes the living with a death grip.
I fears of poets, who the greedy devil drives to bedlam.
I fears of poets, with flailing arms, like grunts on parade.
I fears of poets, who try to keep their ape-selves hidden . . .

The apes corralled.
On the balalaika the ball did sit.
The night of wonders gave the piano
a shot to the kisser and split.

Only there, where windows are,
stoic cats stand guard, eyes wide.
Finches melt in their mouths.
Dead fish inside.

TRANSLATED BY MARY WINEGARDEN WITH PATRICK HENRY

Untitled

Passion's not what's terrible; it's feeling I'm empty,
                              that there's nothing here.
Aizenberg, I'm ashamed to be myself.
I tell you that a fellow convict, convicted of the same crime as I,
    washed this jacket for me,
and, whatever difference it would make, he could as well have been a
    real man.

I can't be myself anymore.
I want this paradise full of sparrows back,
a streetcar in Sokolniki*; give me my childhood suffering
(I'll get it one way or another),

Right now I'm where dandelions curtsey
and schoolchildren want to destroy me —
considering all this greenery, so much of it,
there were so many times I was better, more honest,
so many times I could have been happier.

Right now, I'm full of May and a blue balloon
spinning and whirling as if it were sick[†],
I've got this fresh, opulent, fiery dust,
I've got the fact I never loved anyone,
never bullied Baba Tata and mama —
and I forgive no one for anything.

I made all that up — I was in fact worse,
playing with a blue ball,

---

*A park in Moscow
[†]Playing on the words of a children's song beginning "A blue balloon spins and revolves / Spins
and revolves overhead."

and Sokolniki park, and my Yauza[*],
of which I'm afraid, and don't love, —
don't be merciful and give it all back
(this terrible paradise full of sparrows).
But spare someone from all of it,
someone trusting, beloved, quick.
And yet, you see, in return for whatever that costs
I can give so little in return.

As for you, don't give me . . .
                    life in some asylum,
don't write prison on my palms.
I so much want glory and love.
So let there be no glory, no love,
just dandelions floating in blood.

O Lord, when will I lose my bloom,
when will I fade away in a sweater, gone mad —
will I indeed really become better
like a swallow resigned to the storm.

But if . . . someone . . . demolish these lies,
and life breaks through, the way it was
(the way feathers jut through the pillows at night),
how light and full of holes I'll be,
how crushed, tremendous, unarmed.

TRANSLATED BY EDWARD FOSTER AND PATRICK HENRY

Untitled

Greedy fiery Sin torments me lion-like,
Oh mommy dearest, a moth ate all my coat,

---

[*]A small river in Moscow, feeding into the Moscow River.

And what he's come up with, the gourmand,
Takes my sculpted stomach, a roll with raisins,
Stuffs it tight with slow and sweet madness
Only to smoothe it all down — no joke!

Oh mommy dearest! where's my mommy?

Father says, "Daniel, get ready,
We'll go to the market, they show off a prairie lion,
He's greedy, he's fiery, his eyes a-sparkling," —
I know, Dad, his eyes are all a-sparkle,
I'm shaking out a sweater down in the garden:
It's been eaten up, a hare's fur in springtime,
And I'm a hare in a sweet spring flood.

Oh mommy dearest! where's my mommy?

At night I hear someone calling, "Daniel,
We care not for honey or for raisins,
why did you chase away the lion and kill the moth?"
Thick and fiery, it keeps pouring out.
I answer that I don't feel hot at all,
I'm your roll, stuffed with apple jelly.
And in the morning Dad says, "Let's go to Mickey D's."

Oh mommy dearest! where's my mommy?

And once a dream came: a platoon of horny soldiers,
They let the lion out of his cage,
He's jumping closer with roaring,
As if to play a game of frightening hopscotch,
But what a miracle! — he's meeker than a calf
And gently pokes me, I push his muzzle
With ridiculous defenseless hands,
His eyes like little yellow flowers,
His fiery mane bright and blinding.

Mother's muffled cry comes from a padded barrel:
Wake up, come to your senses quick, oh Daniel,
And I wake up, my little finger bitten off.

TRANSLATED BY VITALY CHERNETSKY AND TOD THILLEMAN

STANISLAV LVOVSKY

White Noise

write, rabbit, write *I will*
I believe you re right   it s better than just sitting here
in the dim room in the heart of the Moscow North-East
    go my letter *fly*, where my love is
waiting for me online where red modem lights
are blinking where I ve never been to
    fly, letter, fly
to the other side of everything   fly —
unsubstantial *pure words* no envelope   even no paper

here it is here I am   knocking some far away *gateway*
open, my addressee, that is me —
that is my unbodied heart weightless butterfly *letter*, saying
good morning my love   that is me
writing you whispering disobedient words of the foreign accents
from the other side of Mebius surface
from the seamy side of the empty Klein Bottle,
which is usually called *habitable universe language love*

so fly letter fly through the mute kilometers miles
take my tenderness to where I ve never been
    go my letter *fly break on through*

she s up very early to take care
of the two little twins love of her life
i want you to be the first to say
them *good morning* it s time
    go my letter fly

TRANSLATED BY THE AUTHOR

Crossing Centuries:

Untitled

all our hopes   on you
pinned, and
you yourself understand
when we officially announce the beginning of Armageddon
you yourself
are to turn out the lights   the gas, lock up the apartment
put the key under the rug and   of course
DON T FORGET TO TURN OFF THE TELEVISION!

*

The crumpled heavens overflowing with snow above
love above speechless winter
America reclining around higher than the rafters
the cigarette, shaking in your fingers, sleepless
snow everywhere and snow without sleep.
not a single word of love, the industrial
european november two silent ones
in the room
in the martial silence of the room.

*

two winters inside one year
are similar to two cigarettes
without a light lit from each other, but
there s nothing to fear, having learned to see
how ephemeral air
ages at night in the lungs, — the winter
of one year and in the heavenly heavens
however God is inside with a stitched lining
we are similar to several different
people completely different similar as twice
two mirrors those angels amalgams damp branches
the day the almighty hemorrhaging wind Sheol.

*

Constantly creeping behind us, again
I don t understand who it is, every day
seeking us, serving us for seven years
on seven streams of migrations and turnings,
in the non-euclidian dark of corporeal corners, away
from us withdrawing, heading nowhere, or to meet,
setting a constant winter on us,
the beast of cold, leading it to us quickly,
to the following causes uncaused, it —
the constant cronost, with a rabbi s hand, again,
devouring us from behind   our heart.

TRANSLATED BY THE AUTHOR

N.

your smile like a banner
kiss is a click
but it s a dead link
always flashing
from inside my eyelids
small animated gift
fairy tale
from the Java s crypt
error *Four O Four*
connection was terminated
access denied
traffic too heavy
try again later

oh Lord, trace my IP
maintain me
update me
reload me

amen

TRANSLATED BY THE AUTHOR

Crossing Centuries:

NIKOLAI PALCHEVSKY

Apparition in the City

Repeat for me this image in surplus hour —
In filthy doorways, in shredded raiments.
Send down to the congress of street and square an eye, the battered
Intermediary that revealed the Word in idiots' rude talk.

And lead heavenward. Through the knife's discriminating guest
Expose the wound clenched fingers can't conceal.
Your guards lowered them to the polluted earth,
Carefully handling the cracked bodies.

That's when we glimpse the direction of continuous love,
Disputed in open air like shouts that pit fist against flesh.
They circumcise newborn thoughts instead of cutting umbilical cords.
They form companies of soldiers, ranks of heroes.

Like giddy children they down glasses of cyanogen chloride,
To induce the shuddering orgasms of long extinct amoebas.
Water thunders through the city's aroused pipes,
Washing over boastful palms its peculiar measure.

Thus like paper other eyes yellow in darkness,
Fading till only a Cheshire grin is visible in the wandering crowds.
Repeat for me, in your unnamed purity, this image,
In the collapse of these faint circumferences.

TRANSLATED BY THOREAU LOVELL WITH PATRICK HENRY

ANDREI TURKIN

In the Woods

I finish my cigarette in silence,
and a pleasant feeling of release
makes me pee on the fern fronds,
take a dump in the skunk cabbage.
I melt more and more into nature,
pissing with the force of the beasts.
I'm a jackal! A boar! I bite! I'm a wolf!
I'm the wolf's wild wife!

TRANSLATED BY PAUL SCHMIDT

Untitled

I bought Lenin's *Works* (Selected)
and the more I read, the more I
stopped being a thorny delinquent
and became an uncluttered young man.

No longer a misfit, a paranoid freak,
I was calm as your pet mouse.
When I save up enough for his *Works* (Complete)
what kind of man will that make me?

TRANSLATED BY PAUL SCHMIDT

Untitled

I moved a book to the table's edge
and brushed against it without thinking.
My lover was sleeping next to the table.
She didn't notice me.

Crossing Centuries:

In her bed, an abundance of leg
between two blankets.
Between the soles of her small
feet, a bunched sheet.

She had bunched it while she slept.
There was a bicycle in her dream.
She was a letter carrier
in the country, only seventeen.

She was delivering a letter to a man
she was in love with
because he had a hairy chest.

Later that morning
I knocked the book off the edge.
It was almost noon.

TRANSLATED BY PAUL SCHMIDT

Untitled

What is it, thick and opaque, the swill that flows
through my pipes, mother of mine?
What plastics are grist for my bristles and bone?

It is blood and muscles, your bristles and bone.

What are these hooks and needles in my body,
mommy dear, mommy dear?

Those are your arteries and veins, sonny dear.
Your cartilage and skin.

But who made it that way, mommy?
Who threaded my needles, bated my hooks, my dear?

We have, child, such a small patch of skin.
He that made the pig made me.

It can't be! Say it ain't so!
Were it not so, sonny, were it not so.

TRANSLATED BY ALEX CIGALE

Untitled

Ninety and nine crannies
are on a woman's body.
And a one is called mouth.

Ninety and nine crannies
are on a man's body.
Just underarms are two.

Ninety and nine crannies
are on Gavrilov's body.
Three are nostrils, throats two,
in the throats are healing grasses,
in the grasses crickets that sing:
their little hairs are rising.

TRANSLATED BY ALEX CIGALE

Untitled

Instead of legs she has two tires,
where her arms were now there are eyes.
She was speeding past the forest
when her emergency breaks failed.

Will her wheels crack and dismember?
Become infected with gangrene?

Or will she, on God-given lubricant
alone, roll all the way back home?

TRANSLATED BY ALEX CIGALE

Untitled

My mother lay dead in a ditch,
my father swung from a tree branch,
but I escaped, lonely and naked,
and here I am with you in the end.

I'll sing to you my sad story,
of how my family and I
roamed the earth as thieves and robbers,
of the many times we shuddered
over our victims' bodies, ate livers,
warm and bloody, the grass growing
through the cracks, how father, mother
and son, all damnable villains,
put to the worst imaginable
torture beautiful young women,
of how we sliced them into bits,
dead and living, how afterwards,
stirring their ashes in the fire,

I decided to string my father up,
having repeatedly stabbed my mother.
And now, that my song is over,
people, please put a penny in my cup.

TRANSLATED BY ALEX CIGALE

Untitled

The wind reels, the cold stiffens
the ripe body, a fruit.
The very cells seem to wither.
Iron in the fire, the matter's alive.
Speed and temperature are one
and the same. The youthful,
breathing chest thumps, afire.
What does it all mean? Here it is —
In the sky there is no place that breathes.
From the universal center the stars blink.
Living people jack-knife together and
by rubbing derive through friction
in two physical locations heat.
And in those spots, animated moisture
emits smoke and the glass perspires.
What does this mean? Well here it is —
Upon the stones ripens the paper moss.
Remember, the good scientist doctor
Koch prescribed us the spirochete.

TRANSLATED BY ALEX CIGALE

Untitled

You have inquired — this blood —
Where is it from? Come here!
I have gulped down a Hero Star
To have it in my chest.

So that it could amalgamate
With me, and drink up all my blood.
And, by illuminating people's faces,
I'd glitter like a symbol!

I'd rise to heaven like a star
And trembling like the savior's tear,

Crossing Centuries:

There I would glitter, burn, whenever
Your eyes would light upon me.

TRANSLATED BY MICHAEL MAKIN

Untitled

Long ago we left the earth.
See the crosses side by side?
You and I — we are these graves.
I'm the left one, you're the right.

On a little bench of green
Our children are drinking Cahors.
And my cross, my cross is casting
An enamored shadow on your mound,

While it reaches toward your cross.
Only sometimes in the crossings
Are our faces similar,
Just on pleasant summer days.

TRANSLATED BY MICHAEL MAKIN

To Yu. G.

He will hang up the receiver.
And what is it now he should do?
Yes! In the kitchen, threshing spuds,
he plants his half-muscular body,
lays his half-overweight trunk,
upon the couch, two chairs, the table,
fills up a plate, pours out a cup.
Something wild contorts his face
and soon he will start to spill blood.

TRANSLATED BY ALEX CIGALE

NINA ISKRENKO

WE ARE THE CHILDREN OF RUSSIA'S DULL YEARS
(on the poetic tendencies of the 1980s, and some of their sources)*

THERE IS A TERM HEARD ON PUBLIC TRANSIT: "standing comfortably." People who often travel at rush hour scarcely think of finding a seat, but rather strive to find themselves a spot on the subway or the bus where, having set down their bags, they can stand with some degree of comfort, leaning against something with a newspaper or a book. About the book, by the way. . . .

Which book do we choose to read, and what do we expect from it: pleasure, fascination, the constructive passage of time, the answer to a question from a textbook or from a personal experience, a shock to the senses, elevation of the spirit, a discovery, or a revelation? The best books are, in principle, able to give us all these things at once. But it is important to keep one thing in mind in this regard: a genuine artist will not undertake the composition of new works for the sake of ideas already sufficiently treated in art, or ideas already established as the norm, if not of existence, then, at the least, of consciousness. As Debussy said: "I do not turn to the fugue, for I know it."

The continuous assimilation of cultural material is as important in art as in any other realm of human accomplishment. The central interest of creative efforts is still focused on humanity as it actually is, and not as it ought in principle to be. Breakthroughs along this path require an active curiosity from the reader, as well as a readiness to participate; that is, a certain professionalism both as reader and observer.

Much has changed in the last two years, if not in life itself, then at least in our attitude toward it (which, properly, constitutes the subject of artistic interpretation). Many of the names that will be the subject of these notes have been introduced into general literary currency. A little something from their works has been published, although with difficulty. The criticism has become both animated and polarized. More has been written in two years about the "metametaphorists" than about some secretaries of the Writers' Union during

---

*This essay was written in 1990.

the whole of their long and productive lives. Moreover, while the word "conceptualism" is rarely spoken in public, even its leaders are on the point of breaking through the iron curtain which has encircled them for years and decades. Perhaps this bitter truth will now lose its currency: "The more we love our mother country, the less we please her" (Dmitry Prigov). In a word might it not it be time to begin a discussion of the processes at work within avant-garde literature, of its various peculiarities and directions? Unfortunately, however, the question of just what makes such art contemporary is far from a resolution, as is the question of how today's authors differ from those of yesterday or the day before, irrespective of the ages found in their passports. What unites these authors one to the other, and what is their place in the general literary context? We are the children of Russia's dull years.

The current attempts to escape stereotypes of thought and the intransigent synonymity of evaluations are, in essence, deeply rooted in Russian literature, as they are, moreover, in the world literary tradition. All great artists of the past acted in this manner, not fearing to go against the opinions of society and the logic of common sense. Neither did they fear being misunderstood or even spurned by the critics and the reading public. "Poet, do not set store by the people's love!" (Aleksandr Pushkin, "To the Poet") We acutely feel this same internal protest in the best works of the artists of the 1980s.

> According to the custom, everything's kept dark here,
> Our deadened life and square-ruled notebooks.
> And slavery's the best defense;
> Don't remove your head, just your cap. (Yury Arabov)

Compassion for our age, acceptance of it as a given, and together with this a keen sense of its incompleteness; desire to change something, and doubt suggested by actual experience, of our own potentialities; experience and naivety, united to the utmost one with the other (let's lay special stress, more over, on this phrase: *to the utmost):* these features are indicative of the outlines of the conflict which, in one way or another, appears in the poetics of the 1980s.

The artists of today, just as the naturalists, are spurred on by one task: the quest for the unity of the world; that is, for concrete signs that confirm the general nature of things. "The worm is a segment of time and blood" (Aleksei Parshchikov). There follows from this a shift in interest, from that which separates the hero (or event) from the crowd, the mass, and from chaos, and which makes him unique, to that which, by contrast, unites him with his surroundings. Such a perception of reality is not connected with concrete particularities of identity or fate, but rather reflects some more general regularities in the spiritual life of man. This does not mean, of course, that poetry or prose should acquire the character of some abstract, obscure discourse. Literature is practical work, experience, an experiment, not in the common sense of poking around somewhere and obtaining something, but in the most direct sense of a verification, with concrete linguistic material, of vague conjecture, hypotheses, ideas; that is, theories, or if you will, philosophies. In the same way that the general, or rather universal, law of the attraction of bodies was recognized by Newton in the unremarkable falling of an apple, so various complex and sufficiently general philosophical conclusions can be discovered in an artistic text as uncomplicated, often amusing juxtapositions or metaphors comprised of the simplest elements.

> though tomato puree flows in my veins
> I will complete the agreed-upon miracle:
> I'll toss myself as a ten-kopeck coin into the change machine
> and drop out as five-kopeck coins.
> (Mark Shatunovsky)

Of course, in everyday life each of us strives in varying degrees to be different from others, trying to catch sight of our personal inimitability and significance, and with this to fulfill and justify our own lives. This is quite correct, although in this we are all alike. In art the motif of inimitability and uniqueness of an individual human life has been worked through for centuries. Whole galleries exist of true heroes, in the classical sense of this word: commanders, emperors, knights, and all sorts of supermen. Then we have the "typical representatives," the half-debunked leaders of Pushkin's age. Finally there are the little people, the humble and outraged, who are unbearably familiar, and at the same time so devoid of worth and talent that it seems a pity they exist. Still, they exist, and an artist of the stature of Dostoevsky or Chekhov could not help noticing. In this manner the hero has in some sense become smaller and more humble, but the intelligent reader follows not so much the object of representation as the reflection of the changes in our relationship to reality (the metaphorical displacement) which it manifests.

The artist is excited by man's re-interpretation of himself, as a result of which the border dividing the world into heroes and non-heroes (in the literary sense) moves little by little. An ever-increasing number of non-heroes find themselves in the ranks of the heroes; the situation becomes ever more democratic. As the markings on the instrument change position, man (the literary hero) loses by degrees his confidence that he is the "crown of creation." He strives anew to become related to the fish or the plant (of which Kuprin dreamt, for example), to the whole of nature, and not only to animate but also inanimate objects, to rocks and metals. What? Lower oneself to the level of a thing? Become related to a button? Let's discuss this.

Until the beginning of the twentieth century, the *thing* was perceived in art exclusively as dead nature (*nature morte*, or still life). The thing played a strictly secondary role, and man's superiority over it was unlimited. But things are man-made, the fruits of human labor, intellect and talent. The thing results from the materialization of consciousness, which somehow attributes soul to it. The thing "wants to have its say," as Marina Tsvetaeva expressed it. This new outlook united the poets of the first stormy decades of this century, that age which for the first time in human memory coincided with space (as in the four-dimensional world of Minkovsky). Mandelstam "measured" that time in pictures of a dwelling uncluttered with accessories, whose coat of arms was a glass of hot water. Mandelstam understood his age in terms of unremarkable details of half-starved city life, of things. He did not say, "two years gone." He pointed in silence to his clock face, where "life began in a wash-tub with a wet, burring whisper, and continued in the kerosine's soft soot. . . ." A handsome, twenty-two-year-old Mayakovsky literally incarnated the world and the real object, appealing to it as if to a living being, and seeing in it not only a living soul, but also living flesh: "The universe sleeps, its enormous ear lying on its paw with claws of stars. . . . The street sat down and bawled, 'Let's eat'" (Vladimir Mayakovsky, "The Cloud in Trousers"). With the arrival of the Oberiu group (Zabolotsky, Harms, et al), the border dividing artistic space into heroes and non-heroes finally came up against its own most extreme contingency: a person collided head to head with a quickly strengthening, full-blooded *thing* grown to obscene dimensions (the sport coat with the manager, the catchword with the drum). He or she had collided with a multi-purpose comb, having themselves turned into a flat name-plate with the inscription, "The Ivanovs have left for work in their trousers and shoes" (Nikolai Zabolotsky, "Ivanovy"). And these marvelously honest and vivacious artists, these masters (with Margaritas and without) had no choice but to cry absurd tears, seizing a moment in which "nothing happened"(Daniil Harms). Nothing happened. This was the sign beneath which passed their entire creative and human destiny. And, unfortunately, not theirs alone.

Time reduces any original idea to a stereotype. The 1960s arrived, and people turned up who were prepared to roll up their sleeves and restore to every small and insignificant person, every event, its lofty primordial meaning and value. "I found you on a scrap heap, but I'll make you shine," promised Andrei Voznesensky, and proposed for this purpose the following model: the hero, in his opinion, is hidden, concealed in the least non-hero. The hero exists as a potential within him, like a sort of anti-world. One need merely look at a person (or thing, it makes no difference) in the right way, that is, create the necessary illumination, to divine its true scale by its reflection. Looking through the oval window at a cinema ticket-seller he might detect the Mother of God, or in a word read backwards he could espy someone's secret, unrealized dream: "There goes solitary Kramer, but he had dreamed of becoming Remark" (Andrei Voznesensky). In this manner appears the sign-reflection, or phenomenon-hieroglyph, which opens a direct path to graphic poetry, to the elevation of the role of intonation in verse (defined by the outline of the text), and to the synthesis of musical and visual scales.

The time of hopes for the internal self-purification of the hero, for the rebirth of human dignity from the trash heap, ended more quickly, however, than these hopes could be fulfilled. The contamination of man's inner, spiritual world, rejuvenated anew at the close of the 1960s, rendered practically senseless the artist's struggle with the phantom called contemporary reality. Attempts to oppose the total ossification, or substantiation, of our consciousness found no room in the context of the bright future that was expected at any minute. As a result the seemingly natural path to new artistic inquiries was crossed out, separated, and forcibly removed from our culture, as the Nobel Laureate Joseph Brodsky was removed, having taught the poets of my generation the flights of romanticism, and a less critical attitude toward our own potentialities. His meditation on "the metamorphosis of a body into a naked thing" is not only devoid of any pathetic element, but also of despair:

. . . A sense of horror
is not characteristic of a thing. In this way,
a tiny puddle won't be discovered by it,
even if the little thing appears in death's presence.
                    (Joseph Brodsky, "The Year 1972")

Let's return, finally, to the 1980s. The notion is quite accepted in our contemporary worldview that the significance of a thing (in both the utilitarian and the wider meanings of this word) is not concentrated within it, but is rather determined by the relations it enters into with the things surrounding it. Any general sign of primordially opposed concepts can serve as a code, a key to the revelation of their unity (that is, as an element of symmetry). In this manner the world is conceived not as a collection of objects, but as a system of links, any one of which could prove to define and unite all of existence.

> I say, what ties us together drives us crazy, in a way.
> Darkness
> of a fast-flying cloud, a trace of glass, the whiteness.
> The clock-faced rim.
> Death's grandeur and insignificance: the stewing
> of garbage in the scorching fog of dragon-flies,
> and some word or other, like a copy of an agreement,
> the world
> is revealed in the mirror-image along the axis of matter.
> > (Arkady Dragomoschenko)

Any old thing, "some word or other" (representing some sort of 'object'), can become the primary element of the world as perceived by the artist. These very objects, which identify and divine solely by their connections with others, become indistinguishable from one another; they become "universal" (Tatiana Shcherbina). Their outlines "become smudged," they lose all distinctness: ". . . and the glass goes to pieces, turning into night" (Ivan Zhdanov). Thought becomes exclusively associative. It can turn into a dense metaphor — a "meta-metaphor" (Konstantin Kedrov):

> The wind off the sea
> and the sun's gradual needles
> knit the white plumage of sunrise.
> > (Sergei Magid)

or an unbroken stream of consciousness:

> until enthusiasm, sweetness, pain, the flow of dream,
> until the flow, dream, hope, swimming, captivity. . . .
> > (Oleg Pavlovsky)

We have grown accustomed to living in an ever quickening rhythm, and we consider this normal. Because of this, instead of the sensation of feverish haste — "There's no time to be human" (Andrei Voznesensky). — and instead of either pursuing disappearing reality or flying from it into the "quiet lyric," there has arisen the metaphor of speed, which imparts to an outwardly tranquil, even leisurely text an inner supercharging of tempo. This acceleration is manifested differently by different authors. It is sometimes distinguished simply by the absence of certain intermediate details, such as connective or purely descriptive words, as in this example:

Each wants to live — criminals, meat,
And the day's still splendid, a sail
Receding over those hills where laughter is ceaseless.
(Vladimir Kucheryavkin)

In other cases the concentration of perceptions is still higher, the fabric of metaphor is thicker, as here:

The sea, clutched in the beaks of birds: that's rain.
The sky, held in a star: that's night.
The tree's unrealized gesture: that's a whirlwind.
(Ivan Zhdanov)

The immersion of the great in the small, the smooth closure and adhesion of boundaries between the external and the internal, between the superficial and the profound, creates a particular spatial structure similar to a page from Mebius. The "lyric hero" is not made concrete. He contains within himself merely general human traits, and himself appears a part of this closed and limitless space:

A river flows inside me, like deaf-mute blood,
A rite's performed, within it, the baptism of the
autumnal fall of leaves goes within it.
(Ivan Zhdanov)

Man's sharply increased speed of perception of a changing reality allows him to liken it to an elementary particle, one "smeared" in space according to the principle of uncertainty (that is, whose coordinates and velocity are impossible to determine exactly). Similarly, in an artistic text object is dashed against object: "street falls into a throat"(Sergei Magid). Events fall from their proper rank and cling to another: "as if a wild gardener had inoculated me with a serious flower leprosy" (Elena Shvartz). Or a sleeper wakes within a dream, and in the dream he falls to sleep:

How does sand move in the hours of the submarine night.
As one swarm? As one crackling of ice?
What is man worth, blanketed in the dirt of the road
blown through the dream's mouth?

What is a man worth, of the age's current
the sole gushing measure?
                    (Victor Krivulin)

The gushing measure is an apt symbol of the relativity of any viewpoint, any system of incrimination, any moral judgement or aesthetic position. The word falls as a stone into water, leaving dispersing ripples of thought.

When aflame, alcohol resembles a young Pioneer girl . . .
When aflame, alcohol recalls speech . . .
When aflame, speech recalls alcohol . . .
                    (Aleksandr Eremenko)

The artist is neither arbiter nor world judge. No one endowed him with any sort of exceptional authority that he might explain to those around him how they should and should not live. His task is more modest: to investigate what exists and what does not exist in the human soul, and in the interrelations between man and the world. He strives to understand what is changing in these relations and what remains, and just what sort of world and man these are. Art brings its educational influence to bear only on those who are receptive to it (and these, alas, are not the majority). A person with a more or less developed imagination is hardly capable of great evil, because it is easier for him to picture himself in another's place, and to appreciate the consequences of his action. This gives rise to the illusion that art can intervene in real life. In fact, however, art is concerned only with the least apparent reality and specifically with human feelings and ideas of what life is (not with life itself). By comparing the perceived commonality in relations, which have been stimulated by various causes and conditions, the artist coordinates all these conditions, and reveals in this way a certain subtle commonality in the world, hidden by the symmetry of events. He or she subsequently reveals the beauty and harmony of this world, or more accurately, the "type" of beauty and harmony most characteristic of his or her time.

The case of the Oberiu group is significant in this regard, with their poetry "of the absurd," the deep, doleful meaning and concealed beauty of which proved safely hidden (alas) from their contemporaries. It is not difficult to understand their reaction, for after all, to a person brought up on the Russian classics, and even more so for someone who simply reads little, a poem such as the following must seem utter idiocy:

The distant future is thicker than what went before.
A sheat-fish is thicker than a paraffin stove.
A sea-screw is thicker than an onion . . .
　　　　　(Daniil Harms)

The poem continues in this vein, offering another dozen similar assertions of the theme of what is thicker, deeper, or sharper. And not a single instruction on how to understand all this. One can only understand this composition as part of a series of similar compositions. In this context something curious becomes apparent: the text, which seems to us uncommonly nonsensical, is constructed from completely logical, sensible statements, and certain completely probable or obvious truths (after all, a sheat-fish really is thicker than a paraffin stove, and a chest really is deeper than a hat . . .). Consequently, there is no distortion of reality here at all; instead, there is utter nonsense. The conclusion suggests itself that it is impossible to get a grasp on reality by means of the logic of common sense alone; this provides nothing, as they say, either to the mind or the heart. Hence the priority of intuitive cognition is confirmed in an implicit form, the advantage of "strange," paradoxical vision over a striving toward cheerless obviousness. The Oberiu group, in essence, struggled with unreal realism, attempting to comprehend this world "like a poor, childish person" (Aleksandr Vvedensky). By restoring several omitted stages in artistic thinking characteristic of Russian culture, it would be possible to spare poets of succeeding generations the necessity of inventing the bicycle, or making an automobile directly from a horse.

Two tiny birds, as one owl
flew over the wide sea
and talked about themselves,
why, just like a chance meeting of indians.
　　　　　(Aleksandr Vvedensky)

People often ask, Well, what's new with the artists of the 1980s in comparison with Vvedensky or Harms? The briefest way to formulate this would be: the Oberiu group communicated to us that human life is absurd, and that this is amazing (ridiculous, humorous, tragic, monstrous . . .). Contemporary post-absurdists assert rather the reverse: human life is absurd, and this is normal. If there is anything really amazing today, it is that amid all the nonsense which surrounds us, there still exist some human feelings, desires, impulses . . .

> I gather myself in the grass before the noose
> but I cannot hang my sonnet.
> It tumbles, and I catch it. . . .
> (Aleksandr Eremenko)

It sounds as though the world tumbles, and I catch it. The eternal values (love, human warmth, mutual understanding) fall, and I like a fool hold out my arms. Perhaps I'll catch them. Perhaps they won't smash to pieces.

Returning to the question of "how this is done," let's bring in another pronouncement for purposes of comparison: "a depth glows in autumn's water, and gravity flows, washing over these objects . . . " (Ivan Zhdanov). What do the "sonnet," above, and this "depth" share? The artist's handling of a process (or property, or symbol) as a real object. Primordially non-material substances become tangible, manual, domestic. The world approaches man, and comes into contact with him in a singular way unknown until now. "Herds of statuettes drag themselves through these parks of culture, parting the bushes as they go" (Aleksandr Eremenko). The gradual effacing of the boundaries between static and dynamic, natural and man-made, everyday and abstract, poetry and prose, culture and "nature," etc. . . . ; these are a manifestation of the general tendency in twentieth century art, the tendency toward the rapprochement of invention and reality, and toward the substantiation of the spirit (as opposed to the spiritualization of the thing). Today, without the slightest embarrassment or curtsey in the direction of daily routine, the poet can remark that, "in bunches, dried garlic expresses itself in Hellenic speech" (Victor Krivulin), or he can gracefully combine a musical instrument, a woman, and a bird:

> He undressed and dressed a flute,
> changing the trained scales.
> It became cold. The flute flew off.
> (Aleksei Parshchikov)

Each new theory of poetry presupposes a change in the conventions of our approach to reality, and a displacement of proportions in the debate between "truth" and "invention," "norm" and "anomaly." This entails a reduction in the degree of strangeness in the world, which gradually leads man to a deeper and deeper understanding of it. A picture did not seem real to Marc Chagall if it contained no element of the unreal. Max Plank seemed unreal to himself when he first pronounced the word "quantum." Today the relations between the artist and artistic space have become much more intimate (as Mallarmé, by the way, predicted when he wrote, "The world exists in order to go into a book"). Bearing this in mind, that which at first glance seems merely shocking becomes more comprehensible, as in the following quotation, the ending of a poem about Peter Brueghel:

He has slept through four centuries
and will wake up quite sober.
And he'll go down. Laughing.
On the road. On the rails.
Past a kitchen-garden.
Past a bath-house/restaurant.
Ah, past a hydrogen bomb.
Ah, past the girls in the port.
                    (Aleksandr Eremenko)

Through the example of Brueghel, incomprehensible and unrecognized in his day, Eremenko reveals to us a certain poet-spirit, or super-poet, as a plenipotentiary representative of the whole race, the entire rank of poets. This conception of the artist as a clot of spiritual energy united for all time, energy which like background radiation does not disappear, but merely crosses from one concrete membrane to another, is extremely characteristic of contemporary poetics. In particular, this conception explains an abundance of unattributed quotations and reminiscences in the poetry of the artists of the 1980s ("Egor Isaev noticed us, and gave us his blessing to descend into the grave" [Yury Arabov]).

Here I'm being prompted to close, although the discussion of the 1980's has hardly begun. The point in all this is that dozens of other authors exist in our literature who have almost no outlet to the reading public. These writers exist, yet they don't. How is it that in our sober reality there are no . . .

long-haired fairies, on their knees

atop the cubes of hard buildings.
>   (Victor Krivulin)

They don't exist, yet they do. They are no less real than their questions:

> Who spat on the street here
> Hardly a fairy, a good little girl.
>   (Yury Arabov)

In order to conceive of the true scale of contemporary strivings, extending from simple candor to profound revelation, and from an elementary capacity for metaphorical thought to the creation of a system for perception of the world, publications are needed, and books, and publishing materials. Otherwise we will never understand that the present craving for new artistic structures is not the fancy of fanatic upstarts incapable of working in a simple style, striving for originality at any price. It is already an event, which reflects definite changes in human consciousness. We must allow it to appear as widely as possible in order that, having better acquainted ourselves with it, we might sense the many dimensions of these authors through the commonality of their queries. In order, finally, to have the opportunity not merely to stand comfortably, but also to understand where we're headed after all.

TRANSLATED BY PATRICK HENRY AND JOHN HIGH

FROM THE UNDERGROUND
INTO THE OPEN
(1980s-1990s)

AFTER THE HOUSE ARREST:
GLASNOST & THE RESURFACING
GAY POETIC

VITALY CHERNETSKY

AFTER THE HOUSE ARREST: RUSSIAN GAY POETRY

Aᴛ ᴛʜᴇ ᴍᴇᴇᴛɪɴɢs ʙᴇᴛᴡᴇᴇɴ ᴛʜᴇ ᴍᴇᴍʙᴇʀs of this anthology's editorial board and contemporary Russian poets in Moscow in June 1997, no issue generated a more heated response from the Russian side than the Americans' stated intention to include in this volume a selection of representative texts of "Russian gay poetry." The very assertion that there was such a phenomenon or trend in Russian letters was contested, and while a number of those who spoke conceded that there existed several important Russian poets who explored gay themes in their writing and were fairly open about their sexual orientation in their work, the idea of grouping them under this "sociological" rubric was deemed suspect. The matter, however, was not laid to rest; more and more speakers posed largely rhetorical questions on the possibility of singling out a distinct gay presence and/or a gay tradition in Russian poetry.

Let us take this question seriously. Is there indeed such a thing as a gay (and lesbian) tradition or school in Russian poetry? The answer is, of course, yes. That it has remained relatively invisible and unrecognized by the general Russian literary community is true, but no drastic archeological investigations are necessary at this point to assert its existence: a number of pioneering investigations already took care of that.

The task of constructing the Russian gay literary tradition, however, until recently, has overwhelmingly been a product of efforts from beyond Russia's borders, which is understandable given the lengthy history of persecution of gays and lesbians by the state both before and after the revolution of 1917 (re-instituted by Stalin in 1933, the sodomy laws were repealed only in 1993) and the pervasiveness of homophobia in Soviet-era Russian culture (in a 1989 opinion poll, the question "How ought one to deal with homosexuals?" brought the following answers: 33 per cent were for "eliminating" them, 30 per cent for "isolating them from society," 10 per cent for "leaving them to themselves" and only 6 per cent for "helping them."[*] Sexuality as such was a taboo topic until the very last years of Soviet Union's existence. Thus the

---

[*]Quoted in Igor Kon, "Sexual Minorities," in Igor Kon and James Riordan, eds ., *Sex and Russian Society* (Bloomington: Indiana University Press, 1993), p. 99. Kon also provides the breakdown of the poll by regions and social groups.

search for the first attempt to trace the gay tradition in Russian letters takes us to San Francisco in the year of 1976 when a prominent émigré literary critic, Simon Karlinsky, published a lengthy essay, "Russia's Gay Literature and History from the Eleventh to the Twentieth Centuries."[*] This essay laid the cornerstone of the canon of the Russian gay literary tradition, initiating a project that culminated in the publication in 1997 of the anthology *Out of the Blue: Russia's Hidden Gay Literature*.[†] While (as it is the case with any anthology) some of the inclusions and omissions there may be contested, we can definitely speak of an established outline of the tradition.

It should come as no surprise that homoerotic motifs in Russian letters have been traced as far back as medieval manuscripts (chronicles, saints' lives, and so forth), and that references to a vibrant gay culture crop up repeatedly in the travelogues of Renaissance-era West-European visitors to Russia. However, as in the West, we cannot speak of a gay community in Russia in the modern sense of the word until approximately the mid-nineteenth century; rather, same-gender sexuality was thought of as a category of acts and desires that do not necessarily "mark" a person who experiences them but rather suggest a partaking of the carnivalesque impulse to revel in the "lower bodily stratum." A poetic testament to that era is the abundant tradition of mostly anonymous bawdy poetry known in Russia as Barkoviana, after the name of Ivan Barkov, an eighteenth-century neoclassical poet whose works in this genre, although unpublished in Russia until just a few years ago, were widely circulated in manuscript and known by many educated Russians; indeed, Barkov's writings influenced many prominent Russian poets, including the central figure of the national canon, Aleksandr Pushkin. Parodic variations on neoclassical high genres, poems of this kind usually offer graphic descriptions of heterosexual acts or stage allegorical conversations among the genitalia. However, several of the most famous examples of this genre are gay-themed, such as the so-called "cadet poems" of another key poet in the national canon, Mikhail Lermontov, and the anonymous narrative poem "Prov Fomich." In Pushkin's own work, gay themes are represented by

---

[*]Reprinted in Winston Leyland, ed., *Gay Roots: Twenty Years of Gay Sunshine* (San Francisco: Gay Sunshine Press, 1991), p. 81-104. A revised and updated version of this essay was published as "Russia's Gay Literature and Culture: The Impact of the October Revolution," in Martin Duberman, Martha Vicinus and George Chauncey, Jr., eds., *Hidden from History: Reclaiming the Gay and Lesian Past* (New York: Meridian Books, New American Library, 1990), p. 347-64.
[†]Kevin Moss, ed., *Out of the Blue: Russia's Hidden Gay Literature — An Anthology* (San Francisco: Gay Sunshine Press, 1997). Yet another revision of Karlinsky's essay appears as the introduction to this volume.

poems of a different genre, namely, by the imitations of classical Greek and medieval Arabic poetry.[*]

While these texts from the late eighteenth — early nineteenth century serve as important precursors to the emergence of self-consciously gay poetry in Russia, its full-fledged flowering came only by the late nineteenth — early twentieth century, the period known in Russian poetry as the Silver Age. By the 1890s there were several prominent poets active in Russia who happened to be gay, lesbian or bisexual, among them Aleksei Apukhtin, Poliksena Solovyova, and Zinaida Gippius; however, the references to sexuality in their writings were veiled and oblique. It is only after the relaxation of tsarist censorship after the revolution of 1905 that we see a sudden emergence of self-consicous, assertive, outspoken gay and lesbian literature. Prominent among its early representatives were the bisexual couple Viacheslav Ivanov and Lidiya Zinov'eva-Annibal: his poetry collecton *Eros* and her works of poetic prose, particularly *Thirty-Three Freaks* (both 1907) provide early influential examples of this trend. However, the two most important figures of the era whose contributions to Russian gay and lesbian poetry tower above everyone else's are Mikhail Kuzmin (1872-1936) among the men and Sophia Parnok (1885-1933) among the women.

Recent decades witnessed a radical reevaluation of Kuzmin's place among Russian poets. Long considered an important, but relatively minor poet occupying a niche somewhere between Symbolism and Acmeism, Kuzmin has been increasingly recognized as one of the major figures of Russian modernism; his prose and drama are now held in high regard as well. His literary legacy contains both the refutation of the excesses of symbolist verbosity and murkiness (although some critics consider him the one "who completed the edifice of Symbolism") and of the normativity and coldness of acmeist poetics (although he admired the Acmeists' striving to render the material and the concrete in their texts). Kuzmin's works undergo an evolution from a light and gracious style that recalls some of Pushkin's texts and that Kuzmin himself termed "clarism" to the dense, hermetic, allusive form of his final masterpiece, the long poem "The Trout Breaks the Ice" (1927).[†]

Kuzmin became famous almost overnight in 1906 with the publication of his poetic cycle "Alexandrian Songs" and his novel *Wings*, the first book in Russia to openly and assertively portray gay characters, a roman à thèse

---

[*] For more on Pushkin's gay-themed poetry, see Michael Green, "A Pushkin Puzzle," in *Out of the Blue*, p. 29-35.

[†] It served as the centerpiece of the eponymous collection, Kuzmin's last, that appeared two years later, which, among others, strongly influenced Anna Akhmatova who borrowed from it the very metric pattern of her "Poem Without a Hero."

comparable to André Gide's *Immoralist* and E.M. Forster's *Maurice*. An enigmatic and somewhat notorious figure, Kuzmin was immediately recognized as an equal by the leading fellow poets, particularly the Symbolists. His first book of poems, *Nets* (1908), is a veritable showcase of formal diversity suffused with emotions both tender and passionate, open descriptions of love affairs with other men as well as recreations of the world of ancient Alexandria and other distant times and places. It was followed by a steady stream of poems, plays and prose works of two major types: brilliant recreations of styles and genres of the past (ancient Greece and Rome, the Byzantine empire, baroque France, eighteenth-century England and so forth) and explorations of life in present-day Russia. An artist of a bright, Mozartian outlook, Kuzmin courageously withstood the daily horrors of starvation and alienation of the old intelligentsia in the years after the revolution. His publications were few and far between, and many of his manuscripts perished in the years of Stalinist terror and the war; however, his writing reached an unprecedented degree of intensity. His late "difficult" works stand up as equals to those of Eliot and Pound, Cavafy and Wallace Stevens, and hopefully Kuzmin will soon be recognized internationally as one of the greatest poets of this century.

The life and poetic career of Sophia Parnok do not abound in dazzling bohemian escapades, with the exception of her very public love affair with another great Russian woman poet, Marina Tsvetaeva, which took place in 1914-16. For the bisexual Tsvetaeva the experience was intense and traumatic, and later she tried to suppress and even erase her memories of it, although it had inspired one of the best poetic cycles she had written, "Girlfriend"; Parnok, while also known for her passionate character, turned out to be more restrained and eventually more forgiving after their breakup. As in the case of Kuzmin, however, the notoriety of this affair for a long time eclipsed attention to Parnok as a major poet in her own right. The relative neglect suffered by her work can be partially explained by the lengthy period of her poetic apprenticeship. Like Kuzmin, she published her first collection of poetry when she was already over thirty, in 1916, and some of her best work was written in the late 1920s-early 1930s, when her books appeared in just a few hundred copies and much of her writing was unpublished for being "unsuitable" for the Soviet era. For all the many differences between them, Kuzmin's and Parnok's poetics have a few points in common. One of them is the masterful recreation of the tone of classical Greek poetry — Sappho, naturally, in Parnok's case — and the other is a striving for a simplicity of form that is simultaneously able to convey great emotional intensity (hence their shared rejection of symbolist clichés and a complex attitude towards the Acmeists); indeed, while the two of them were never close personally, Parnok's approach to writing strikes one as similar in many ways to Kuzmin's proclaimed "emotionalism" of the 1920s. She was equally forthright in decribing her passion for other women, and it was a final great love of the last year and a half of her life that both brought us some of her best poems and sped up her death, since her health was weak. As was the case with Kuzmin, her writing was consigned for oblivion in the Soviet Union, and any attempts of reviving interest in her life and work were greeted with accusations of "false scholarship" and "pathology"; a comprehensive edition of her poetry appeared in Russia only in 1998.

In the case of other prominent Russian poets of that era who at various points explored gay desires and homoerotic imagery in their writing, we also see a pattern of forced erasure of that aspect of their legacy (in the case of Tsvetaeva, Sergei Esenin, Nikolai Gumilev, Nikolai Klyuev and many, many others). Even the émigré literary circles proved extremely reluctant to tolerate, let alone encourage gay voices, especially in poetry: gay characters in prose works can be mocked, marginalized or demonized; however, in poetry, traditionally so strongly linked with authorial self-expression, gay themes were met much more awkwardly — which explains the neglect suffered by the talented poet of the Parisian school, Anatoly Steiger, and especially by one of the most fascinating personalities among the émigré poets, Valery Pereleshin (1913-1992).

Born in Siberia, Pereleshin found himself in Harbin, China (one of the major centers of Russian émigré life until the end of World War II), at the age of seven; after the Chinese revolution he moved to Rio de Janeiro and lived there for the rest of his life. Having developed as a Russian poet in such unusual circumstances, he not only introduced the themes and imagery of Chinese and Brazilian culture in his writing; his poems are fascinating in their combination of conservative strict metric forms and of a very contemporary, lively and rich vocabulary. His ninth and arguably best book of poems, *Ariel* (1976), a collection of sonnets inspired by an epistolary love affair with a young literary scholar in Moscow, offers some of the most intense gay love poetry in Russian, ranging in its tone from tender to sadomasochistic. Pereleshin tirelessly combines the utterly mundane experiences, the most daring sexual fantasies, and diverse literary allusions to build in a seemingly effortless fashion his formally precise texts. A poet of great technical skill and passion, he is the leading Russian gay writer of the generation shaped by the revolution of 1917. Writing in distant China and Brasil, Pereleshin formed a bridge between the flowering of Russian gay literature at the beginning of the century and the rebirth of gay writing in Russia in the final years of the Soviet empire.

Evgeny Kharitonov (1941-1981), the leading fugure of this renaissance and the oldest of the Russian gay poets included in this anthology, lived in the tragic and paradoxical condition of not being able to publish a single line of his writings in his lifetime, and simultaneously enjoying almost a cult status within the Russian literary underground of the 1970s and 1980s. Belated public recognition of his talent and accomplishments, culminating in the publication in 1993 of the critical edition of Kharitonov's collected writings, and public references to him as "Russia's last literary genius" were combined in his home country with insistent attempts by the cultural establishment to divorce Kharitonov's writing from his homosexuality, while his uniqueness in Russian letters is due not merely to the fact that he never denied his homosexuality: for him his sexual orientation became the lens for perceiving and representing the world around him.

Kharitonov is better known as a prose writer, even though poetry makes up a sizable portion of his work, and even his prose texts, especially the cycles of fragments he wrote in the final years of his life, challenge the preconceived boundaries between genres. Kharitonov's fragment cycles have been frequenly compared to the writings of a prominent and somewhat notorious Silver Age author, Vasily Rozanov, famous for his prolific and outspoken discussions of sexuality and the focus on the minutiae of day-to-day existence. However, unlike Rozanov, Kharitonov's fragments are multi-voiced and playful, each possessing a tone of its own, very loosely identified with the autobiographical narrator. He filtered the text through the intimate, personal experience of himself as a discrete individual, but simultaneously with that he perceived himself as a spokesperson of an underrepresented (indeed unrepresented) social group: gay people. Kharitonov courageously chose this path, although this made him even more acutely aware that his status was that of unpublishable writer, a subject on which he reflected in one of his texts. Kharitonov's key innovative contribution to Russian literature was his choice of homosexuality as a basis for cognitive universalization. As a fellow writer has noted, in Kharitonov's texts "all reality is saturated with the homosexual sentiment."

According to reminiscences of Kharitonov's friends, he began writing at the age of twenty, and throughout the 1960s he was writing imitative quasi-acmeist poetry. However, approximately in 1969 he renounced most of what he had written by then, and embarked on developing a new manner of writing. The manuscript collection of his writings that he prepared shortly before his untimely death and titled *Under House Arrest* (and which was reproduced as the first volume of his collected writings) was structured to showcase his new approach to literature.

One of the central themes of much of Kharitonov's writing is that of unrequited desire and failed projects to find "the boy of his dreams": the hero's passion builds up, but he often lets the chance to act on it to slip away. In these texts, the author/narrator is simultaneously inside and outside the text, directing the action and taking part in it. His is the position of someone who claims he controls the course of his and others' lives, at the same time knowing only too well that that is not the case. These early quasi-autobiographical narrative works are succeeded by "Roman" ("A Novel"), a text written as an assemblage of mostly brief fragments that combine explorations of the limits of textuality with a strong autobiographical coloring. The pages of "Roman," filled with experiments in spacing, offer sequences of words that become magic formulas, next to "draft" texts with words crossed out — all of them saturated with gay themes and desires. Side by side with these are fragments similar to earlier narratives — stories of the narator's personal acquaintances, together with personal letters, observations, reflections.

Upon completing "Roman," Kharitonov experienced a creative crisis that eventually led him to adopt a new writing style, that of the cycles of fragments mixing descriptive sketches with musings on literary, philosophical and religious topics. Without resorting to the pathos of a Solzhenitsyn, Kharitonov writes with great pain about the repressive totalitarian machine, its cynicism and humiliation — next to descriptions of glory holes, representations of the affected language of "flaming" queens, and moments of highest erotic tension. Never in Kharitonov we find remarks to the extent that he hated himelf for being "hopelessly homosexual," as one fellow writer has put it, or perceived his homosexuality as a sin, as others suggest. His sexuality for him was a given, and to apply to it moralizing value judgments would simply be a category mistake. The cycles of fragments increasingly turn more subdued and introspective. Reflections on the impossibility of producing a narrative text, on the faculty of writing itself, form a thread running through these texts. Kharitonov's late texts still include masterful mini-stories, "scraps" of Proustian detailed remembrances of childhood, but analytical backward glances on life and reflections on death occupy a much more prominent place.

Kharitonov must have had a presentiment of the nearing closure, for in his final days he was primarily preoccupied with carefully assembling his final tome and searching for a definition of his own "gay textuality." Kharitonov asserts that it is homosexuality and its textual representation that provide the transformational momentum for reality, both textual and extra-textual: "if we [gay people] write about them," he insists, "about their monstrous deprived norm, then one should close one's eyes and cry that some final screw has not been placed into them."

The French lesbian writer Monique Wittig has written that to be effective, a text by a minority writer must "make the minority point of view universal." She stresses that this is what enabled the work of such gay writers as Proust and Djuna Barnes to become "a war machine with a delayed effect" and "transform the textual reality of our time." It would not be an overestimation to describe Kharitonov's contribution to contemporary Russian literature in similar terms, thus making the very fact of him being read and discussed in contemporary Russia a significant contribution to the breakdown of the citadel of homophobia in Russian culture.

Kharitonov's writing has had a lasting and profound effect on the younger Russian poets whose writing contains gay themes and homoerotic imagery; traces of his influence can be found, to various extent, in the work of every one of them. For instance, in the texts of Aleksandr Shatalov we see a development of Kharitonov's position of public intimacy, a hyperrealistic focus on the seemingly random details of day-to-day experience combined with a pained search, an unquenchable longing for the perfection of a union both bodily and spiritual of two men. In his poetry one also senses traces of influences of a number of Western poets, most notably of Lorca and Frank O'Hara. His focus is frequently on attempts to seize the sensory and emotional makeup of a fleeting moment, to release its traumatic outcome by transforming it into a poetic text. Dmitry Kuzmin's impressionistic, quasi-diaristic sketches likewise partake of oharaesque "personism."

The poetry of Yaroslav Mogutin, while also anchored in this mode, more properly belongs to the tradition of writing that intends to shock and confront the sensibilities of the poet's audience. His texts are brimming with much more assertive, aggressive energy, and are strongly rooted in performativity. For all the imagery of graphic sex and violence that appears in his texts, there is, however, something peculiarly uplifitng about them. Speaking from a stance of a *poète maudit* in the tradition of Rimbaud and early Mayakovsky, while at the same time influenced by the Americans Bukowski, Ginsberg and Dennis Cooper, Mogutin mobilizes his audience to embrace the new cultural possibilities in all their diversity, calling for a "radical sodomization of Russian culture." The linguistic makeup and imagery found in his texts are unprecedented in Russian writing in their energetic polymorphous queerness; his writing may serve as one of the clearest instances of what Hal Foster has dubbed "postmodernism of resistance."

Other poets who explore homoerotic motifs and desires do so often in a more circumspect fashion, mediating the subject position through a web of allusions or sometimes deliberately obfuscating it. Thus, in Sergei Kruglov's writing we see a fascinating amalgam of the poetics of Kharitonov with that of Joseph Brodsky, in its combined skepticism, melancholia, and rootedness in Mandelstamian "yearning for world culture." In Aleksandr Anashevich's texts the authorial voice is overlayed by multiple defamiliarizations and a hermetic withdrawal that is nevertheless unable to contain the pierrotesque, theatricalized, yet very palpable pain of the speaking subject.

The St. Petersburg-based Aleksei Purin disclaims influence by Kharitonov and is much closer in his writing to the earlier poetics of Kuzmin and Pereleshin. Like them, he favors graceful, precise classical forms while suffusing them with dense literary allusions, visions of worlds long gone and remarkably open, at times graphic, modern vocabulary. Another native of St. Petersburg, Dmitry Volchek, constructs his poetics by experimenting with small, ellyptic forms and intertextual references, evoking by some of his strategies a comparison to the American poets of the Black Mountain school. However, Kharitonovian voicing of intense intimacy and incisive observation is ever-present in his texts, which particularly in the recent years have been shifting to the more thematically transgressive mode reminiscent of Bukowski or Genet.

It would be an exaggeration to claim that all of these poets form a clear-cut, coherent trend or movement; however it would be equally erroneous to deny their sharing a certain common ground not only in their extra-literary experiences but also in the way their subjectivity filters into their writing. The diversity of their voices testifies to the prominent position of writing that touches upon the non-heterosexual experiences in contemporary Russian poetry (unfortunately, this work so far has been pursued overwhelmingly by men; a similar flowering of lesbian writing is yet to occur). The opportunity offered by this anthology to introduce it in a coherent, representative fashion will hopefully be followed by badly needed further attempts to explore and assess this dimension of contemporary Russian writing.

DMITRY VOLCHEK

from The Talking Tulip

the further it is the faster   what will be   what used to happen
an anxious kiss faster under the blanket
to writhe there to submit
to shameless piercing waves

was trying on a wig or looking at medusa
all the tight billiard pockets all the cracks and moans
who could have thought they'd come
from such a chest so slanted so manly

love i have lost and also the grass and the blanket
what had drowned was much more difficult to raise
under the canopy a young eye opened up
filled itself with water

short stocky
downed a glass of vodka
how   why he turned up here
at a dacha kitchen
a shack — some twenty years ago
they lit a fire here
now daffodills the porch
take off your pants let me touch
the firewood narrow alley
a bicycle frame
studiously cleaned the fingers with a brush
must keep them clean
an iron sink
blue

Crossing Centuries:

and now   the skies:
they were shining

in this land of officer delights
i'll go to parades
like a soldier who's just sucked someone off
with a glassy gaze

i'll watch army movies
in a wretched state doghouse
squeak on my fragile bed till morning
blinded by raw arousal

so that this heart-rending squeak-squeak
rustling of shameful rubbish
stuck like a thick-lipped fish
to a serene angelic choir

TRANSLATED BY AARON SHURIN AND VITALY CHERNETSKY

from Daemon Meridionalis

"i don't understand a thing,"
he says rising up a little,
"where are all these waves coming from?
where's the radio gurgling from?

who's plucked the naked strings
set them ringing like a spent bow
who's blown into this wire
all these strange american words?"

the rapist answers him,
"at least give me a blowjob
go ahead! no one will know"
the plot's slipped out like a lily of the valley

then came a whiff of old man's sweat
under the ceiling the tower clock is ringing
but the frequencies keep on screaming
like a rattle above the poor head

and the stars having pierced the ether
burn down the incomprehensible world

TRANSLATED BY AARON SHURIN AND VITALY CHERNETSKY

from Germany

4

again i saw destroyed dresden
there the cold ship-boys lie
i'd gnaw on bloodied chocolate
stuck in an iron shack

underground the faces are merging
the portable phone keeps crying
waldemar leans down to fritz
and says "i kind of like him

who'd have thought it's such sweet torture
to caress a dying man
kiss his flaccid hand
torment his arian hips"

you are all mine "from sideburns to genitals"
and let the soviets make noise
in our ears like plebeians at the carnival
the soldier is not asleep

he strokes his hair with his left hand
and with the right — down to the emerald crotch
where sleepy israel is warming up
inside my lips

TRANSLATED BY AARON SHURIN AND VITALY CHERNETSKY

SERGEI KRUGLOV

Untitled

So close, our time
together, drinking tea in silence —
my house on the edge of town,
it's always quiet here.
You were drawing on a table
with a burnt match, a face, part
of a neck, a rose, the rest implied.
You are still so young, Ganymede — why
did I let you go into this night?
But then, there's no way you could
have stayed. You finished your tea,
crumbled a match, never to light another.
Purity of style joined us together.
Art made us enemies during our rare
meetings over tea. Antagonism, passion,
secretive glances, the tea-stained tablecloth,
your youth, your strong teeth, the saffron-
colored cups, the glass stick you used
to stir the hot tea, like a myth, Ganymede,
that's what you were like — but why did you go?

With pride you told me you were going to die — how sweet,
how sad! But I know better than you. I can see
into the future & all tomorrow's parties, even
though I cannot draw with a match as well as you.
You are the envy of all the gods. Those
who don't die in their youth play different
games, believe me. Why didn't I realize
what you were like, then, at night,
when without turning back you ran out
of my house into the darkness
onto a deserted country road!
I called you from the door

but you didn't answer. You walked
a short distance and then the odorous
wind engulfed you, & a bird with giant wings
sank its claws into your back;
upwards, you flew, into the depths of
space, the horror of the interior landscape
where everything is muddled & confused.
I know where you are now, Ganymede.
It's a different night, and I follow your path
by the movement of the tea
leaves on the surface of the
water. Soon we'll meet again. The
unfinished tea in your cup never
grew moldy. One after another,
I burn the matches & finish your
drawing: the face, the rose,
the cry of horror & indignation,
the wind, the eagle & the boy.
Art is a preface to the games
of the gods, the coming together
of youth & age, the night, the necessary
absences. Youth is cold
& doesn't know anything about
love, but travels higher
& higher into empty airless space.
I have finished the picture, but
you could have drawn a better one.
Come back soon. I will make you some tea.

TRANSLATED BY LEWIS WARSH AND VITALY CHERNETSKY

from Dialogues with Phaedrus

4

". . . but with what degree of sin, Phaedrus, do we measure beauty?
In ancient writings we read

about the siege of Troy, Achilles
encased in purple marble & foam-like Hector:
the lightning-like tenderness between heroes,
the boiling of blue ice in a copper cup,
the pulse of loneliness, the dryness
of muscular fingers intertwined
on the battlefield, the sweat
& steam, skin against skin, the deadly
embrace — the sorrow of the battle flute
when the wounded body, dragged
at the back of chariots, flies through
dust & ashes. Isn't this a sign that you are
one of the immortals? Isn't this
the desire & the heat of life, something
to be envied by the Olympic gods?"

"But Andromache . . ."

"Frail Andromache! what could she see
looking at the field of divine heroes,
white eyes swollen with tears?
A woman wasn't given the power
to create a myth or kill a friend. Here
we find the classic triangle
on the map in the great atlas.
The sum of these two catheti, Phaedrus,
is always greater than the hypotenuse.
Similarities attract, it's like that
everywhere. This is the divine law
from the beginning of time . . ."

"Well, I believe
in God, but don't trust him.
Other writers say that after
St. George killed the serpent
& fell asleep after the battle, the
corpse of the snake rose up in the
night & the warrior's stallion crept

secretly to him, the saint's stallion,
without even removing the harness,
& that they possessed each other, inflamed
by deadly yearning, & that from the union
of the horse's body & the serpent's seed
modern humanity was born, saturating
the heavens with its poisonous
breath, & that there are no more
saints anywhere,
& that there are no more men
or women. When the triangle
disappears, what remains
is the straight line
between the end & the beginning.
But then these ancient writers, possessed
by too much imagination, tell a lot
of tall tales, & who knows what
is true?"

In early gray spring
you smoked in bed, the purple blanket
pulled down around your waist. The wind
sifted dust through the branches
of the broken poplars. You
looked at me through the blue-grey
smoke of your cigarette, responding
to me in the white light, until
your pupils became invisible — the
interior of the eye a sphere
coated with a drop of alien
substance, spilling into a cup
filled with oil, Gainsborough blue.

Then the sphere shrinks down to an infinite point.

No, it wasn't your fault.
You were here by accident,
nothing special, & left without
drinking your tea. I doubt
that you even wrote down
my number. But looking into your
eyes, this spheric moment, was
like entering a cavern in the fabric
of illusion, the intersection
of the angelic & the demonic.
There are only three or four
such points in existence. One doesn't need
to possess a refined mentality or
the sensitivity of the erogenous zones
of the imagination to see it. But once you've seen
it, there's no way to survive.

The magic of concrete, the dense
layers of oil paint, rotting wallpaper,
the color of your age and mine.
These rooms have died long ago
but we, having grown old, are still alive.
At night the wind howls through
the elevator's dried bones. It's been
six years since we passed
in the bathroom or hallways, or
by the darkened windows, &
now we are like alien shadows,
dead to the world. In the icebox
a crust of mica has grown on
our feasts of devotion.
When you look into its gaping
mouth there is nothing to see,
& the fingers no longer leave
prints on the door. The porphyry
is incurable, having been inspired

by the gray skies; it has eaten
away the heart, so you no longer
recognize it. Do we really remember
each other? What have you become,
my changeling concubine, the tenant
of a dead house passing through
the shadows? There's the lamp, the
dust on the floor, the ticking of a clock
in the darkness, the clasped jaws
of the front door, the keyhole, the emptiness
of the draft as it crawls through
the keyhole, the draft that has infected us,
my dear, with the sickness that makes
it impossible to recognize the forgotten fragrance
of the art of choosing the right key,
the art of entering or leaving, of staying
forever or saying goodbye.

TRANSLATED BY LEWIS WARSH AND VITALY CHERNETSKY

Untitled

The mythology of reputations hard to pronounce breaks off like a piece of ice.
Swallow it and you're pregnant.

Draped in silk, the fallen statues of women stop you somewhere between
a dead mother's voice and an unhappy puppy's squeal.

Forget about it!

Entertain me, distract me, screw me. What else could I want?

Great sailors come to party all night in the flickering port.
The wandering Genet seduces me in French:
his chimpanzee brain like thinking jelly in a jar,
my slim Beaumarchais between black leather and champagne.

"Figaro. Figaro. Figaro." Figaro here. Figaro there.
Get a guy. Figure this!

Jean, I beg you, sign "La Marseillaise" — no silence, no restraint.

We play in waterproof makeup a Porgy and Bess
who know the audience they address.

Translated by Charles Cantalupo and Vitaly Chernetsky

from So Many Traps

See the beautifully formed letter handwritten out of original thought
for the exclamation point of a small black soldier standing on his head.
Smell the perfume incomprehensibly named in Arabic with a bitter tobacco
    scent.
Touch the hand, clean and fresh as a peach.

Once I was little. Hear: "Such a cute little boy!"
With eyes two different colors and living in books
about armies with unshaven lieutenants and every poet searching
for the ascetic and losing his virginity.
Everything bloody after childbirth, taste this bloody letter.

Suspended from above by what I've read of Whitman,
I study sleepy men in wrinkled pants
who smoke and grip their tokens like a cure.
Night flecks their skin,
boys with dull razors attack a row of seats
and the otherworldly signals
through such irreplaceable meaning.

How do you die
when your heart stops
if the cause of death
on the death certificate
is a heart attack?

At first during the two weeks I knew him,
he confused Andre Gide with the Wandering Jew,
yet only to raise my self esteem
enough so that I could be taught
patience, how to cook pilaf,
take good pictures,
kiss,
dress well
and avoid cheap perfume.
I learned self worth,
how to speak English
and to function on three hours sleep a day.
Trusting people,
and liking animals

were not necessary
to choosing not to harm others
and calmly accepting death.
He also taught me this song:

"Once I was married
And lived high in Spain.
Get what you need
But you don't want pain.
No, my boy, you don' t want pain."

Full of trust and handsomely smoking, you always have nice days:
a snip, a stitch, a tuck and the proverbial glass of red.
One sip and I die — theatrically, of course — for you
in the orchestra pit, amidst the strings and woodwinds:
a Humbert Humbert with his secret and all empty glass in hand.
Strings. Woodwinds. The moon!
Let's pin it to a swing and fly.
Do with me what you will, I'll never tell:
your ballet sylph, my prince, my girlish fingers with no rings.

Translated by Charles Cantalupo and Vitaly Chernetsky

Don't I Look Happy?

Uncomprehending and unsuspecting, why should you care
about my subtexts, hidden messages and exquisite cryptograms?
The columns, lines and dots are Greek, humorous at best.
But who needs them
or the pretentious pipe, striped jacket and silk shirt of their author,
silly as his pseudo French fairytales.
What a bouquet! Perfect for hiding my grenade.
I'll pull the pin and wipe everything out
to kiss you, sniff you and pick every flea out of your fur.

Crossing Centuries:

Look. I can even spin and dance on my fingers.
Why would you want to leave? Look closer.
I can cross out the whole alphabet, crumple the paper and. . . .
See: one letter remains, the key.
Now watch me squirm.

TRANSLATED BY CHARLES CANTALUPO AND VITALY CHERNETSKY

from Petra's Notebook

I too dreamed of walking, rocking on my stiletto heels,
down Gorky Street
in a long skirt, smearing
tears and eyeliner all over my face,
and then, using a powdered cotton ball
to bring my face back in order,
of snapping mincingly at the stare of a passer-by,
"Young man, have you never seen
a girl put on her makeup?"

And I am tired of being a person of extreme
Conditions,
Of eccentric life,
Of lonely,
As if beyond the grave, sex

Look for me, for you almost found
Me yesterday, and the sweet thin elbow
Touched thirstily the palm of my hand,
And thus you and I froze for a moment,
Kissing each other in the midst of a crowd in our minds,
But having turned our faces away from each other . . .

A DRESS

I bought it after all; beyond the river
Was it not made for me by Fate itself?
A perfect fit, all jolly flowers,
And when I put it on, I got all soft — oh my!

Oh dress, my dress, I waited for you,
As if I found you beyond the river,
The world is burning with its need for me,
As a poet, as Petra, a woman, a wife.

I kissed a man's face for the first time,
And the coarseness of the lips and cheeks was so sweet for me,
As if gentle pine needles were pricking me
On the stomach and by the crotch . . .
I felt so good because a man
Was with me, with me, just like truth itself.
And unfamiliar sensors were suddenly turned on
By my desire — I was all in your hands.
Your phallus was hard as a rocket,
Erected by my breathing,
When I whispered touching it with my hand,
"I beg you, please don't be afraid of anything."

TRANSLATED BY VITALY CHERNETSKY

EVGENY KHARITONOV

TEARS ON FLOWERS

fragments

I T WAS JUST NOW, just now this time, and it's all evaporated, the groups have regrouped, we're no longer in the mood, and friends have stopped being friends.

There are already other forms of life in the world, and it's too late for me to find out about them. The trade school, the rock group, the Swedish family. Life has hemmed me in on all sides, and there is no happy place for me. Youth will say: you are no longer of any interest to us, but for understanding us you'll do very well. So come on, we'll show you our genius, and you try to understand. But when it comes to my performance at last, they'll run away or politely remain. Furthermore, the ones who run away will be *the right ones*, and *the wrong ones* will remain. I, when I'm an old man, I don't like everything new. Or they'll come up with some new invention, all just to replace us. The flowers have turned away from me, though I planted them facing me, and turned towards the Sun. And I'm in the second row from it.

I went once to sit on my grave. To eat an egg for my health. And I see. And what do I see. I don't see anything. And I can't see. Only hear. And smell. And I smell: a flower is flying towards me, waving its paws. Hello, my dear flower. What do you want from me? I want, it says, all of your life. Here, take my life and give me my whole death. Here I died, and it grew on me.

Is it really possible that everything in my life has been calculated and known. And there is no side from which to expect *something*. But this is why there are fresh and young people. But it's time for me to grumble.
—You like to grumble?
—Oh, I grumble like God. Wait! don't leave! I still haven't finished grumbling at you.

Today I turned 100.

Everything that can be said I have already said and thought in my life.

Yes, the poet can say only a little and says one and the same thing all the time. It's awful to read his complete works. It's awful, you think, how much can one go on about one and the same thing!

My low energy level was already noticed by S. in 1961. So what can one say about now. And it was already taking shape both in school in phys ed and in my coordination. Because I'll never manage the swing. Swing people have elasticity, they feel the pulse and still allow for different rhythmic figures through it and around it. God grant that I manage to keep even the steady beats. Arhythmic me.

But in my compositions I strive to gather a lot together drop by drop, so the result is a spectacle of taut saturated twisted into a ball concentrated compressed life to console myself and show people how well tautly tensely elastically I apparently live.

There is an art that is fragmented, filigreed, many-many pieces, all glued together and united into something; collect the separate pieces and insert something else as well in there. Or else exhale! a song! somehow just ah! and everything in one stroke, — and this is real talent; but the former, subtlety, let it be; yes, you can put on your glasses and examine it or carefully, very carefully listen for what you may hear. But talent is ah. Talent catches you up and carries you on its wings.

There — oh! there it tears you from your seat and calls you with it to battle or to love. There you can hardly keep from singing along. But here you can't sing along and it won't even occur to you; but you'll be fascinated, subtly lost in listening. Here you have to listen closely to the quiet and distant-distant music, while there you almost have to stop your ears to its pressure, or say — oh, take me! Here you have to pick up and carefully examine the page with its words, while there oh! there you remember it on first hearing and beat yourself with your fist, ay, how you said everything! and join in. Here is something peculiar, some marvel that fascinates you like the life of fish in an aquarium. Here, you say, is such a subspecies. People look at this or hear it as something distanced from themselves. But there is something that grabs you into its circle, infects you, squeezes tears out, forcing you to dance and sing together. That is directed at and calls out to people, while this is separated from people, is itself immersed in its marvelous mysterious pattern and has to enchant people who look at it through glass. While that tears people from their seats, forces their hearts to beat stronger. This has to be penetrated, and the pleasure is in the process itself of reading and penetration. But there it penetrates you itself, grabs you, goes through you and pulls you with it; but later, maybe, it will seem empty.

There is no sweet impossible heart-stopping love. For fastidious me. I have an apartment, an evening, a summer, a little youth, but not a nice guest. That's the way my recollection of four months will remain. It's more and more untruthful. Forgetting that even then it was wrong. No, no, it was right, leave me this at least, if I think it was there, it was. Only it hindered my writing and one thing couldn't combine with another in my life. Because with writing like mine nothing that keeps you from living alone can be combined. Only if I get a cat and turn him with a spell into a 17 year old tenth grader. Like me (only better looking).

I would put out a saucer for him in the kitchen, take him for a walk in the morning. He'd scratch at the door, meet me, lie curled up at my feet, while I write these words. I would conduct experiments on his body and take down the data from my own heart.

I need a younger brother who needs an older brother.

I thought I heard the door open and I came in. I came over to me, we embraced with our dry careful bodies, afraid of being too hot and climbing onto each other, such close people, who know everything about each other, real lovers. We had the same childhood, he and I. Only there can be no children.

I once got from one world to another. So I live on the gap between two worlds. The world of family, faithfulness, and cares for me, and the world of familylessness, unfaithfulness; and take care of yourself on your own.

Terrible. Old age ahead. There on the whole old men look like old women, little old women like little old men.

Something (You Know What) keeps me from doing something apparently good and successful; there has to be nothing in life, no successful affairs or well worn circle of friends, and then! and then! only then is there what there should be in your soul. And you have that pallor on your face. In spite of the red spot on your nose, for example.

But *if only*, then that's all. Life would take a different path. But if only doesn't happen. Because melancholy is my home.

Well no, there is no happiness for me, I don't know how to feel it. For some reason I see it inside out all the time; and there's no point; and I'm irritated that I know there's no point; and I know that I shouldn't know everything, but I know it all the same. Yesterday, it seems, I had come very close to what I need, but no, I deflected it with my knowledge. Oh, my demon. When will it depart from me.

Everything is forms, everything is relationships between objects, but what kind (namely) of objects makes no difference. Everything is functions and schemes. There may be spirit here, but there is no soul! And there is no heart. If there is a heart, it has to grow onto something. And not just to something, but to this: who are you, what do you love, what makes you cry, what makes you close your eyes for happiness, what were you taught as a child, how were you spoiled.

A man has to attach himself to something and share some faith. And not to something and some faith, but this one and that one. Our faith and us; or if just some faith, then be gone, for example, to the Devil. But God is with us. And not for example to the Devil, but to the Devil. And God is with us. God, this one here, not some one. I'm not a mathematician!!

I should have been a military man. And they recruit new soldiers every year. And for the Motherland. And the regulations weren't thought up dubiously by you.

Nothing gets you hot like the skilled movements of young men as they jump, rage, hang on crossbars, turn somersaults, their t-shirts ride up, their pants fall to their tailbone, the records of their youthful hot energy. Where there is health and youth, there is war!

An idea of happiness.

It's going, for example, to the bathhouse and meeting somebody simply and easily. But unfortunately, I can't, I don't know how to start a conversation. Here you have to be able to be clever. Not like me once at 19 when I came up and honestly asked a pleasant divinity on a suitcase. And he took me for a crazy man. Instead you have to do it with cleverness and a certain approach. Which is contrary to the Soul of the Poet. But how, how? And you have to avoid going too far, read him right, not investigate him too much, or how would it be if he thinks — what's he talking to me for? You can't be afraid that he'll reply rudely or laugh, you can't be afraid of getting burned. Remember that conquest, courting is not an aristocratic affair, it requires both resourcefulness and a certain amount of ingratiation and, maybe, everyday common vulgar words, and you have to know what people live by today, have to be able to keep the conversation up, or what will happen. B. there can talk people up on buses, right away in the crush puts his hand there on their zipper and the other often gets an erection and presses against him himself, a 15 year old, and if he pulls away and says something rude, he doesn't take it to heart, he may act offended himself, as if to say what's the problem? If you believe his stories. So, the bathhouse. You have to know how, to know how. Not to be shy, yes, it's slippery sit down and start talking. If he answers rudely, leave and don't consider yourself beaten and your dignity insulted. This would be life's happiness, for the prey to be yours, won by your own hands, rather than having been someone else's, and you got it second hand, somebody found somebody, then did you a favor. Instead you look, look yourself. Don't be a Chekhov, a man in a shitty case. But you need strong nerves. Not to fall into an inescapable mute sadness, but act, act, move closer, squeeze, be a scout, a Jack London, even deceive him in something, promise something, make him interested; act! And don't be satisfied with the beauty of your sadness. All the same at this moment no one can see it. Instead what do I do, always rely on humanity. I take them as if through understanding. And you understand them so well, that if he doesn't need it, then I won't, oh, of course. Well, and who's that good for? So much for seeking and the rotten morality of waiting. We find consolation in the apparently attractive tragic pose of Death in Venice. But in reality this is just cowardice and lack of initiative. After all, there is no audience for your tragic paralysis and your hopeless gaze at the beloved object. It's one thing to show Phaedra in theater, frozen in the hopelessness of her passion, and Phaedra achieving her goal will still look beautiful; but everybody left or fell asleep at Conversation Piece.[*]

"Them."
So, behind the armor of masculinity each one hides a soft melted heart. You understand that in order for him to open like a flower, you have to encourage him, indulge him, flatter him. That's the way it is, after all, it may be that every man wants to open up, but out of caution, lest it be taken advantage of to his detriment, he doesn't open up. In the interest of self-defense he's protected by such thick armor of defensiveness.

You know, there is a certain age when they want caresses, but somehow there's no girl handy, and he willy-nilly sits with his arm around a friend or stretches out in his lap, but this — no, this is not homosexuality. This is having no outlet for your warmth. And you want to lean on a friend temporarily. I never wanted to leave that temporarily. I wanted passionately to stay in that divine temporarily forever.

Reading has made me a dreamer; or the opposite, disinclination to outdoor games saddled me as a reader and dreamer. At any rate, the circle is closed. I started to live in dreams. And with age came the additional fact that my hopes diminished. And vanished altogether.

Oy, how the pillow pulls me. It just pulls me so to lie down on it.
—Hello Divan Blanketovich!
—Hello Sheetyan Humanovich!

I thought up wiring the doorbell to a button next to my pillow, and while I lay in the dark falling asleep and thought now someone would come visit me, secretly pushed the button and in the silence the abrupt bell rang out through

---

[*]Visconti's film *Gruppo di Famiglia in Interno* (1974). [KM]

the whole apartment. That's how I played with my heart, and it's true, it skipped a beat.

You have to be ready in advance for something bad, and it's easier to get through. When I was little, I always, when I put my feet in slippers, thought, just in case, that maybe a mouse had gotten in them. At least, if it was there, I wouldn't be suddenly frightened. And if it wasn't, of course it never was there, you'd think, well, thank God, how nice. But what's bad is that there's always readiness for the mouse in your soul, and no serenity. And now when I pick up the phone I'm ready for the investigator to call. And if not, once again, thank God. For daily peace of mind it's bad that there's an investigator living in my soul. But Christian feeling requires that you be the accused for life and not have fun.

2 unlying books are being written, we are writing and they are writing against us. Kitchen writers, we write in the bedroom and read to guests in the kitchen, but there is an even more secret book being written about the kitchen writers *by them* and it is kept behind 7 seals, and no one shall read it.

The 2 main questions in these books: who is to blame? and what is to be done? And the 2 answers to them: no one is to blame, and most importantly, you don't have to do anything.

A writer must imagine very well the distribution of power in the city for the KGB to dream of getting hold of him. And you have already done it a service in that it has found out about you. Everyone the KGB is interested in is already its helper. If it has called you in, it has found out about you at least.

But you shouldn't think that if they, then we too; after all (what *after all?*) ah! After all they (them) for us (we) — **we** what? what **for us**? Oh!

Tomorrow that guy will call again (Jailov).

Maybe they won't put you in prison, but they have to keep you scared.

I gave a guitar to Gulya for her to take my manuscripts to the West. And for this I've been punished three times, ten times over! Both for giving away a guitar that was a gift to me, and for giving it not simply, but so that she would take them. And for all this the singer in me has perished. I didn't even learn

to play the guitar, and I never will, because now you can't buy one anywhere. Now I'm left with forever writing only subtle prose, of no interest to young simple hearts. But everyone would have loved songs. How precisely God has determined my fate.
The singer
in me
has perished.
(Caw! Caw!)

No, all this is not talent, that some young man, amazing us with his freedom, can sing or write up in a minute a pile of poems. Talent is faithfulness. When nothing turns out, but all the same you don't want to do anything else in life, and I won't, even if it doesn't turn out my whole life.

Oh, at least to fill this one page. You're already thinking, in the light of the task set, not what to fill it with, but only to fill it. There are still three fifths of the page left. And I won't fill it. Only with the words that I won't fill it. Such weakness (heroic). And no one will understand my heroism. Will anyone understand my works? Of course they won't. No, here is something bigger than they will or they won't. A strange labor (they thought of me, seeing how I write something down on the page with pauses, — Hey, you, on the balcony, behind the pansies —). And I'd better think something about them. Oof. Thank God. No, not thank God yet. Here we'll write two more lines, then it'll be thank God. Now there's already one. Now there's half of one. Now there's who knows how much. Now that's all.

The first five years or so I'd work on one poem for a month or two; and once I took half a year to write one poem — even working only on that, didn't party, didn't get distracted, only composed it for half a year and somehow got it done. And I would have told no one that it was all so much work for me. But now I'm delighted I had such exceptional instincts for diligence.

Because what used to happen continues to happen: what I am doing is all the time thinking about something and rethinking it; always about one and the same thing, one and the same; and only when it's not about one and the same thing do I take note and insert it in the collections. That's it, only new and fresh things work.

I'm a mouse. I'm running around quickly-quickly looking for a cracker.

The New Generation in Russian Poetry

How many layers, unnecessary, that have become heavy over a lifetime. But one needs an unencumbered, light structure, though one with twists. And one also needs children.

Weak boys (and girls), spread a rumor, please, that I am a tyrant. And I will love you.

So is this all ME or NOT ME (I said, for example, taking a look at my designs). It seems it's me. But also not me. When it's in a journal among other writers, it would be me, but when it's here on the desert island and there's nobody else, it's still me, and therefore already not me too, but *in general*.

Oh why, why can't I completely fly off into the beauty of marvelous words. And unsad ones. And dove-like. And cloudmaple and soulringing and brightbrowhazel and scrollsweet seventeenautumnal and starryredfleet ones.

Oh stop your doubting. Everything you write will be beautiful (and what you don't write even more so).

TRANSLATED BY KEVIN MOSS

⬦⬦⬦ ALEKSANDR SHATALOV ⬦⬦⬦

from Poems on Love and Death,
Texts Addressed to Victor Escobar

the plot's plot drags me into the vortex
i bite my lower lip — no out-of-place smile, not here
i've already touched the arm outstretched towards me
how many more times do i have to test this, my fate

meanwhile, it's totally terrific just to sit close and not listen to music
your eyes peck around me as if for the last time
souls cooing like pigeons in the window of morning
I am taken aback by your eyes, sleepy, alien-shaped

it's summer and the shirt has faded, the skin roughened
fingernails clipped short
                        sensitize the fingertips
the body narrow and lively, a tadpole
always aroused, always dancing

the twilight breeze barely ruffles your hair
uh-oh — is someone nibbling my ear
say a young stranger slips on your shorts in the morning, by mistake
maybe I saw it wrong, heard it all wrong

giddyup, taxi, giddyup
            I don't want to see it, don't want to hear
the plane will get lost in the clouds, the insane leaves will cover the pavement
my ears are stuffed up but I've gotto climb higher and higher
up to the snowline, where the rosy mountains are like tongues of all-day suckers,
                                                            Escobar

let there be dark! let it be blue I
can't see anything familiar not
even through your dynamite eyes they
won't leave your skull like night moths
hand over the razor the scritch of the
first streetcar who cares I do I love
to love your narrow hips rolled up
in our little blanket let's do it three
times tonight the squawking and coughing
soundtrack through the wall, communal
gears and the slopbuckets of midnight
but it is our night it is your hips I love
your narrow hips paint paint it's no
use just a pre- pre- pretext for possessing
a means of stressing the size the random-
ness the indirectness of touching meeting

TRANSLATED BY BOB HOLMAN AND VITALY CHERNETSKY

from Moscow Poems

if at night I dream mommy brother Slava touches me
I will fly in a dress a simple one of crèpe-de-chine
with polka dots on powder blue or leaves on navy
and buds and birches flowers on a grave
playing with my pale blond braids with one hand
with the other holding brother Slava
'cause in a dream people come to hug each other tenderly
or in bell bottoms a pale pink shirt
sandals or shoes only the heel mustn't break off
father shoots the ball into my gate I catch it and my dress
rises up to the waist everyone laughs you are so
funny today Sasha because there's wind a poplar
dandelions mother says that in the gate
I should jump faster and do my exercises
in the yard near the dumpster Slava kisses me on the cheek
starts caressing me his fingers are like a girl's and he himself
is like my little sister Olya and a little brother too because

it's a dream I dream of all those dear a small town the trees
so far away far mommy daddy brother and Slava
I kiss them all in turn because I'm in a new skirt
So beautiful now if at night I dream of mommy

TRANSLATED BY VITALY CHERNETSKY

from Poems to T.

1

in germany's hands the age of air or
jasmine bird cherry so that breathing stops
to melt to expend if we haven't loved yet
fear makes one shiver as if the blade of a knife's passing between fingers
in germany's hands never to wake up
to kiss or only touch lightly
close one's eyes never look back
squeeze but in such a way never to fall out of love
but the wind wind it seems to smell of you
summer haze finally approaches
air rhymes well with your blue shade
opened lilac blossoms if such a thing happens
taking the shirt off so hot can get burned
and the flower's body the seed the opened tip
squirting so to kiss means distraction
to love so strongly that not to come once during the night
hands pages movements partings
germania mania one simply cannot confess
you think or gaze and there are only distances
but I don't want to don't know how to part

TRANSLATED BY VITALY CHERNETSKY

Untitled

a working man eyebrows knitted fists hairy the broad shoulders
stooping the chin rough and pimply the mouth always half-open: a worker
legs crooked the chest bulging arms long fingers coarse all of
this made for hugging clasping pressing into hairy belly squeezing into
groin: then mine could be pulled at turned around opened up
transformed into a drawing or simply the filling of space into time or
historic events to use up whole or in parts: the muscles tight the balls
taut member hard well proportioned a tatar man in baggy pants a
hunter with a knife in his boot a young worker in dirty overalls

Translated by Vitaly Chernetsky

from Garcia Lorca

i am going to cry because
i am going to cry because
i don't need anything anymore
i can't do anything about it

i'll sit on a balcony
i'll lie on a couch
maybe somewhere in bologna
coming and going and rocking in nirvana

maybe it's the silent sluice of san francisco
rolling in bed and just when I want it to
in my mouth your purple penie
pops up in my dream

but you don't know anything about it because
you're lying down holding somebody else's
body you've forgotten me as completely
as a lipstick trace dissolving on a foggy mirror

the fragile folds of your foreskin
I am sitting down as if
I'm the one who's dead
examining the blood on your collar

TRANSLATED BY BOB HOLMAN AND VITALY CHERNETSKY

from JFK Airport

well of course life is all snowstorms or no like this the snow burns the face
i wrap myself in a scarf and try to sleep pressing myself into the corner the seat
it's all the same so it is moscow even in this snowstrorm lonely a suburb
or forests ditches moscow environs far away
the car jumps on bumps the city asleep long ago
christmas lights like firearms a protection
teeth chattering as if the nutcracker on the tree ready
to bite your nose for nothing an apparition of you when
my lover from the american embassy politely calls me every holiday
and invites for *lunch* or *dinner* his chest
covered with curls sweaty when he starts breathing into my ear passionately
stroking my hand america is there already after just one glass of whisky
that's what you'll say you'll be wrong as always just looking for a chance to
                                        say something nasty
i dream in turn of the suburb the smell
thawing pine needles i know there'll be snowstorm again at the airport
and planes grounded i'll be dialing your number
in the departure area hanging up after the first beep
just like you always get my answering machine
well this just needless reflection and passion to think about actions
was it right and the right way the word the look did you turn away on purpose
dropped a card in the mailbox and why
didn't get an answer manhattan covered with snow just
like natasha medvedeva grinding her teeth in a cold bed in the morning
the knees touch the wall and the hands ran away into other rooms
or hiding in the corner of the bed i'm at Astor place by the granite cube
decided to freeze my balls off finally risking it all showing off
to yourself suddenly you appear in the crowd of dimwits
you pass i pretend not to have noticed

only the cufflinks fall on my bed with a melodious
here is the belt buckle hitting me on lips drawing blood again the smell of
                                                                        whisky
this city in the morning is like bed sheets covered with yesterday's sperm
having started off in chinese i'll continue in english
i have studied the miuss cemetery forwards and backwards looking at neighbors
i stuck plastic tulips into snow let them glow as if they're alive
tongues of the dead not twisted twitching and indecent
a heap of dicks protruding from earth melting snow swelling
i'll circle around my eyes closed the face turned up to the sky
catching the slow falling snowflakes with my lips and then swallowing them
the skin have become see-through like a long sucked lollipop
trace-paper waxed transparent
                              all tender
                          flaccid
                          lifeless

                         TRANSLATED BY VITALY CHERNETSKY

Untitled

> I love bathing in the river; you see
> your own body through water,
> gold light reflects the suface, and
> when you dive in an open your eyes
> down there, everything is so green, so
> green, and you see the little fish rushing
> by . . . And it is not true that the body
> is sinful, that beauty is sinful . . .
> —Mikhail Kuzmin, *Wings*[*]

> I don't know how to swim . . .
> —Nikolai Sapunov, last words[†]

---

[*]Mikilail Kuzmin (1872-1936) was Russia's most prominent gay poet and prose writer; *Wings* (1906), his first novel, is a manifesto calling for the social acceptance of homosexuality.
[†]Nikolai Sapunov (1880-1912), a painter, was one of Kuzmin's lovers; he drowned in a boating accident.

the age of aquarius mineral water taking a bath
in the river that smells of dampness the body's contours distorted
fragility of extremities
         and suddenly transpired well proportioned body
the rainbow of splashes near hands
            as if a butterfly passed by the eyes
or weeds rushing up from the bottom
towards light again toward quick and strong male body
the greenness of backwater reminds of a place for seduction
chilly and young there is no limit to perfection
i see contours the outlines breaking i have to make do
with little such as the hits of a whip
on muscular shoulders the lips tingle a rushing
movement so fast the throat chokes on old
vomit the instinct of self-preservation
but in the morning the icy water will burn me again
and movements of the heavy male body at night
rhythmical just like blood's explosions in the heart

Translated by Vitaly Chernetsky

Untitled

Our hairdresser friend
clipped your hair above forehead
just the way the rave kids wear it,
you immediately started whining —
no clothes to match this haircut,
a full closet of shirts but nothing one could wear to work
and the skin on the face is no longer
the way it should be to match such a haircut
silly to show up at work with such a haircut
a haircut like this should go off club hopping
and it's too late for us, the clubs
these idiot DJs make us puke
and so do the kids who fashion their lives after
                              Araki's and Van Sant's characters,
sorry for them all but what's the use,
some overdose and croak at abandoned construction sites,
                              others go into business,
you can't be of any help to either the former or the latter,
we're home together every evening
each doing his thing
looking at each other from time to time, compassionate
I master the basics of web design,
you put photos into albums,
you still have long hair there,
perhaps right there one doesn't notice
dryness of skin, wrinkles, shadows under the eyes,
but then, during this vacation, you didn't get up early,
half a year passed, it seems more than that,
one can't understand, time seems to fly
just yesterday we met in the subway, and now it's our seventh year
     together,
and the certainty about tomorrow, and the day after tomorrow,
if, of course, this obscene country doesn't blow up in a big way,

if the police don't fuck us over residence permits,
if they don't move from looks to something menacing,
the imbeciles in leather jackets that hang out in our stairway,
and I too now have bad skin under my eyes,
but to hell with it, this isn't the meaning of life,
by the summer, if you want, you can let your hair grow,
they promise new arrivals at the vintage store,
show me, a professor asks, a happy gay person,
this, the professor says, tougher to find than a cheerful corpse,
corpses are not our business, so what shall we tell him?
a) here we are, open your eyes, you fucked-up idiot!
b) show us a happy person, period.

TRANSLATED BY VITALY CHERNETSKY

❧ ALEKSEI PURIN ❧

KUZMIN[*]

A Dutch hat — just like Kostya
Somov's?[†] And with the steamship bass,
the smoky Chaliapin,[‡] the guests are going.
Volga. A slope. These verses give off a smell
sometimes of Cliquot, sometimes of kvass, sometimes of stage makeup . . .
So, let them! Sometimes of canvas, sometimes chalk.
And the dolman on his beloved
Wouldn't it move us, on the sweet, the brave,

the ready to death V.K.?[§] How strangely
was the place of their reckoning chosen —
in Mann's mountaneous novel!
Only the spine is different — the Carpathians.
The future slaughter and shiver of the past
Blissful madness. And the trout breaks the net.[¶]
The Lepages lie there in velvet happiness.
It seems: reading these books

Is like using a broken shower,
suddenly icy, and then very hot.
Clio, and what about warm? . . . For those whom we've befriended, let us
cry together, Kuzmin!
Yurochka's on a barge?[**] Fouchet's in Paris.
Gilette's blade has grown again . . .

---

[*]Mikhail Kuzmin (1872-1936), Russia's most prominent gay poet, was an avowed aesthete who promoted the cult of Hellenic Alexandria and eighteenth-century Mannerism.
[†]Konstantin Somov (1869-1939), a Russian painter and member of the World of Art group led by Diaghilev, was Kuzmin's friend.
[‡]The grear Russian singer.
[§]"V. K." is Vsevolod Kniazev (1891-1913), a minor poet and one of Kuzmin's lovers; he committed suicide. His life story has also served as a source for Akhmatova's *Poem Without a Hero*.
[¶]The trout is an allusion to Kuzmin's final and arguably finest book of poems, *The Trout Breaks the Ice* (1929). "The Lepages" are duel pistols.
[**]"Yurochka" is Yuryi Yurkun (1895-1938), an artist and prose writer who was Kuzmin's partner for more than twenty years.

How to find it now in a bloodless niche?
Where is the eighteenth century of Miletus?

TRANSLATED BY VITALY CHERNETSKY

Amsterdam

In a special little shop, located, pardon me,
on a canal, the entire Netherlands
I would have bought naked. Please wrap up for me
all these veins, glands, hatches, tonsils,
the cramps and lines of all Holland,
its convex waves, its shallow boats

full of genitals! The delirium
of Amphitrite*: splashes rising, temptation oozing,
sweat flowing . . . Wipe at least your pearl!
Why is it not in the gill but on the collar bone?
The quicksilver fish market, the rows of Aphrodite.
This is where Snyders should go learn!†

Oh, the Utrecht of condoms! Oh, I am blushing . . .
Oh, the hybrid of Sodom and Senegal . . .
But I read somewhere about the orchid
and the bee‡ and I've little to do
with Lot and his angels — was it not the bee
that winked and buzzed the idea to the sinners?

The sweet winged brother,
chocking on our passion's petal
drowning in our slime: calves, armor
and the dragon in the cave of the flower's muzzle,
in the tender yawn. Mary, whom did you let
to drop their pollen, collide the parts?

---

*Amphitrite is the Greek sea goddess, wife of Poseidon.
†Snyders is the most famous of Dutch still life painters.
‡The orchid and the bee is an allusion to Marcel Proust's *The Cities of the Plain.*

And the Creator, twisting all these waltzes,
undoubtedly would end his life in bedlam —
on a sunflower, if his fingers
of pure gold were caught by us.
He is a Dutchman. A lens wriggles in a little canal —
and a diamond. And a windmill with boulders.

TRANSLATED BY VITALY CHERNETSKY

The Army Elegy

To the soldier Seryozha, whom I discharged from his post at four o'clock in the morning, having introduced myself as the son of Russia's Defense Minister.

The scent of a soldier's cock is beyond comparison
Which is well known in New York Berlin and Nice
There they know all about tenderness
When taking a sniff of the crotch

Terrains of alien pillows
Stains of alien sheets
The disparity of guns' caliber
Grows in viciousness and length

I did not have anyone except the Army
Rosy-cheeked soldiers fall out of windows
Like Kharms's old women[*]
When they try to gaze at the sky
Their resilient bodies are dragged away
(And there's something farcical in it)

The intoxicating smell of the barracks and dirty feet
The creaking tenderness of several pairs of entangled combat boots
(What to do — I couldn't do otherwise any more)

Foreign queers are aroused by Russian soldiers
Russian soldiers are not afraid of foreign queers
They bravely gaze at the sky
Many of them did not have anyone except the Army
They fall out of windows
And their able young bodies fall into foreigners' hands
They are dragged across the border
usually to Paris Berlin New York or Nice

---

[*]An allusion to "Old Women" by Russian absurdist writer Daniel Kharms (1905-1942).

Smuggled by a firmly united lusty gang
Getting through customs with difficulty
(The creaking and scent alone could drive one crazy
Were it not for the tenderness
That squeezed the crotch in the final gasps
Of disparate guns alien sheets and pillows)

TRANSLATED BY VITALY CHERNETSKY

My First Man: Sentimental Vomit

I have never written or reminisced about it
as if this part of my memory got blocked: the recollections are vague and dim
as if it had happened in my infancy long before I became who I became —
A DEPRAVED UNBRIDLED MONSTER
I think I know what happened: I made myself forget about it
my first experience with another man
that guy at whose place I crashed in leningrad
I do not even remember clearly either his face or his cock — just a shaky
        eroded image
I was 17 he near 40
things did not get to fucking
everything was quite innocent: I was lying like a log giving him complete freedom
of action but he was delicate and courteous perhaps too much so
nervous and stiff so I couldn't come no matter how hard he and I tried
he liked my body even my skinny legs he called
sexy it must have been from him that I first learned I was beautiful and this
knowledge turned my world upside down
in order to shock my teenage imagination he took me
to a beriozka hard currency store where we solemnly acquired
a bottle of vodka my imagination was indeed shocked it was bitterly
cold we were dying to get warm so we split the bottle between
the two of us that night I did not have anything to eat except some
solyanka soup that was a bit off and I got sick I puked all over him his bed
                                and his bedroom
it was a terrible snafu I vaguely remember how he started undressing me
and when I was already naked he tried to take off my neck the little golden
cross I was wearing I got baptized shortly before that and was very

religious at the time I got ravenously angry called him a faggot
a pervert and proudly fell asleep in my own puke while he
offended went to sleep on the sofa
(a couple of months later I was arrested by the militia for a drunken row in the
                                        subway in moscow
the cops in the sobering station having beaten me up and stripped me naked
emptied my pockets and expropriated my golden cross and watch then threw me
onto a concrete floor to relax under an icy cold shower where I understood that
                                        god
had turned away from me and that my religion was not even worth my vomit)
upon my return to moscow I sent him a few of my poems full of adolescent fears
depression and of a vague foreboding of the future knockout life
he wrote to me mad love letters at my mother's address — the letters which I read
already after his death when he either slipped or jumped off a balcony
one of them reported that he "cannot live without me"
these words meant absolutely nothing to me
later on things happened this way more than once

the only thing that I did remember clearly and forever is the scent of his cologne
drakkar — the scent that I can unmistakably distinguish from any others even
                                        though
I myself never use perfume
now it seems to me he was even good-looking as a male of the species
back then anyone could have taken this place
I was waiting to be seduced and used the first one who came in handy (even
                                        though
he was sure it was him who was using me — so young and innocent!)
he was only part of the faceless crowd of extras — one of those who later in my
                                        life
were countless
MY FIRST MAN
THE FIRST OF THOUSANDS
a half-poet/half-journalist/half-playboy who did not leave behind anything
                                        except a
slim little book of poems and some rapidly ageing boys who to this day preserve
memories of his embraces
I entered his life and unceremoniously appropriated it
I adopted his identity and developed it to the point where he no longer existed
my adolescent depression grew into something greater than a simple yearning
                                        for a

good life and someone's strong arms
even now I am writing not so much about him but about the vomit with which
essentially everything had begun
since then whenever I see vomit I get sentimental

TRANSLATED BY VITALY CHERNETSKY AND THE AUTHOR

SPEAKING THROUGH THE VEIL:
THE DILEMMA OF WOMEN'S VOICES

LAURA D. WEEKS

SPEAKING THROUGH THE VEIL:
The Dilemma of Women's Voices in Russian Poetry

A S A GARMENT AND AS A SYMBOL, the veil is a purely female object. In all its incarnations — the Chador, the bridal veil, the nun's habit or the veils of Salome — it is the exclusive province of the female. It makes visible the quintessentially female urge to conceal while inviting further revelation. The position of the woman behind the veil, forced to speak through a device which both deflects and attracts attention, accurately describes the position of Russian women poets writing today. Most Russian women poets are reluctant to be immediately identified as women. True, there is an active and articulate feminist movement in Russia with a long tradition behind it. True, there is a growing body of gendered lyric. But the majority of women poets avoid stepping into this charmed circle for fear of several things: that their female-ness will be dismissed as "femininity," that their poetry will somehow become circumscribed as "female experience." They would much prefer to be poets without gender, who deal in the realm of universal experience. To achieve this exalted status means overcoming certain barriers, such as the fact that both the private and public dissemination of poetry is largely controlled by men. Beyond that, there is the barrier of language itself. The Russian language carries grammatical markers in the past tense of verbs and in all adjectives that automatically identify the speaker as either male or female. As a result, the history of Russian women's voices has always been in some sense a game — using the veils available to them as a series of subterfuges to distract the male gaze long enough to convey their message and to assure that their poetry will attract serious consideration.

One of the most effective veils, used both early and late, is that of tradition. In the first decade of the nineteenth century, Elizaveta Kulman invaded the traditionally male bastion of the Classical ode with an alien sensibility. In her view Apollo takes second place to Diana, who is exalted as the protector of poetry and women poets. Especially illuminating is her treatment of Corinna, the woman renowned for her victory over Pindar at a poetry festival. At the contest, Kulman's Corinna begins as a demure demoiselle, advancing shyly, requesting to be heard. But she ends as something entirely different —

a poet, crowned by Pindar, and welcomed as an equal among poets. This early attempt at establishing an autonomous female poetic voice failed, because as Diana Greene has pointed out, it was quickly subsumed by the male myth of the dead virgin-martyr. Elizaveta Kulman, poor and erudite, child prodigy of Prof. Karl Grossheinrich, died at age seventeen. Critics immediately transformed her into a victim, attributing her death to any number of causes: poverty, overweening erudition and Grossheinrich's pedagogical excesses. The critic Nikitenko even suggested that she died in order to remain pure: "She was an angel on earth and died at age seventeen in order not to stop being one." Thus the veil has become a kind of shroud.

In the mid-nineteenth century, the "virgin's shroud" became the mantle of majesty and mystery donned by Karolina Pavlova, the finest Russian woman poet of the century, and the first to insist on her status as a professional poet. Pavlova did not shrink from adopting the pose of the Romantic poet — the divinely ordained bard aflame with the holy fire of inspiration. She even identifies herself in a late poem as "izbrannitsa," the "chosen one," giving the noun a marked feminine ending. But her confident assertion of self met with stiff resistance largely, we assume, because she did not fit the reigning paradigm. The Romantic ethos was a predominantly male ethos dominated by images of "manly writing" and the "virile pen." Accordingly, Pavlova's content-laden verse, with its accent on intellect rather than affect, was labelled the product of a frustrated blue-stocking, and even her declamatory style, appropriate for the period, was ridiculed. As Romanticism declined, however, and the Russian national consciousness turned its attention to social issues and its medium to prose, she was able to forge an identity in harmony with the declining movement — the identity of an isolated, alienated intellect who speaks with the powerful voice of memory.

Pavlova's case brings up an interesting point. Catriona Kelly has demonstrated that Russian women poets do not fare well whenever the vectors of power, poetry and politics converge, when, as she puts it "poetry is the medium of politics" which happens in Russia more frequently than elsewhere in the European tradition. In Pushkin's day poets were the spokespersons of politics and not infrequently its martyrs, witness the number that suffered in the aftermath of the Decembrist revolt. Pushkin's passing, itself a political act, evoked a powerful response from the young Lermontov, whose ode "The Death of the Poet" immediately earned him the status of heir apparent of Romanticism. Thus was established the "first line" of Russian poetry, in which women poets do not seem to figure largely. Conditions (which had been tolerable during the pre-Romantic period) would not again be favorable to women poets until the last decade of the century, when previously submerged philosophical currents surfaced. At this time the so-called "second-line" of Russian poetry came in for reexamination. This was a more meditative strain of poetry which originated in the philosophical and metaphysical lyrics of Tyutchev and Fet. At this time there was renewed interest in the German Romantic concept of the eternal feminine. The man responsible for cultivating these concepts in Russian soil was the mystical philosopher Vladimir Solovyov. He posited the existence of a female principle in the creation whom he named Sophia, or "Divine Wisdom." In this exalted atmosphere a belief in women and women's wisdom blossomed. Suddenly there emerged on the Russian cultural scene a phenomenal number of world-class poets, many of whom were women.

In this period, which lasted well into the present century, the mantle of the Romantic poet was transformed into a coat of many colors. Abandoning any pretense of a single, universal "female" voice in poetry, women poets indulged in a dizzying display of archetypal masks. They paraded as Amazons or woman-warriors, cabaret singers or street musicians, gypsies, peasants, sorceresses, princesses, harlots and nuns. Such archetypal creations were also very much in vogue with the male poets of the period, but in the case of the women poets they had an added dimension. For them the "masked ball" was not just an exercise in camouflage but a deliberate attempt to confound all the traditional markers of gender, including those native to the Russian language. The prominent Symbolist poet and philosopher Zinaida Gippius used exclusively male pronouns and adjective endings, as well as writing criticism under a male name, Anton Krainy. The poet Poliksena Solovyova also used masculine grammatical markers and wrote under the pen name Allegro, which in Russian is neuter. Another indicator of the intent to escape the confines of gender is the importance of the Sybil, most notably in the poetry of Adalaida Gertsyk and Marina Tsvetaeva. As the maiden who rejected Apollo and whose body withered away leaving only her voice, the Sybil is the prime example of a truly liberated female poetic voice.

Even in this favorable atmosphere female creativity was in danger of being subsumed by male myths. The main line of attack, adopted by Trotsky and by the Symbolist poet and chief arbiter of taste Valery Bryusov, was to dismiss all women poets as emotionally unstable and ideologically backward. But these frontal attacks were successfully countered. Bryusov will always be remembered for his "Evening of Poetesses" (nine women poets chosen to represent the nine Muses, topic limited to the prescribed female topic of love) where he was bested by a young world-class poet, Marina Tsvetaeva. More subtle and more deadly were the mythological creations by the men who worshipped women. The greatest of the Symbolists, Aleksandr Blok, created a series of mysterious veiled women who float across his urban landscapes sowing spiritual turmoil as they go. Predictably, these ephemeral anima creatures have no voice. Enter the world-class poet Anna Akhmatova, with her finely-honed female sensibility grounded in the physical details of ambiance and dress (beads, feathers, shawls, a recalcitrant fringe of bangs). Exercising the utmost formal restraint, Akhmatova gave these silent creatures a psychological identity and a voice. No longer the passive objects of admiration, it is they who view men through the veil of irony.

The major achievement of women poets of this period was the creation of the vatic voice. The vatic voice combined a psychological unity lacking in the mask figures with the greatest possible consistency and cultural resonance. Part of the Symbolists' philosophy was the concept of the poet as prophet and priest. This, coupled with their celebration of "women's wisdom," that is, their priviledged access to the mythic domain, lent a certain authority to their prophetic utterances. This was especially true of the two greatest women poets of the period, Akhmatova and Tsvetaeva, as they abandoned the intimate lyric and became the chroniclers of their tortured age. Speaking through the veil is also an ancient metaphor for communicating with the dead, and they spoke — as only women could — for the dead. Thus Tsvetaeva, surveying the bodies scattered on the battlefied of the Civil War, speaks with the voice of God come to judge the quick and the Red and the White alike. Thus Akhmatova, in the majestic opening of her *Requiem*, written for the victims of the purges, speaks with the voice of history and the voice of pain, singing in the unresisting flesh.

The reign of Socialist Realism, that Stalinist gothic monster, was less congenial to women's voices in poetry, largely because the real poetry was being written "underground," and the dominant image was that of the poet as Christ-like martyr, spilling his blood in defense of the truth. For obvious reasons, the role is traditionally filled by men, leaving to the women the role of mourners. The role of mourner was an established female voice in the Russian pre-Christian tradition. The lament, for example, was traditionally a female genre as opposed to the epic or lay, which was male. This perhaps explains the greater cultural resonance of Akhmatova's persona of the grieving mother at the cross from her *Requiem*, than the "anonymous victim" persona of Anna Barkova, a poet who actually suffered more at the hands of Stalin's henchmen and in the camps than did Akhmatova.

The 1960s was a period of silent gathering of strength, and by the 1980s the female voice emerged from its temporary retreat with renewed vigor. This newfound vitality stems partly from the poets' recovery of their lost heritage. Because so much of the poetry of the "Silver Age" (the period described at length above) has only been widely available for the last twenty years, it is not surprising that it hit the Russian cultural scene with the force of a revelation. What is interesting is that certain parallels are emerging between that period and the contemporary scene. In the Silver Age it was quite common for poets to establish themselves first as painters, designers and graphic artists and to migrate to poetry as a second occupation. Among contemporary women poets there are several, such as Tatiana Shcherbina, Faina Grimberg, Sveta Litvak, and Natalya Chernykh, who are similarly bi-talented, with a background in the fine arts and a love of fusing word and image. Their work presents a heady blend of the visual and the verbal, from Grimberg's startling transformations (a fur cap into a live grinning fox, a flowering tree into a crowded subway car) to Shcherbina's "drawn book" entitled, appropriately, "Space."

The poets of the late Silver Age also delighted in playing with language, breaking up words into morphemes and recombining these to create radically new clusters of sound and sense. This kind of verbal play is visible today in the work of Lyudmila Vyazmitinova, who uses a similar technique of breaking up words into syllables separated by dashes, thereby producing an illegal (at least in traditional Russian prosody) stress per line and at the same time creating new words and associations of the fragments. Elena Katsyuba takes this technique one step further: in her work the verbal dislocations are reinforced by the poem's graphic incarnation on the page. The interplay of shape and sound also harks back to the earlier period.

But contemporary women's poetry is no slavish reproduction of past achievements. Along with the increased vitality comes a new sense of confidence and a willingness to discard old cultural baggage. A good example is the treatment of Ophelia, a popular figure at the "masked ball" described above. The poets of that period were chiefly interested in providing a rebuttal to Hamlet's overweening male arrogance, consequently, their poems had Ophelia attempting to engage Hamlet in dialogue. In Evgeniya Lavut's stark reworking of the myth, by contrast, the figure is dismissed, albeit not without regret: "Ophelia, alas, who needs/Your carcass caught in snags. . . ." With a single image, the meaning of a powerful male projection such as Ophelia is called into question, and the veil of the virgin-martyr is ripped away to reveal her terrifying mortality.

Contributing to this growing confidence is the sense of writing within a female tradition. In the nineteenth century, Karolina Pavlova had to look to a male mentor, the poet Evgeny Baratynsky. In the Silver Age, women poets had male mentors too, but they also consciously derived power and inspiration from Pavlova. The greatest of them, Akhmatova and Tsvetaeva, used Pavlova's poetry as epigraphs to their own works. They in turn became so influential that Yunna Morits, writing in 1975, could refer to womens' voices as being caught "between Scylla and Charybidis, between Anna and Marina." And with the weight of tradition comes the burden of history. Contemporary women poets have an acute sense of historical development. Their vision encompasses both the past, as when Kondakova speaks of the bleak and bloody Stalinist era: "realism's landscape . . . a chapter of heads forever lost," and the future, as when Polina Barskova addresses the coming age: "The last age is here. And it will be a time When the word turns into a moan. Not an age of love, hiding Its nullity under a wig of sin." Barskova's authoritative voice, surprisingly mature in a very young poet, demonstrates to what extent the vatic voice has been assimilated by contemporary women poets. Predictably, it is not history in the abstract that concerns them, so much as Russia's historical destiny, Russia's place in the coming age. History, in other words, is a means of exploring the Russian identity. The paradox of Russian identity, split equally between repulsion and attraction, estrangement and loyalty, is expressed in the poetry of Yulia Kunina, one of the most powerful voices in the growing diaspora: "Moscow, unbearable, is more familiar to me than my own body. . . ."

By far and away the richest harvest has sprung from the rediscovery of spirituality. The current spiritual revival in Russia affects virtually every poet, from Aleksandra Petrova, whose imagery is as dense as a Medieval Allegory, to Natalya Chernykh, who writes poems as strong and simple as psalms. Sometimes it takes on a quieter, more introspective tone, as in Olga Martynova's metaphysical reflections on the nature of God and time. The almost transparent quality of her verse, coupled with the fine detail, show her to be a descendent of the "second-line" of Russian poetry, the line originated by Tyutchev. The true nature of Russian spirituality may come as a surprise to Westerners. This is not religion of the tame, kitchen-garden variety. For that matter, it is not even purely Christian, but an ecclectic mixture of Christian symbolism, Russian pagan ritual and Eastern metaphysics. Its full range is captured in the poetry of Elena Shvarts. With Shvarts the dance of the veils comes full circle. In her cycle *Winter Muses,* the decorous dance of the muses becomes by turns a wild Gypsy habanera, a Russian peasant circle-dance, a drunken orgy, and finally, a mystical procession before the Mother of God. With each turn, she lifts the veil of tradition just enough to reveal another veil concealed underneath. Posing as the tenth muse, she confidently manipulates all the standard rhetorical figures: the dedication of the poet to Orpheus, the invocation to the muses, the eulogy, the lament.

It used to be a commonplace to use the Biblical figures of Martha and Mary to define the antipodes of existence: the one representing the active life, the other the life of contemplation. So it is with Shvarts and her colleague Olga Sedakova, who shares with her the honor of being the finest living Russian woman poet. Shvarts's fierce lyrcal energy is counterbalanced by Sedakova's introverted, intellectually sophisticated voice. At her most meditative, for example, her *Fifth Stanzas*, Sedakova offers a serene vision of the universe where things have consciousness, and each thing speaks in its own language. Strings of images hang together like a set of amber beads, mirroring a creation which is both transitory and permanent: "My friend! Everything we cherished, like life, will pass away. And like a star, the **unknown** will rise. . . " And with the rising of that star, she reveals the final veil, which is the joint property of all mortals, the veil which Tiutchev named the "thin cloth" — the veil that separates this world from the next.

⬡⬡ FAINA GRIMBERG ⬡⬡

Untitled

For a long time I haven't seen such a young face,
Rejoiced over a boyish, naked body.
And it's not a dead cap, but a living fox
That rounds his black-haired head.
Traces of bird claws are mysteriously written
        in bold strokes across the cap's tag.
The subway's filled with inhuman, guttural bird voices.
And the fox
      keeps a hard, sharp smile perched in its native tongue.
Its eyes curiously cover me.
As if emerging from a movie screen
        at that moment when the tall & green tree
      and all of its leaves suddenly
    crumble into those sitting nearby.

His jacket's tiny green squares
    glitter, as if it too were brilliantly animated —
      a malachite stone now resurrected from so many
        books of photographs.

And the boy himself —
A complete, joyous smile flickers with his dark & radiant eyes.
The apple shaped face breathes in, so alive —
             & silent.
And though this clearly variegated & rattling music
Doesn't sing the flaccid lips,
        slightly ajar — the thin
& shabby clothing suggests a body rejoicing,
And it makes a nest inside me,
And like rain-washed leaves, the green jacket shines.
The white pleasure of large teeth instantaneous & sparkling
         & the whiteness fresh
      because spring's apple tree branch is in blossom.

For a second we all live in
                    someone else's immense breath.

Delicate fir needles over the dark, widespread eyebrows,
How I quickly glanced into the darkened lashes, glinting there
          & saw his swarthy eyelids, raised —
Then at once looked down
At the black shoes made for a man, tightened without shoelaces,
Though light green strings hung from the jacket's collar. . .

Winter & Spring, alive & holding hands
                    step directly toward me.

O apple in the face
                    hear me out —

    these shy slow lips want to kiss both cheeks.

The boy's Adam's apple,
                    a living small bone beneath skin —
                          lean & hard,
The body's strength & length
                    a budding & quick paced heartbeat.
His black pants narrowly furrow at the knees
                    the slender & long adolescent legs.
Darkness of woolen slacks — rumpled
          & the sharp small ankle hairs visible there.

He doesn't notice me, know anything about me
                              & he'll never want to
And if his lips open fully & pronounce a word —
It won't be from what's human,
                    it'll be a terrifying animal's snout.

So does it mean I have to live with closed eyes,
                    sleep as if without dreams?

No, I'll open my eyes & begin
                to weave myself the sun's rays.
Because all this is here so that I can suddenly appreciate my own.
This Lazarus unofficially sent by someone
Sent to me
                so I could awake & rejoice
While riding in this car from one stop to the next,
A kind of wonderful & boundless precept &
          we can't understand it
            anymore than we can suddenly embrace one another.

The doors already closed &
              it's hard for me to breathe now
           because a dusty childish sunshine
         grows momentarily visible
             across this empty leather seat.

TRANSLATED BY JOHN HIGH AND IVAN BURKIN

from the cycle Marginalia

1.

Marginalia . . . Here's how the day begins:
with a whispered exchange of barbs,
with bells sounding in darkened railway cars,
with needles of frost scribbling on your cheek, with knocking knees,
spilled over in patchy sleep from paper platforms.
Jingling from splashes of muted piano keys,
from greedy fires of the station's black maple,
there a rusty stream of leaves is scattered on the wind,
sweeping the parched lawns like rain.
There emerging dawn swims like a pinch of salt;
like a flabby body the warming city shakes.
Like a broken fingernail grating along the skin of space,
a nameless pilgrim stands, pregnant with a stone of light.

2.

Between two interludes, between two autumns —
the yellow and the black,
there are two states of movement:
one born on the wind, the other —
at the bottom of the reservoir.
Between them lies a pause where one cannot hang on
you fall head down into the leaves without waking.
The wind rises — songs of angels
scattered over the stony earth
make funnels and vortices of fiery leaves, of charred sparrows.
The voice insufficient, the moist meat of premonitions,
of greedy events — along the edge of reason, along the selvage edge,
scattered seeds of September's bitter poppy
swarm, humming in the lashed and ragged sky.
Father and Mother, sister, all the same you will leave them;
we're closer to where the rooks and ravens nest.

Boy of piano-wire, running along the edge of lightning,
be it a dream, or a net, or a dusty, pale drawing,
traveling for the first time is a ripe ear ripped out with the roots.

5.
A rusty wheel creaks,
snowdrifts smell of straw . . .
What would it take for a man to stretch out
sprawling over the sled like a wolf's dead pelt?
gunfire's reflection, salty drops of buckshot,
a fishing-line of rainbow from the fire to the icy ravine
An empty casing, nothing more, that once was pain —
do you remember, my soul, clothed in rushes and nets,
how we ran in the brittle tracks,
how they showered us with light and food,
do you remember words, remote as footnotes,
clumps of hoarfrost before the tightly locked door?
Now a wild animal steps cautiously into a thawed patch;
the air boils, everything melts away in rings and rivulets.
A cast stone leaves circles in the sky.

8.
It must be April
scraping its claws along the marble,
leaving no trace.
Stifling city dust
clings to the sound of birdsong.
You, who were leafing through the prayer-book,
couldn't thread your way through the rosary of gardens —
skin flickers in the hunger's twilight
Whom will you speak to? What will you find to rhyme
with your tidy harmonies?
You're burning with note-fever;
you're breaking out in typhus spots.
Flax still burning, and there's no one
to smother the smoke

to touch the strings with a yew bow,
waking a tremor in the resonant pause.

TRANSLATED BY LAURA D. WEEKS

Untitled

I bar-gained sky and earth
It turned out money was ex-changed

and we shake the civil servants' goatee
over the enigmatic I-ching
and we blink — heads or tails
and we play — fathers or ciphers
and we shift — a wife over next to a husband
a husband — in a wife's orbit.

I slips over the rings — either or
I dreams at least of wings
for soaring, while we chase
death's history, between firm-
ament and firmament

and we draw — angels with — wings
and we draw — devils with — wings

what was there — don't remember — they forgot —
either I — or what then — am I a w-i-n-g-s?

nothing above, nothing below
white light
in the crimson speck of an eye turning
un-over the frequent blinking of its lid

eyelid — flutters
lid — obliterates
eyelid — sutures
the entire wide world.

TRANSLATED BY ELENI SIKELIANOS AND LAURA D. WEEKS

Untitled

monk-libertine
sky's eyesocket
call to crucifixion
in smoke signals
in orgasms, orgies
they've slipped past
smoke's not enough for us
we need to eat him

beautiful youth
beautiful youth, pure
to Him — it's crystal
to us — it's aching

wreath Eros in-
to the spokes
of the carriage
wheel, pierce him, crooked
doll in sky's eyesocket

close the lids, lashes

Absolute absent
a desert of snow
a body unclothed
Hamlet embodied
live or not live
shade of Absolute
naked I

TRANSLATED BY ELENI SIKELIANOS AND LAURA D. WEEKS

from the cycle Rachel's Verses

to Daniel Davidov

1.

Monday arrives unannounced
accompanied by all the rest
and Tuesday sends up smoke
and everything becomes unnecessary
Wednesday at midday a crack is sensed
and the smell of a canvas' age
a colorful fragment of depression
graphically delineated
Thursday makes attempts
welcomed by both sides of the acquaintance
because it's still a half-week to Sunday
and the postcards are journeying
under Tuesday's blanket stirs Friday,
builds hideaways and walks backwards
objects begin to talk
the word for Saturday recalls the word for work
and the need to remember something
similar in color to preserves
— and Sunday expires.

2. The Conversations of Objects

like dogs they know their places
can bark and make compliments
in their spot survive to maturity
worse then men suffer illnesses
therefore exceed them in longevity

she speaks who is the biggest
—the outlines of a square circle
the spring of decency's busted

she speaks who in silver shines
like a needle in the rug

objects perk up and speak
all together at once

arranged along the perimeter
of the only room that's been mopped

at first, we were only five
then we were turned inside out

but who'll explain to whom in this world
one plus three is not four

that every sign rises up to god's name

we were essential
now we are many.

Translated by Alex Cigale

from the cycle The Fifth Holiday

Has everyone left me?
   Well, I'll be a seed then.
And bore through the scorched horizon.
The last age is here.
And it will be a time
When the word turns into a moan.
Not an age of love, hiding
Its nullity under a wig of sin.
An age of truth, which is deaf.
An age of soaring light verse,
Which raves but doesn't pine away.
Will everything be there? No! Not us.
A different filth will adorn the dissolving world.
In the lover's hands in the hour before dawn
The rustling of Holofernes' curls.

The bass strings of red pines.
An astonished squirrel's Chinese eyes.
Far off, an acrobat's underskirt flies up.
The children's room. Little beds and nightlights.
Through a fine fringe of gray fur
A gravestone regards the others.
Warm needles, copper and steel,
and the long vicious stingers of mosquitoes.
It smells of garbage, slippage and fire.
All other death pales beside these esteemed ashes.
I tear the legs of my pants, I crush glass.
Off with the descriptions of the shameful interior!
The squirrel's pink fright, the terrier's pious anger.
Don't trust your secrets to diaries or children
Or you'll offend the proud dead.
Don't wash the poison pill down with a glass of juice.
Living at all at among these stones is lonely and full of shame.

> "Even one-stringed, it's still a Greek lyre."
> —Georgii Adamovich

Seedy demon, get dressed. Hurry up, country boy.
The burned-out soul needs new pastures.
Let the hunchback sell the skinny candles of pagan grass
For a nickel — as lately on Bald Mountain.
Let the speckled hen ask the giggly cook, "What's up?" —
Who brings vanilla wafers on a salver
After a long series of sleepless nights . . .
What then?
Get comfortable with your own reflection.
Don't mix first-class simplicity with
Getting something for nothing.
And the organ pipes of fat frogs in the haze.
And candy sown on the table by a thin hand.

Soon the Muse will tire. The cuckoo will rust in the clock.
Dappled ashes will settle in the darkness of your hair.

TRANSLATED BY JEAN DAY AND LAURA D. WEEKS

from Christmas

In that enchanted land,
 Which no one can describe,
I know each and every thing,
Love every face.
God lives
Just a minute's ride from my door.
But everyone drives and passes by.
I know what's inside every earthenware jar,
What the stone fence conceals.
I'd buy some apples at the market
If they weren't so full of poison.
And despite what I know
I could fall in love with an idiot,
Do something really mean,

Burn an icon to ashes at the icy gate.
And paradise would become it's own inversion. A slick mire.
Live and let live.
   Hell maybe. Possibly liberty.

TRANSLATED BY JEAN DAY AND LAURA D. WEEKS

Café Philology
for Lev Lossev

Traces of the people left here
Have slipped tight around my throat like a killer's
Rope circling up out of the dark.
On a scrap — a one-eyed dog.
So these creatures die symbolically,
Like mucus on a little red eye,
Like cellophane, glinting on a slice
Of plain sausage under a hot nose,
It's not pity but panic they install
In the cells of the cerebellum of an idle loafer
Who preferred a visit here to Homeric
Questions . . . "How can I?!"
You cry out here. This way. Alone
The universal term "jerk" will determine
How you look to the world, the way you cry, head down
On the wet slope of a March day,
So inconsolable, yet so out of place.
Your stillborn tear
Won't amuse the dog we said before
But will slip by like life, easy and gone,
So you can say, "I too was here.
Ate my salad and downed my beer,
Expounding on the fire in Rome."

TRANSLATED BY JEAN DAY AND LAURA D. WEEKS

EVGENIYA LAVUT

Untitled

Luther sleeps, and his big head
On the pillow is round as a stone.
He dreams of places, faces, words,
Murmurs, rumors, crowds, an axe.

On the pillow, next to his head — two fists.
His round neck is damp.
His sides stir anxiously under the cloth.
In the window hangs a blue moon.

Midnight. A mouse tries first his shoe,
Then a candle stub. Christmas is past.
Enter, the devil, quietly, with a bag of nuts.
Sits down at his feet.

But Luther has fumes in his head.
He's got the shakes, the sweats. The devil
Roils in his bag, finds, crunches a nut
As if this were business as usual.

The preacher's tormented body shivers
His damp forehead is laved
By moonlight, from the sky where in anguish
A gray bird circles,

Now rising above the spire, now falling,
Now screeching, now sighing,
Like the siren on an invisible car
From which God will emerge.

Translated by Natasha Efimova and Laura D. Weeks

Ophelia (Variations on a Theme of Rimbaud)

Ophelia on white sails
Drifts with the broad current,
Sees the dance of the planets overhead
Her eyes covered with heavy lids
And duckweed in her hair.

She drifts. She hears the speech of birds.
She drifts, not spoiling the idyll,
Along the bank, and her breast is sweet.
Ophelia, alas, who needs
Your carcass, caught in snags.

When you wash up somewhere,
Full of water like a wineskin?
So little time has elapsed
Since your youthful beauty
Melted the ice of rejected hearts.

Either you are, or you no longer exist.
But the roses on your breast do not fade.
Your gaze is fixed on a swallow —
Above you, stretched taut, the kerchief of the heavens —
Which he slices to ribbons.
Roll, river. Ophelia, die.

Translated by Natasha Efimova and Laura D. Weeks

In Memory of a Certain Inhabitant of America

That two-piece suit, scarlet, green and black —
he who wears it can never outgrow elegance.
In Arizona summer, lazy day,
children go with their parents to church.
they know how to read and conceal it,
happy to be small.
Everyone wants to live a long time.
He lived long, and died one fine day
encircled by a large family, like the ending
of an old, or all-too-new novel.
There, he will still be remembered after fifteen years
(such fifteen years!) Here, he's known already.
Here, everything runs smoothly,
and spots shine on the seedy side of life
and a voice speaks, "Today is the beginning of the week,
only the beginning." To forget time,
this and this, and the lines of your hands,
with greater valence, like a three-figure IQ.

TRANSLATED BY HARRIET MOORLAND AND LAURA D. WEEKS

Anya, Anna, Annie

anya is in the last class of special studies
evening streetlights wandering like high-beams
parents anya how are things at school
today a lecture in metrology on the freedom of bones
anya closed her eyes and with her inner vision
contemplated her indistinct skeleton whispering to herself
this bone I will call anna
anna of the Beautiful Moon
anna wrote a letter to whomever

anna wrote You with a big tail on the "y"
anna always made mistakes in all the same words
anna received a thoughtful, condescending reply
Beautiful Moon will I call the bone anna
    for three days anya was not called to the board
on the staircase anya thought up three historical words
révolution rêves révélation
    the gymnasium was packed
anya grabbed the climbing rope but it was the wrong time
    evening streetlights white weightlessness
anya buried herself in her fur coat until her hands were warm
into the subway she hurried her shoulder got pinched
the train knocked thunk, thunk, and the tunnel yum-yum-yum
    annie wrote almost no one is ready
to sacrifice something for a good cause
in her youth our annie was excessively shy
but she has made great strides and is now incomprehensible
anna of the Beautiful Moon emerged from the cave
anya who are you just a junior in high school.
and the excarnation is the long worn-out
forgotten device of sketching bodies on branches

TRANSLATED BY LAURA D. WEEKS

Childish Sonnet

What's age? Eight or nine or ten.
"Grow big and strong. Don't be a lefty.
You're still so small, uncomprehending,
And every second, someone's whim

Plays the dickey with your soul."
All by itself , the sky is frightened.
And you, finely-chiseled cypress,
Palms upward grow into your role.

Crossing Centuries:

There, the grain-heads fall away;
And all with silence interwoven.
Beneath the blows of deadly boredom
I call to mind the droll sixth case,

The prepositional: Of whom? Of what?
A smell of milk mingled with blood.

Translated by Laura D. Weeks

Yehudah Galevi looked up at the sky and saw
the Maiden-Night in a robe sewn with stars,
but she, in order to make fun of the poet,
turned the robe inside out

A stray comma
Lacking a place,
The golden moon stands
Cast off from the text,
And the darkness stands all around,
As if a Negress
Had wrapped herself
In a starry cloak; but to us
It's wrong-side out,
And to a warm body — the light
Of cold, prickly type.

Suddenly — there's nothing there,
Only the wind dancing?

But Galevi saw the face
Of the menacing black maiden,
And his heart cleaved to the night,
But heavenly hosts, where are you?

Gazing into the dear night
I say, "Hold on a minute.
I can overcome my fear,
But what's there, behind that comma?"

TRANSLATED BY LAURA D. WEEKS

Untitled

When a child searches in the dictionary
For a word overheard by chance that day,
He clumsily leafs through "i," "l," "r,"
Turning back, — "Here's 'p'" . . . and freezes, as if
It weren't a list of words scanned in haste
But his own brightly colored plastic legos
He submerges in his outsized forehead
And forms a thought — the whole solar flare
Seems now a constellation, now a flower,
Now a mineral transformed in vain
Into all the words he knows,
And the world trembles under the dictionary's cover.

And it may be, when in daylight
Or in night-light, in the light of dreams
In the fire of imagination, chasing
His blood round in a circle, some vague genius
Suddenly freezes in mid-soul,
And a man with the shakes in his leg
Suddenly finds himself so far out in the Styx,
Where it's not just that he's lonely,
He's not even born, but the grownups
Catch him, almost by chance, in his shame
And it may be, at this moment, in the egg-shaped
Shining fission, chewing his pencil
God sits weeping over the letter "C."

TRANSLATED BY LAURA D. WEEKS

Untitled

Sounds, colors, smells and silhouettes
Of trees and houses only interfere with staring
into nothingness And listening to the rumbling

of time, Continuing to rub against us.
Someone's hands move, and the doors of time
Suddenly fly open — the hidden doors
From some clumsy gesture,
And we remain without a place
Among the infinite reflections
of time, and we think, "Does this signify
Our immortality, or our absence,
And, in general, who's dreaming of whom?"
But, as is only proper, this camera-flash
of time is senseless. The door slams shut.
Life begins to rustle and laugh,
A laughter with the chesty notes of sobbing.
It's useless to stare and to look around —
Only sounds, colors, smells and silhouettes
Of trees and houses.

Translated by Laura D. Weeks

Untitled

Time sways like the moon
On an invisible thread,
Like an ocean wave:
Watch it, and it crawls ponderously backwards,
Turn away, and it flies forward;
Then again —
It spreads out like a snail shell.

Unseen by anyone, it is
Lit from within with a sinister light,
It's tough there, in its commander's grip . . .
And what can we say to the One,
Who, it seems, is not subject to it,
And in what tongue?

When night slips down over the earth,
When day crawls up into the sky —
There is a pause, an emptiness, a punc-
tuation mark in which to trap time's shadow.
But a wave of fragrant dew,
Or the sprinkled flour of stars
Or an angry string of bees,
Or the faint shiver of the wind
Will distract, confuse, drown out with talk.
And you hear — owls fly to the woods,
And you see — snow falls on the city.
How tough this cloth — without seam or tear . . .
This harem without door or windows
how tightly woven. Even time
is in Your hand. Out of it
Did You not weave this inexplicable design?
I could howl for its terrifying beauty
It's the same as, turning my gaze on You,
Saying, "In what tongue?"

Translated by Laura D. Weeks

⊠⊟⊠ ALEKSANDRA PETROVA ⊠⊟⊠

Untitled

He relies on N in all coffee matters.
"Mocca," "Romano," "Turkish (with water)," "Caramel"
He begins to sound axis mundi, when her profile
cuts darkness, and becomes their two.

Third, undomesticated, darkness peeped through the magic lantern of the café.

Warming the window, he said, noiselessly, to her,
'D'you have a sulphur match? We'll have our own auto-da-fé,
and lend our colour to autumn fog.
We'll fire the crimson settlements of the Old Believers
from all they badly placed there
in furnished rooms of biased memory.
Is it wish you we roll mercury balls,
bombarding the conscience of the mulberry educator at all those look-alike
reflections?"

———————————

In the big hall, pioneers, o pioneers, raise aluminium spoons,
light lies crosswise,
from window one shaft, icon the other,
and, catechumen, I am not a laggard

———————————

Paradise of panty childhood,
ether and Eleusis of fever,
wall-shadowed — it's what you could
inherit of winter

Briar- and grain-fluff,
half-hearted avenue, baldpatch turf,

moss stretching along trunk mass,
kid stuck to the glass —

Watching rain darken prickly grave,
and a rake's sparse trace,
and, from above, unravel
a hooded face;

Concierge — mister pasha or gate keeper?
Sanitarium stuntling, milksop,
you're raised in a glass retort
to ponder the momentum of a leak

in both funnels. Watery overflow
a little retards perspective slide.
Give me, Euphoriun of flanneled childhood,
a view from the wiped window.

Our engine winged and circular,
d'you recall the blizzard singing at night,
when you look through the window
everything's beaten flat.

———————

Clutching the scroll of last days,
quicker stalk to the blaze.

Addressing the other, he didn't note the exit of N
carried away world-centre to Lebanon slope.
'Didn't again contrive discourse or spark renouncing fire.'
Darkness, summoned, entered, involved with the cafe' murk.

He called over the waiter.
Sipped what was left in the cup
and played with a fancy that the inauspicious
sisters of Chekhov drank coffee not tea.

A long time ago Uncle Vanya might have lived in Europe.

And, stepping aside for a reflection, exits cheerfully almost
to the humdrum of morning, to the heaven of Sheol.

Translated by Dennis Silk

from The Lady and the Saracen

III

1.
In the wastelands of Judea
in the marshes,
Moira sat washing her white feet.
Green slime drifted by.
Three toads sat looking on.

2.
"Slime, where are you drifting to?"
"Nowhere," it answered, "I'm thickening."
To the toads: "And you, my friends?"

3.
The singer-toad, a pea in her throat,
sang in a husky voice,
"We keep watch here in the mountains
over the chilled body of time.
It swells ever greater.
We retreat ever further.

Time — until it dies — is called hope.
So volatile
etching a smile in the fiery pollen.
But the unity's thin veneer
now shifts toward its dead twin.

People and things long-gone
cluster in the wrinkles
on its body and face.

Now it's crowded there.
The hollow 'has been'
Outgrows what will be.

Here in the earth's sonorous core
we want to reset the clock.

A sandstorm stirs up the particles,
and the lifescales are balanced.

After all, not everything is meant to be obedient.
We'll go out with a raised lantern
and in the cast-off, sunken void
we'll find the day that has just set."

4.
But Moira, heeding the desert beast
hesitated:
"Why should we seek?
Behold the crayfish and the crab —
alive, yet in a dead house.
We must do likewise.
The inanimate is our shield.
Without it, we're orphans."

5.
O, Maria, eternally meek and mild,
Look at the fading orb.
Do you see the red foam,
the flamed retreat?
Even in motion, verbs change their tenses.
Now they're in the past tense — pillars of salt.
Look at the blind, the voiceless, the naked —
Time, the vampire, sucks out their blood.

6.
Maria sat sadly,
warming her feet in her palms.
Blackness narrowed the gorge.
Choking back a damp trill,
far-off beasts fell silent.
Only Maria's feet
shone a bright ivory light.

Translated by Laura D. Weeks

Inconsistent Self-Portrait

Half-Jewish, 30, maintaining matriculation
Five-six, a credit history, a c.v.,
excerpts from an encyclopedia, fragments of a thesaurus,
three languages, to be brief,
Here are my eyes, said to be beautiful,
here is my long nose,
lips, color prune, blackberry — or lipstick,
who cares?
Here is my profile, said to be Nubian
but maybe Jewish, and maybe just Russian
that is, who the hell knows what.
here are my traits: a magpie of joy.
Here is my decisive chin,
determined to do it, by whatever means,
whatever it's worth.
Here are my shoulders, collar bones protruding,
I'd like to be compared to Natasha, but
a bird in the fist becomes
mere down and feathers.
The downward journey, said to be filled with temptations.
I contain multitudes,
old maids, women with a reputation,
Renoir's dames, and ambiguous personages,
suffragettes, faithful wives, and those benighted
souls of the pre-feminist era.
But I'm just bragging.
All the above is just a frog's pimpled skin,
a thing loved by a Jew or hick,
and that's all there is to it.
To tell the truth,
I am heaven in a wild flower
I hold infinity in the palm of my hand.
I dribble through my fingers like a grain of sand.

TRANSLATED BY RICHARD SIEBURTH AND THE AUTHOR

from The Poems for Elena Shvarts

"On a cloud I saw a child"

2.

On a cloud I saw a child
And that child said to me
I have seen many a thing
And have died a grape vine
And have grown again
And you, remember,
You complained you never fly
As you sped over the forests
and fell into the rhododendrons
In their summer bloom
All this happened somewhere
But where is the place
Where is the dream
And like an avenging angel
on the Last Day
he appeared to me
from a mirror
in a communal apartment's
dim hallway
and I asked him
to lead me
into this mirror inferno
where on Tavricheskaya
the linden trees used to rustle in unison
and where everything now
is so clear, so vacant

TRANSLATED BY RICHARD SIEBURTH AND THE AUTHOR

After Bergman

And suddenly I understand
that the taut tethering of my people
its dense infusion of kindness
& little nothings
are dearer to me
than all the Sound & Fury.
But I keep gazing, as children do, at shopwindows
& this disinterested show
is a miraculous vision of the Nativity.
I've never had such a Christmas in my life.
But, God, if that were only the point.
Moscow, unbearable, is more familiar to me
than my own body:
my silenced friends' telephone numbers,
and the scarlet buds of the future
on the predatory stems of the present,
& the addresses that no longer exist.
Go thunder: excruciating piano,
trolley, Ark, smashed to smithereens & light!
My people are only a people. But this is more
than enough. I no longer care
that they were out of step with the World,
that they were filled with themselves like a vessel,
that they were no fishers of men,
and this is stronger than all the draw
of the New Testament.

TRANSLATED BY RICHARD SIEBURTH AND THE AUTHOR

ELENA FANAILOVA

Verses for Maria S.

Marie was the wife of B, the poet.
He was a Nobel Laureate, and she
Could have spoken from the scaffold
About him. But life is full of irony:
B was confined to a mental ward,
Avidly developing the theme of the flesh,
Focusing attention on himself.
He talked about their strange relationship,
And all the mad listened — believing every scabrous word.
He took the part of Gorbunov, then Gorchakov,
And then Chaadaev. At that he disappeared,
Leaving only a vague impression.
But this semi-intelligible confession
Hardly defines a vassal's duties:
The astral marriage — beyond the bedroom walls.

Marie was given to B, the poet.
What can one do? Neither regal disdain
Nor time could shield her.
Displaying enviable speed
He flattened her with a blow to the left.
Then he wept over her and refused
To let her be buried, and I swear to God,
He kissed the bleeding wound
On her beautiful severed Gorgon's
Head — without a shield — but wouldn't you
Be terrified before the trembling lava?
And if so, wouldn't you bury yourself in glory,
Sobbing and retching in despair?
Here — this is only her mocking blood.
He got her with just one blow to the right.

Crossing Centuries:

Many lusted after Marie.
(Those who got her were small-fry.) She managed
(B. described this) to give the pitiful impression
Of being at an execution. But death
Didn't get them between the eyes, and she shrieked,
Because — she's a woman. (She was ahead of her time,
She injured her own self; she fell into a net
She herself had spun.) And what about you, o sons of England,
Standing before the executioner, didn't you shit in your pants?

Marie had a poor understanding of power
(Or, rather, of passion), with all its seductions.
Fervor, the Oedipus complex — all of this
Amounts to no more than sarcastic spasms
Generated by B., who made use of the fact
That the role of victim can also be sweet.
He studied Russian degeneration,
And was, in his own way, bound to it, like a flaneur
With nothing to do; but he who breathes in the miasma
Of his native bog can't help but sink into it.
If he'd taken idiocy into account
He might have avoided doing time.

To Maria, however much you call out, "Marie!"
However much you shriek at the arrogant Scot,
However much you yell at the horse
Until bloody froth bubbles forth,
She cannot, she will not, let go of the shafts.
What else is in her but blood?
Her dessert turned out to be vast —
Meager ends demand meager means
And meager qualities. Anyone who, like a snail,
Reaches the long-desired threshold
Will be covered in empty shells
And think he's been seeking the name of God.
There was no one to comfort Marie,
And no one to relieve the throbbing of the wound,
To calm the rebellious citizens
In time of plague
With a dash of mercury, a splash of acid.

Marie should have gone to India, with its so-so climate,
Blood and water around the same temperature.
And if passion provokes a sigh,
It's transformed at once into culture,
Religion, morality, and so forth.
In the North, a single catastrophic delta
Gets us into trouble,
Cold on the outside, fire within,
And this needs resolution, but Marie
Listened only to a simple Celtic song.
She might have been a Buddha,
But she turned to rust, typographer's ore,
A grasshopper's wing, stained glass made of mica.

Thus, in the conflict between inner fire
And a show of perfect manners
the tragedy went on. A loving couple:
Marie plus B. — not one to take half-measures
(As opposed to, say, Chateliar).
They were sure the body's merely packaging,
Shaking when venturing across the grassy square
From the building with its bars.
Who might escape this nightmare
In the garden, its chimerical statues in decay,
Each taking some fantastic pose.
Marie plus B. — in sum, metamorphosis.

So, try to muster troops,
To cross this desert of Marie's
Spread with a delicate touch,
To vanquish the treasured sands
On solid, airy bridges,
And share the hardships of the march with them,
Only to discover that some fatal sadness
Has suddenly overcome your troops.
The soldiers mark time, they rub the dry ground
With their socks. A barrel pointed at your temple

Will signal you to end the terrible campaign.
You will have reconsidered who was the main character here.
And the goal, as before, long-desired, is near,
And the brain like a grindstone casts sparks as it turns.

TRANSLATED BY LYN HEJINIAN AND LAURA D. WEEKS

from Two Journeys There and Back

How infinite are Your circles!
I am the earth beneath Your heel.
I am the grass beneath Your scythe.
I am your winged pain.

Cut me down, I arise.
Persecute me, I sing.
I am a pilgrim, wandering
Among unearthly cities
Across this Earthly hell
Following Your white tracks.

How infinite are Your circles!
Earth looks like swarthy flesh.
Surrounded on all sides, I am
laid low by bellsong.

My raw voice, scraping along ice
Shouts my grief out loud.
Like a black chalice, I drink
My unutterable sorrow.
Lord, while I still have breath left
I ask for one thing only:
Remember these bitter days
In your song.

TRANSLATED BY LAURA L. WEEKS

Yet Another Metamorphosis

In the attentive topsoil I greet
each and every seed by name, by name.
Fate wills that we should turn towards a voice,

and that we should perish from a voice.

Silence, the last link has fallen,
dropped from a bird's beak, like a gash.
Thus, at night, a window slips through the cosmos fingers
shards scattering the echoes.
Earth, I have drunk you like bitter wine,
hell will be a hangover for me.
I had hoped to live like any seed,
wandering the underground routes.
But Poor Yorick in a white kimono
shone in the night, waving a cigarette.
Shooting a movie in black-and-white
I didn't shut my eyes til dawn,
observing the swarthy face
and the white nervous movements.
They tell me: He was your father.
He was your Father; he begs to be avenged.
I have drunk you like bitter wine
go away, no more burnt offerings!
Just to love You, and to remember this:
curses in this world call out the ghosts
Just to love You to forget myself:
to become a skull, a gravedigger, a desert.
You are God-the-Father, who has forgotten his progeny.
You are Abraham, bending over his son.

Silence. Now it's quiet. Quiet, now.
Ashes, ashes fall on your shoulders.
Don't talk. Be still. Every sign
is terrible, even the air of human speech.

Translated by Laura L. Weeks

The New Generation in Russian Poetry

Untitled

If your kisses are so bored
then blow me one baby
I'll whisper sweet somethings in their ears
and watch as they pucker up
and run away.
That's right baby
smile and kiss me again
now that your boredom
has pulled itself together
and straightened up.

TRANSLATED BY KRISTIN PREVALLET AND LAURA D. WEEKS

Untitled

Me and the girls we ski on trails
that will not end
smoke in toilet stalls
and with our husky voices
laugh at our
physics instructor Savelev
who is young but hides
it behind a beard
and who does he think
he is knowing
I believe in God
just in time
the bell rings

TRANSLATED BY KRISTIN PREVALLET AND LAURA D. WEEKS

Untitled

The old city is so bloody cold
and white — it must be spring as usual.
Madame Esperaille sips tea and yawns
while a metronome drops ticks
on her mangy sweater.
The windowsills are all in bloom
and everyone is growing the same rose.
Petals drop into wet ledges
and here you are
slumped in your stinking vodka
home from a faraway land called "the army"
but not feeling at home.
I couldn't care less
I'm leaving tomorrow.

Someday everything in this world
will make sense, not to us
but we'll be ok.
Do you remember
how we slept
through the Brezhnev
years of stagnation
our shoes were soaked with rain water
yet on our hammock
we slept soundly
high above the ground?

Ok I'll stay, my darling, I'll stay
I won't block your passes any more.
You're my line-driver, my quarterback, my pro
and you're holding my heart.
I'll stay, my darling, I'll stay.
We'll go to the movies with Madame Esperaille
The incomparable Liza is starring in Cabaret.
Things can't be so bad. I'll stay.

TRANSLATED BY KRISTIN PREVALLET AND LAURA D. WEEKS

Untitled

Memory
My Chinese box
What are you hiding?
What will you serve me for breakfast?
In that parallel world
flocks swirl and skitter away.
New ones take their place
In the black, bottomless drawers.

TRANSLATED BY LAURA D. WEEKS

Untitled

A stone in a column's base knows nothing about the Greeks or about the very column itself, and if you say God is questionable, that's for you alone. Only a river remembers in its sleep, and everything that remains with you afterwards becomes a reprieve like a verdict thrown on the fire. You'll throw it out, and opening the door, you'll forget that there, in yesterday's room, is only darkness.

If memory returns in sleep, the second column over from the entrance will continue on its way along a burning wall, washing its black marble in the salt of a sandy lake that has taught you not to wade barefoot in the water, but to laugh — tossing up a pair of stone boots together with the wooden echo of a carelessly thrown open bridge.

TRANSLATED BY MICHELLE MURPHY AND AUTHOR

Untitled

And to go to a Codfishing village, to sit near a table-lamp, where a frying hot summer is assembling a fountain of ostrich feathers while keeping an eye on the road.

A dream is spilling over like water in the yard, and soon it will enter the little white hut as firm ripe cherries. Ask the old man sitting on the doorstep, and you ll be taken to the shore and shown a place ready for salt pillars. Here each has his own business, and they will propose that you do the same come every Sunday to a deep underwater cave and wait for Dante near the entrance to Hades. And whether you wait up for him or not, they will pity you and release you, but forget your name and go ask for rain from a Tartar Khan who spread his camp near the village. And when you go back, narrow brooks will stop you, which are rushing towards evening's milk and a clay cold jug's narrow throat. All roads lead to this narrow mouth along a way leading through blue wormwood to a Codfishing village with its little reflective life.

TRANSLATED BY MICHELLE MURPHY AND AUTHOR

Untitled

You know you shouldn't touch butterflies by their wings, you know that a rain gutter (where your dear worm lives) can be seen from this window. You know many things, and you don t like it when you're asked bizarre questions about yesterday's weather or a broken umbrella.

And just earlier on the street, you noticed a lone eye staring from a wall past you, and since that time you ve stopped noticing what settles in your room.

TRANSLATED BY MICHELLE MURPHY AND AUTHOR

Untitled

Do you remember how rain dropped on your tree and the chilled blue drops died, choking in dark puddles near the benches. And only an astonished tram stood at the next-to-last station and decided not to enter this town over water and roofs, where you no longer were, where you remained under a different name, and I can't find out that name or you, even if I cover the entire town from the water-tower to the flooded bridge. But you will sit in a dry room and think not about this, but about the transparent, prickly, laughing eyes and faces, gathering the sun and dust of this town in your cupped hands, the smiles and clean cobwebs of hair through a transparent rain coat. And when she comes out, you will see her through rain stretched along the walls and the long March week.

And you ll return, settle in, begging, speaking through the viscous air of a morning dream which leads you home. And the stone framework of a house in the big stupid city will not save you from her cautious answer within the stone well of a water tower frozen in snow.

TRANSLATED BY MICHELLE MURPHY AND AUTHOR

WAITING

```
w       ceilingceilingceilingceilingceilingceilingceiling        s
wa      ceilingceilingceilingceilingceilingceilingceili         ls
wal     ceilingceilingceilingceilingceilingceilingcei          lls
wall    ceilingceilingceilingceilingceilingceilingc           alls
walls                                                         walls

walls   ALL EVENING YOU FLY AROUND THE RO-                     walls
walls   om, clearly the floor is heavy today                   walls
walls   here comes a paper snake flying by                     walls
walls   with painted eyes, and your memor-                     walls
walls   y's tied up in knots                                   walls
walls                                                           walls

walls   YOU'RE TETHERED          BETWEEN FLOOR                  walls
walls   and ceiling, you cir-    cle the room:                  walls
walls   wall, window and be-     yond the window h              walls
walls   ouses ranged like i      vory dominoes....              walls
walls   You open the fr          ame, read in the               walls
walls   fissured traces of r     ain:  nothing,                 walls
walls   except wait              ing, nothing el                walls
walls   se to be read there.     Once more papery               walls
walls   rustle of flight         past the mirror,               walls
walls   books, doors, win        dows...Silent                  walls
walls                                                           walls

walls   the telephone's cocoon,  like an unborn                 walls
walls   butterfly, the doorbell sleeps                          walls
walls   WALL  —  WALL  —  FLOOR  —  CEILING                     walls
walls   WALL  —  WALL  —  FLOOR  —  CEILING                     walls
walls   WALL  —  WALL  —  FLOOR  —  CEILING                     walls
walls   WALL  —  WALL  —  FLOOR  —  CEILING                     walls

wall    floorfloorfloorfloorfloorfloorfloorfloorflo           alls
wal     floorfloorfloorfloorfloorfloorfloorfloorfloor          lls
wa      floorfloorfloorfloorfloorfloorfloorfloorfl             ls
w       floorfloorfloorfloorfloorfloorfloorfloorfloo            s
```

TRANSLATED BY LAURA D. WEEKS

Portrait

```
***********************************************************
*                                                         *
*                                                         *
                        If
                    not for the
                     artists
                     of the
                    Renaissence
                  we would still
                think that the liver
                     is a moon
                        and
                     love is
                an arrow in a heart
              The main thing in a woman is
              a glass slipper; a ball gown
             strewn with pearls.  It softens
           death from love's fever, introducing
              into it the equilibrium of a
                    ball game.
*                                                         *
*                                                         *
***********************************************************
           But if you're      going to put
          us back into              a frame
           Better kill        us outright.
```

TRANSLATED BY LAURA D. WEEKS

BEYOND THE RING ROAD

THOMAS EPSTEIN

THE MIRACLE(S) OF RUSSIAN POETRY

LIKE POETS EVERYWHERE, Russian poets of the second half of the twentieth century have had to forge a language to express the bewildering diversity of its experience. What has given this diversity and this bewilderment its particular richness are the daunting facts of twentieth century Russian history. (And of course this is true of not only the Russian experience: all poets, all people, participate in history — but when history barrels off the tracks, continuity is lost and culture must, apparently, reinvent itself.) Russia, not-incidentally, entered the twentieth century in the midst of a great poetic revival, led by the Symbolists Bruisov, Bal'mont, Ivanov and Merezhkovsky; soon they were to be joined by Bely and Blok, and somewhat later by a further flowering, producing the pellucid talents of the Acmeists Akhmatova and Mandelstam, and the ultra-Modernist revolutionary experiments of the Futurists Mayakovsky, Pasternak, and Khlebnikov. (Interestingly, two of the most talented poets of this two-generation movement, Tsvetaeva and Khodasevich, fit neatly into none of the just-outlined categories.) The Symbolists however, and Bely and Blok in particular, sensed a coming catastrophe amidst the splendor of this poetic renaissance; and of course it did come, in the form of World War I and the ravages wrought by the Bolshevik revolution. Not only was the organic development of Russian culture short-circuited, but the aristocratic element — both spiritual and material — was suppressed. With it, the exalted understanding of culture and its role, so cherished by all the poets of this so-called Russian Silver Age, was reduced to a primitive caricature: culture was to serve as but an ideological bulwark to the plans of the Soviet Communist Party. Not surprisingly, lyric poetry itself was subjected to "demotion" by Soviet aesthetics, replaced by the cult of an anti-subjective, ideologically overdetermined brand of prose, Socialist Realism. Those who served the new State, particularly after 1932, not only betrayed the essence of poetry as a free act of the human spirit but erected a cultural bureaucracy that, in its very denial of the spiritual, betrayed the idea of culture itself. It was an appalling spectacle that Russians even now have not fully come to terms with.

In the 1930s and 1940s poets died by the hundreds, citizens by the millions. Yet in spite of this unparalleled barbarism, the human spirit, the Russian spirit, could not be snuffed out — perhaps particularly because of the rich poetic and artistic traditions on which future generations could rely. The Gulag could not kill it — indeed the drama of total dehumanization only served to reaffirm the values of spirit and moral autonomy among those who managed to survive. In prisons and in battle, under repression and blockade, then through another wave of repression and thaw, repression and stagnation, Russians *remembered* — and they especially remembered their poets, as their poets remembered them. Here and there, in Moscow and Leningrad, in Isk and Saratov, Tomsk and Ekaterinburg, from the 1950s into the late 1980s, small groups of them kept the flower of memory alive: indeed, as this anthology attests, they not only kept it alive but added their own fuel, taking the Silver Age and other traditions on new and productive paths. They did so without support, social or material (a fact that should not be forgotten when comparing the homogenized, tenure driven poetry of the American creative writing program with the Russian poets considered here*): indeed they worked in the face — and behind the back — of hostile authorities and an increasingly uncomprehending public. Although culturally impoverished in comparison with their exceedingly cultured Silver Age predecessors, the post World War II generation of Russian poets could look upon itself-at least in part-as lucky, even blessed: few of their number knew the hunger and starvation of the 1920s and 1940s; fewer still suffered the horrible deaths of a Mandelstam, Tsvetaeva, or Harms — or the humiliations of an Akhmatova.[†] Their fate, when it was happy, was to lead socially invisible lives, devoted to poetry, to reading (literature has always been better than life in Russia) to spirituality and vodka. Some of them followed — or challenged — Silver Age models, others looked to Europe and America for inspiration. In large measure they wrote for each other, creating homemade, hand-distributed literary magazines, collected 'forbidden' books, turned their apartments into art galleries and literary salons. Instead of living in the official world of Soviet materialistic culture, they lived at its fringes or beyond it, between worlds, eras, voices. And when, at last, the Soviet system collapsed under the weight of its own essential emptiness, they found themselves hailed by many as the most authentic voices of post-World War II Russian poetry.[‡]

---

* The Soviet academic system did produce its own version of the writer's workshop, and with a vengeance; but very few of the poets in this anthology (and all of them of the younger generation) could be considered its products.

† Brodsky is an exception here, as he is in many ways. It should be remembered, however, that Brodsky was born in 1940 and is thus technically not part of the post-War generation.

‡ There are many signs of this, the most recent being the publication of *Samizdat veka* ("Samizdat of the Century"). This huge tome, edited by the leading avantgardist Genrikh Sapgir, presents an alternative canon, in conscious opposition (down to the book's cover) to Evgeny Evtushenko's

Crossing Centuries:

In the few pages allotted to me here I cannot aspire to anything approaching a complete overview of the poets and poetries I have been charged with editing, not to speak of trying to contextualize them within the overall plan of this anthology or as they relate to post-World War II Russian and Soviet-Russian poetry in general. Nevertheless, I will try here to indicate several general lines of development I consider important and leave it to the reader of this book to draw the broader conclusions.

For nearly three hundred years, ever since the founding of Saint Petersburg in 1703, Moscow and Saint Petersburg have been cast as antagonists: the new capital as masculine, aristocratic, rational, and European, the old one, Moscow, as feminine, mercantile, irrational, and Byzantine or even Asiatic. But the "rationalism" of Petersburg has always been suspect, shadowed by madness and mirrors; and the sheer size of Moscow, its labyrinthine circularity, has allowed it to accommodate all and every form of Soviet-Russian and Russian culture. Thus, Moscow and Petersburg have served — and continue to serve — not so much as real but mythological poles, imaginary East and West, between which all Russia's people mentally — and thus for free! — travel, trying to make sense of the tragically contradictory nature of Russian society.* Nevertheless, the twentieth century has seen the material fate of the two cities continue to move in opposite directions: entering it as one of Europe's great imperial capitals, Saint Petersburg-Leningrad suffered a series of catastrophes that has left it, at century's end, as a dirty, suffering, "provincial" center whose grandeur is in large measure a function of its awesome ghostliness. Moscow, by contrast, having shed the atmosphere of fear that reigned during the Soviet years, has become a bustling, aggressive, cosmopolitan capital where money talks and image is power. Yet Leningrad-St. Petersburg, along with its many calamities, was spared of at least one thing that plagues its bigger sister: the unbearable ideological weight — the Kremlin being the literal geographical center of the city — and vulgar careerism that mark modern Moscow life. While Moscow, brash and extroverted, brought us both the socially-engaged poetry of Evtushenko and company, and the perfectly *au courant* phenomena of *Sotsart* and Soviet Conceptualism[†],

---

1996, equally massive anthology of twentieth century Russian poetry, entitled *Strophy veka* ("Stanzas of the Century").
*The advent of the internet has only strengthened this tendency toward "virtualizing" the Moscow-Petersburg opposition. Dmitry Kuzmin, poet and editor of the magazine *Vavylon* (its internet site is www.vavylon.ru), has a made a point of crossing all "boundaries," geographic, sexual, mythic and national.
†The former was an attempt to bring a Pop Art sensibility to Soviet culture; the latter a brilliant but no less derivative movement in the visual arts and poetry that originated in the West in the 1960s.

Leningrad-St. Petersburg turned inward, introverted and brooding: in content its poetry has been marked by the lyrical and spiritual, in form by an engagement with the Silver Age and other, sometimes foreign, models.[*]

In this Soviet underground a poet like Sergei Stratanovsky was able, in the privacy of his own imagination, to combine the everyday and transcendental-religious in a way that might qualify him as the first Petersburg Beat poet; in Yelena Shvarts, perhaps the most talented poet of her generation, we witness the search for the divine-sublime amidst the convulsing ruins of her native land; in Victor Krivulin a voice that seeks the meeting point of the everyday and the other-worldly; in Arkady Dragomoschenko, whose intense engagement with American poetry has brought him to the attention of an international audience, we can perhaps discern Russia's first Language Poet (a trend that has proven productive: witness his younger friend, the highly talented Aleksandr Skidan). The Petersburg poets who are currently in their thirties and forties range in many directions; from Sergei Zavyalov's neo-modernist encounter with the Classical heritage to Svetlana Ivanova's simpler but mystico-spiritual honesty; from Valery Shubinsky's highly formal engagement with the Russian Silver Age tradition to Aleksandra Petrova's no less formal but more personal voice; from the lyrical grace of Kononov and Purin to Golynko-Volfson's unabashedly post-Modern joy in language games.[†]

Moscow, as this anthology attests, is the homeland — and heartland — of Conceptualism. But it is also home to the highly refined, religious-inspired lyrics of Olga Sedakova; to the sizzling metamorphical energies of Alexei Parshchikov, Aleksandr Eremenko, and Ilya Kutik (only Parshchikov is a Moscow native); to the quiet assurance of Mikhail Alzenberg; to the dark brilliance of Ivan Zhdanov; and to a pleiade of younger poets who write in every possible mode.[‡] Indeed to speak of Moscow is to speak of a plethora (and at times chaos) of poetries: from the most radically post-modern to tradition-bound lyric; from the profane to the sacred; international and hermetic; stridently ideological and equally stridently mystical: a modern melting pot.

Outside the capitals lies a vast, impoverished land known as the Russian provinces. For the poets of these regions, the choice has often been stark:

---

[*] This can also be seen in the generation that proceeds the eldest one represented here: I have in mind the Leningrad poets Brodsky, Sosnora, and Kushner.
[†] I make no pretense here to offering anything like a full catalogue of Petersburg poetries: just a sampling of some of its tastier victuals.
[‡] The division of labor required by this anthology has excluded me from working with many poets whose work I value highly — let me here just mention Aristov, Vodennikov, Kondakova, Martynova, Rubinstein, Kekova, Volchek, and Fanailova.

Crossing Centuries:

either make their mark on the capital or suffer the fate of obscurity. Nevertheless, cities like Samara (Ulanov, Ermoshina, Kekova), Chelyabinsk (Kalpidy) and Sverdlovsk (Mesyats, Kurytsyn, Tkhorzhevskaya), to name but a few, have produced vital poetic communities and poets of real worth. Indeed some of these "provincial poets" have demonstrated more poetic freedom than their capital-bound counterparts, some of whom can be said to suffer from the provincialism of the capital (that is, the illusion of being at the center of "everything that matters"). Poets like Ulanov, Zhdanov, Abdullaev, Kalpidy, and Mesyats have used their experience in the capital as a pole, not of imitation, but tension. Of equal significance, one can see in them the sheer diversity of Russian poetry and therefore the limitations of the very rubric "provincial." This matter of rubrics, of multicultural groups, is one that has bedeviled this project since its inception: have we simply forced our model of poetic 'production' on a foreign culture or brought to light unacknowledged but authentic realities? Moreover, are poets (are people) Muscovites, Petersburgers, Provincials, women, men, left-handers, first, last and always (are they bodies and nothing more?); or is there something else, something untidy and perhaps unsayable, some *autonomy of the imagination* that lies beyond all determinism and is the foundation of all our corporeal schemes? In a word: is poetry, is culture, merely a deterministic reflection of social forces or an image of our ability to be free, creative beings? And is it not this freedom that makes authentic *communication* possible? Does poetry not prove it with an alchemical geometry that violates the obvious arithmetic of the individual social body? How else to explain why some of us live for poetry, for mere words? How else to explain why some of us live? Perhaps some answers to these cursed questions are lurking in the pages of this book.

Untitled

This — the steppe, and the dry expanse, like an onion dry,
its shell cascading down upon the pasture of heat.
This — intestines of depot, a glimpse of a curtain drawn high,
anorexic thinness of kids — only faces and ribs
bridged by pearly-grey dirt.
Hens in barns — like the cackling pillows.
This — the sun-driven halo
of sprouting, pulsating, breathless,
maddened meters of earth. Where the dragonflies battle blizzards,
and the old women nestle inside — reminiscent of lizards.
Nothing sadder than these brick factory outskirts,
or the desolate sight of the limestone suburbs.
How do people exist here? how? how do they survive?
especially after their dinners? smell of stew? this half- life —
how does it go on? and why don't they die
from the breeze, from humidity, or the thought of the ocean —
they just wipe off their sweat, they just sigh . . .
This is simply a gaze of detachment. Of those that pass.
It's a view from without — impartial and passive.
Thus the eye doesn't soak in the tender,
the invisible forces, since life dissipates, squanders
into itself . . . Nevertheless,
this — the steppe, the burning skin of the dry expanse,
suntanned, greasy hands that the children exhale
of mechanics, of train operators — sinewy, lithe,
this — through dwarfy and dusty leafage rustling mice,
this is all that has thirstied itself to the limit —
from a town whose name makes one's teeth screech — a convict
who will choke on the brook. He will lick out its bed.
He will drink for three days, so it won't be as sad
to die in these parts that hallucinate storms as a price
paid to fill mouth's hollow — in order to rise, to rise.

TRANSLATED BY YANA DJIN

Crossing Centuries:

Untitled

Speak looser, please, speak freer,
by feel, by heart, unleash,
a tramway track steers
like a spinal cord of a fish,

a tramway track, no fears,
the soul takes off, un-wept,
un-sung, un-whined, un-teared,
at heart, just to the left,

let go, unwind your ear,
the streets let go, unchains
in yellows, lean and hear
the flow of words through veins,

in yellows the street lets loose,
pulsates cathedral-shaft,
between us plies the news,
like draught,

a trembling branch, a breath
rekindles all the fire,
now, are you still afraid of death . . .
be freer, life . . .

Translated by Yana Djin

Untitled

I will take that winter's illuminated square
(like a neon splinter of a Christmas tree at night)
A squander that exceeds our salaries, leaves us bare,
I will take the humble dailiness by the flickering light
of a lamp. (A needle nestled in the crack had gathered dust)
What's more longevious than our sense of must?
So, rejoice in your grief, by God, you feel no lack.

Closer, closer to that window I will shift my eyes,
to that window, whose cross
throws a shadow onto a neighboring house. To loss,
or oblivion this yellow light will never be rendered.
I will see the oval of your face and a tender,
slightly crazy curve of your hand:
". . . have to wake up so early tomorrow,
O, this is the end, the end . . ."

Drunken screams from the street,
or the soldiers's taurpalin screech in a morning hurry,
I'll pick up at the corner — dark and blurry,
in a corner that resembles a grave, or a ditch.
I will take the dawn — leftover from yesterday's brew and pale,
in the kitchen — then, it's off to work, it is time . . .
we'll sleep it off on a Saturday, love of mine . . .
But the Saturdays never come. They fail.

And when we are covered by the polar night,
covered by its officer's topcoat,
when the snowflakes perform in the circles of light,
and when our daughter wakes, fearing for our sakes,
remember? it's a holy, it's a fiery labor — being an infant.
suddenly, that instant, to redeem the fall,
holidays will come to bend over her bed
and save everything. Save it all.

TRANSLATED BY YANA DIJN

Untitled

Getting dark. Getting black. And the river is mad as a hatter.
Tears its clutches away. Its shores stutter.
Autumn rips at one's throat. Hands over the face.
The cloakroom is empty. Not a soul. Not a trace.

Crossing Centuries:

Now it's dark. The platform is getting wet.
Ashes from garbage-cans — short-lived tornadoes — litter.
Late night cashier gives out tokens of wit.
This place dissolves and becomes a street.

Searching about on a different end of the earth,
in the abyss of my coat — like boredom wide — I fumble for cents.
This land wasn't made for my hide, it just doesn't fit.
Hell, what's the difference, I would easily say in heat.

A bit cleaner, perhaps. But the same old tide.
Same hysterics of trains. After all, I'm not blind.
If to be without you — then I'd rather not be at all.
Life — is the fall of philosophy. Of any. Of all.

Either an old man is dozing. His dried out body leans.
Parents torture a child with their violins.
Or else a sound was heard — known before.
A door was slammed shut. And I was no more.

TRANSLATED BY YANA DJIN

Untitled

What's there behind this dread . . .
One can look at the wall . . .
Sounds like they're moving a bed . . .
Life's broken heartbeat — that's all.

Frightful to think that there
Is the same. Not a thing otherwise.
Someone is following someone.
Following someone, cries . . .

Where did the hat disappear
Out of this coffin-like commode . . .
That's where it was. It was here . . .
But it no longer is. No more.

TRANSLATED BY YANA DJIN

Untitled

Give me a word, meaningless, tender,
fresh like branch with a crack,
a bundle of tree vessels, inevitable,
is trembling in the homeless air.
Between the two it is more fearful
to be the last one who feels attached,
it's the sheer horror of the branch,
whose force is still pulsating in dark speech.

TRANSLATED BY ANDREY GRITSMAN

Cimmerian Letters

1

Greetings, Vardgesovich,
My hand is shaking as I write this:
I drank a great deal
yesterday
As the barbarians stormed her city.
I heard some escaped,
but I doubt she's among them;
after all, she's very fond of death
and her city.

2

Vardgesovich, my friend,
I'm sure you'll agree that it's pointless
to write about what has already passed,
but also agree
that it sometimes happens
the past does not depart
and the future does not arrive.
My friend, I am not speaking of today.

3

You know, Vardgesovich,
I do have a refuge — in the crowd.
Only there can I conceal
my intellect and the beauty of my body,
only there does my uniqueness dissolve,
only in the crowd can I distinguish
crazed Cretan-Mycenean women
from the clever ones of the Inca tribe.

Don't ask me to be brief
and don't get angry:
I've been inhaling the marijuana-laden air
of eternally-living women.

4

All would be well, my friend, Vardgesovich,
if trifles from our past
did not recur in our new life.
I'll give you an example: love,
With which I'm sure you'll agree, drawing your Egyptian woman . . .
But you remain silent . . .

5

The gulls here are so serious, Vardgesovich,
I haven't even heard them laugh,
I haven't had a drink of the electrifying juice
of grapes or women,
but I saw you near Neapolis of Scythia,
was it a dream?
I didn't dare approach: you were arguing with Giorgione,
and she was laughing so hard at the two of you
that I suddenly wanted her.

6

Vardgesovich, my friend, why
do you ask what's she's like?
Is it not enough that I love her?
Take a look at yourself, at me in your self-portrait
and draw the cooling day, with its sky full of birds . . .
Oh yes! she has very thin legs.

7

If you only knew, Vardgesovich, how hot it is here.
Fortunately, there's plenty of water
and shade.
The fish in the sea behave strangely:
overly trusting one moment, overly cautious the next.
I've grown to like them.
That
for me
holds a mystery.
It holds me.
The coffee they brew here is good,
and it's quite interesting to make
love at noon.
I almost forgot:
the most beautiful woman
on this island
is my wife . . .
And finally the island is teeming with Hetaeras, which
is tolerable,
but there isn't a single Pythia.

8

I'd like to see you, Vardgesovich,
but the capital is so sober and so
permeated with lust
that I think I'll stay here till winter.
Please explain it to my family — they open up to you.
It's a well-known truth: not to love is a sin.
A crime.

9

My friend, I must distress you:
The Saligir has grown so shallow over the last century
that it seems to have died.

It's painful to outlive friends.
And even more painful to outlive oneself.
Hold on a bit longer.
I'll try to do the same.
This way we'll be of enormous help to each other. . .
And yes, she also has wild hands;
it wouldn't hurt if she wore less make-up
and either died or was enlivened
by at least one-fourth.
Yes, Vardgesovich, I'm spoiled,
not by someone else, but by myself,
you must agree: it's very pleasant.

TRANSLATED BY NATASHA EFIMOVA AND THOMAS EPSTEIN

Crossing Centuries:

Area B*

Area B. Departures. Reunions. The revenants
appearing from the stardust.
Sinful faces of semitic beauties
reflected on the screens of the past.

It's usually cloudy this time of year.
The skies are full of myths,
which reappear
as we are born twice,

emerging from the lost cities,
from letters, from the heavenly mist,
condensed somewhere in close proximity
to the East.

We are waiting here, in Area B,
"Shadows in Paradise,"
covered by time's patina.
Where time becomes space,
and we grow extinct,

as memories break through the sound barrier
and then fade, like, remember,
our invincible fighter planes
above the May Day parade,

disappearing like the dreams of youth,
fleeting, untouchable.
We are the now "Eternal Jews,"
gliding along the Long Island Expressway
like Flying Dutchmen.

---

*Area B: international arrival area at the JFK Airport in New York City.

staring at the lights streaming
in every direction.
closing the circle.
New York at night is a forest fire,
a fire of resurrections.

And we are closing our circle too,
actors leaving the stage,
leaving a fallen foliage of letters,
turning yellow page by page.

TRANSLATED BY THE AUTHOR

Going Back

In this town words are worthless, all
objects having been named.
The river's backward flow is habitual,
its light a gaseous glow.

Lime-soaked, graffitied alleyways, driveway
stench. The nameless
shroud of inexhaustible happiness,
where we are joined.

Life's pendulum, bisection of destiny,
the mirror's beyond.
And so we're forever fated to love
the illusory,

the unattainable, phantomlike revenant,
the wonderful, dopey ache, irrevocable
by the tram tracks, by the station's stands,
where repeatedly
I exit myself and hang from the train window gargoyle-like,
and drink to the rumble of the right-of-way, to Glier's theme.[*]

---

[*] Reinhold Glier, Russian composer whose theme announces the departure of the daily midnight train from St. Petersburg to Moscow.

This place is such that if you gulp
the converging air
it will ooze all of your life from your soul
through your speech.

TRANSLATED BY ALEX CIGALE

Provincial Notes

It is that time
when your breath is visible.
Time, when the evening
glimmer, unnoticeably
slips in the dark crevices
of the platform with the clock
stopped at half past five,
when the past is audible —
go for a walk and imbibe.

There, the gestalt of the passengers
is not according to Jung or Freud,
a hybrid of Perov's and Bosch's realism,
on the embers of ice mixed with urine,
and the station's palisade
cuts the landscape in half.

We walk on the rails
toward the black box of the post office
and mail out letters
to the silhouettes on dream analysis.

Wild dogs by the bottomless puddle
tear apart the deathless kitty,
our stroll becomes a theater,
the way of the cross to the kiosk.
Departure's yearning is endless.
It's a bit cold. Resonant.

The reflection of Moscow beyond the forest
floats toward morning away from us.

TRANSLATED BY ALEX CIGALE

from Like You

3

When we at last become our name
and in the leaves rustling
we splash above the damp roofs,
will you recognize us?
Outlasting everything,
will you, kindred stairway,
tin of dawn courtyards,
stone walls, rough and living,
will you understand that we're here?
Tender bog and silent wave, will you,
concealed from the darkness,
will you hear our breathing, our breathlessness,
will you recognize the true us?

TRANSLATED BY THOMAS EPSTEIN

Untitled

Who will write these letters on the outside?
Who will read them, in the dark?
Winter no longer hears a thing,
Soon even the sky will have thawed.

Gold summer leaves already
Glitter bluish-gold. Before
My eyes you're already a dead sister —
A butterfly — before dawn.

And you remain like shadow
At the bottom, a blood-bearing sea-weed
Like he who flew a lifeless ladder
Rushing about like dust frost-covered.

Who will blow away mortal anguish
One mortal to another,
Melting like a cloud on a black heart
Of yesterday's friend.

TRANSLATED BY THOMAS EPSTEIN

⊠ SHAMSHAD ABDULLAEV ⊠

A Taste for the Coast

One season: and we arrive here
too late, having come from south to north,
on the way back. Past the window lattice
smoke sputters and the stone house
catches fire, like a pale yellow mirage in a fruitful field
honored
on special days by the calm. From the outer wall
amidst marketplace junk, there's less coal than eyes
winding up walls from the Sunday crowd
where ears of harmsir* grow amidst the yellow.
It was not the river that flowed,
but the things reflected in it that rippled in cadence,
and clocks and clouds took off upstream, as if
you were heading for the wide water
amidst whirling park wasps and women, when
the bilious awn bowed before the bazaar fire pit, and
to your father's unclean shadow. The picture
pelted backwards, into the thick
of the quiet emulsion. Wind and waves.

TRANSLATED BY DARLENE REDDAWAY

Week's End

Bridge, horizon, or wall in the distance — it's not important.
We, thank God,
are banished from the city — if only for a time; a serious step.
But as before, we're so helpless
we can't worship nature, so instead we worship
the Personlessness in which we abide

---

*a kind of grain

this entire waning day. And neither by prayer, nor frenzied
naiveté, nor fleeting artlessness
can anyone be saved
who boasts of too useless an anonymity,
having chosen impassable roads. We survey the world,
for now unfamiliar — and because of this we seem to see
nothing at all (or has the thing seen
deprived us of our sight?). The glade,
the reservoir, the pellet, the mulberry, and the wagon,
overswept with weeds, and suddenly, —
God knows from where she came — a churchgoer
who adjures us: "Silence."
And right away: a click of the Spidola,*
where, a moment ago, were muttering voices,
women and men in various languages,
making it seem we had an archetypal
audio map of the world, — a sign offered
to the Sunday silence. We turned the noise off.
A lone breeze rustled an old piece of straw
and vanished in the colorless air. Nettles
swayed below and lay down — under them
a small oval of earth was exposed, like a wound,
and in an instant it was hidden again and overgrown by the grass:
windlessness, no sound. I held my breath.
You touched, as per a script, my breast
with your palm. Then, like inevitability,
a girl walked along the low hill (limping!)
and froze at the end of the glade, as if the silence
had already foretold the childish figure on this spot
or had sent her ahead to meet us.

How can all this be saved? For whom are you waiting?

Translated by Darlene Reddaway

---

*A brand name Lithuanian radio manufactured in the 1960s.

A Propos of a Greek Photograph

Sea, insect, horse. To gaze,
torturing the eyes. Flies
were minted along the center — snuffed
air. Stone,
a small mainspring, worm under hand —
untouched earthly trifle. He
fell asleep in Belaqua's pose; neither alive
nor dead. A tear,
as if a needle, catches the elusive swelling of lips
on a scorched face. Without a cry
he opened his eyes — or rather, they themselves,
for his lack of concern, surfaced from his lids. An unseeable essence
stared through the millennium
at the road sign. In the end,
not stirring, he licks drops from his lips
and feels the aftertaste of melancholy —
in God's right hand, in a dead tavern, in someone else's bed.

TRANSLATED BY DARLENE REDDAWAY

Week's End, Film

Landscape: like a gift. The spirit streams
past domestic twilight (Dreyer
forged whiteness above the northerly mold —
this take is for redemption, the Irish
monk said and plunged into the water
where the mud sloped downward and at foggy midday the depth steamed
above a distant drowning victim). So flows
the Comforter.
Livestock eat something like communion wafers
but the sun drives dogs and gray window panes out of
their mind in the neighboring yard. Friends, hands dancing in a summer café.
Only
the concrete has a name. The river, rising, endures

the phosphorescence of workers' quadrants; nowhere.
And behind the house dust careens
in a granular prism: the local
dead end will scarcely dry out. We go still further
talking under our breath or
humming "The Salsbury." Not chaos,
but controlled chaos, like a river whose current
raises the dead in vain:
fish, suicides. The ancient ray
streams from one street into another. Long
shadows descended into the cool room from southern
roofs: opposite. A moment
consists of a thousand dark leeches,
its facet work lengthens.
Sunday dust is all in our eyes.

TRANSLATED BY DARLENE REDDAWAY

Week's End: Walk with a Friend

So they walked, out onto the hilly vista — so broad that
the worn path became more visible, while the frayed curve
of the fence with its pungent-green, mossy covering
and the dirty gust of wind, arising from the dead end
to overtake us, as it always does, from behind,
worked together, deafening the epic decor, like Paris,
as first seen through the eyes of Rousseau
in all its fat, cackling lackluster.
Compressed by creeping dust and shaggy sprouts of
shrubs
the cheap expanse is exactly here.
We slow our step, infected by the silence. Everywhere
It breathes. A Something.
A comforting duration, a blazing sun, beetles
shift heavily like sullen pilgrims on the stubble
to expose — each time suddenly — while bursting
into flight, their pale, very pale-rose wings.

You think we'll be saved this way,
constantly holding our own, like "them." I'm stuffed
to the gills with the feigned ordinariness of summer's
expanse.
We lie, having spread our arms on the trampled field —
two crosses
from a bird's eye view; I grope a young reed,
clutching at evasive fragility with my nail; and you
read about how Rimbaud died (is dying):
words, prompted by pain, — "*allah karim*"
but the angel is already up for grabs (every
Sunday.)

TRANSLATED BY DARLENE REDDAWAY

SHAMSHAD ABDULLAEV

ATMOSPHERE AND STYLE

Y OUR WORK IS MUCH RICHER than reflections on it. This is the kind of wealth that affirms: the poet is only briefly aware of his being let loose into the world. This, it would seem, is the illusion against which the claims of poetry are shattered — but not only in that brief instant when a new person is created in you. You gather matter into a tight center, giving it a name appropriate in and for that moment. The weakness and ambitions of the contemporary Russian lyric are in large measure a result of its submission to extraneous theoretical temptations: to step back, and then from another distance to step back again, the text forming a compact line of rapid evasions. This is the shamanic way: being not with the object but casting a spell over it from a distance. It thus becomes easy to get caught up in the letter and conventions of dead laws, which demand illusory judgement and even history; and you turn up in a strange environment, unconnected to you — the usual case. The author fears but one thing: to approach the indubitable reality of passing states of being, for there is nothing more unbearable than to have to limit the obviousness of the empty flux that daily forces us to get out of bed, have breakfast, speak, look, return home, go to bed. Man dies each day. The atmosphere that accompanies him to the end of this road is permeated by the currents and echoes of ephemeral experiences. However, they cannot be taken in at one fell swoop: they are more evasive and varied than any exposition of merely literary adventures. The most difficult thing of all is to grasp them within a poem, where one must remain within the limits of two or three lightning-quick decisions, describing only that which cannot be secured in action. A mood without plot — it passed near us and was forgotten, only to return again sometime later; but now we are exiled and defenseless, and it is difficult for us to refuse because therein lies a choice. The point is to allow powerful meanings to pour forth while at the same time filling the outer object and the unconscious act with a breath of freedom, never for a moment letting actual reality out of sight. A slightly open spontaneity can be controlled, but only to the extent necessary so that its elementality is not encroached upon. Such meticulousness, doomed from the start to failure in creative effort, suddenly seems to be a form of madness, which it is not. It sometimes happens that an effect can be had quite cheaply: it is enough merely to name objects, anomalous by nature, taking note only of the most obvious, vectoral traits.) Thus on occasion a work is created almost instantaneously, as if dictated by the motion of the hands themselves — a sudden prophetic impulse; but what is being prophesied? Simultaneously death and eternity. This in part explains the muffled aggressivity of some of our best poems. But they don't accept you. Individuals are torn apart, and the fear of arriving late falls on the heads of the innocent (you envy Robinson Jeffers, who built a house on the ocean and lived in it until a ripe old age, writing gloomy and long poems in free verse). Of course, you are a member of poetic sect; as a rule, every little group is initially defensive, arming itself with utmost rigidity and the discipline of form. Nevertheless, these days many write unclearly, making constant use of a slippery set of stylistic devices, as if they were ashamed of the subject of their verse, or else have not mastered this lack of clarity itself, confusing the texture and essence of completely opposite and vaguely sensual definitions. In truth, what they are doing is akin to using words to adorn and cover an already prepared foreground, thereby feeding the demon of deafening repetitions. They are turning language into a stone fool, an ecstatic metronome that transforms fate into philosophical Substance, thereby avoiding all practical embodiments: thus hacked into everyday numbers, into an illegible sketch, it is doubtful that the mystery can be heard. These kind of lines are reminiscent of rays of sunlight groping around an empty street, full of passers-by. Others, far away, determine plot, prosody, plan. As for us, we are left to see only long days and several duplicate faces in the slowed flow of Asian time.

Thus, as Montale wrote, "style comes to us from good manners," and the value of the poet is not in speech, quickly soldered into a lyrical yoke, but in the ability to squeeze out something like material proof of an uninhabitable wholeness, or rather to cover a painting (that's how you're caught red-handed), provided by the powers-that-be in order to resurrect the found image. A kind of internal precision of verbal experience shuns aesthetic fact, which is transformed into exaltation. Tranquillity must be ensured and constantly nursed. The pay-off is in a correspondence to one's own claims. What flickers across my memory is not the linguistic phenomenon of a fading era but a wave-like signal sent, tribulation of a new world, to individual experience in the here-and-now, in defiance of the false witness of never-ending norms. Nevertheless, it is probably necessary to rely on this mythical pressure, which is ground down and contained by the tranquillity of writing and by a set of your favorite states of being, which can change at any time with a change of purely literary provocations: room, climate, the human figure, earth, a hot wind, light and night. An objective material ripens before our eyes, and its greater palpability is apparently a result of the ability to situate the material within a slightly aberrant context that denies neither the duration of the inspiration nor the truthfulness of authorial behavior. The ideal text is perhaps analogous to a river whose source and mouth cannot be encompassed by a   glance — what is perceived instead are scraps of the passing disorder, which the banks both conceal and goad. Striving vainly toward it, we remain unchangingly — and unfortunately — within the limits of our initial hopes and conjectures. We are left with a slice of day's light on a table, and in it all the passion of the glittering world shudders. Air, burdened with longitude. An empty landscape. A final refuge. The sun.

TRANSLATED BY THOMAS EPSTEIN

Untitled

Bonfires are burning, a crowd on the square.
Hunched around the fire, bums warm their hands
Hurrying to the theater, an anonymous n'er do well
Tries to keep the mud off of his clean pants

He has passed by the lobby and the cascade of stairs.
Under his nose, testaments to the evening's wealth
Glitter and shimmer, and the heady scent
Of exquisite perfumes adds to the attraction.

But it's another trail that has led the n'er do well to the Opera:
Nervously, he waits for the appropriate moment
And then it arrives. Heading towards the box, taking out a pistol
He fires, seventeen times in a row, at the President.

While the conductor of the orchestra, oblivious,
Calmly turns the pages of the score
And it all starts up on stage, determinedly, gloomily,
The choir starts singing, building to a crescendo . . .

And the President collapses . . . His young wife
Follows him down and so to the accompaniment of trumpets and harps,
His confidants, desperate, hysterical,
Haul away down the aisle the bleeding corpse.

TRANSLATED BY SIMON KENT AND ALEKSANDR KALUZHSKI

Untitled

O you deepening shadows with cloth rags,
Charming floor-wipers
Your driving force, your majestic genius
Deserves both words and music
Especially, most especially in July,
When oblique beams gild
The columns of dust in a roomy lobby
And sunset is reflected in your buckets;
When the full moon is swimming
Slowly across the sky
And in heavy steams the liquid silver
Pours down your mop.
Due to their own choreography,
Unassisted by propeller or wings,
The cleaning ladies of public buildings
Fly from the dark, stark naked
Filling the corridors with their song,
Circumnavigating fire-extinguishers
Neither filing cabinets nor lamps obstruct them
Nor security, dozing at their watch.

TRANSLATED BY SIMON KENT AND ALEKSANDR KALUZHSKI

Untitled

. . . And Pushkin, strange beast with lilac-colored
Fingernails, drops in on us, sits down at the table
And carries on a light-hearted conversation,
While behind him a music steals past the door
Poisoning everything with its buzzing poison:
Death is sent us by home delivery, in a colorful cover.
The poet is the servant of feline complaint:
Not for nothing do all things sense in him their enemy.
Brother of iron stars, in love with a simple life,
He is a weapon of wide expanses, picked clean
When matter was created from the rumbling din.
He came into this world to extract
Things, odors, memories, and faces,
Came to hide them where they could not be corrupted,
Where it's senseless even for the living butterfly
Not to become damp earth and a drop of rain
But to sleep, like a maiden, in a crystal coffin,
To glimmer, a rotting tree stump at distant millenia
Until bodies cease to burn in earthly fire
And the tamed beast secures a wing.

TRANSLATED BY THOMAS EPSTEIN

On the Streetcar Tracks

And so you and I will take a walk on the streetcar tracks
We'll sit on the pipes at the beginning of the ring road*
The black smoke from the factory smokestack will become our warm wind
The yellow plate of the traffic light will be our guiding star

If we're lucky we'll return to our cage . . . before nightfall
We'll have to be able to hide ourselves underground in two seconds
In order to lie there while the grey cars drive over us
Taking with them those who couldn't and wouldn't play in the dirt

If we succeed we'll continue by crawling along the railroad ties
You'll glimpse the sky, I'll glimpse the earth on your soles
We'll have to burn the clothes in the oven, if we get back
If the blue-caps don't meet us on the way

If they meet us, you better shut up,
don't say we went for a walk on the streetcar tracks
It's the first sign of a crime or schizophrenia
But from the portrait Iron Felix† will smile at us
It'll be a long imprisonment, it'll be very just
The punishment for walking along the streetcar tracks
A just punishment for a walk along the streetcar tracks
They'll kill us because you and I took a walk on the steetcar tracks

TRANSLATED BY SARA MOORE

---

*Perhaps the Ring Road around Moscow.
†Felix F. Dzherzinsky, head of the first KGB

Burn, Burn, Bright[*]

You won't catch up: you can't understand, you didn't catch up:
   they didn't steal a thing.
Without work you won't break teeth, won't sell out, won't fuck someone over
You won't even begin to suffocate or kill this song.

   The house burns: the jerk doesn't see
   The house burns: the jerk doesn't know
   That he was born a jerk
   To answer for yet another jerk

Burn, burn bright to keep alight

On the way I fell, dirt diluted with tears
They ripped apart my new skirt, and stuffed it in my mouth
Glory to the great proletarian people
The invincible powerful people

   The house burns: the jerk doesn't see
   He got drunk and started a fight
   He doesn't remember
   Who called who a jerk first.

Burn, burn bright to keep alight

Howl, my song, in the expanse, fly away to the oven smokestacks
Threshing knives like black smoke along the beauty that is earth

The sun is laughing with loud red laughter
Burn, burn bright so it doesn't go out

TRANSLATED BY SARA MOORE

---

[*] A saying from the Russian folktale "12 Months"

Only the Universal Rain

Only the universal rain will comfort us
Only a real fear will help us
A soul-substitute is our redemption
We'll not remember: they'll forget us too
   Our tears are stones falling on the tops of others' heads
   An act of love in a big cold sauna
   Just the wind in sleeves and hats
Only a house in which it's very quiet
A yellow world of which there's always more
   Eternal path: to the border and no further
   Dreamy fear forgives us with tears
It's really simple when an island sinks at sea
It's really true if it doesn't give an answer
It's really perfect if you're alone

TRANSLATED BY SARA MOORE

ANDREI SEN-SEN'KOV

The Secret Life of a Toy Piano

1.

Snow was falling
like squadrons of badly built paper airplanes
might fall.
Straight down.
He was in pain.
In pain was he:
unshaven, skinny and trembling,
like a line from an unfinished poem.
Or a piano key, vibrating . . .
Vibration — incisions in the air,
air preparing to become sound.
Incisions correct and incorrect,
embraced and lost,
abbreviated and magnified.
About jazz,
the panic between inhale and exhale.
About bed sheets
(white carnations
crushed by bodies,)
about a cup of hot rain for breakfast,
a lining of Chinese tea,
stuffed sugar optics.

About a toy piano,
a piece of wood
dolled up in White.
About music playing,
appearing within us
in the form of a little,
just-hatched dream,
on whose shoulder sits
a tiny snowflake,

resembling a white parrot's fledgling
and the South Pole of a white keyboard.
Incisions about how from music
anything can be constructed:
Winter, the island of Lesbos,
pebbles and small sea rocks,
the fifty stars of the American flag . . .
As to what was created first:
jazzy candy,
heard in weepy sniffles, movie clips,
and the voices of consterned constellations.
About how later a Wrapper appears
for the Candy,
introducing the jazz
Principle of Vagueness
in a jar of jazz Dust,
in a bitten-into jazz Pastry . . .

And still later — a Drawing
Resembling some kind of Map to search
for reflections sunk into mirrors,
It is the sapling of musical branches.
Twig Number One:
an attempt to use insect noises.
Flies playing
"September: the laying bare of August,"
based on the sound
produced by flies in flight
from September to August and back again.
Limb Number Two:
the dripping crotch of broken glass.
Limb Number Three:
the completely possible bifurcation
of the fingers of a pianist.
Limb Number 4: the transition to Limb Number 5,
intertwining with limb Number 6,
which is Limb Number 4 . . .

2.

The snow disappeared.
The vibration disappeared.
what remained was a yellowed
page of crooked paper, full of dots
of different sizes
and a strange text:

> . . . dots — literary pies
> dots — concave zeros
> dots — tiny dirty moons
> dots — chronic commas
> dots — eyeballs of a microgypsy
> dots — marbles of typographic ice-cream
> dots dots dots dots dots . . .

and verse,
which stuck to the window
on plastic suckers
Their form reminscent of
brightly-colored tropical
plants, only very small.
Whose are they, these prematurely born
lines of free verse?
Whose cracked teardrops?
Whose temporally mutuable
philological landscapes?
Are they magical little truths?

3.

Mountain snow
buries the crushed dead rain
gathering frozen poems
on the slopes.

> It's quiet. You can hear

The ants — black snowflakes —
Yearning for summer.

Autumn in the mountains.
Fog, like a ripe purple plum,
Smearing my hands with its spray.

Can't sleep.
The moon — a little puddle of white rain —
Hangs over us.

In the mountains there's no autumn:
September, October and November —
An orange winter.

4.

It's the season when girls' tears freeze,
turning into birthmarks . . .
The music sounds.
"What's that?"
"That?"
        "A *svirel* * made of seven thin reeds of unequal length,"
        Ovid's gift.
But a new limb appears
on the musical tree,
or rather, seven small
parallel-growing twigs.
The jazz rainbow.
Seven magical inspirations.
Seven clean, small pages.
Seven taut pearls on a string.
The jazz rainbow,
played on a reed pipe,
comprised of seven thin reeds of unequal length . . .

_____

* a reed pipe

5.

The dream: a painting in lemonade
in an empty goblet, from under which
dream and reality
change place.
Like lovers in bed.
Dream: lemonade ecstasy.
And ecstasy happens —
Africa,
the mask of the Yoruba,
native to brown Algeria.
The masks:
rebellion of the red-headed imagination,
which the Negroes conceal
in wooden clothing.
These masks are furniture for faces.
These maks are vertical legends
about horizontal lines,
about women with taut faces
that resemble a month
32 days long,
about nagana,
reminding one of incurable
little lumps of matter,
about the Sun,
and the fairy-tale beauty of animals
in an African village,
how they turn under the spell of magic,
soil the bedding with their splinters,
subdue the heartbeat of divine grace,
heal discolations in little indoor hidden places,
whispering of love at twilight,
when shadows exit
and finally fall silent

Like tears into a kerchief
Like badly built little paper airplanes
They fall.

TRANSLATED BY SARA MOORE

In Memory of Valeria Simina

A crow is eating snow and cleaning her beak against a branch. Honesty of high temperatures. Winter presses against the river's elasticity. There's not enough space for everybody; everyone has their own hell. Yellow fanfares, notes of wheat grains. Only for the stone hurled down is everything transparent. A gleam of lonely snow is a splinter though the other five are the same. A is a letter, aa a question, aaaaaaa a cry. A barberry tree strokes the air with its branches, pulling the air slowly to its trunk. Captives of fatigue with their hands on the backs of their heads. It becomes the past when one understands that it no longer is. What no one can change no longer exists. A thousand flickering eyes of water. The old one, by night, won't stumble against the sea.

TRANSLATED BY MICHELLE MURPHY AND THOMAS EPSTEIN

Untitled

Winter slowly surfaces from the comet's first snow. Night pulls the horizon into a soup bowl of thickets. The snow grows bolder, fevers crumple and fall. No waterlogged telegrams come from September's harbor, telling of the golden siege in the leaves' voices. Now the windows are losing their hinges — every night — and a fly is crying in a petrified garden.

Farther on there are walls of elastic dust, cold salt, on which the elbows of light are leaning. Still farther, a lost moth and cherry mice. However why are they measuring the dull east, when a face is getting cold under a net, when an acrobat is standing in the doorway of a scream on the very brink of a ravine and the crater is filled not with wine but steel filings.

But next to evening there are the shoulders of trees, a whisper of cold raspberries. Seduce me or transform me. Night is the promise of moon snails; a frog swallowing stars left floating on the river. Sails flapping over chalky water. Beyond the pyramid of frozen copper, weeks of sun are coming, the sun is biting through leaves, a salt temple stands over a cheek of landscape.

But, somebody's canvas is thawing, the cold is cocking its trigger, street lamps are scattering, and a mirror is breaking on knives.

TRANSLATED BY MICHELLE MURPHY AND THOMAS EPSTEIN

Untitled

Time moves steadily, in the body of a snake. Not like stairs or a wheel-rather like scarcely visible waves under its rough skin, the same undulating trace. Achilles won't catch up with the tortoise — the snake will, effortlessly enduring, and slipping away at every point. Time contains all, a snake knows all. She writhes through narrow paths, striking precisely. The sound of her scales is the rustle of fine sand.

Time rests, rolling up into a snail. In her hushed padding it dreams. The quietest dreams are under water, and for that reason sea shells are the most beautiful. Clots of time are scattered on the sea bottom, on vine leaves, on pages, hiding in O and moving out of V, hornlike.

When a snake and a snail meet, they remain quiet. A conversation between the one awake and the one asleep is impossible. The snake knows the snail — like everything else. The snail often dreams about the snake — with all the snake's knowledge. Therefore they smile and skim along, each going its own way.

TRANSLATED BY MICHELLE MURPHY AND THOMAS EPSTEIN

Untitled

1.

Wind becomes bleached after fire, when it rouses itself from the hills. It has two sides — stone and water. Rain tests the knife-air with its tongue. Eyes are turned inward, a bush drums. The east is tightly drawn, there's no west for it, no place to put a jug on a broken town square. Night can happen, like an ever-widening column of Crete. Near the ankles of a birch lies a snake, lighter than first spring leaves.

2.

From a one-eyed feather, a voice from the north — about rain's old age, the loyalty of birds. White-eyed fish tales, stolen skin and the burn of forgiveness. They should ask a door about its street, a field about its town. Time lives behind doors of rooms, but a year isn't time, only a dash on memory. A flicker of light shows only a face, leaving everything else to the warm dark. Where is there a point without length or breadth? In the prick of a needle. When a man dies, the thread that's drawn him slips.

3.

Sometimes I want to be in compact and less transparent surroundings, to walk, moving it apart with my arms. But the air's too empty.

Night's brought on by the tips of their fingers, and they study it for a long time, like practicing the flute. Eyelashes are longer than the night, a light brown tree of a redlipped snake. Fireflies appear at the touch. Afterwards, you glance at a puddle on the street — there are reflections of a Gothic church or a tree which are absent here. And you aren't reflected either.

TRANSLATED BY MICHELLE MURPHY AND THOMAS EPSTEIN

Untitled

Your bones are made of glass, and fish scratch their foreheads on them. Old air yellows on the inside. After a night where no one touches, the morning's rough. Rejected apples and tattered heels pursue you and your sky says it's ten minutes to seven.

All you can do is go to the river. What joy it would be for you to sleep in a stranger's home, having the day for yourself. However, your rounds are circular, birdlime is scattered over your dreams, and papers blow over your titmice.

If you know everything — say my name.

A perfect snow is in your hands.

TRANSLATED BY MICHELLE MURPHY AND THOMAS EPSTEIN

ALEKSANDR SKIDAN

POETRY AND THOUGHT

And I've told you about this: no works of art, no language, no speech, no
reason, nothing. —Antonin Artaud

1

IF WE WERE TO UNDERSTAND (or continue to understand) thinking as the act of
representing the representation of the object or as a series of logically
infallible judgments resembling mathematical operations that embrace the
world in its presence, that is if we were to remain inside the territorial waters
of classical discourse under the flag of Self-evidence or the Transcendental
Signified, we could readily ascribe to poetry the merit of steering steadfastly
away from re-presentation.

In a poetic work, then, the signified is endlessly deferred, and words, as
Saint-Jean Perse once wrote, lose their meaning at the threshold of bliss (the
threshold of bliss that is a vertiginous entry into pure duration, the apocas-
tasis that can never take place, an apocastasis without Apocastasis, that
prolongs itself in absence and gaps into an impossible beyond): this is un-
doubtedly the case. The case seems even clearer when we become aware of
the scrupulous and exacting analysis of its own foundations and strategies
that modern poetic practice has been pursuing ever since Mallarmé, from
within the very space of the text.

Yet how are we to think the astonishing affinity, to which Adorno had
already pointed, that obtains between the discursive movement of a lyric
utterance and that of a speculative utterance? The turn from an art of reflexion
to a reflexion of and by art, on art's own territory and by deploying its own
weapons, is an overt proclamation of the new status accorded to poetic
writing, or better still, of the new sovereignty claimed by the poetic sphere.
This turn falls within the history of the West — that is, it is historical, just as
the essence of poetry and the essence of thinking are historical. Every true
poet, every poet of the present, establishes the essence of poetry anew. And
the thinker? Let us listen to Heidegger, whose interrogation remains, despite
everything, still to be overcome: "Insofar as we perceive an entity in its being,
insofar as we, to use the language of the New times, represent objects in their
objecthood, we are already thinking. In this way we have been thinking for a

long time. But we are still not truly thinking as long as that upon which the being of the entity is founded remains unthought, when it appears as presence."

The thought of silence calls to oblivion, to a light that has ceased shining.

What is thought? What is poetry? This question, as always, keeps blinding me. This blinding, as always, keeps forcing me to the writing table, where I am plunged into a clairvoyant sense of nothing, into the ineffable. And this, as always, only so that I might once, on emerging from this ruthless insight, be filled with the darkness of this night. Poetry thinks non-thought.

2

How can a person who has nothing to say not try (for *destitute time* has also been exhausted, the time of the gods who have fled and the god Who is not coming: a double lack), to begin speaking, and by virtue of its very impossibility, express this impotence, this shortage of self?

Dif-ference makes one. The source of thought and poetry is one — the unthinkable. Nothing. But the thinker asks: why is there something rather than nothing? But the poet says, hiding behind the same screen: I will compose a history text book for you, or a sacred text, like the Koran or the Vedas; and it is certainly true that he composes cosmogonies and morals, theologies and kings of France, and clowns who jingle their mourning bells of the universal madness and dishonour to come. Perhaps poetry owes its origin (here and now) to a certain insuperable defect of thought, an affect that robs me of myself. Only in the poetic act, only in the power of a writing powerless to express anything, can I emerge as one who could emerge in no other way than through the self-asserting act of writing. A tautology that can make you go crazy. It is in breaks that speech comes about, like bad blood that won't clot: a loss that makes your head spin. And there are no works of art, no language, no speech, no reason, nothing. But an absence, a hole, cold suffering, "without images, without feelings, like the indescribable thrust of an aborted foetus."

Maurice Blanchot writes with extraodinary perception about the "case" of Antonin Artaud, about the torment of the ineffable which this despot of ecstasy undergone, and the desire to undergo: "With a depth granted to him through the experience of suffering he knows that to think is not to have thought, and that the thoughts he has merely make him feel that he 'has yet to begin thinking' . . . It is as if, despite himself and through a pathetic error from whence come his cries, he touched upon the point at which to think is always already to be able to think no more. . . ." Here, at the point where an extreme suffering becomes an extreme poverty of thought and drowns, by destroying the physical substance of he who thinks, any effort to solicit more, all are forced to fall silent. Because . . . because who else would dare to shout so loudly with a mute voice, when the word never comes into play (Aleksandr Vvedenskii)? Thought has thought its surface.

That ecstacy (of poetry and of thought) is linked to this impossibility of thinking that there is a depth to thought — "this is a truth that cannot be revealed, for it always turns away, thereby obliging him to experience it below the point at which he would truly feel it. This is not only a metaphysical difficulty, it is a delight in pain, and poetry is this constant pain, it is the 'shadow' and the 'darkness of the soul,' the absence of a voice with which to scream."

TRANSLATED BY HARSHA RAM

Delirium

> We are riflemen creeping blindly towards
> the heights of night.
> —Georg Trakl

(. . .) the loss of the murdered echo. lot,
    falling like a stone in the oblivion of a sling,
conceives the unknown, led by
the degree "of fall"; the daughter enters unto him and again —
the daughter, another. A
daughterly darkness,
crashing down, covers Israel; a leaf
    praises utopia
to the heavens, the book
questions pale fire, licking its tongue. Tribes. Whence
the loss
    in these desert places,
my people? Even catching fire, I no longer pronounce
"I"; taste the rustle of this grass from nowhere: waste
of dust. Scattering. My mouth. To behold,
how winter blazes, how
the fruit of the wilderness opens, trembling,
burning.
    Immensity.
      Low
clouds. The Host of the "alexandrian" winter; intoxication as if — never. The
                night beats a
dark wing,
as if it would hoist itself up to the bosom of the goddess. The letter
    weeping
enters the poem ahead of time, pressing close
to the shoulder of absence. Who keeps silent here? Potlatch, he said. this
            when there is no
one to, but they

corrected him — to no one. on paper
the holocaust reminds
        (nothing
reminds one of nothing) of an exercise
in funeral art: a genre, whose style likewise
"made verse-writing *useless*,"
his italics. even so,
it continues, the phrase, the lament, or the wall, clings to metonymy. he tastes
        the heady delight of her
manna: thus the knife
    offers up
a prayer to the whiteness of dough, torturing; literally
it would be "I love you" — like a key in the moist
opening of the lock the tongue turned,
spitting out and commanding, to incest, to the seed.
Before the wall of fire she comes, it would be literal
to live

I

        like winter,
the thirteenth, we go out
into the ice, it has still not begun to grow light,
and he strains on the harmonica
with a German accent: ach
my darling, and so forth. And afterwords
all the first, all the balls, all the tinsel,
all the nonsense, all the firs with a bombastic
planetary motto — into one
tent, and . . .
no, not everything, still not everything,
ach, and so forth; how it will flare up
and "ah, my darling augustine," and

(. . .) a clear-toned call, talk of mortals. bright
are the pilgrims' clothes; white scrolls of clouds.

From soundlessness rises up the fine-fleeced
stem of melodies, the silk-worm weaves its web,
devouring poppy seeds of writing; hand,
mimesis. A fine hoar-frost on the trees. To smoke
grass, being penetrated by dust
the pollen of painted kimonos
                              to droop
downwards,
        expelling madness; night's gentle. And
not a drop of rain. In the lungs — heartfelt warmth,
shroud of sad runes — in the eyes; moist chill of eyelashes strikes
                                              the pagoda of the jade
stalk, entering
the slow turn of the neck, ah how the collar squeezes
the dream, lifeless. Sing
the star sailing across emptiness.

Dust. How strange are
        the locks of hair, letting out the weather,
a segment of glass, the song. A fragment
of the casement. And
the Jordan flows. But again
the circling of birds hails a black circling,
their stigmata, the light-bearing lad with woman's
hand, in yellowing moons, sisters behold!
Birth of dawn's shadows.

———————

love?
what of love — it starts
like a bent needle in the heart

        ———————

II

But these dances by the fire fire the
incineration swarming

above the ancestral skirmish play
funeral gathering for the idle urn
pyromaniac unicorn mephisto
"library a den in essence
let even the Alexandrian the heterae
like bread-and-butter or a book
but they too strive to fall face down
or open on a piquant place
and in each little letter of the despised
paternal alphabet our oedematose god lives
and corrodes that which is tastier
as the worm the spiritual of deep red lips"

"thus mentor Leibnitz life-guard of the monads
above or face down but with the tick of mathematics
and with a guard's pelisse of immortality in mind —
. . . in my hands I hold hamletism like a skull
and weigh the poor" ah

incineration swarming

They saluted by lifting up their legs
deep in the Siberian ores of the cartesian
shaft not so the naughty child
should freeze a little finger
like the blueblooded radical
and the blind force thinks everyone and all
and everyone and all they lay into ambiguous
queen-size pencil-boxes
do not be tempted friend of petrarch tasso's friend
needlessly
and in general

and GAS!

above the ancestral skirmish play
senselessly like a kamikaze
the blessed cry banzai
the painfully emaciated comic

rushing by the acheron he
no crowned head — alcoholic of the lung
so as not to be rid of the pleroma trauma
and not be fulfilled
not to fulfill
ah, my darling augustine
augustine augustine
ah, my darling Augustine all has passed

all

Translated by Daniel Weissbort

Untitled

Wind the spindle
  crumple the vegetable clock
above the icy crust above the edge
  with trembling force alone it's given us
to offer up the tapir's dumb speech
  to the cinema where the ballroom pianist laps
to guild the remains of the world
  the celluloid marquee
grows grows full of love
  and subsides like a belly
then — it grows dark. then lacking a shadow
  I enter it like broken glass
somnambulistically I gaze as if
  anaesthetized — the performance grows dark
and I leave (here's when) the sun
sets like a throat

Translated by Daniel Weissbort

Untitled

In the underdusk I lay down
    with a madwoman in a siamese bed
and with claws withdrawn from the loops
    caught hold of the soft air

what's not to be found in the soft cry of salvation
    already appeared dimly in the fear . . .
I learnt to tear the plaster slightly
    above the wife's lymph

and to nurse the quilted alphabet with my lips
    while it stratified itself like a pagoda
when the levite like an almond tree
    bent with his scalpel over the dream

and in the substantial little sieve where we bind
    the sky and calico captivity
the expended OM of the eyeball
    is such a fluent reading! —

for all to hear it uttered . . .
    an eyelash trembled and I came to the pain
recognizing I was seeing the dream's continuation
    with halved love

TRANSLATED BY DANIEL WEISSBORT

Crossing Centuries:

Passing the Church of the French Consulate

Suddenly someone entered — and, through the din of voices,
said: — Here is my bride.
Aleksandr Blok

1.

O Jesu, darling, damn my nativity in the Year of Bull.
A glossolaliac I sibillated your mass,
Garden-snaked into your fate, faded into it like an otter,
Counterfeited a demon — & that's what the dames named me.

2.

I stole gooseberries, crowfoots in the municipal gardens of Tartu,
tried on the pike skeleton of the mahogany cathedral
in place of my vertebral column — the card I got, got topped,
the Mammy of God placed into my hands a vial — it shattered

3.

into seven pieces: in its firmament are reflected
the gavel of the judge Semina, the despondent cawing of a "canary,"
a wood demon's miter, the ditty about the sacraments of the grave,
the crown of Stakenschneider's palazzo in a beautiful maiden's skullcap,

4.

simmering Lesbian gardens, the Olympian torso
horseshoed, tonsuring with hoof-clippers the brazenfanged serpent . . .
And all this is past. Like a yuletide needle my discourse
knits, for the sake of the past, the caparison of a prayer:

5.

....
....
....
....

6.
Sear, o blacktail maiden, me-without-a-droplet-of-lamb's-blood,
set loose in a bulbous crib or a hot-air balloon,
with a cord of flax wrap length and widthwise my nappies
to the pitiful salvos of piano-forte or pop-guns.

7.
I'll have neither the ire — [caesura]— nor the dark force, nor the gesture
at the decline of life to wank off the fattening, pock-marked period
with a schismatic's pointing diaresis: "Here is my bride!"
and so turn her into a comma, glaucoma, coma.

Translated by Eugene Ostashevsky

from Sonia, A History

The night before her arrival
I fell into the hands of a dream
astringent as the witch-hazel berry.

I dreamt: Sonia
was my death's gaping touch-hole,
under a polyester blanket

the undulations of our bodies
interpreted a psalm by Handel
or the chants of schismatics.

Interwoven, our torsos and limbs
resembled the treble clef
or the crotchets of Old Believers.

Sonia reached for a smoke,
torqued a knife from aluminum foil,
and severed my head from its shoulders.

She put the head's uncombed cabbage
on a tray of Limoges enamel,
my mouth on a latch of topaz,

in my forehead a candied lemon,
in each of my eyes a marzipan,
and asperged me with heavy cream.

And in a lunatic trance
carried it automatically
to a tennis court.

As a farcical farewell,
she waved her hand, grasping
not a handkerchief, but a racquet.

Let us stress the visual complexity
of my unfortunate head's
following the flights of the shuttle-cock.

Describing nooses & loops
over outdoor discotheques
in a tarantella of torments,

it let fall the ballast of tears
onto the buhl of the Bourse
and the kohl of the Colleges.

In the ionosphere
is my head now; the orbit's
stationmaster salutes it.

A rival of Micromegas,
it rolled like a laughing Gouda
on the plastic tablecloth of the universe.

And, with a BANG! of a pop-gun,
plutzed on the pillow's square
which tears had slightly moistened.

That dream was prodigious.
Afterwards everything shot
to Tartarus   to the devil

TRANSLATED BY EUGENE OSTASHEVSKY

Corvus, Corvus

> and the fire-mighty eagle,   drowsing,
> droops his head on Zeus' scepter
> folds his swift wings   over the valley
>
> Vl. Ivanov

O how short   Il paeon c anacr
even this incandescent   December day   pher   ia
   no snowfall   ba
but clouds over the bay   feathery-winged   hem hypercat 2d

      now the raven   cho
of the night takes wing   No   pher
      it's the raven of death has taken wing   glyc inv
            beating, beating the air   teles

You can forget yourself   Il paeon c anacr
in May foliage   the green of grass   2 cho
      and then   ba
if you're lucky   the close-set breakers of the Black Sea 5 d cat

      but your heart races   pher
and the funereal raven flies   albeit unnoticed   hem c anacr ad
      albeit a barely distinguishable   pher c anacr
                  speck on the horizon hem

You can lie to yourself   2 d
delude yourself   with light wine   4 d cat
      or flowering flesh   reiz

but there's no refuge   teles
      from the terror of the clear call   hem hypercat c anacr
wings slicing   slashing   Il paeon c anacr bis
            is it the air or   }hem
                  time

Once again -- Christmas Eve   hem
Peterhof   year's end   anap cho
            same old decorations   pher

| but in this | imminent night | ba | Il paeon c anacr |

```
but in this                  imminent night            ba       Il paeon c anacr
with its last-to-be-extinguished                     4 d cat c anacr
          celestial dot                              sp
you distinctly hear                                  reiz
the approaching flight          not Pindar's eagle   2 hem
      but the raven   of extinction and death        ba pher
         corvus, corvus                                         Il epitr
```

TRANSLATED BY LAURA D. WEEKS

Second Helonic Ode
Trenos

In memory of Brodsky

1. Archa

Strophe

```
                         Black shades of exodus
         choristers             their heads shrouded in mantels leave
    this circular stony space            paved
           with worn flagstones  where in isolation
              the flower-strewn altar of Dionysus rises
```

2. Metarcha

Antistophe

```
                         But even the god
    takes no joy in the rich offerings      besides, his eyes      are dry
    his servants                   just now whirled madly
         in an emmelic dance   pounding their breasts
            with blows of their cruel palms
```

3. Catatrope

Strophe

```
         Sun            on the threshold of setting
    They still have to light the torches
    They still have to hear the flute
            in the fourth play, keeping time
               for the sikinid
```

AntistropheAnd the fake tails

```
            And the fake phalluses
    of the satyrs                    will sway
            to the orgiastic
               phrygian refrain
```

epode

```
                    and the actors will divert
    the stunned spectators                from the horror of the spectacle
    so that       it won't be so unbearable
    to return with the tragic burden
               to their houses hidden
                  from the street
```

4. Omphalos

extra metrumHow can we endure these things?

Oedipus' bloody eyelids

Iphegenia's childish neck -- slashed

Antigone's white feet swaying in the wind

5.Metacatatrope

6.Sphragis

The poet stripped the earth   naked like a corpse   just grown cold
And without covering it   leaving that job to the extras
Without keening over it
Without wringing his hands from compassion

Turning away, he left

And this same earth   which we all   love out of long habit
this tender   body, only moments ago emanating
spasms of desire
lies on the ecciclem   all in bloody slashes

unnaturally laid low   by a fatal tremor.

TRANSLATED BY LAURA D. WEEKS

Elegiarum Fragmenta
Ex Ponto (?)

Fr. 2

spring - at last

and you vanish, as if
     falling into one of your former (lives)
if only you could peek....................................from that (past)
   into today's air
..............................hear
   today's heart beating
....(Corinne)
   how it hurts............................her memory
when she breathed beside you.......................................
   she didn't seem..
capable of showing up.......................................ten years later
   (in a dream) obscured by tears

TRANSLATED BY LAURA D. WEEKS

The Course of Airing Out

On the centennial wind, the thunder of cellophane birds
above roof cornices turns loose horror
from the hungover heart onto ribs of framed houses,
forcing them to shine hoarsely.
The long sub-zero thermometer
roams in the cracked mortar of nighttime New Jersey
like a dead crane, like
a naked mast without arms.

Repairs are beginning on the whole world.
And have been finished forever.
Don't ever complete an entire picture of misfortune,
     even if it belongs to somebody else.
You won't be able to.
And it's funny to speak of your own.
     (More natural to keep silent in such depths
     of our restored silences).

These rough repairs on trees grown old
overnight on the blackening river, scaly
with electric waves,
my last repair before
sleep, before laughter, before a distant voyage
                to a city called Thistle,
so awkward it's more appropriate to recall
the geography of it — it too a creaking repair.
Its biography is also.

At night, familiar cold glances into your paper-made coziness
with its worried (like old age) tear-soaked eye
                                of King-Kong,
leaving iron drops on the edges of crystals,
unsolidified, helpless wax.

At the window, yellowed by smoke,
we doubt even the proximity of the large poplars —
they enter as shadows,
here, they touch each corner with their quiet branches,
and possibly, are not at all happy with this corner.
Bodilessness usually frightens.

Like sorrowful evening fires over the churchyards of fish.
Like tricky automobile beaches
inside the concentration camp wires hung around them.
Like everyday dreams.

I don't feel death.

It means that hope and horror,
just like any other illness,
    are gone with the wind.
It makes no sense for me to say
that there exists a border in the fog.

Maybe, a mood? A sensitivity?
A blindness that doesn't distinguish happiness from non-existence?

The snivelly headcold of water on the concrete
                bonfires
of a setting sun (some cooled-down plasma)
allows you to feel your own build as planklike,
Dust running as if it trapped in sunbeams at the corners . . .

Getting used to wobbliness as if it were basic movement
could hardly be considered science,
but in the wind
it's the path to purity.
As if your sad silhouette
were being cut out of the dense cardboard of giant houses
and you becoming just a black hole for the wind.

(I would love to make such a memorial on the shore,

just the long screen of Manhattan,
            where along its length
I could cut out palisades of silhouettes. But they say that
less is better.
In the same way, a community of thinking reeds
conjures up ultimate Asia for me).

Here, in the darkness
left in pieces of a damp factory washcloth,
it's somehow easier to understand the lifeless, cellophane crunch . . .

We thunder even worse. We're cracks in eyes of fish.

Half my life, I've been taking off this synthetic sweater
somewhere in Gram's dark corner, spilling needles
on dried coats, unsewn guests.
I will keep the floorboards creaking
until I finally fall asleep.
In this sense, somnambulists are more controversial.
Bringing their dreams like others' unborn infants,
they'll be able to, regardless,
take a step of their own.

To drop a vase on the floor, to open the window onto poplars. . .
And their eyes grow like children on drunken palms,
because in them, there's no more (at the very least, for this moment)
one-dimensional time.
But there is a solid room.

Time's dear substance, too vivid,
like a light blast of limp lime deposits into Saturday's ribs.
And all the threads that link time to the galaxy's spray
have finally become a completely common thing.

When on the wind.

Undergo the process of airing out. Out of the skin.
Bones. Out of any evolution

480   *Crossing Centuries:*

of death or life. Out of anyone's biographies and stone cities.

Gigantic rust of these passing villages
gives away bitterness of a dam's burning sugars,
substantial, like rings of winter
on shavings of soaked pines.
    In its height
the wind is feeding off decrepit green steel,
sometimes more significant than molecules
of running water.

The impossibility of repentance is pounded into us
                      by the round moon
like a strange, sensible calm after a long scream.
By the incomprehensible fighting of cellophane birds with twigs
on the crests of hot gas.

April will just about be arriving.

I love you.
I have remembered this love, that could make one
flow as a snuffbox through mercurial autumn,
freezing in a hospital shell, lost in the sea
of Magellan's crude oil, rocking the marble of wheels.

A person who crossed dawn in the clockworks
deserved more than this gray memory
of the damp basement amidst the mixed perfumes of *Je Ose*
and the violent smell of fried sprats.

Most likely, I love you only on account of the ambiguity of words,
awaiting whatever repetitions, whatever instructions,
returning a white handful of aspirin berries
on the centennial wind.

I don't know *whom* I am talking to, but I know — *where*,
as if we're listening to noise radiating from the earliest Universe
like a spy

with a radio on his knees
which broadcasts only the past — no matter how you adjust it.
White noise, forever alien to a surprise snowstorm,
grows in the springing up of their spirals, raw mushroom spores,
the capillaried space of the soul, on which parting
is printed from the beginning, a birthmark.
That's why we like to hold on to last year's leaves
with the still surviving winged skeleton — this other sort of eloquence —
in order to prove confusingly
that yes something was there.

To prove it to yourself.
Surely they shouldn't exist in nature.

A person squeezing hot sand in his fingers
is reminded of gunpowder or possibly, snow,
which once melted, easily evaporates on the eyes,
instantaneously turning into that elongated northern spectrum.

A person, drinking water, tracking movements of ships.
This, a form of the river's silence, getting hungover
with the ordinary frankness of actual presence.
It's necessary to be quiet
and to swallow these waves, to glance in the pitcher's reflection
so that the most rank and good-for-nothing canoe
would drag out as far as the station whose sign says
                    Thistle.

I love you, as if repairs are beginning
in plank-built universities unscathed by thunder,
where a kitten rolled a tangerine through deaf corridors
and receptionists are knitting orange sweaters.
Where the usual spider wore the name Holy Volvoks,
and when it came down on the globe with its paw,
we couldn't have believed that autumn had already come —
we took it as only a short night.
That out of the reign of drying oils and glances, smoothing down the parquet,
it's possible to step out into the fresh air with old man

Herodotus's splended tome.
   — And was he the blind one? Or was that someone else?

The spring flood often brings up dead people
with incomprehensibly bent clay hands
squeezing a tiny piece of chalk
consisting of small Mezozoan era crabs.
You want to pick up their steel pince-nez
and clean off the slime, and maybe, even try them on,
for the souls of teachers, killed by thunderstorms,
are infinitely pure.
The reflection of lightning on their chests
allows you judgements about the nature and power of discharge.
Thus, an anatomist hands over his corpse for his students to do with what
   they will.
Thus, a biographer lacks a biography, like a whistle.

Dearest, do you remember what Aristotle once said?
That Earth was twice as big around at the equator.
He couldn't go wrong, he saw a different planet,
one of those seven. It is said that we will return there.

This thought will lull everyone to sleep, even in the cold mugs
of the infinitely empty gathering, where a stone of melancholy towers with
the feminine coarseness of old Sphynx
arched over the horizon;
where the eye looms, like a wilted red flower;
where on the tablecloth, sodium is spinning crumb by crumb
like a little demon from a roadside cigarette butt.

And some kind of glass launch with a guilty numeral,
bricked up, like a child's eyelash in amber,
scattering to smithereens
as it meets the eye
of a person standing on the pier.
         (Our glances are far more dangerous than Old Testament psalms.
         They contain the sobriety of interference
                              and incest.

A sharp quantum, causing multicolored swelling of a cancer
on relaxed lungs of inexplicable words).

This thought will lull to sleep everyone who agrees to cross
through the oval aperture, answering miners' calls,
hacking straight paths out of Jersey City depths
to the native round-the-world river.

To that river, where Dutch yachts flapped their wings,
where shreds of the New York Times swim like a hunchbacked duck,
where a neglected, dispersed stream fades away from the fibrous river
of the not-so-distant Story of the Constellation Libra . . .

And now here's all that's left —
                only the racket of a well's oarlock,
only perforated rope ladders, their raw plumblines
water trough of Ay-Dag, riddled with termite paths,
drunken seagulls bawling over the fish market of Everything.

Repairs march on the whole world. And in their damp creak
it's become easier to go, shaking the former horror
of raw mint liquors and bitter goat smoke,
lentil soup
           solo for a birthright.

This is a simple fairly-tale. When a boiling teapot
promises us a tempest in a teapot, seems we need to wait for that tempest in a
                                                         teapot.
In the wind you forget about everything — who you were, or will be,
or will you be at all, but the main thing is: you are.

Life looks too haughtily towards traces of particles flying past,
leaving behind the legacy of fleeting empires'
lead water pipes, whose essence would have been like a gasp of breath,
if only someone had responded to the echo of a repeated gasp . . .
And on the extra narrow pier which greets all ships,
I'll bury my nose in your cloak, like in darkness of a theatrical dressing room

after catching sight of a homeless old man with an African grin
withdrawing into darkness with a black cat in his black arms.

This thought will lull to sleep everyone . . .

TRANSLATED BY MARGARITA ZILBERMAN

▨◈▨ VYACHESLAV KURITSYN ◈▨

The Craft of Lettering

Meanings concealed by rows of letters and other symbols of writing are accessible only to God and our loved ones. We ourselves have nothing to say about it; we are not given the language to speak about sublime meanings.

If we can talk about beauty, it is only by granting as a pledge of our sincerity and devotion, the thoroughness and accuracy with which we cover the white soil of the page with signs. Let our fingers go white with tension, clasping the nib; let the tip of our tongues, clenched between our teeth in agitation, quiver intensely. Let the addressee of our devotion see how hard we try. How can we know which thoughts, passions, and ideas about the world he is expecting from us? Little man can so easily make a mistake in those fine matters — little man, who knows only the craft of composing words out of letters and sentences out of words. Let the criterion of our love be the desire to inscribe beautifully the way our letters look on the page, so that we should not insult the radiant eyes of the one to whom they crave to belong.

Once one used to write by hand with a quill or a ball point; one copied entire books by hand, including the very voluminous ones. One's hands were freezing in a cold scriptorium and one had to breathe on them to warm them. Now one writes by tapping the keys of intelligent machines with the tips of one's fingers, and the letters flicker across the screen; but no matter who is writing, the letters come out uniformly and the accidental delight of an error or a uniquely exquisite, calligraphic flourish does not breathe in them.

But it is all right; there are many more ways of friendship with the eternal craft of writing in the world. Letters can be tattooed on the hot bodies of our beloved. They can be thawed with a patient finger in a frozen design of a winter window pane. Letters can be baked out of dough in the shape of fluffy, tasty breads and eaten with those who need them.

TRANSLATED BY YULIA KUNINA AND CHARLES BORKHUIS

Mirrors and Optical Glasses

From time immemorial, mirrors and optical glasses have been confusing people: they double essences, change the quantity and location of objects, and create the illusion of the proximity of another world, the path to which would be greatly facilitated by these magical devices. But all too often conversations about these matters have an abstract, mystical nature.

Many are afraid of looking into the mirror. But what if, already gone, the reflection lives an autonomous life wherever it pleases? Many are afraid of being looked at through a magnifying glass, but what if our image has already flaked off and is wandering elsewhere, playing dirty tricks on us without our knowledge?

Mirrors seduce by the idea of symmetry, by fostering thinking within the framework of the categories of "left" and "right," the "original" and its "reflection."

Optical glasses rehearse the idea of infinity, convincing us that at some point symmetry will inevitably be violated. The lens will fall, the microscope will crack, the magnifying glass will break, and nobody will remember about the symmetrical tapeworm of the Mobius strip.

In mirrors and optical glasses the world boasts of its ability to reflect itself, transcend itself, spread into light waves, and hide itself in the folds of the spectrum. If something horrible happens and the world starts to disappear, it will flee to a remote star, perhaps spending a thousand light years in its flight.

But the world can also be rolled into a faceted, crystalline lens and hidden within the curvature of one's eye.

TRANSLATED BY YULIA KUNINA AND CHARLES BORKHUIS

Tricks

The following tricks are known: pulling a live rabbit by its ears out of an empty top hat, sawing a box in half with a live woman inside (with the subsequent putting together of the halves and extraction of a whole woman), walking through walls, and turning water into alcoholic beverages. In all cases, the effect of the trick is related to the violation of this or that popular law of physics — something emerges out of nothing or dead matter comes to life. The spectators present view something like the act of creation — tricks, demonstrated hourly and daily in different corners of the world that are reminders of the wondrous nature of the universe and the mystery that is always present. The priests of the mystery — the magicians (aka illusionists and prestidigitators) who wear oriental costumes or are accompanied by the dance of Bengal fireworks and spotlights appear to the audience as creatures that indeed interact with the gods.

The rather commonsensical point of view accepts that these magicians do not saw up women. They do not pull rabbits out of otherworldly nothingness, but rather hide them in a secret box or up a sleeve. The necessary deception played upon the audience is produced by ingenious optical effects and various hidden springs; the illusion of the cancellation of "laws of nature" is predicated upon the assistance of specific physical devices.

The deceitfulness of tricks and magicians is no secret to anybody. The knowledge of the principles of manipulation used to be passed down from teacher to disciple and was of an esoteric nature; now books about the art of deceit are widely published. Magicians often disclose their methods at their own shows and demonstrate how the use of cunning devices have made the tricks possible. The audience grows accustomed to the idea that in magic, deceit as a practice is not a taboo, and that such deceits are capable of being decifered. But who can guarantee that, as he discloses his method, the magician is telling the truth? Maybe he is precisely lying, distracting the public with his secret mirrors and levers from the ultimate truth: the woman has indeed been sawn in half and put together again, and her severed tissues have magically grown back anew.

TRANSLATED BY YULIA KUNINA AND CHARLES BORKHUIS

Lyrical Treatise on the Book as Such

Gloss angel, the numbered rustle of your wings
smells sweet, of mildew, consumed, compressed
felled angel . . . into the palm of my hand; I'll refrain
from saying, "fatted calf, fed on cellulose,

sacrifical lamb." A book: papyrus-osiris and stalks of rice;
a book: the skins of wild horses, elephants and bison.
A book, like any miracle, is in the beginning
destruction (cf. the decay of o² in the trinity of ozone).

A book, a gesture tossed off by the right hand (Whose?
Take a guess!) trampled by the coupling, copulating, naked throng.
A voice tatooed onto the pages —
a stupid trope, but a right hand has neither timbre nor throat.

A new heaven slipping sunset's snakeskin
is not a book at all, but so like, so like . . . A book is not exact-
ly the ghost of Pasternak, although it once might have been,
and there's nothing more hackneyed

than this pointless analogy wrenched from dark
by the author's fertile ecstasy (much he cares how many
obscure passages you don't get). I'll consign this portent
and the dead adage about two rabbits to a post-mortem.

Virgin piece of vellum redeeming the illustrations' gloss,
a book briefly reminds you of the vows of the Ursulines.
In Cheliabinsk in winter, an old maid named Rita —
a book, burned at night (noted by me).

It's undoubtedly what they've been writing — lengthy, unbound —
Ecclesiastes, Bianchi, the pimply kid from Bobriusk,
Brodsky (keep him — whoever's up there — from running off
at the mouth, and from attempts to spout Russian in English.)

It's what they're writing. Undoubtedly. Uncensored,
in the UNESCO library, and in the (motherfucking!) gulag.
The author of under-lines, author of pauses (caesuras
that is) all of them fuck as the equal of Blake.

Black on white, white on black, everything on anything.
"Raven" in splotches, "Horseman" in bronze, in mildew, in neon —
It's what you're writing even when screwed by cancer,
or screwing yourself — makes no difference.

A spit wad on my tongue, I bend over the paper
to scribble over the water marks on the cabbage-moth's wing;
so often the pattern destroyed by a sharp zig-zag
of the slate pencil, a crumb of which is the ghost of Jericho. . . .

all of which is errant nonsense. Here we must add
not "by the way," but quite intentionally,
while reading, haven't you more than once been seduced?
As if the book suddenly opened and read you

right down to the epithelium, down to the nimble crows feet
around the eyes, warmed by reading, (our respects to the tear-making process)
From the blind, as from the most degenerate types
the book takes an imprint, in preparation for

judgement day? O, gloss angel, not amply feathered
judging by your leaves — autumnal, paper angel
I bend over to drink from you. By mistake
I bend over, but that's just a drop in the bucket.

TRANSLATED BY LAURA D. WEEKS

Untitled

Do not scrutinize a sleeping man after a night of love.
He isn't tired at all, but for a little while he dies
of tenderness. The shadow secret of sweat cast on blood
illumines the final syllable of sun —

after which . . . dark. He lies spread-eagled, not breathing,
only the slight pressure of lungs exudes a piping stream.
Lean over him, you run a risk: the modest God
leaning over him, might miss and kiss you by mistake.

Eyelid slits . . . the crystalline depths of his eye
filters a gaze. Your man will regain consciousness,
but not all at once. Not all at once. For a full two minutes
you will utter prayers, swear devotion in your quick-tripped speech.

His arm, bent at the elbow, will suddenly describe a half-arc
in the dark, vainly searching for cigarettes.
Putting your ear to his rippled back, you hear
someone throwing newspapers against the screen door.

And the next time you comingle the dampness
of your drenched bodies — fortiesh, lightly rimed with frost,
do not look at him, because it well may be
that for these last two years he has longed to die for just that.

And the next time he expires from his own tenderness
look out the window where the branches' metastasis plays,
and feel how he shivers, his dried-out mouth half-open . . .
but God forbid you look at him, even with one eye.

TRANSLATED BY LAURA D. WEEKS

AFTERTHOUGHTS

EDWARD FOSTER

ITS OWN ECONOMY

"We tire of the forms we impose upon space and the restricted identities we secure from them. We tire finally even of the act itself of imposition."
—William Bronk, *The New World*

CROSSING CENTURIES was from the beginning meant to be the principal and most ambitious of several projects outlined when the Russian/American Cultural Exchange Program was established in 1993. Despite its all-encompassing name, the program was created primarily to bring Russian poets and poetry to America and American poets and poetry to Russia. Perestroika gave poets in both countries an opportunity to know each other's work more intimately than had been possible for many generations, but communication requires money, and poetry, unlike other arts, rarely operates in a cash economy. Poetry had been hugely popular in Soviet Russia, but Perestroika put an end to that, and Russians rapidly learned that in capitalist countries, things with little or no cash value are largely invisible.

A few mainstream American poets found a limited audience in the new Russia, thanks to their publishers and the USIA, but much of the more interesting and innovative American work remained all but unknown. With a few exceptions — notably Kent Johnson and Stephen M. Ashby's *Third Wave: The New Russian Poetry* (1992) — developments in Russian poetry were at the same time rarely recognized in the United States. The Russian/American Cultural Exchange Program, which has been generously supported by the Russian Academy of Sciences and the William and Mary Greve Foundation, arranged to have major Russian poets such as Ivan Zhdanov, Nina Iskrenko, and Arkady Dragomoschenko visit the United States, while coordinating reading and lecture tours for Eileen Myles, Nathaniel Tarn, and other Americans in Russia.

Major conferences that brought together Russian and American poets were held in Moscow and the United States, and a series of books were undertaken, including a bilingual anthology of contemporary Russian and American poetry, *The New Freedoms* (1994), edited by Vadim Mesyats and myself; *Contemporary American Poetry in Russian Translations* (1996), edited by Arkady Dragomoschenko and Vadim Mesyats; Ivan Zhdanov's *The Inconvertible Sky* (1997), translated by John High and Patrick Henry; and a selection of Mesyat's work in English translation, *A Guest in the Homeland* (1998).

Contemporary American Poetry in Russian Translations made works by a number of major American innovative poets — John Ashbery, Susan Howe, Michael Palmer, Alice Notley, and Leslie Scalapino, among others — readily available for the first time in Russia. A few had been published there already but only in limited, hard-to-find editions. The anthology was distributed free to Russian libraries and universities.

John High agreed to coordinate the anthology of Russian poetry in English translation. His journal, *Five Fingers Review,* had been one of the first to publish many of the new Russian poets in the United States, and together with his principal co-translator Patrick Henry, he had been largely responsible for most of the English versions through which Nina Iskrenko and Ivan Zhdanov were known outside their own country. He had also translated Alexei Parshchikov, Aleksandr Eremenko, and other key figures in the Russian poetry world. An editorial board of distinguished poets and academics was chosen to select the poets and poems to be included, and work on the anthology began.

The various conferences and publishing ventures organized by the Russian/American Cultural Exchange Program made it increasingly clear that in Russia as much as in America, experimental poets — particularly younger ones — have few opportunities to reach a public and are often not well known outside their country or even their communities. The problem is especially acute among gay and women poets. Their work was being done, but it was being done almost without exception in isolation.

Arrangements were made for the editors to travel to Moscow and St. Petersburg to meet with editors, publishers, and writers, especially younger ones, in order to get a better sense of contemporary Russian poetry than would have been possible even through the extensive network of Russian friends shared by the editors. All but one of the editors had lived, or spent much time, in Russia and knew well the course that Russian poetry had followed during Perestroika and the decades immediately preceding it. But poetry, like all of the arts in the twentieth-century, changes rapidly, and the course it had taken in Russia during the last years of the century was less clear. The emergence of a strong community of gay writers, for example, as well as a great increase in the number of women poets was still, for the most part, unknown in the West.

Interest in the new Russian poetry was, at least among American poets, far more than academic. Innovative poetry in America during the last generation has been for the most part cloistered — aligned with, at most, two or three other poetry communities, notably the French, and certainly not deeply affected or much altered by others. In part this is the result of the fact that translation has been largely confined to the academy rather than to poets. This may have resulted in translations that are "correct" but that also miss the reason the work is a poem and not merely a record of feelings or ideas. Most of the translators chosen for *Crossing Centuries* are poets who, respecting the "strangeness" of poetry from another culture, have tried to recreate in English equivalents for what they considered distinctly poetic in the original.

.   No one believes that *Crossing Centuries* or any book can, at this late date in our history, significantly change the role, or lack of role, that poetry plays in the United States. But the book can perhaps change the way poetry is understood and written there. Poetry operates according to its own laws and often within an economy that has little to do with the marketplace, but poets need always to be aware of transformations in the ways language is being understood and used elsewhere. It is said that the essential problem with the world economy is that it is an American economy, absorbing and transforming other cultures with little regard for what they have been. Poetry, however, can't, or shouldn't, operate in that way, and *Crossing Centuries*, like the Russian/American Cultural Exchange Program, exists to change, among other things, American poetry — not simply by importing something for distraction or pleasure, as one might import a cuisine or wine. What poets know is that finally there is, or should be, no such thing as "Russian poetry" or "American poetry." There are only poems and poets and, occasionally, an audience.

Some readers and poets have been incensed by Jack Spicer's argument that "poetry has nothing to do with politics," but he was fundamentally correct. Poetry can operate as successfully in one political vocabulary as in another, and can be put to use in any political context or in none. Poetry as such does not succeed because its politics are "useful" or "correct" and is, in the end, supremely indifferent to these distinctions. It has nothing to do with "authority" or "property," but rather with the perpetual flux that characterizes any given language. There is nothing essential to one culture that will make its poetry superior to another.

A few years after Russian authorities gave the Orthodox church permission to begin its work again, I stood in the sanctuary of one of the great cathedrals in St. Petersburg and heard the liturgy chanted with fervor and strength. This was a poetry of colossal conviction, making most of its "avant-garde" cousins in the recent West seem attenuated and pale. Notions that guide much "innovative" poetry, particularly in the United States, it seemed, were not enlightened insights into language and the mind but components of belief systems geographically and historically discrete. Denying even the possibility of transcendence, the American poet was trapped in a linguistic flatland in which poetry could no longer find possibilities other cultures took for granted.

I had recently been constructing English versions or "imitations" of poems by Ivan Zhdanov, who had spoken of Russian literature not within the critical terminology inevitable in the West but as "a new patristic literature." Perhaps in this he echoed traditional views of Moscow as the successor to Constantinople, but he also was proposing for poetry possibilities more serious and ambitious than those to which one is accustomed in the United States. Grander visions do not assure greater poetry, but they open the prospect, and in the work of a poet as accomplished as Zhdanov, they permit rich metaphorical and musical textures that call for translation and imitation:

> . . . the soul speaks out from that void once more:
> The eclipse complete, its aureole flares,
> the crescent sickle shines: and in its voice,
> the wail you hear when one is born again.
> > —from Ivan Zhdanov, "The crescent moon, its seas eclipsed . . ."

If *Crossing Centuries* does the work I hope it can, it will help to keep the domain of poetry various. Poetry's greatest enemies are poets who protest that poems cannot do what in fact they have always done.

VADIM MESYATS

FINE TUNING THE GREGORIAN CALENDAR

To whom is this book addressed, for whom is it meant? Inevitably, no arrangement of vectors can produce the single, unified effect that will please everyone. In the present case, disappointment, even resentment will follow, especially for the specialist in Russia, believing that he knows the details of Russian poetic discourse and the Russian language better than the visitor, "a man of different taste." But this book sees things from the outside, so to speak, and is aimed not so much at Russian but more particularly at American readers, notably those concerned with Russian culture.

All anthologies should strive for academic objectivity even when they deal, as in the present case, with "underground" poetry that uses material outside any social context. Inevitably, anthologies present a particular point-of-view. Ideally perhaps, an anthology like this should give an author attention in proportion to his or her reputation, and that's not what happens here. Nor, in this case, is it necessary. Many contemporary Russian poets are already well known in American poetry circles and, like Joseph Brodsky, do not need to be "introduced" to the American reader. A great many deserving authors like Brodsky are, therefore, not represented here, and to take into account the wishes of everyone who supported this project would be impossible. One can't do everything.

For example, Russian poetry from specifically a woman's perspective is unknown to American readers and, given the cultural differences, can't be accurately represented in English translation. Nor are the ethnic criteria that divide one Russian poet from another obvious to the outsider. This is a book of translations done for the most part by American poets, for whom literature is a single entity. As Lyn Hejinian says in her introduction: "The task of the editors and translators of this anthology was to move the realities of realities." Or as Edward Foster says in one of his essays, "No single poetic is superior to others, except in so far as it is useful to the working poet."

I recall the amusing point-of-view suggested by Boris Groys in an interview with Alexei Parshchikov a few years ago. Groys said that in order to understand an artist's strategy at a given point in relation to his culture, one had to see it in terms of its market, particularly questions of "import" and "export." Some creativity is directed at the domestic market, which means it is concerned with "importing"; in Russia this means grouping it with jeans, free verse, performance, video, Foucault, and Derrida. Other artists try to make their living on the international cultural market. For example, Nikita Mikhalkov tries to market his patriotism; his business is export. "Pushkin was a pure importer; that is why is absolutely uninteresting for the West." The reason many poets in this anthology are marketable is that they are translatable, indeed extremely translatable. (Saying that, however, it is important to remember that a poem's origin does not necessarily have anything to do with the way it is distributed.) If you want to sell dreams, try to dream commercially.

In Russian poetry, all of the props associated with postmodernism have been imported from the West. This is not to say they haven't been renamed and rethought. But Vyacheslav Kuritsyn is not Jacques Derrida, Arkady Dragomoschenko is not a Language writer, Yanka Diagileva is not a punk-rock poet. Nevertheless, something similar to the postmodern sensibility with its use of quotations, intertextuality, and found objects is present. Perhaps even Americans have had a chance to breathe the air of Chernobyl. But if Dmitry Prigov writes a pseudo-scientific article no one outside Russia may notice that the vocabulary was borrowed.

In June 1997, a remarkable poetry festival took place in Moscow — the festival described in the essay by Leonard Schwartz that follows this. The occasion was unusual, perhaps even naive in its ambitions. It was, in any case, a step forward, an attempt to discover what in recent Russian poetry is new, young, bold, gay, and deeply of the provincial depths of Russian. For a few days, Americans heard what they had never read. Poetry in Moscow, they found, is not part of the international community; it leads a separate existence, breathes a different air.

There is, of course, as I have said, much that is missing in this book. I am sorry that nothing by Yury Kazarin, Vladislav Drozhashchikh, Yury Belikov, Sandro Moksha, and Dmitry Baturin found their way into this anthology. Evgeny Asimov's list of Ural poets is not represented. On another issue, Thomas Epstein is certainly correct when he writes in his essay that "poetry from the provinces" (and Russia, in general, *is* provinces) demonstrates more poetic freedom than that produced by the two competing capitals. And yet, necessarily, it is the capitals which are represented here. Every anthology has its limits: not everything can be done at once. Not everything. Imagine a parallel situation: a group of Russian editors and publishers coming to New York to seek out the "hottest new poets" and the poets lining up at St. Marks to read one after the other.

Let us remember the times when Russians in this century could provoke positive interest in American intellectuals. First, there was the October Revolution and the enthusiasm and economic energy that followed the first Five Year plan, a subject of great interest in the West, especially during the Great Depression. "What are those 'Russkies' doing?" Americans asked. Then came the alliance of World War II and Gagarain's flight on the other side of the "Iron Curtain" — Krushchev banging on the podium with his shoe — the so-called peaceful coexistence of the 1970s during which almost all the Soviet "Village Prose" writers were translated and Russians began to appear as virtually human. (John Billington, a renowned American Slavist who is currently the Librarian of Congress, wrote in his introduction to the writer Valentin Rasputin's diaries that in Siberia there were not only concentration camps but cities and towns in which good, sincere people lived.) Ronald Reagan reportedly told Gorbachev that in his spare time he enjoyed re-reading Bulgakov's *The Master and Margarita*.

Only two poets have achieved the rank of official Russian poets in our own era. Evtushenko gradually gathered enough translations of his poems to publish, in English, the bulkiest volume of its sort I have ever seen. Voznesensky, to name the other, rests his hand on Allen Ginsberg's bald head in a photo published in the Russian magazine *America*. Only two, so far. Perhaps, with Brodsky, three.

Then began the Gorbachev period. The 19th Communist Party Conference. The dawn of a new kind of Sovietology and Slavistics: "Romantic perestroika." Rybakov's *Children of the Arbat* was translated, published, and widely discussed followed by *The Hunt for Red October* and *The North Star*. In America it was the "Russian season." There was even room there for new poets. Contacts were made, people were introduced to each other, invitations were exchanged. John High, the chief editor of this book, was in fact married in a church on Moscow's Swallow Hills. There were poetry readings in St. Petersburg and even in Moscow where poets were treated like rock stars. Parshchikov took up graduate studies at Stanford University. Arkady Dragomoschenko shared a bottle of wine — diluted with water — with Lyn Hejinian, explaining his inexplicable verse to her. Aleksandr Eremenko impressed everyone with his free drinking and powers of speech, Nina Iskrenko with her knowledge of the truths of life, Elena Shvarts with the beauty and lucidity of her dreams, the Siberian Ivan Zhdanov with his aristocratic nature, Dmitry Prigov with his artistry and the shape of his ears, Vladimir Druk with the virtuosity of his meanings and his irony.

Finally readers acknowledged even Vsevolod Nekrasov, Kholin, Rea Nikonova, and Sergei Sigei; it realized that Genrikh Sapgir wrote more than children's poetry. And on and on. Readers found pleasure in novel forms and the most incomprehensible meanings in the *Literaturnaya Gazeta*. There was a flowering of the arts, of religion and philosophy. And yet Russian postmodernism was of no real interest to most Americans: what was interesting were those who wrote more or less comprehensible verse somewhere beyond the "Iron Curtain."

And then that era ended. The flea market was wide open: jungles á la Pablo Escobar. And then children, who were raised or less properly by their parents, felt disgust and bewildered toward what was going on. Hopes were dashed, so to speak, and the poverty began.

No one cares about poetry — which is why the Quixotic enthusiasm behind this book is so impressive. Everyone else, it seems, has already thrown up their hands. Among the editors, Patrick Henry lived and worked in Moscow for several years, Gerald Janecek and Tom Epstein travel to Russia several times a year, Laura D. Weeks was a student in Moscow, Vitaly Chernetsky was born in the Ukraine, Lyn Hejinian and Edward Foster have been to Russia several times. For them, this work was necessary, and they may not altogether agree with my account of the current situation.

Twentieth-century Russia drew to a close with the image of Yeltsin standing on a tank turret. With the fall of Communism. The failure of Perestroika. And with the end of twentieth-century Russia, twentieth-century Russian poetry also ended. Changes had to be made in the Gregorian calendar. I don't know how it is with the Western calendar but such is the case with ours: changes had to be made. We live differently. Conceptualism, Metarealism, Polystylistics: when Konstantin Kedrov and Mikhail Epstein pioneered these concepts and saw them take root in Russia's poetic culture, the general population demanded only a list of names. A short list, if possible.

The bombings in Belgrade can serve as a final marker. Russia is a different country, a Byzantine mind-set tethered a dominant civilization. Poems can now be written as they used to be written. As the soul commands. We don't care that nobody's listening. There aren't many listening to Americans either.

Ten years has passed since the era of "Romantic perestroika." The poetry exported during that period continues to be much better known than anything that has been written since or at least better known that work with strong political or sexual overtones. The dialogue between East and West that Russians were counting on have not come off . But there remains the possibility of continued dialogue in venues like the Stevens Institute's Russian/American Cultural Exchange Program, the organization which in many ways has worked to make this book possible. A certain enlivening of Russian culture has been observed since the economic crisis of August 1998. People who were trying to make money in the mass media suddenly remembered that they used to write, publish magazines, and the like: perhaps, in a few years, we can evaluate the results. But that will be in a different century. For the time being there is what's known to the editors and translators of this book but, until now, poorly known elsewhere in America. We should be grateful to them.

Translated by Edward Foster,
Thomas Epstein, and Andrei Gritsman

LEONARD SCHWARTZ

MOSCOW IN JUNE:
Russian Postmodern Poetry at the End of the Century

W HEN POETS TRAVEL they tend to travel alone — or else as romantic pairs, or possibly trios. A group of poets converging for the singular purpose of poetry, in one of the most contested and chaotic cities of the century, Moscow, presents us then with a singular test of human patience. But patience, that protracted delirium, is one of the chief qualities required in the discovery of what comes next.

The occasion was a conference entitled *Closing the Millenium: Russian Poetry at the End of the Twentieth Century,* sponsored by the Russian / American Cultural Exchange Program and the Russian Academy of Sciences and held in Moscow from June 9th to 15th, 1997. Organized as an encounter between Russian poets and several invited American poets and Slavisists, in back of the conference was a proposed anthology of Russian poetry in translation to be published by Talisman House with the generous support of several public and private foundations in both helping to get some of the Americans over in the first place and in making the book possible. The poet invitees from the States included John High, the general editor for the proposed anthology, former Fulbright Scholar in Moscow, and prolific translator from the Russian; the publisher Edward Foster; the Chinese poet Zhang Er; and myself. Also invited were the Slavisists Thomas Epstein, a fiction writer as well; Laura D. Weeks; Vitaly Chernetsky, and the former Moscow Times reporter Patrick Henry, each of whom would be editing a section of the anthology, and whose interests run from "the metaphysical" (Epstein), to the question of poetry and gender (Weeks), to gay writing in Russian (Chernetsky), to the "Moscow Poetry Club Scene" (Henry). (Lyn Hejinian and Gerald Janacek would also be involved in the editing of the book, although neither could make it to Moscow for thc conference.) The poet and translator Alex Cigale was also on hand to provide insight, translation, and interpretation for non-Russian speakers like myself. A discussion of the issues of selection and translation the anthology raises, the warring claims of various aesthetic factions, meetings with journal editors, evening readings of the American poets translated into Russian and marathon readings of the Russian poets themselves, made up the substance of the week. Vadim Mesyats, Russian poet and Visiting Fellow at Stevens Institute of Technology, was the impressario and general organizer for all of this exchange, while his father, Gennady Mesyats, a physicist and a branch head of the Russian Academy of Sciences, provided the conference with support and prestige.

For a non-Russian expert like myself perhaps the place to begin is with a line from St. Petersberg poet Arkady Dragomoschenko:"Everything begins / with an error of vision, with the disintegration of the thing affixed to its inevitable unity": this from "Accidia," published in *Sulfur* in Hejinian's translation in 1985, one of the first translations of contemporary avant-garde Russian poetry to appear in American circles. (Although Dragomoschenko didn't make it to Moscow, we did meet with him later in St. Petersburg.) "Everything begins / with an error of vision": this line parallels the phenomenology of travel in a foreign land in which you know your perceptions are going to be distorted and strange . . . and at the same time, that they have subjective validity. It also parallels poetry, in the sense that composition is dependent on creative misreading, as well as translation — that necessary betrayal. Everything begins with an error in vision — and the poem, a fragment of that error, seeks in truth or in error to reverse it, in truth or in error to salvage the whole.

Is the poem up to the task? At the Pushkin Fine Arts Museum in Moscow, at which the Gold of Troy is displayed (having been stolen from the Ottoman Empire by the excavating Germans, and from the Germans by the Soviets), I am struck by the fact that this wealthiest of legendary cities, basic to Western myth, is now most memorably present in the tiniest of its earrings, the most delicate of its jewels, while all the great walls and loud chariots have vanished. Will our culture, too, be remembered by its tiniest fragments, its poems, those little gleaming pins of a Simon Pettet, the jewels of a Robert Creeley? And what of the Russian literary landscape, charged now with the energy of a political release but completely bankrupt in terms of any poetry economy? As Patrick Henry put it in the English language newspaper *The Moscow Times* in 1996, "the government has allowed literature, once the most policed of the arts, to develop or degenerate according to its own internal logic, to find its place in Russia's collapsed and cutthroat economy without providing significant support or opposition." Whatever is to emerge out of this latest of errors will itself be a new vision, as the "inevitable unity" of the Empire breaks up further and further.

The eradication of the given was also a note struck in a May, 1997, letter from Hejinian to John High, which John read in Russian translation at the opening night of the conference at a packed Central House of Writers: "In American post-modern poetry, 'borders' have been at stake, under scrutiny, and up for reshaping, transgressing or destroying — borders delimiting genre, borders delimiting style, borders delimiting 'personhood' (who speaks when writing is written) — a question which inevitably queries the borders delimiting gender. American post-modern poetry involves a lot of border-crossing. Is this true of Russian post-modern poetry? And what else is at issue in current Russian poetry? Reality?" That evening each editor gave a short presentation on his/her interests. In the press after the formal presentation, I was inundated with books from different Russian poets, none of which I could read. I met a nuclear physicist who hadn't been payed in six months, had taken on a second job as a school teacher, for which he wasn't payed either, and so had taken on a third job as a nightwatchman at a hotel, which did pay. If the economy is so bad that the nuclear physicists are working as night watchmen, where does that leave the poets? Interestingly, however, I met several other scientists during the week who claimed that since their technical, equipment-oriented fields had been defunded, the only way to carry on their research was with "a notebook and a pen," that is to say, through poetry, whose very lightness of material accoutrement has recommended it from the start. Poverty equalizes. In his poetry, Wallace Stevens recognized this as well. As he puts it in "An Old Philosopher in Rome," "It is poverty's speech that seeks us out the most."

Ivan Zhdanov, a major figure and a poet available in book form to American readers (translated by High and Henry), was in attendance, even though he'd recently been forced to leave Moscow for his native Siberia (where he'd famously been born the"eleventh of twelve children"), not for political reasons but for economic ones. Along with poets like Alexei Parshchikov, Lev Rubinstein, and others, an older generation of writers, perhaps already familiar to Western readers, was well represented at the conference. But the afternoon and evening readings or June 12th and 13th at the Chekhov Center revealed many other interesting poets of the very sort the anthology proposed to uncover.

Aleksandr Ulanov, a younger poet from the Eastern city of Samara, was one poet that stood out. Conversant in both German and American poetry (he has translated both Ashbery and Duncan), several of us felt an immediate infinity with him. Janacek says of his poetry that "a lyrical-musical element is present uppermost," and that in some cases "the antecedent for a pronoun is puzzlingly ambiguous, an effect hard to render in English, where one must choose, for instance, between 'him' and 'it,' when both might be meant." Here was one of the few translations avaiable at the time. It was done by Janacek.

And he who was walking on the left
will step to the right,
and he who was walking on the right
will step to the left.
And each of my steps has its own dust
It settles on me
and becomes part of me.
And steps towards other dust.

Maria Maksimova, a historian by training and a member of the Moscow Writers Union, also was of immediate interest. The following translation is by Laura D. Weeks:

And now the same thought, the same words
again suck feeling into the region of the solar plexus,
again the grass
swells with green light, exudes lemony grief.
Look, there under the tree, on the red fallen leaves —
the same two people

In a session at the headquarters of the literary journal, *Arion*, at which editors of many journals spoke, Anatoley Kudrevitsky, the editor of *The Archer*, himself a poet and translator, spoke of the lingering influence of Joseph Brodsky on literary aesthetics, and of the idea of a "poetics of silence" in which the words count as much for the silence they make possible as for what they say themselves. Kudrevitsky, a samizdat poet who had to put up with a good deal of abuse during the Communist period and who has only been able to publish openly in recent years, argued that the role of the literary journal was to "anticipate a future or even read one," over and against Alexei Alekhin, *Arion's* editor, who claimed his journal offered a reflection of Russian poetry's total present. In the two readings for the Americans, one at the American Embassy and the other at Shakespeare and Company, an English language book store owned and run by Mary Duncan, John High was able to conjure up the presence of Nina Iskrenko, a leading Russian poet who had died two years earlier of cancer.

Ultimately of course there were as many points of disagreement and dissonance as there were moments of recognition. From an American point of view, it is no doubt astounding that so much time is still spent in Russia arguing about metrics vs. "vers libre." (Perhaps it is of significance that Eliot's "The Waste Land," as an example, was first published in translation in the 1970s. By comparison, "The Waste Land" was published in translation in China in the 1920s.) Nor was this argument generational: if anything, many of the younger poets were the ones making the arguments for the centrality of rhyme and traditional systems of measure. In a double sense, then, the Russians and the Americans were speaking two different vocabularies.

Of course it is also problematic for me to look only for the markers familiar to my own vocabulary. Indeed, if the question of enthnocentrism is always the central one in the encounter of literary constructions and catego-ries, this was especially the case in the Russia of 1997. That is because on the larger scale Moscow was awash in Western consumer imagery; MacDonald's, Coca-Cola, and Cindy Crawford have newly come to dominate the cityscape from every billboard and corner. And while a high official could conclude a talk at the Academy of Sciences with the remark that "everything Marx said about Communism was false; everything Marx said about capitalism was true," the prevailing mood was certainly one of a capitalist and Western-corporate embrace. What was our relationship, as "rich American antholo-gists" (rich in that High could pull off an anthology of Russian poetry that the Russians themselves probably could do not at this point) to the commodity culture so clearly exerting its influence on the Russian scene? ("Rich American poets" — what am I saying?) To the extent the American editors were actively seeking women and gay writers, "provincial" and "younger poets," all rubrics the Moscow crowd seemed to want to wholeheartedly reject as extraneous, I have no qualms about our asserting a potentially progressive influence. (The sexism of the Russian literary scene was startling.) The further questions of poetry, history, and economic power remain perplexing.

It is true that the force of the icon is a two-way affair. If I was conscious of the ways in which our arrival coincided with the corporate makeover of the cityscape, I also noted the influence of the Russian icon on ways of thinking about American poetry. However imperceptibly, some of us were altered. The churches are on the upswing, and while it may be alarming that after eighty years of Marx, the Big Crutch still hasn't been thrown away, all the same the churches do house the icons: images that don't *represent* the Saints, but through which the Saints are made manifest, or so the tradition says. So too the iconostasis — a frame for the idols, a dynamic series of manifestations, from behind which the voice of exquisite Russian choral music emerges, the faces of the singers hidden as the faithful bend. So Edward Foster can argue that the poetry of Jack Spicer, for example, can best be understood in relationship to the theater of the iconostasis: the potential for a poetry that is communal and impersonal, Being itself, beyond language and any of its representational distortions. So Russian poet Mark Shatunovsky can write while discussing Ivan Zhdanov: "At the rupture of two eras — the old lie weakened and the new lie not yet in force — he saw in the emerging dawn not a distorting mirror but a genuine eternity where modernism and realism, avant-gardism and conservatism, 'the eleventh son of a peasant family' and the refined intellectual all were reconciled. And in the reflected light of that eternity all the new deceptions now raining down on our heads continue to be invalid." If we can use this "eternity" toolwise to get out from our own downpour of untruths, our poetry altered to other hearing, then what began as an error of vision will transform itself into subversive song. What impact will the poets anthologized in this book have on the American poets that have translated or read them?

THE POETS

SHAMSHAD ABDULLAEV, poet and essayist, was born in Fergana, Uzbekistan, in 1958. During perestroika he edited and published *Zvezda Vostoka*, a quarterly magazine devoted to contemporary Russian and international avant-garde poetry. He is the author of two books, *Promezhutok* and *Medlennoe leto* (1997). In 1998 he was awarded *Znamya* magazine's prestigious poetry award. He lives in Fergana. ≈≈≈ GENNADY AIGI was born in 1934 in the Chuvash Autonomous Republic. Regarded as the Chuvash national poet, he has translated many works into Chuvash and has edited an anthology of Chuvash poetry (translated by Peter France and published by Forest Books, 1991). He has worked at the Mayakovsky Museum, organizing art exhibitions, but most of his life has been lived in poverty, earning his living through translations into Chuvash. Though little published in the Soviet Union until the late 1980s, his work has received major acclaim throughout the rest of the world and has been translated into some twenty languages. He currently lives in Moscow. ≈≈≈ MIKHAIL AIZENBERG, poet, essayist, and editor, was born in Moscow in 1948. He writes frequently on contemporary Russian poetry for various Moscow magazines and journals. He has published two volumes of poetry, *Ukazatel Imen* (1993) and *Punktuatsiya Mesta* (1995) as well as a book of literary essays, *Vsglyad na svobodnogo khudozhnika* (1997). An issue of *Russian Studies in Literature* (Spring, 1996) brought together English translations of his essays on contemporary Russian literature. He lives in Moscow. ≈≈≈ IVAN AKHMETEV was born in 1950 in Moscow, where he now lives. His poetry, often in short poems of free verse, is in the style of Vsevolod Nekrasov and especially of Yan Satunovsky but is also overtly philosophical and personal. His first major collection, *Poems and Only Poems* appeared in 1993. ≈≈≈ ALEKSANDR ANASHEVICH was born in 1972 and lives in Voronezh in central Russia. His first collection of poems, *Stol'ko lovushek* (*So Many Traps*), was followed by *Signaly sireny* (*The Siren Signals*, 1999). His poems and plays have appeared in numerous literary periodicals. ≈≈≈ YURY ARABOV, born in 1954, is a poet, screenwriter, and essayist. Head of the cinematic drama department at the All-Union State Cinematography Institute, he has worked as a professional screenwriter since 1978, and twelve of his screenplays have been filmed. His poetry was first published in 1987. A year earlier he emerged as a leader of the Moscow Poetry Club. He is the author of three books of poetry, *Avtostop* (1991), *Prostaya zhizn'* (1991), and *Nenastoyashchaya saga* (1992). His poetry has appeared in many journals and collections, including Evtushenko's *Strofy veka*. His novel *Yunye gody Danta* appeared in 1994. He is a member of the Union of Cinematographers of Russia, the Union of Russian Writers, and the Russian branch of the PEN. ≈≈≈ VLADIMIR ARISTOV, born in 1950, graduated from the Moscow Institute of Physics and Technology. He principal work as a poet began in 1967, but he did not publish until 1987. Two of his books have appeared, *Otdalyayas' ot etoi zimy* (1992) and *Chastnye bezumiya veshchei* (1997). His work has been translated into Serbo-Croatian, English, German, French, Romanian, Swedish, Italian and Polish. ≈≈≈ NIKOLAI BAITOV, born in 1956, is a postmodernist who writes poetry and prose in a variety of styles ranging from the traditional to the avant-garde. His "holey texts" are works in which pieces of the page on which they are typed are cut away or otherwise obliterated to create one kind of what he calls "adventures of information." He was a founder in 1996 of the Moscow Literary Performance Club, created for the "archiving, study and popularization of literary practices which go beyond the traditional concept of the literary object." He lives in Moscow. ≋≋ ALEKSANDR BARASH, born in 1960, lived in Moscow until 1989, when he emigrated to Jerusalem. From 1985-1989 he published, jointly with Nikolai Baitov, the literary journal *Epsilon-Salon*. His own books include *Optichesky fokus* (1992) and *Panichesky polden'* (1996). He co-edited the *Jerusalem Poetry Miscellany*. His poetry has also appeared in various journals and anthologies. ≋≋ POLINA BARSKOVA was was born in 1977, the daughter of Oriental scholars, and is currently a graduate student at the University of California in Berkeley. She has been writing poetry since the age of eight and publishing since she was ten. Her books include *Christmas* (1991), *A Squeamish Race* (1993) and *Memory* (1996). ≋≋ EVGENY BUNIMOVICH, born in 1954, is a poet, essayist, secondary school mathematics teacher, author of mathematics textbooks, newspaper columnist, and a deputy in the Moscow city duma. He was a founder of the Poetry Club. His poetry and essays have appeared widely in Russia and abroad in Russian and in translation. His books include *Prosto net takogo goroda parizha* (1990) and *Potomu chto zhivu* (1992). He has written a column for *Novaya gazeta* since 1996, winning the Independent Press Prize in 1997 and the Union of Journalists of Russia Prize in 1998. ≋≋ NATALYA CHERNYKH, born in Cheliabinsk, lives and works in Moscow. By profession a librarian, she is also a poet, a prose writer, a translator from English, an artist working as a graphic designer, a painter, and a book illustrator. She is the author of *Refuge* (poems, 1996). ≋≋ YANKA DIAGILEVA was born in 1966 in Novosibirsk. She is known primarily for her songs but published poetry as well. Her first album, *Ne Polozheno* was recorded in 1987. She performed both as a solo act, accompanying herself on the acoustic guitar, and as part of the punk band "Velikie oktiabri." Her poetry was published in *Russkoe pole eksperimentov* (1994). A collection of articles about her life and works, *Pridet voda*, was published in 1998. She died on 9 May 1991, possibly a suicide. Her body was found in the river Inia, a tributary of the Ob. ≋≋ ARKADY DRAGOMOSCHENKO, poet, essayist, editor, and journalist, was born in 1947 in Kiev, Ukraine. After moving to Leningrad in 1965 to attend the university there, he began his writing career as a journalist, essayist, and poet. Over the years he has published hundreds of articles, essays, poems, and five volumes of poetry, two books of non-fiction, and a novel. Three volumes of his work have appeared in English translation, *Description*, *Oxota*, and *Xenia*. He has also translated contemporary American poets, including Olson, Creely, Ashbery, Duncan, Hejinian, Silliman, Warren, and Howe, among others. He is considered to be one of Russia's most innovative poets. He lives in St. Petersburg. ≋≋ VLADIMIR DRUK, born in 1957, received his M.A. in educational psychology from Moscow State University in 1980. He is the author of two books of poetry — *Narisovannoe yabloko* (1991), and *Kommutator* (1992) — as well as four plays and ten screenplays and scripts. His poetry has appeared in various journals and anthologies in Russia and abroad. He was one of the founders of the Poetry Club. Druk now lives in New York City, where he works as an internet entrepreneur and webmaster. ≋≋ ALEKSANDR EREMENKO was born in 1950. Dubbed the "King of the Poets" in 1989 by a convention of "unofficial" Moscow writers, he is closely associated with the poets Ivan Zhdanov and Aleksei Parshchikov. After the publication of his *Stikhi* in 1991, he virtually ceased writing. He lives in Moscow. ≋≋ GALINA ERMO-SHINA is the author of three books of poetry, *Windows of Rain*, *Hail*, and *Time Town*. In 1998 she was named poet laureate of the First Russian Prose Poem Festival in Moscow. She lives in

Samara. ⚬ ELENA FANAILOVA was born in 1962, lives in Voronezh, and works for Radio Liberty. She has published in various journals and the almanac *Mirror*, published in Israel. Her poetry is collected in *Journey*. ⚬ VLADIMIR GANDELSMAN, born in 1948, graduated from the Leningrad Institute of Electrical Engineering. He has published five books of poetry: *Shum zemli, Tam na Neve dom, Vechernei pochtoi, Dolgota dnya*, and *Edip*. He currently lives now in the United States. ⚬ DMITRY GOLYNKO-VOLFSON, poet, essayist, and theorist of postmodernism, was born in Leningrad in 1969. A graduate of the Department of Russian Language and Literature of the Russian State Pedagogic University, he is doing post-graduate work at the Russian Institute of Art History in St. Petersburg. The author of the poetry collection *Homo Scribens* (1994) as well as multiple publications on new technologies and culturology, he was the co-ordinator the 4th St. Petersburg Biennial, and the organizer of the conference "Modern Art: New Strategies and New Ideologies" in October, 1999, at the Russian Institute of Art History in St. Petersburg. He is a contributing editor to *The Moscow Art Magazine*. ⚬ FAINA GRIMBERG, poet, prose writer, dramatist and graphic artist, is by training a philologist and Slavist. She has written a number of historical/conceptual works, including *Bulgarians and the World, The Existence of Concept and Doctrine, Pretenders and Pretension, Mythical People, or Confessions of Wandering* (a history of Judaeism), *Notes Towards a History of Russian Philanthropy,* and *The Romanov Dynasty*. She has also written a number of books using fictitious and historical masks. Of these, she considers her book devoted to the life of Andrei Yaroslavich, brother and political adversary of Aleksandr Nevsky, to be the most significant, since it offers a non-canonical interpretation of the Russian Middle Ages. She has published a collection of poetry entitled the *Green Weaver* (1993). ⚬ ANDREI GRITSMAN, born in 1947, is a physician originally from Moscow who now lives in the New York area. A poet and essayist, he writes in both Russian and English. He has authored two books of poetry: *No Man's Land*, and a bilingual collection, *View From the Bridge*. He holds an M.F.A. in poetry from Vermont College. ⚬ YULY GUGOLEV, a native of Moscow, was a member of the Moscow Poetry Club. In the past several years, he has been close to the poets formerly known as the "underground" group: Aizenberg, Gandlevsky, and Kibirov. His work has appeared in numerous Russian periodicals, and his first collection of poetry was recently published by OGY Publishing House, allied with Moscow's Literary Club. Until recently, he was employed at NTV and currently works for the International Red Cross. ⚬ IGOR IRTENEV, born in 1947, graduated from the Leningrad Cinematography Institute. He is the author of ten books of poetry and is a member of the Russian PEN Center. He currently works in Moscow as the chief editor of the satirical journal *Magazine*. He was a president of the Moscow Poetry Club. His poetry has been translated into English, French, Danish, Polish, Serbian, and other languages. ⚬ NINA ISKRENKO (1951-1995) was the daughter of a physician and an engineer. She earned a degree in physics from Moscow State University and worked until 1989 as a translator of scientific literature from English into Russian. In 1986 she joined the Moscow Poetry Club. Following the failed putsch in 1991, she became a member of the Union of Russian Writers. Three books of poetry appeared in 1991, *Ili, Referendum,* and *Neskol'ko slov*. Her work has appeared in numerous newspapers, journals and anthologies in Russia and abroad. A book of selected work in English translation, *The Right to Err*, was published in 1995. ⚬ SVETLANA IVANOVA was born in Leningrad in 1964. She is the author of three books of poetry and has recently edited an anthology of Paris-based Russian poets of the 1930s entitled *Russkaya Atlantida.* She is also a noted water-colorist. She lives in St. Petersburg. ⚶⚶⚶ VITALY KALPIDY, poet, editor, publisher, was born in Chelyabinsk in 1957. The author of numerous books of poetry, including *Resnitsy* (1998), for which he was awarded the Smaller Apollon Grigoriev Prize in 1998, he is the editor of *Nesovremennye zapiski,* the managing director of *Ural'skaya nov'* and the director of *Galleriya,* a publishing house devoted to the works of the poets of the Ural regions. He lives and works in Chelyabinsk. ⚶⚶⚶ ELENA KATSYUBA (Kedrova) was born in 1946. Her first publications appeared in Kazan in 1963. In 1969 she received her degree in journalism from Kazan University and moved to Moscow. In the mid-1980s she and the poet Konstantin Kedrov formed the poetry society VSPD (the Voluntary Society for the Preservation of Dragonflies — Russian acronym "DOOS"). She published little before the emergence of independent, non-government sponsored publishing ventures, although the many successful appearances of DOOS made her an influential figure in the political underground. The poem "Svalka," published in the almanac *Labyrinth-Eccentric* marked the debut of a new verse form created by Katsyuba and christened "linguistic realism," a synthesis of anagrams, meta-grams and combinatrics. At the recommendation of Andrei Voznesensky and Genrikh Sapgir she was accepted as a member of the new independent Writers' Union in August of 1991. In 1995 she published the collection *Ad Verbum,* written in collaboration with Konstantin Kedrov. In 1995, the Moscow State Museum of Vadim Sidlur issued a separate printing of the poem "Svalka." Her *Complete Collected Works* has been published. She is currently preparing for publication *The First Palindrome Dictionary of Contemporary Russian Language* with roughly 9000 entries. ⚶⚶⚶ KONSTANTIN KEDROV was born in 1942 in Rybinsk. He has graduate degrees in philology and philosophy. As an instructor at the Moscow Literary Institute from 1971 to 1986, he served as mentor to a number of young poets, especially metarealists. He is a poet, theoretician, literary scholar interested in the deep mythological origins of words and thought patterns. His book, *Poetic Cosmos* (1989), is a major document of metarealist thinking. In recent years he has headed his own Poetic Lyceum and advocated what he calls "squat-poetry," in which poets are free to write whatever and wherever they want. ⚶⚶⚶ EVGENY KHARITONOV (1941-1981) was born in Novosibirsk, Siberia, and moved to Moscow after graduating from high school. He studied at the Institute of Cinema Studies (VGIK) where he received a Ph.D. in art studies in 1972. He worked as a researcher at Moscow State University and as the director of a theater company of deaf-mute actors. He died of a heart attack before any of his poetry or fiction was published in Russia or abroad. Selections from his work were published in the 1980s, first in the West, and then in Russia, and an edition of his collected writings appeared in 1993. His writing has been translated into a number of languages; a selection of his prose in English, *Under House Arrest,* was published in 1998. His work was also featured in several anthologies, including *The Penguin Book of New Russian Writing, The Penguin Book of International Gay Writing,* and *Out of the Blue.* ⚶⚶⚶ NA-DEZHDA KONDAKOVA, born in 1944, lives in Moscow where she is a member of the Writer's Union. Her first book of poetry, *Miraculous Day,* was published in 1975. A second book, *I Love—Therefore I Am Right,* was published in 1989. ⚶⚶⚶ KIRILL KOVALDZHI was born in 1930 in Tashlyk, Bessarabia. A graduate of the Gorky Literary Institute in Moscow in 1954, he began publishing poetry in 1947, his first book appearing in 1955. A collection of poems from his first four books (1955-1975), *Kniga liriki* (*Book of Lyrics*), appeared in Moscow in 1993. He served as a teacher and mentor to many young Russian poets, edited *Yunost* (*Youth*) magazine, and is currently editor-in-chief of Moskovsky Rabochy (Moscow Worker) publishing house. ⚐⚐⚐ PETR KRASNOPEROV was born in 1946 in Leningrad. His published collections of poetry include *Autumn Jogging* (1983), *Bird's Eye Pupil* (1989), *Golden Chariot* and *Elevator to Venus* (both 1996). He is best known for the transgender poetry he published in such periodicals as *Znamia* and *Eshche* in the mid-1990s. ⚐⚐⚐ VICTOR KRIVULIN is a poet, essayist, and journalist. Born in Leningrad in 1944, he was one of the leaders of Russia's underground culture in the 1970s and 1980s. He is the author of more than ten volumes of poetry, including a two-volume selected works, *Stikhi* (1988). In 1998 he published two books, a collection of poetry, *Kupanie v Iordane*, and a collection of essays, *Okhota na mamonta*. An associate of the assassinated liberal leader Galina Starovoitova, he was also in 1998 an unsuccessful candidate for St. Petersburg's city duma. His poetry has been translated into numerous languages. ⚐⚐⚐ SERGEI KRUGLOV, born in 1966, lives in Minusinsk, Siberia where he works as a journalist. His poetry has appeared in numerous periodicals. ⚐⚐⚐ EDUARD KULEMIN was born in Yaroslavl in 1960. He is an artist, poet, and author of many "realized and unrealized projects outside of definite esthetics." An active organizer and participant in various arts organizations as well as poetry readings and seminars in Moscow, Smolensk, Riga, Tallin, etc., he is the author of three books, of which *One-cocked Ulysses* (Crimea, 1995) is the second. He lives in Smolensk. ⚐⚐⚐ YULIA KUNINA (Trubikhina) was born in Moscow and graduated from the Faculty of Philology at Moscow State University. Her first book of poetry, *Kairos,* was published in 1991 by Kniga. In addition to scholarly articles, she has published translations of English poetry of the seventeenth century, and her poetry has appeared in numerous journals such as well as in anthologies on both sides of the Atlantic. The poets to whom she feels closest are Vladislav Khodasevich, the consummate Russian classicist of the early twentieth century, and Gavrila Derzhavin, the great Russian neo-classical poet of the late eighteenth and early nineteenth centuries. She is currently a doctoral candidate at New York University writing a dissertation on translation theory and translating H.D. into Russian. ⚐⚐⚐ VYACHESLAV KURITSYN, a critic, was born in Novosibirsk in 1965. Known as the *enfant terrible* of Russian postmodernist literary criticism, he publishes extensively in the daily, weekly, monthly, and "thick journal" press. He is the author of *Kniga o postmodernisme* (1992), *Liubov' i Zrenie* (1996) and *Zhurnalistika, 1993-1997* (1998). He lives in Moscow. ⚐⚐⚐ ILYA KUTIK, a poet and essayist, was born in Lvov in 1960. He is the author of numerous books, the most important of which, *Ode on Visiting the Belosairaisk Spit on the Sea of Azov* (New York, 1995), translated by Kit Robinson, was published in a bi-lingual edition. Since 1994 he has lived in the United States and teaches Russian literature at Northwestern University. ⚐⚐⚐ DMITRY KUZMIN, born in 1968, lives in Moscow. He edits the literary almanacs *RISK* and *Vavilon*, the bulletin *Literaturnaia zhizn' Moskvy* (*Moscow's Literary Life*), and the poetry series of the publishing house ARGO-RISK. He also runs one of the most important websites dedicated to contemporary Russian poetry, www.vavilon.ru. ⚐⚐⚐ EVGENIA LAVUT was born in Moscow in 1972. She has a degree from the Department of Romance and Germanic Languages in the School of Philology at Moscow State University. Her first published book is *Poems about Gleb the Good Gentleman-Landowner, about King David, Foma and Erema, Luther and others* (1994). ⚐⚐⚐ ALEK-

SANDR LEVIN, born in 1957, graduated from the Moscow Transport Engineering Institute, then worked as a computing technology engineer and a literary editor and features editor for an independent press syndicate. He began composing music at thirteen and poetry at twenty. He is the author of three books of poetry, *Stikhotvoreniya* (1985); *Lingvoplastika* (1987); and *Biomekhanika* (1990) and has composed music for his own poems as well as poems by Vladimir Strochkov and others. His CD, *Frantsuzsky krolik*, appeared in 1997. ◆◆◆ SVETA LITVAK, born in 1959, graduated from the arts college in Ivanovo, then taught at Yukhnova. She worked as a stage decorator at the Soviet Army Theater in Moscow. Two books of poetry have appeared, *Raznotsvetnye prokazniki* (1992); *Pesni uchenika* (1994). In 1996 she founded a literary performance club with Nikolai Baitov. ◆◆◆ STANISLAV LVOVSKY was born in 1972. He graduated from Moscow State University with a degree in chemistry. He works as a copyrighter, writing advertising slogans. In 1989 he was one of the founders with Dmitry Kuzmin of the Young Writers' Union ("Vavilon"). In 1993, he was awarded the first prize at the 4th Moscow Vers-Libre Festival. He has published poetry (*Blank Noise*, 1997), prose, essays, and translations of English and American poetry by Charles Reznikoff and Charles Bukowsky. He lives in Moscow. ◆◆◆ MARIA MAKSIMOVA was born in Moscow and is an historian by training. A member of the Moscow Writer's Union, she has published poetry in various journals. She participated in the Bosporus forums on contemporary culture and the conferences in contemporary poetry in Moscow and the United States and was awarded a prize at the All-Russian festival of free verse. ◆◆◆ VADIM MESYATS is a poet and prose writer. Born in Sverdlovsk (Ekaterinburg) in 1962, he was trained as a physicist. He is the author of three books of poetry, including *Vyxod na more* (1996), and a volume of short stories, *Kogda nam stanet veselo i svetlo* (1994). He currently lives in the United States and is a co-director of the Russian/American Cultural Exchange Program. A volume of his works in English translation, *A Guest in the Homeland: Selected Writings*, was published by Talisman House in 1997. ◆◆◆ PAVEL MITYUSHEV, born in 1957, is the author of the *Belaya kniga*. Thirteen collections of his work appeared between 1990 and 1996 and comprise the so-called *White Library*. His books have been translated into numerous languages. ◆◆◆ YAROSLAV MOGUTIN was born in Kemerovo, Siberia, in 1974 and grew up in small towns in central Russia. He moved to Moscow at the age of sixteen and began his work as an essayist and journalist in 1991. He has published numerous journalistic pieces, critical essays, and interviews. In 1993, he edited the first edition of Evgeny Kharitonov's collected writings. In 1995, due to repeated harrassment by the Russian authorities, he left for the United States and applied for political asylum; he now lives in New York. His first collection of poetry, *Uprazhneniya dlya yazyka* (*Exercises for the Tongue*), was published in 1997. Recent books include a book of prose *Amerika v moikh shtanakh* (*America in My Pants*, 1999) and a collection of poetry, *Sverkhchelovecheskie supertekshy* (*Superhuman Supertexts*, 2000). His poetry, prose and translations have also appeared in many literary periodicals. English translations of his work have been published, among others, in the *Harvard Gay and Lesbian Review*, *Index on Censorship*, and the anthology *Out of the Blue*. ◆◆◆ ANDREI MONASTYRSKY (Sumnin) was born in 1949 in Petsamo in the Murmansk region and studied at the Stroganov Art Institute in Moscow. He then worked as a docent at the Literary Museum. A central figure in the Collective Actions Group from 1976 to the 1990s and a member of the Moscow conceptualist group, he is a painter, a poet, and a theoretician,

KEEPING YOU POSTED

NEXT TIME, USE A FLAT RATE BOX.

UNITED STATES POSTAL SERVICE®

Just $8.10 to ship Flat Rate Boxes.
$4.05 to ship Flat Rate Envelopes.
Hey, what's to weigh?

With easy, flat rate packaging, shipping almost anything to anywhere is simple!

- Choose from two box sizes – either shoebox or shirtbox.

- Just fill it and seal it (no need to weigh, or calculate postage).

- Go to usps.com/clicknship to pay postage or pay at the Post Office.™

With Priority Mail® Flat Rate Boxes and Envelopes – if it fits, it ships.* Order yours free at usps.com/flatrate1 (or pick 'em up at the Post Office).

*Certain limitations on content apply. See retail clerk for details, or visit our mailing standards Web site at pe.usps.gov

085509D*12380**********AUTO** 5-DIGIT 98502
POSTAL CUSTOMER
2115 CONGER AVE NW
OLYMPIA WA 98502-4503

most noted for the "Actions" he designed as a kind of outdoor performance often in an isolated field in the Moscow region with the participation of invited spectators. He now divides his time between Moscow and Germany ❧❧❧ REA NIKONOVA (Anna Tarshis) was born in Eisk in 1942. She grew up in Sverdlovsk, studying music there and in Leningrad. She returned to Eisk in 1974, where she and her husband, Sergei Segay, lived until they emigrated to Germany in 1998. Since the 1960s she has worked as both a painter and a poet. Her works in the 1960s include some of the early manifestations of conceptualism in Russia. She and Segay created the Transfurist movement and its samizdat journal *TRANSPONANS* (1979-1987). ❧❧❧ MIKHAIL NILIN was born in 1945. By profession a psychiatrist, he is an important poet in the Lianozovo tradition of colloquial verse. His first collection, *Accidental Selection* appeared in 1992, followed by new volumes of poems published in 1998 and 1999. ❧❧❧ RUSLAN NURIDINOV (Elenin). Both a poet and a publisher, he was born in 1962 and lives in Moscow. His poetry has appeared in many periodicals and in three collections of poetry, *Versograph* (1994), *I was Just About To* (1995), and *From Kirn* (1996). His poetry also appeared in the anthology *The Samizdat of the Century*. He is a member of the Russian Writers' Union. ❧❧❧ NIKOLAI PALCHEVSKY writes that he "began at an aviator's school. A pilot in the sky, that's cool. But I had to give up the school: it seemed to me that something was lacking in the sky. And I entered a pedagogical institute. Only half-educated I went into the army. Later my dream of the sky gripped me all the more strongly. As a train conductor I traveled all over Russia's Far East. I found no road to the sky there. I grew my hair out, grew a beard, smoked marijuana, drank vodka — never settled down. Acted in a community theater, but this sky wasn't mine either . . . I CANNOT DO WITHOUT THE SKY! I shaved my head, gave up smoking and drinking. And then She appeared! And poetry with Her! It was a miracle. O heavens! We married. Now I love my wife, I draw, compose poetry, and in my free time I'm a metal worker at a factory. So that's who I am, a simple Russian poet. I could have gone to waste, but was saved by the sky. . . ." ❧❧❧ ALEXEI PARSHCHIKOV, a poet and essayist, was born in Kiev in 1954. A graduate of the Mosow Literary Institute in 1981, he also holds an M.A. from Stanford University in Russian literature. He was a leading figure in the Moscow poetic culture of the 1980s and 1990s. His *Vybrannoe* was published in Moscow in 1996, and he has been widely translated, including a volume in English, *Blue Vitriol* (1994), translated by John High, Michael Molnar, and Michael Palmer. He currently divides his time between Cologne and Moscow. ❧❧❧ ALEKSANDRA PETROVA was born in Leningrad in 1964 and graduated from Tartu University. She has published widely, including journals in Russia, Israel, and the United States. She has published one book of poetry, *The Edge of the Precipice* (1994). She left Russia to live in Israel and now lives in Rome. ❧❧❧ DMITRY PRIGOV was born in 1940 in Moscow and studied sculpture at the Moscow Stroganov Art Institute. He is noted as a prolific poet, performer, artist, essayist, and installationist. One of the core members of Moscow Conceptualism, he was arrested in 1986 for 'manifestations of insanity' following his performance at a workers' club and was incarcerated in a psychiatric clinic. He was released only after protests from the Moscow literary community. Earlier that year he announced that he had already written 10,000 poems. He has published numerous volumes of poetry and other works both at home and abroad and, while remaining based in Moscow, has lived and traveled in Germany, England, the United States. ❧❧❧ ALEKSEI PURIN, born in 1955 lives in St. Petersburg. He has published four collections of poetry:

Lyzhnya (*Skiing Track*, 1987), *Evraziya i drugie stikhotvoreniya* (*Eurasia and Other Poems*, 1995), *Sozvezdie ryb* (*The Constellation of Pisces*, 1997) and *Arkhaika* (*Archaics*, 1998). He has also participated in the collective project *Trudy Feognida* (*The Works of Theognides*, 1996) and published a number of critical essays, many of them collected in the volume *Vospominaniya o Evterpe* (*Reminiscences of Euterpe*, 1996). He co-edits the literary almanac *Urbi.* ፠፠፠ LEV RUBINSTEIN was born in 1947 in Moscow, studied philology, and until the end of the 1980s worked as a bibliographer. In 1974 he began the series of poems on index cards for which he is now famous. He was one of the founders of Moscow Conceptualism. His poems have been widely published, but his collected works, *Regular Writing*, did not appear until 1996. He has lived and traveled in Germany and the United States and presently lives in Moscow. ፠፠፠ GENRIKH SAPGIR (1928-1999) was a leading figure among the Russian absurdists. His many books iclude *Sonety na rubashkakh* (1978, 1991), *Stikhi dlia perstnia* (1980), *Moskovskie mify* (1989), *Stena* (1989), *Litsa sotsa stikhi* (1990), *Izbrannye stikh* (1993), *Videomy* (1993), *Liubov na pomoike stikhi mart* (1994), *Letiashchii i spiashchii rasskazy v proze i stikhakh* (1997), *Armageddon mini roman povesti rasskazy* (1999), and *Sobranie sochinenii v chetyrekh tomakh* (1999). ፠፠፠ YAN SATUNOVSKY (Yakov Abramovich) was born in 1913 in Yekaterinoslav and died in 1982 in Moscow. By training a chemist, he was leading member of the Lianozovo group of poets and artists. During his lifetime he published only a few children's poems in the Soviet Union and in a few in anthologies abroad. His collected poems appeared in a German edition in 1994 and in a Russian edition in 1992. ፠፠፠ OLGA SEDAKOVA is a poet, translator, and essayist. Born in Moscow in 1949, she is the author of numerous volumes of poetry, including *Vorota, okna, arki* (1986) and *Stikhi* (1994). Known for her essays religious and religio-aesthetic thinker issues, she is also the distinguished translator of Pound, Celan, and St. Francis of Asisi. Her collected essays were published in 1999. Among the prizes she has received are the Paris Prize for a Russian Poet (1991) and the Schiller Fund Award (1993). Her poems have been widely translated. She lives in Moscow. ፠፠፠ ANDREI SEN-SEN'KOV was born in Tadzhikistan in 1969. He graduated from medical school in Yaroslavl and now works as a pediatrician in Borisoglebsk. A poet, prose writer, painter and photographer, he has published three books of poetry and visual poetry. ፠፠፠ ALEKSANDR SHATALOV, born in 1957, lives in Moscow. He has published four collections of poetry, *Pryamaya rech'* (*Direct Speech*, 1985), *V proshlom vremeni* (*In the Past Tense*, 1991), *Drugaya zhizn'* (*Another Life*, 1996) and *JFK Airport* (1997). His poetry and critical essays have also appeared in major Russian literary periodicals and in the anthology *Portfel'.* He founded and continues to run an important independent publishing house, Glagol, and anchors a television program on literary topics. ፠፠፠ MARK SHATUNOVSKY, born in 1954, is a poet, essayist, playwright, and translator from the English. His verse first appeared in print in 1987. A year earlier he helped found the Moscow Poetry Club. He is the author of two books of poetry: *Oshchushchenie zhizni* (1990), and *Mysli travy* (1992). His play *Trajectory of a Slug, or an Anecdote about the Death of Stalin* was performed by the Moscow State University Theater in 1991 and 1992. His novel, *The Discrete Continuity of Love,* was published in the journal *Postscriptum* in 1995. His essays and poems have appeared in numerous publications, and his poetry has been translated into English and French. ፠፠፠ TATIANA SHCHERBINA was born in Moscow in 1954. She was very active in the independent avant-garde movement in the 1980s and had five books published in samizdat by 1990, *Swan-Song, Colored Grillwork, New Pantheon, Still-life with Transformations, Nothing-Nothing.* A selected edition of her poetry, *Shcherbina*, appeared in Moscow in 1991, and a novel, *A Spy's Confession,* was published in 1988. In 1989 she was invited to represent the alternative "second" literature at the International Poetry Festival in Rotterdam. At that time she also began working as a commentator for both Moscow and Munich for Radio Liberty, and until recently lived in Munich. She now lives in Moscow. ᛫ᛋᛆᛋᛆᛋ VALERY SHUBINSKY was born in Kiev in 1965. He is the author of three books of poetry, has published dozens of book reviews, short fiction, and longer theoretical pieces. He is head of the literary society and publisher Utkonos and translates extensively from English. He lives in St. Petersburg. ᛫ᛋᛆᛋᛆᛋ ELENA SHVARTS is a poet and prose writer. Born in Leningrad in 1948, she was one of the leaders of Russia's underground culture of the 1970s and 1980s. She is the author of more than ten volumes of poetry, including a volume in English, *Paradise.* Her *Selected Works,* a 500-page volume in Russian, was published in 1999. She lives in St. Petersburg. ᛫ᛋᛆᛋᛆᛋ ALEKSANDR SKIDAN is a poet, translator, essayist, and novelist. Born in Leningrad in 1965, he is the author of two books of poetry, *Delerium* (1993) and *V povtornom chtenii* (1998); a book of essays, *Kriticheskaya massa* (1995), shortlisted for the Anti-Booker Prize in 1997; and a novel, *Putevoditel' po N.* (1996). His translations of American poetry include works by Olson, Howe, and Coolidge. He has also translated Paul Auster's novel *City of Glass.* He lives in St. Petersburg. ᛫ᛋᛆᛋᛆᛋ YULIYA SKORODUMOVA (Yuliya Gomazkova) was born in 1964. A poet and member of the Union of Russian Writers, she holds a degree in Russian language and literature from Moscow State University. After graduation she worked as a translator and journalist was a participant in many theater, poetry and music events. She is the author a series of texts for the Moscow rock-band Lombard. At present she is working on stage versions of her poetry — theatrical-musical compositions using various light and sound effects, pantomime and folk elements. ᛫ᛋᛆᛋᛆᛋ SERGEI STRATANOVSKY was born in Leningrad in 1944. A leading figure of the Leningrad underground culture of the 1970s and 1980s, he was a co-editor of the samizdat literary journals *Chasy* and *Obvodny Kanal.* The author of the poetry collection *Stikhi* (1993), he currently works at the St. Petersburg Public Library. ᛫ᛋᛆᛋᛆᛋ VLADIMIR STROCHKOV, born in 1946, graduated from the Moscow Steel and Alloys Institute, then served two years as an officer in the tank corps. He later worked in ferrous metallurgy for the electronics industry and for the past decade has worked in the publishing business as a computer graphics designer. He has written poetry much of his life and began publishing at the end of the 1980s. Two books have appeared: *Glagoly nesovershennogo vremeni* and *Izbrannye stikhotvoreniya 1981-1992.* His work has also appeared in numerous journals, miscellanies and collections. ᛫ᛋᛆᛋᛆᛋ MIKHAIL SUKHOTIN, a poet, translator and theoretician, was born in Leningrad in 1957 and lives in Moscow. He is most noted for his "cento" poetry in which poems are built on quotations ranging from pop songs to political slogans and famous literary texts. Individual poems have been published in periodicals and anthologies since the 1980s, and his first major collection of poetry, *Giants (heroic tales),* was published in 1995. Sukhotin wishes to add that he differs from Mikhael Epstein's remarks on his work in "Like a Corpse I Lay in the Desert." ᛫ᛋᛆᛋᛆᛋ ALEKSANDR TKACHENKO, born in 1945, is a graduate of the University of Crimea and the Moscow Literature Institute. From 1963-1970 he played soccer professionally for clubs in Moscow, Leningrad, and Simferopol. The first of his seven books of poetry appeared in 1972. In 1977 he became a member of the Union of Soviet Writers. From 1988-91, he headed the literature and arts department of the magazine *Rabotnitsa*, followed by a one-year stint as poetry editor of the journal *Yunost'*. He served as chief editor of the journal *Novaya yunost'* from 1992-1994. Since 1994 he has been the director of the Russian PEN Center. VITALINA TKHORZHEVSKAYA was born in Sverdlovsk in 1971. She first published poems in samizdat and in the journal *Ural*. She has two published collections of poetr,: *A Bird's Memory*, (1991) and *Journey to the Other Side* (1994). She now lives and works in Ekaterinburg. VLADIMIR TUCHKOV, born in 1949, graduated from the Moscow Forestry Institute. He works as an arts columnist for the newspaper *Vechernyaya Moskva*. His work has appeared in numerous journals and anthologies. Tuchkov is the author of a collection of poetry, *Zabludivshiesya v zerkalakh*, and a book of stories, *Zapiski iz klinicheskoi palaty*. He is a member of the Moscow Poetry Club and the Union of Russian Writers. MARINA UKHA-NOVA is a young Moscow-based poet whose work has appeared in *Vavilon*, among other journals. ALEKSANDR ULANOV was born in 1963 in Samara, where he currently lives and is a professor of physics. He is author of the volumes of poetry *Napravlenie vetra* (1993), *Sukhoi svet* (1995), and *Volny i lesnitsy* (1997). He also writes frequently on issues of culture and poetry. Since 1994 he has been a lecturer in contemporary Russian poetry and the avant-garde at Samara Humanitarian Academy. LIUDMILA VIAZMITINOVA is currently a student in the Gorkii Institute of Literature and a member of the Moscow Writers' Union. She has published critical articles on twentieth-century poetry and three collections of poetry, *the Space of Growth* (1992), *News from the Thrice-tenth Kingdom* (1997), and *Coin* (1997). Her interests include philosophy, especially Descartes. DMITRY VODENNIKOV, born in 1968, lives in Moscow. His first collection of poems, *Repeinik* (Thistle), was published in 1996. *Holiday* appeared in 1999. His poetry has also appeared in a number of literary periodicals. He works at Radio Russia, where he hosts a program dedicated to contemporary art, *In My View*. ANDREI VORKUNOV was born in Moscow in 1957. In 1973 he graduated from Moscow State Metallurgy University and has worked as an engineer and a businessman. In the 1980s he took part in the workshop of Kirill Kovaldzhi and joined the Moscow Poetry Club. His poems and songs have appeared in periodicals, and his book *Trojan Cat*, was published in 1995. DMITRY VOLCHEK, born in 1964, was born and grew up in Leningrad. He was the founding editor of one of the most important samizdat literary periodicals of the 1980s, *Mitin zhurnal*, which now continues under his editorship as a major literary journal. His collections of poetry include *Govoriashchyi tyulpan* (*The Talking Tulip*, 1992), and *Poludenny demon* (*Noontime Demon*, 1995). He has also published a number of literary translations. For the past few years, he has been working at the Russian service of Radio Liberty and living in Prague. He won the Andrei Belyi Prize in 1999. ARKADY ZASTYRETS, born in 1959 in Sverdlovsk (Yekaterinburg), has published in many journals. He is the author of *Pentagrams* (1993), *Magician, Hermit and Jester* (1996), *Deus ex Machina* (1998), and *Hamlet* (1998), as well as a volume of translations of Francois Villon. His work is included in the anthology *Contemporary Ural Poetry* (1996). He lives in Yekaterinburg. SERGEI ZAVYALOV, a poet and essayist, teaches classical philology. Born in 1958 in Leningrad, he is the author of two volumes of poetry, *Ody i epody*, and *Melika*. In 1998 he organized an important poetry festival, which included readings in Moscow and St. Petersburg.

Crossing Centuries:

His essay on contemporary Russian poetry appeared in 1998 in *Novoe Literaturnoe Obozrenie*. He lives in St. Petersburg. ⚜⚜ IVAN ZHDANOV was born in Barnaul (Altai) in 1948 into a peasant family. One of eleven children, he moved to Moscow in the mid-1970s. He was the first of the metarealists to have a book published under official auspices, *Portret* (1982). He won the Apollon Grigoriev Prize for poetry in 1998 for his book *Fotorobot zapretnogo mira*. An English volume, *The Inconvertible Sky*, translated by John High and Patrick Henry, was published in 1997 by Talisman House. Zhdanov currently lives in Moscow. ⚜⚜ OLGA ZONDBERG, born in Moscow, has a degree in chemistry from Moscow State University and has taught chemistry in high school. Her work has appeared frequently in periodicals and anthologies.

THE EDITORS AND THE TRANSLATORS

ELENA BALASHOVA, born in Moscow, now lives in Berkeley, California, where she works in the University of California library. She has been translating with Lyn Hejinian and Jean Day since 1985. Among her translations with Hejinian are Arkady Dragamoshchenko's *Description* and *Xenia*. ⚶⚶⚶ CHARLES BORKHUIS, a distinquished playwright as well as poet, is the author of *Hypnogogic Sonnets* (1992), *Proximity (Stolen Arrows)* (1995), *Dinner with Franz* (1998), and *Alpha Ruins* (1999). *Mouth of Shadows*, a collection of plays, is scheduled for publication soon. He was nominated for a Peabody award and is the recipient of a Dramalogue Award. Originally from Texas, he now lives in New York City. ⚶⚶⚶ CHARLES CANTALUPO is the editor of *The World of Ngugi wa Thiong'o* and *Ngugi wa Thiong'o: Texts and Contexts* (1995) . He is the author of *A Literary Leviathan: Thomas Hobbes's Masterpiece of Language* (1991) and *Anima/l Wo/man and Other Spirits* (1996) a book of his collected poetry, 1987-90. He is co-author with Reesom Haile of *The Voice We Have*, a collection of Haile's poetry in Tigrinya with English translations (1999). Cantalupo lives in Bethlehem, Pennsylvania. ⚶⚶⚶ VITALY CHERNETSKY is an assistant professor in the Department of Slavic Languages at Columbia University, where he is also affiliated with the Center for Comparative Literature and Society, the Harriman Institute, and the Institute for Research on Women and Gender. He teaches Russian, Ukrainian, and East and Central European literature, film, and culture. Born in Odessa, Ukraine, he was educated at Moscow State University, Duke University, and the University of Pennsylvania, from which he received his Ph.D. in 1996. His translations and essays on contemporary Russian and Ukrainian literature and art have appeared in many journals and in *Rereading Russian Poetry* (1999) and the anthology *Out of the Blue* (1997). He is now completing a book manuscript entitled *Second World Postmodernity: Literary Paradigms of a Cultural Transformation.* ⚶⚶⚶ ALEX CIGALE was born in Chernovtsy, Ukraine, in 1963 and lived in Leningrad, Tel Aviv, and Rome, before coming to New York in 1975. He lived six years in Ann Arbor while attending the University of Michigan. In the summer of 1997 he returned to Russia for the first time in twenty-five years to take part in a conference of Russian and American poets in Moscow in connection with this anthology. The editor of the multimedia journal *Synaesthetic* , he is the author and translator of poems and essays in English and Russian. ⚶⚶⚶ JEAN DAY is the author of five books of poetry, the most recent of which is *The Literal World* (1998). Her work has been anthologized in *Moving Borders: Three Decades of Innovative Writing by Women* (Talisman House), *From the Other Side of This Century: A New American Poetry, 1960-1990*, and other collections, and a selection of her translations (with Elena Balashova) of works by Nadezhda Kondakova appear in *Third Wave: The New Russian Poetry*. She lives in Berkeley, California, where she works as associate editor for the journal *Representations*. ⚶⚶⚶ SARA DICKINSON is a doctoral candidate in Russian Studies at Harvard University. ⚶⚶⚶ YANA DJIN was born in Soviet Georgia in 1968. She emigrated to the United States in 1980 and writes poetry in English. She currently lives in Washington D.C. and is working on a novel. ⚶⚶⚶ JOSEPH DONAHUE is the author of a number of collections of poetry, including *Before Creation* and *World Well Broken*. He is co-editing a history of innovative American poetry since 1970, *The World in Time and Space*. ⚶⚶⚶ THOMAS EPSTEIN writes extensively on contemporary and modern Russian literature. He is currently preparing a volume of translations of the poetry of Elena Shvarts. He teaches at the Rhode Island School of Design and Boston College. He lives in Providence. ⚭⚭⚭ EDWARD FOSTER's recent books include *Answerable to None: Berrigan, Bronk, and the American Real; boy in the key of e; All Acts Are Simply Acts,* and critical studies of the Black Mountain Poets, Jack Spicer, Allen Ginsberg, and Jack Kerouac. A professor at the Stevens Institute of Technology, he has also been a visiting professor in the graduate program at Drew University and a Fulbright professor at Haceteppe University and the University of Istanbul. With Vadim Mesyats, he co-directs the Russian/American Cultural Exchange Program. ⚭⚭⚭ PETER FRANCE, born in 1935, teaches at the University of Edinburgh. He has written extensively on French and Russian literature, and has translated works by Blok, Pasternak, & Brodsky. He is also the primary translator of Gennady Aigi, having translated Aigi's *Selected Poems* (1995) and Aigi's *Anthology of Chuvash Poetry* (1991). ⚭⚭⚭ FORREST GANDER's books of poetry include *Science and Steepleflower* and *Deeds of Utmost Kindness.* He lives in Rhode Island. ⚭⚭⚭ For ANDREI GRITSMAN, see entry above "poets." ⚭⚭⚭ PATRICK HENRY has been translating contemporary Russian poetry and prose for eleven years. He is co-editor and translator of *The Right to Err* (1995), selected work by Nina Iskrenko, and of *The Inconvertible Sky* (1997), selected work by Ivan Zhdanov. Henry received his M.A. in Russian literature in 1990 from the University of California, Berkeley, and returned there in 1999 to pursue the Ph.D. He worked as a newspaper reporter in Moscow and Little Rock from 1994 through 1998. ⚭⚭⚭ LYN HEJINIAN is a poet, essayist, and translator and lives in the San Francisco Bay Area. Published collections of her writing include *Writing is An Aid to Memory, My Life, Oxota: A Short Russian Novel, A Border Comedy,* and a collection of essays entitled *The Language of Inquiry.* She has travelled and lectured extensively in Russia as well as in Europe, and *published* two volumes of her translations from the work Arkady Dragomoschenko, *Description* and *Xenia.* Hejinian and Dragomoschenko collaborated on the script for the award-winning documentary film, *Letters Not About Love,* directed by Jacki Ochs. ⚭⚭⚭ JOHN HIGH is the author of several books including *Ceremonies, Sometimes Survival, the lives of thomas–episodes and prayers, The Sasha Poems: A Book of Fables,* and a poetic trilogy of novellas, *The Desire Notebooks.* A founding editor of *Five Fingers Review,* he has also co-translated collections of works by the Russian poets Nina Iskrenko, Aleksei Parshchikov, and Ivan Zhdanov. His selected poems will be published by Talisman. He is the recipient of numerous awards and fellowships, including three Fulbrights, two National Endowments, and poetry awards from the Witter Bynner Foundation, Arts International, and Arts Link. ⚭⚭⚭ BOB HOLMAN, one of the best known performance poets in the United States, is the author of numerous books and the co-editor of *Aloud: Voices from the Nuyorican Poets Cafe.* His CD, *In With The Out Crowd,* appeared in 1998. ⚭⚭⚭ GERALD JANECEK was born in 1945 in Brooklyn. He holds a doctorate in Slavic languages and literatures from the University of Michigan. A professor of Russian at the University of Kentucky, he is the author of articles on Andrei Bely, Russian Futurism, and contemporary Russian poetry and the books *The Look of Russian Literature* (1984) and *ZAUM* (1996). He is the translator of Belyi's novel *Kotik Lataev* (1973) and his long poem *The First Encounter* (1979), as well as various contemporary Russian poets. ⚭⚭⚭ LISA JARNOT is the author of *Some Other Kind of Mission, Sea Lyrics,* and *Heliopolis.* She currently lives in Boulder, Colorado, where she is writing a biography of the poet Robert Duncan. ⚭⚭⚭ ANDREW JORON lives in Berkeley, California, where he works as a freelance proofreader and library assistant. He was raised in Germany, Massachusetts, and Montana, and attended the University of California at Berkeley, majoring in the history of science. He has translated the

German philosopher Ernst Bloch's *Literary Essays.* ⚜⚜⚜ GREGORY KAPELYAN was born in Leningrad in 1940. He is a prose writer and a graphic designer as well as a poet and translator. He lives in Jersey City, New Jersey. ⚜⚜⚜ J. KATES, poet, writer, editor, and internationally known translator from Russian and French, lives in Fitzwilliam, New Hampshire. With Stephen Sadow he co-translated *We, The Generation in the Wilderness* by Argentinian poet Ricardo Feierstein and is the editor of the bilingual anthology of contemporary Russian poetry, *In the Grip of Strange Thoughts: Russian Poetry in a New Era* (1999). His translations of Tatiana Shcherbina's poetry have been widely published in literary journals and anthologies. ⚜⚜⚜ SIMON KENT, British by birth and New Yorker by choice, publishes his books under a different name. ⚜⚜⚜ ALEKSANDR KALUZHSKI is a Russian translator, poet, and musician currently living in Los Angeles. ⚜⚜⚜ THOREAU LOVELL was born under the sign of the Cold War. He reports that he is not a friend of crows — except as they appear in literature. Simpatico scavenging for any shiny object that can be picked up against a dark background and fit into a simple story. He hasn't moved very far from the long valley surrounded by mountains where he began. Starting point: Fresno, Central California. Where raisins were king. Not much time spent in Paris, none in Buenos Aries. A moment in Moscow. Some poems written in English published in different magazines. A book, *Amnesia's Diary*, on Ex Nihilo Press. More time in Thailand, Mexico, Canada, Alaska, New Mexico, Arizona. Almost two decades spent in San Francisco. Quite a bit of editing *Five Fingers Review*. More than this cannot be easily stated. Except that this bio note was composed during a reading by Michael Palmer given at the Attic Bar in San Francisco, February 1999. ⚜⚜⚜ SCOTT MacLEOD completed his first novel, *Anne Frank in Jerusalem*, during a residency at Villa Montalvo in January 1998. Excerpts have been published in *Attic, POTES-POETZINE, e-Juxta* and *Lost and Found Times* and are forthcoming in *gestalten, Tight,* and *Neologisms.* He also has work forthcoming in *Chain.* Some of his poems have been translated into Russian by Igor Irtenev and Evgeny Bunimovich. ⚜⚜⚜ For VADIM MESYATS see the entry above under "poets" ⚜⚜⚜ MICHAEL MOLNAR studied Russian literature in Leningrad and elsewhere and has published translations of Arkady Dragomoschenko, Victor Krivulin, Aleksei Parshchikov, and Elena Shvarts, and a monograph on Andrei Belyi. He is affiliated with the Sigmund Freud Museum in London. ⚜⚜⚜ KEVIN MOSS is a professor of Russian Language and Literature at Middlebury College. He was educated at Amherst College and Cornell University, from which he received his Ph.D. in 1984. Among his recent publications is the anthology he edited, *Out of the Blue: Russia's Hidden Gay Literature* (1997). One of the pioneers of gay studies in Slavic studies, he has also published on a number of topics in twentieth-century Russian and East European literature and culture, and on the work of the Russian philologist Olga Freiden-berg. He is also the founder and director of the acclaimed Middlebury Russian Choir. ⚜⚜⚜ HARRIET MOORLAND lives and works as a poet "north of Boston." ⚜⚜⚜ MICHELLE MURPHY's book of prose poems, *Jackknife & Light* was a recent finalist in the PEN/WEST Literary Awards. Her work has been published in numerous American journals as well as in Russia and Japan. ⚜⚜⚜ MARK NOWAK is an associate professor of humanities at the College of St. Catherine-Minneapolis, where he teaches courses in folklore and writing. The founding editor of *Xcp: Cross-Cultural Poetics* (http://www.stkate.edu/xcp/), he is the editor of Theodore Enslin's *Then, and Now: Selected Poems* and the co-editor, with Diane Glancy, of an anthology of postmodern Native American poetry and poetics, *Big Myths Die Hard.* Nowak's first collection of poems & "micro-ethnographies," *Revenants*, was published recently. He is also currently at

Crossing Centuries:

work on a full-length folklore book, tentatively titled *Sing to the Lord a New Song: Fr. Frank Perkovich and the Iron Range Polka Mass.* ᴁꙅᴁꙅᴁꙅ KATYA OLMSTED's translations of contemporary Russian poetry have been widely published. She formerly headed the American Library in Moscow. ᴁꙅᴁꙅᴁꙅ EUGENE OSTASHEVSKY was born in 1968 in Leningrad and grew up in Brooklyn. His verse has appeared in *6,500, Lungfull!, Log, Beehive,* and other magazines; translations of his work by Alexei Parshchikov were recently published by *Kommentaryi.* He is the co-founder of San Francisco's 9X9 Industries and can be found through their website at www.paraffin.org. His article on Dmitry Golynko-Volfson, with an earlier version of "French Consulate," can be found in *Shark* 1 (shark@erols.com). ᴁꙅᴁꙅᴁꙅ MICHAEL PALMER is one of the most admired poets of his generation. His selected poems, *The Lion Bridge,* was published recently. ᴁꙅᴁꙅᴁꙅ EVGENY PAVLOV received an M.A. in German and English and German from Moscow Linguistic University and did graduate work at SUNY Buffalo. He received his Ph.D. from Princeton and currently teaches at the University of Canterbury in New Zealand. ᴁꙅᴁꙅᴁꙅ DAVID POWELSTOCK, an assistant professor of Slavic languages and literature at the University of Chicago, is currently completing two books on Mikhail Lermontov and Russian poetic culture in the 1830s at Harvard University's Davis Center for Russian Studies. He has published critical articles and translations of poems, stories, and novels from Czech and Russian. His translation of the late Czech author Karel Pecka's novel *The Passage* will appear soon. ᴁꙅᴁꙅᴁꙅ KRISTEN PREVALLET's book of poetry, *Perturbation My Sister,* was published recently. Her translations are primarily from the French. She lives in Brooklyn. ᴁꙅᴁꙅᴁꙅ STEPHEN RATCLIFFE's most recent books of poems include *Mallarmé: poem in prose* (1998), *Sculpture* (1996), and *Present Tense* (1995); *SOUND/ (system)* is forthcoming. *Listening to Reading,* a collection of his essays on contemporary 'experimental' poetry, will be published in 1999. He teaches at Mills College in Oakland. ᴁꙅᴁꙅᴁꙅ DARLENE REDDAWAY is a doctoral candidate at Stanford University, finishing a dissertation entitled "Russian Literary Manifestos: 1910-1914." She is the editor of *Estonian Short Stories* (1996), and has edited, translated and designed *Niche,* a bilingual journal of contemporary Russian culture. She has also translated works by various Russian poets, artists, politicians, scientists, and scholars, including Mikhail Gorbachev's 1990 speech at Stanford University, various poems by Alexei Parshchikov, memoirs of Victor Frenkl, and, together with Joseph Gitelson, the director of the Biophysics Institute at Krasnoyarsk, parts of a book on closed ecological systems. ᴁꙅᴁꙅᴁꙅ KIT ROBINSON's books include *Windows* (1985), *Ice Cubes* (1988), *Counter Meditation* (1991), *The Champagne of Concrete* (1991), *Balance Sheet* (1994), and *Democracy Boulevard* (1998). A resident of the Bay Area, he has been the literature director at the New Langton Arts in San Francisco. ᴁꙅᴁꙅᴁꙅ STEPHEN SARTARELLI is the author of a number of collections of poetry, including *Grievances* and *In the Skies.* He is a leading translator from Italian and French. ᴁꙅᴁꙅᴁꙅ LEONARD SCHWARTZ is the author most recently of *Words Before the Articulate: New and Selected Poems* and *A Flicker At The Edge of Things: Essays Towards A Poetics.* He also co-edited *Primary Trouble: An Anthology of Contemporary American Poetry* and *An Anthology of New American Poets.* He has received grants from The National Endowment for The Arts, The New York State Council of the Arts, and Arts Link. Schwartz, who teaches at Bard College, has translated from French and Chinese and lives in New York City. ᴁꙅᴁꙅᴁꙅ AARON SHURIN's selected poems, *The Paradise of Forms,* was published in 1999. One of the principal poets of his generation, he is also the author of, among other works, *Unbound: A Book of AIDS* (1997) and *A Door* (2000). ᴁꙅᴁꙅᴁꙅ RICHARD SIEBURTH is the translator of Friedrich

Hölderlin's *Hyms and Fragments*, Walter Benjamin's *Moscow Diary* and Gerard De Nerval's *Selected Writings*. He is a professor of comparative literature at New York University. ⚜⚜⚜ ELENI SIKELIANOS, poet and translator, lives in New York, where she formerly edited *The St. Marks Poetry Project Newsletter*. Her books include *The Book Of Tendons*. She has translated from French and Chinese as well as Russian. ⚜⚜⚜ GERALD S. SMITH is a Professor of Russian at the University of Oxford and Fellow of New College, Oxford. He is author of *Songs to Seven Strings: Russian Guitar Poetry* and *Soviet Mass Song*, the translator of *Alexander Galich: Songs and Poem*, and the translator and editor of *Contemporary Russian Poetry: A Bilingual Anthology*. ⚜⚜⚜ COLE SWENSEN is the author of *Try, Noon, and the New Math*, among other books of poetry. She has translated extensively from the French. ⚜⚜⚜ TOD THILLEMAN, poet, is the author, most recently of *A World of Nothing but Nations* and *The New Frequency*. A resident of Brooklyn, he is the editor-in-chief of Spuyten Duyvil Press. ⚜⚜⚜ SAM TRUITT is the author of *Anamorphosis* Eisenhower (1998). He lives in New York City. ⚜⚜⚜ JOANNA TRZECIAK's translations have appeared in numerous periodicals. She is the translator of Tomek Tryzna's novel *Panna Nikt* (*Miss Nobody*), recently published. Trzeciak is a doctoral student in Russian Literature at the University of Chicago, writing on Nabokov's translations and self-translations. ⚜⚜⚜ GYORGY VLASENKO, born in Pyatigorsk in the Ukraine, moved to San Francisco from Moscow in 1989. A poet, translator, and filmmaker, he has taught comparative literature at San Francisco State. ⚜⚜⚜ ANDREW WACHTEL is Herman and Beulah Pearce Miller Research Professor in Literature, the chair of the Department of Slavic Languages and Literatures, and the director of the Program in Comparative Literary Studies at Northwestern University. He is also the author of a wide variety of books and articles on Russian and South Slavic literature, culture, and society, the most recent of which is *Making a Nation, Breaking a Nation: Literature and Cultural Politics in Yugoslavia* (1998). He is the editor of Northwestern University's acclaimed series "Literature from a Unbound Europe" and is widely known as a translator of contemporary Russian and Slovenian poetry. ⚜⚜⚜ JULIA WARD's poetry has appeared in *Faucheuse* and *Seneca Review*. She lives and works in San Francisco. ⚜⚜⚜ LEWIS WARSH, poet and novelist, is the author of many books, including *Avenue of Escape*. He is one of the principal figures in the so-called New York School of Poets. A founding editor of United Artist Books, he lives in Brooklyn. ⚜⚜⚜ LINDSAY F. WATTON is an assistant professor of Russian in the Division of Languages and Literature at Bard College. In addition to translations, he has published articles and reviews on topics in Russian Modernism, sexuality, and Russian culture, and on the interplay of the verbal and visual arts. ⚜⚜⚜ LAURA WEEKS is a defrocked professor of Russian language and literature. Formerly the acting chair of the Russian Department at Wheaton College, she holds a B.A. from Wellesley College and a Ph.D. from Stanford University. In addition to a number of scholarly articles and a book, she has published translations of Tsvetaeva, Bulgakov, Shvarts, and Petrova. She currently lives and works in Portland, Oregon, as a translator, editor, and consecutive translator. ⚜⚜⚜ DONALD WESLING, a professor of literature at the University of California, San Diego, served as the Otto Salgo Professor of American Studies at Eötvös Loránd University in Budapest during the 1997-98 academic year. His many publications include *The Chances of Rhyme: Device and Modernity* and *The Scissors of Meter: Grammetrics and Reading*. ⚜⚜⚜ MARY WINEGARDEN, a writer and translator, lives in San Francisco and teaches English and comparative literature at San Francisco State University. ⚜⚜⚜ MARGARITA ZILBERMAN